CONVERSATIONS WITH HITLER
OR – QUID EST VERITAS?

**APOSTLES & VICTIMS
VOLUME I
REVISED EDITION**

"Were I to philosophize on moral questions, I would never have survived one say in the SS."

SS-Standartenführer Seibert –

"The nervous strain was far heavier in the case of our men who carried out the executions than in that of their victims. From the psychological point of view, they had a terrible time."
- [Paul Blobel]

YAD GHARRAWI MA

Copyright @2021 by Ayad Gharbawi

All rights reserved. No part of this book may be reproduced in any form or by any electronic or mechanical means, including information storage and retrieval systems, without permission in writing from the publisher, except by reviewers, who may quote brief passages in a review.

This publication contains the opinions and ideas of its author. It is intended to provide helpful and informative material on the subjects addressed in the publication. The author and publisher specifically disclaim all responsibility for any liability, loss or risk, personal or otherwise, which is incurred as a consequence, directly or indirectly, of the use and application of any of the contents of this book.

WORKBOOK PRESS LLC
187 E Warm Springs Rd,
Suite B285, Las Vegas, NV 89119, USA

Website: https://workbookpress.com/
Hotline: 1-888-818-4856
Email: admin@workbookpress.com

Ordering Information:
Quantity sales. Special discounts are available on quantity purchases by corporations, associations, and others.
For details, contact the publisher at the address above.

Library of Congress Control Number:
ISBN-13:   978-1-956017-65-6 (Paperback Version)
            978-1-956017-66-3 (Digital Version)

REV. DATE: 20/09/2021

Conversations with Adolf Hitler

Or

Quid Est Veritas? - Interviewing Apostles & Victims

VOLUME I

~

Ayad Gharbawi – 2021

Contents

1. Contents
2. Introduction & Synopsis
3. Introducing Me - Myself!
4. **Daddy**, Poverty, A Life of Hell, Boredom, and Fantasies
5. Daddy and **General S. George Patton**
6. Man's Cruelty to Daddy
7. Hearing of A Job Opportunity - To Be Sent to Germany
8. Daddy Tells Me Why I Must Take This Job - *If* I Want to Find the Meaning of My Life and Why God Allows Evil
9. After Fighting Daddy So Much, I Choose to Think About His Words
10. Job Interview with **Anonymous DC Official** — December 1944

   I. The Anonymous Interviewer Says The Fuehrer Insisted The Applicant Must be a Young Female With Minimal Education

   II. Yours Truly, Attacking *His* Lack of Aptitude

   III. Anonymous Interviewer Asks What I Know About Hitler

11. What First Deepened My Interest in Adolf — A Human I Was Hitherto Uninterested In

12. The Differing Types of People I Interviewed

I.   Actors Denying Any Knowledge of the Holocaust

II.   **Ted Bundy** - Seducing His Executioner, **Judge Edward D. Cowart**

13. Why Were My Books Never Published?

14. Are My Memoirs Unique? If so, Why?

15. Why Did I Finally Decide to Write My Memoirs?

16. I'm Going to Berlin '45 Baby!

17. Unnatural Effects of Being in Berlin — Mixtures of Jackson Pollock, Renoir, Egon Schiele & Edward Hopper

18. Four Unexpected Twists I Experienced in Berlin

I.   Differences in Realities Between Berlin, The Bunker, Hitler, and My World

II.   The Unique Nature of the Russo-German War

III. Hitler Is History's Most Unique Characters in Modern History

IV.   *Hitler Was Not Just Evil -How Many Times Must I Say This &, Yes, He Had Great Qualities!*

19. Portraits of Berlin 1945

    I.   Evolving Lives of Corpses

    II.   Sounds of Lovemaking & Sounds of War

    III.   Procedures of Death and Dying

    IV.   Obscene Odours, Some Weirdly Enticing

    V.   Civilians Between Madness & Stoicism

20. Dawn of the Battle of Berlin

21. Nothingness *is* Berlin

22. When Evil *is* Good & Good is Evil

23. Giving You An Impression of Germany's Destruction

24. First Impressions of the Bunkerites; Feeling I May Not Be Up to The Job Given the Disgusted Looks I Was Getting from Them

25. Idling While the Titanic Sinks

26. Sick Contrasts Between Innocence of Happy Children and Suicidal Adults

27. With the Passing of Every Hour, Ivan Was Getting Closer

28. Conversation With **Oberscharführer Rochus Misch**

I.   Misch: "What are Our Only Means of Communication? Randomly Calling Anyone. If They Speak German, We Know the Area is Still in German Hands!" And the *'Unknown Pre-Raphaelite Woman.*

29. Peace of a Tomb's Life While Outside Is Hell

30. The Master Race Squirms with Fears

31. Conversations With Oberscharführer Rochus Misch

II. Misch: "The Carnival of Finding Anyone to Defend Berlin; Or What's Left of It!"

III. Dorothy — "Uncanny How Similar My Life Is to The Wizard of Oz!"

IV. Dorothy — "I Cannot Accept We're Living in an Alice in Wonderland World and All Germans Have Become as Automatons."

32. Contradictory Thoughts — Kansas Virgin Country Girl Sightseeing in Gay Berlin

33. Conversation I - **Three Soviet Officers** — Squabbling Among Each Other

34. Conversation With Oberscharführer Rochus Misch

V.   "War Destroys All That Is Good, Sane, Virtuous, Leaving Only Evil and Insanity."

35. My First Battle Wound - The Horrific & Absurd Existence of the **Anonymous Katharina Esser**

36. Conversations with **Gruppenführer Fegelein**

- Fegelein: "Nazi Germany Is Structured on Sand, Thanks to the Fuehrer's Disinterestedness in Governing."

- Dorothy: "So Who Is Defending Berlin Now and With What?"

37. Conversation With **Three Female German Teens** I - Discussing Each Other's Concerns & Needs

38. Conversation with **Gruppenführer Fegelein**

- Fegelein: "Where Are Our Great Generals? — No, Worry, Here Comes Himmler the Great!"

39. Finally! My First Impressions of Hitler — He Does Not Look Like *'Hitler!'*

40. **FAQ I** - "Can You Tell Us How Mad Hitler Was?"

41. **FAQ II** - "What Were His Eyes Like? Did They Hypnotise You?"

42. Disquieting Excavator of My Hidden Needs, Hopes, Sensitivities & Aspirations

43. Conversations with **Hitler's Inner Circle**

- Dorothy — "Did Hitler's Personality Change During The War?"

- Dorothy — "Who and What Caused Germany's Defeat?"

44. Goebbels Gives Sage Advice to A Woman Who Lost Her Home — 1945

45. Conversation with **Hitler's Inner Circle**

- **Halder** Is Accused of Disobeying Hitler's Orders and Thereby Causing the Defeat of the Wehrmacht

46. Conversation with *SS-Gruppenführer* Hermann Fegelein

- Dorothy: "I Want To See A Surgical Operation Room Where The Wounded Are Being Treated."

47. Satan's Majestic Symphony

48. Conversations with **Hitler's Inner Circle**

I. Goebbels: "The Fuehrer Ought to Have Exterminated the Aristocratic Wehrmacht Generals!" and Guderian Vehemently Disagrees

II. Hitler's Highest-Ranking Men Cannot Understand Why Britain Fought a Suicidal War Against Germany and Dorothy Answers Them

49. Goering's Response to Dorothy's Argument on Why Fighting Germany Is Pointless

50. Goering- "In the Eyes of the Hypocritical World, Our Greatest Sin Is Racism. But Do You Think the West Is Not Racist, Given Their Segregationist Laws and Colonies?"

51. Goering - On the Supposed 'Criminal Nature' of American and Russian/Soviet Culture

52. Dorothy — "The Only Reason Why the 'Herrenvolk' Did Not Build the Atom Bomb Is Because You Expelled or Murdered Jewish Physicists — Which Proves You Were Far Dumber Than the Jews!"

53. Conversation With Three Female German Teens II – "What Is Happiness?"

54. Guderian – "Goebbels Is a Nothing Man!"

55. Dorothy Rats on The Rat **Speer** - And A Dreary Detour with **General Keitel** ...

56. Conversations with **Himmler** – Explaining His 'Historic' and Most Difficult 'Burden' That None Could Bear Nor Do

    I.   Himmler: "Do You Think any General, Officer, Diplomat, or Minister Could Have Done What I Achieved Without Having a Nervous Breakdown or Committing Suicide?"

    II.   Dorothy To Himmler: "Since So Much of Your Ideas are Rooted in Biology, Can You Explain How Exactly Does the 'Degradation' You Speak Of, Occurs in the Medical or Biochemical Sense?"

    III.   Himmler Insists Katharina Esser Was A 'Moron'

57. **Guderian** – "The War Is Over! My God, What Is Wrong with Some of You Fanatics?"

58. How Hitler Seduced Everyone Around Him

59. **FAQ III** - "Did I Just Sit There & Ask Questions and Hear His Answers?"

60. Finally, I'm Allowed to See Hitler During His Military Conference, Though I May Not Speak.

- **Military Conference** - Evening Situation Report. March 2nd, 1945: Tedious Numbers

- **Military Conference** - Midday Situation Report – March 24th, 1945

    Hitler [Shouting]: "Are We Blind? Is That What you Wehrmacht Geniuses are Telling Me? If you Cannot Even Produce One Report That You Can understand On Our Frontline Situation, Why Then are We Having This Conference?"

61. Watching and Observing Hitler, Trying to Think What He Was Thinking & Feeling

62. What Were the Remaining Options for Hitler by April 1945?

63. **FAQ IV** - "How Can One Man Mesmerise Millions of Germans and Not Only in Germany?"

64. Finally, Interviewing Hitler! And My Lousy Start ...

65. Dorothy to Hitler – "Why Did You Force Jews into Concentration Camps, Where Thanks to Your Restrictions, the

Majority of Jews Either Starved to Death or Were Worked to Death?"

66. Dorothy — "Herr Hitler — What Do You Think Your Legacy Will Be?"

67. Dorothy — "To Be Blunt, Herr Hitler, Are You Aware of Your Crimes?"

68. Conversations with The Infanticidal **Adele Sorella**

I.   The Background — Adelle Murders Her Two Daughters And A Day Later Stages A Car Accident Whereupon She's Taken To The Police & Thinks She's Been Investigated for the Car Crash

II.   Dorothy - *"I Regret to Inform you Both of Your Daughters Are Dead."*

III.   Switching To Playing Good Cop

IV.   Dorothy — "Don't Your Daughters Look Beautiful, with Rigot Mortis Having Their Arms Outstretched to God, With Lividity and Decomposition Eating Their Faces?"

∼

'Then *Jesus* said, "Father, forgive them; for they do not know what they are doing." And they cast lots to divide His clothing.'

- Luke 23:34 New Revised Standard Version (NRSV)

~

Conversations with Adolf Hitler - Volume I

Introduction & Synopsis

In 1945, I was a twenty-year-old German immigrant living in a hamlet called Goodland in Kansas. I wanted to be a famous Hollywood actress — money, fame, and fortune, nothing less.

I'll speak more about my life later, but I'll get to this point now. Some day I came across a job vacancy ad requiring German-speakers to be sent to Germany. After talking to Daddy, we understood that Hitler wanted his final words to be heard. I guess the man didn't trust any of his Master Race people to safe keep and preserve his words for future generations to read. The Germans were the ones who initiated contact with Washington, and a deal was reached whereby the latter could only send a young, relatively uneducated female to Berlin and interview the man. On our side, we insisted all questions can be asked must be answered. To the surprise of Washington officials, military, and diplomats, Hitler agreed.

At first, I was repelled by the job as I had no interest in politics in America, let alone German politics. But, in brief, Daddy explained it to me this way — I was a mixed-up girl, with pent-up, repressed self-shame, low self-esteem, despising my gender, sexuality, body, and brain. I was a fragile bundle of emotions, instincts, and needs, mutually fighting each other, day in, day out. And that's the top of the tip of the proverbial iceberg. Don't ask me how Daddy figured that out, but he knew me in every manner and angle. And I hated him for that. I mean, knowing me. I'll tell you now; I was a straight-up nasty, obnoxious, and rude daughter with him. Just him. I don't know why. But to use today's language, only he triggered me, and boy did I explode in raging verbal lava.

Anyway, the old man's solution was odd. Going to war-torn Berlin, I'd gradually see an evolving authenticity within my mind — where at? — where else, but in Berlin, of all places on the planet! Bit by bit, surfaces self-confidence, he claimed - self-love, serenity. Thus, he presumed I'd get to know myself, and that creates a blessed mind.

Ha! Did the fool waste his worthless time! And on and on, he'd echo back the same trite garbage. My reactive emotions swayed from boredom to irritation to rage, and finally, he needed to be vengefully reminded of his idiocies most mercilessly. To cut it short, as I said because this part is just a summary. So, anyway, I took the job because Dorothy's brassy brain realized once my interviews are made public, I'd be instantaneously famous, and that means Hollywood will be screaming for me to come and be the greatest actress in the history of movies!

So, I was interviewed and chosen for that job. Flown to France and escorted by our soldiers somewhere near the frontlines. From that point, I was picked up by this man, SS-Gruppenführer Hermann Fegelein, one of Hitler's high-ranking men, who would later marry Eva Braun's sister, thereby becoming Hitler's brother-in-law.

I interviewed the man in question, but in my spare time — for there were many days when the leader was unable to see me – I decided to expand my job by interviewing his followers, men, and women, such as Goering, Goebbels, Himmler, Keitel, Guderian, Eva Braun, Fegelein, and others. I'd also leave the Bunker, escorted by Misch or Fegelein, to observe how Berliners coped with their difficult circumstances. I managed to speak to some of Hitler's victims, such as Sophie Scholl. She was sentenced to death because she distributed anti-Nazi leaflets.

The essential function for my interviews is to *understand the mind of Hitler*. Every book written on that man described the events of his life, the Second World War, and the Holocaust. But no one focused on the question of the *"Why?"* I regarded myself as an anatomist, like Dr. Frankenstein, believing I'd eventually discover the ways he thought and rationalized; how and why he was possessed with that unparalleled homicidal rage against Jews and other so-called 'Undesirable Races.' And to do that, I had to place myself inside Hitler's brain. I admit that was Daddy's idea. I had doubts. Of course, I did. Because none of it made sense. Actually, I thought it impossible. How could I be 'in the mind of a mass murderer'? Wouldn't that mean I'd have to 'be' him? Wouldn't I have to accept and believe his evil thinking?

I had no idea what Daddy meant.

There were numerous other questions I had to ask given the multiple contradictions in his life. For example –

1. Why did he refuse to study architecture or painting when the Vienna Academy of Fine Arts rejected him?

2. How can he justify a preference to being homeless and living in homeless shelters rather than actually work?

3. Why was he so bitter with hate during his youth, admitting that others saw him as an "eccentric"?

4. Why and how did he become an anti-Semite?

5. It was one thing to be an anti-Semite; unfortunately, there are too many anti-Semites throughout history and many nations. But to be a *genocidal anti-Semite?* Why did he create, organize and manage a European-wide physical annihilation of Jews from Paris to the Caucasus in Russia?

6. Why did he invade Russia when his intelligence knew next to nothing about Stalin's military strength and war economy?

7. Why did he needlessly declare war on America when he had no contractual obligations to do so?

8. Why did he not surrender when the war was lost, specifically after Stalingrad?

9. Why did he insist on diverting precious resources for his SS in their exterminatory policies when he knew his armed forces were desperately in short supply of men, weapons, fuel, trains, and in every attribute a functional army needs?

All these questions are one more step in my hope of painting the most accurate portrait of the evilest man in modern history. I don't know if I succeeded. I'm now in my nineties. But my memories are crystal clear of those months I spent in the Bunker and outside the Bunker in Berlin. In addition, I wrote copious notes of every recorded interview as I thought about what I had experienced and what I felt during our conversations.

Finally, I'll tell you about my writing style. Primarily uneducated, I write whatever comes to my mind. I make grammatical mistakes. I know that. I use slang because that's who I am. So, if you want words that no one says in their private lives, don't look any more here. I'm authentic. And. That's how I write. I write freely with an open mind and heart without caring for a historian's superficial niceties, rules, and regulations. Or, a scholar, I suppose. However, I'll tell you when interviewing the Nazis; I tried as much as I can to speak in a formal manner.

I'm the first telling I'm no scholar, historian, or academician. The same goes for my interviews. I write and think. Follow my flying mind: no constraints and no restrictions ordering me *not* to say this and *not* to employ that phrase. However, I did read tons of material on that man. While *I* think *he* was meeting a bumbling young farm girl, *I* was prepared to ask him hardball questions.

~

Introducing Me – Myself!

I ought to introduce myself, if only briefly.

My name is Dorothy Gale. These are my memoirs for a brief period in my life—a few months, to be exact. Barely twenty years old, I was sent to Berlin to interview the Third Reich leader, Adolf Hitler.

I was born in Germany, where Daddy was wealthy by inheritance, allowing us to live in outrageous opulence. Daddy never worked, preferring to spend his money profligately and allowing us to spend as much as wanted. At the same time, he never considered the potent reality that if you've got no income, no matter how rich you are, your millions will eventually dwindle to zero.

When the economic depression hit the world in the late twenties, Weimar Germany suffered catastrophic economic consequences, with businesses going bankrupt and unemployment soaring in the millions. Daddy didn't lose his money because of any companies – he had no business except for maniacally spending his diminishing money. As far as I remember, which is obscure, we became impoverished overnight. One day he came to our house and faintly spoke, "I'm broke."

Unable to cope with being poor, we emigrated to the United States – the Land of Milk and Honey! My excitement was unbounded, thinking we were somehow going straight to Hollywood itself - and just being there means I'd become rich, glamorous, and famous!

Now my 'real' or I should say, originally, I was named Dorothea Sturm. But Daddy, knowing we Germans weren't a popular lot, anglicized our names once we arrived in the United States. Remember, the Great War wasn't so far ago, and many Americans, especially Anglo-Saxon protestants, hated us Germans. And so yours truly, 'Dorothea' became 'Dorothy.' He also translated our family name. In German, our name was 'Sturm,' so he translated that into English, 'Gale' — and there you go, I become Dorothy Gale!

I'm not sure why my Father settled us in a rural area outside a small 'town' called Goodland in rural Kansas. I say 'town,' but in truth, it was nothing more than a squalid hamlet. Further adding to my dismay, our economic status did not change a penny in America. So much for milk and honey.

My Father, though highly educated, couldn't find any job, successfully rejecting in every application he made. And I understood why — he had no work experience because, as I said, the fool never worked in his life. Who'd hire a middle-aged man with not a day's work of experience? Therefore, poverty remained firmly wedded to the cursed Gale family.

My own education was limited up to High School. I was a non-starter. Uninterested in anything academic. My only passion and ambition in those hazy days was to be a famous Hollywood actress. That was a dead-end hope since I had no idea how to be a Hollywood actress when you live in Goodland. But I clung to my fantasy. That was it. Fame was the aim of my game!

When I was twelve or thirteen, my troubles began. Life was empty. I only read on Hollywood stars. Gossip. Empty words. I noted anxieties waving and rumbling. Overnight I changed from a dolly, edible, fuzzy girl to a sullen, temperamental girl. I was 'losing out' from not being joyfully alive, while a door or a few miles away, everyone else in the

United States were in their throes of unstoppable excitement and merriment. I thought the entirety of America was outside Goodland.

Why wasn't I famous? Hedy Lamarr. Vivien Leigh. Ava Gardner. Fetish goddesses. Nothing else mattered in life. People philosophize on the stupid question, *"What's the meaning and purpose of life?"* Fame, glamor, being loved, rich — what else? Stupid Gilgamesh, searching for the impossible. Stupid Icarus. Seeking the impossible. I knew my pursuit was practical and grounded on sanity.

Think of this. A juxtaposition, I mean. I'll speak of your times. Famous model, actress Cara Delevingne and any of the glorious Kardashian sisters. Let's take the most famous one, [I think] Kim Kardashian. Who are they, these immensely renowned people? Why are they so exceptionally famous people? In some ways, I suppose, you can say or ask or question, "Who cares why they're famous? They're famous, and that's it." That was me. I can't remember knowing, but we even had the so-called 'It-Girl' — famous for being famous in some decade. Mind you, that one I never understood. Because the Kardashians created something, and Delevingne was a model, the It-Girl, by definition, is famous, though never having achieved nor made anything.

Looking back, I have no answers as to why I never made a serious effort to be an actress. That answers my question, "Why wasn't I famous?" I made no effort. Not at all. I mean, I could've traveled to Los Angeles, as many stars did before me. But I never thought of doing that, despite my astronomical revulsion against Goodland.

Anyway, following school, I worked as a secretary with the local Goodland police station. Why did I do that? For prestige, I guess. And to get the hell out of the terminal boredom of lifeless 'life' in rural Goodtown.

But, the boredom didn't go. The nickel and dimes we were paid was peanut currency, as far as I was concerned. And prestige? Nobody noticed nor cared I was working with the police. That's another example of youthful stupidity. You see, everyone knew what Dorothy was doing. I was no detective, nor was I in a high position with the police department. I was a secretary. In other words, I may as well be a secretary for any firm or company, and no one would regard me with any greater esteem because I'm still just a dumb typing and tea-making secretary.

A mind genuinely unconnected to reality. Naïve in its emoty depths. My God, how naïve I was!

I had to be. *How* did I know I was naïve? For an impressive start, physically, I never walked beyond the glittering gutter hole of my unknown miniature pig town, Goodland, except once. I was uninterested in any subject, be it from the arts, going all the way to zoology. Nothing interested me. Once Daddy insisted on taking to the library in Topeka. The idea revolted me, but being in no mood to argue yet again, I just went.

Jacob Gale: Which department would you like to see?

DG: What do you mean 'department'?

JG: Girl, which subject? Libraries, like bookshops, are divided into different categories.

DG [Angrily Shouting]: I still do not understand you!

JG: Shush, idiot! You aren't even allowed to talk in a library, let alone —

DG [Angrily]: Just get on with it.

                {Tense Silence}

JG: I mean subjects. Do you know what 'subjects' mean? For example, astronomy, biology, cooking, fiction, non-fiction, and so on. That's how they're divided.

DG [Angrily]: So what's your point?

JG: I love your rage.

                {Tense Silence}

DG [Fuming]: Don't push me, I swear …

JG: Which topic interests you?

DG: Nothing. Absolutely nothing.

                {Tense Silence}

JG: Do you mean you're not interested in any topic, ranging from 'A' to 'Z'?

DG [Surly]: Well done, now you understand!

Recalling that conversation, I'm shocked at how anyone is uninterested in any subject on earth and the universe. But that was Dorothy. You can mention any subject, topic, theme — I'd be turning away. And that's a staggering illustration of stupidity. Looking back, how could I be that person? And Daddy would remind me of that day, and at the moment, he'd repeat it —

JG: Girl, that was the moment I realized you have no mind. Because if a human has no interest in anything on this planet, then they have no interest in being productive in life.

Now you can easily understand when sophisticated, suave city people saw me, why they snickered and said to each other, "Will you look at that! What a sad example of an iconic redneck, bumkin, hilly billy country girl!"

Dorothy's mind lived, enjoyed, and thrived only on matters such as talking with my girlfriends about dancing, movies, gossip, and doing the daily routine chores, and constant anecdata. Nothing more swayed me. Nothing less.

∼

Daddy, Poverty, A Life of Hell, Boredom, and Fantasies

I was imbued with an *angry* sensibility. And it was the enigma of not knowing the causes nor the origins of that anger that eventually shoved me to find answers. My emotions were a haphazard grid of anger and hurt. Uncomfortable fusions of changing complementary and contrasting energies trying to cohabitate in my mind, in my brain matter, or God knows where and yet failing to achieve any peace. Niggling self-feuding obsessional thoughts. Endlessly picking on myself. You could say there was a Civil War in Dorothy's mind. A mind wilfully scouring every worriment I had. With nothing resolved, ignoring my desperate needs for any resolution. Anxieties fracturing my self-confidence, my self-esteem. There were abstract whirlwinds in my mind actively and daily seeking to degrade, humiliate and scorn my totality and composure, especially when I was out in public with people.

Hurt. How can I define that? Hurt. I know it's there. Inside me. One day or night, I realize something embarrassing. How can I find answers when I don't know the question? What a joke. I was, I am a joke. Prevailing overwhelmingly miserable self-loathing feeling. Why is this perpetual life-murdering hurt that forever causes my uncontrollable mind to be driven into suicidal needs? How can I understand anything in my mind, say 'hurt,' when I cannot define it as the physical parts of my body, such as my nose, legs, etc.? How can one deal or interact with the abstract mind when it is abstract and therefore indefinably untouchable?

I know what you're thinking. Why exactly is this girl telling us about her problems? We're only interested in reading her interviews with Hitler and the people around him. And now she's going on and on ... about her mental problems ...

Daddy.

Did you know my Daddy was the kindest man you would ever be lucky enough to meet? Not when he was living, though. I was a mortal bitch to him. Well, he's no longer with us. Of course, I regret screaming at him, swearing, and you name it, I did it. I was to tell you not *once* did Daddy ever raise his voice in anger or never spoke bad language in his life. Would that tilt your mind and opinion? Peaceful as Jesus walking on the calmest, glassy waters. There he was, Daddy. But like all humans, he was not a one-dimensional cartoon character. And 'cartoon' was one aspect of his personality.

∼

Daddy and General S. George Patton

As I said, no one employed my old man except for one beastly son of you know what, hiring him to work on his pig farm. At first, he avoided talking about his job. But I was incessant. I was hoping he had a high-ranking position in pig farming, which would mean we'd be getting good money again. Well, Daddy being no liar, told me the truth of his employment status. His role was cleaning up farm dirt. And then, in time, he refined his words, as per his job description, clarifying his actual job.

He cleaned pig poo.

It shocked me that he wasn't deemed competent enough to be a proper pig farmer. No, my old man was only good and able to be a first-class shit shoveler.

For you readers in your modern world, what I'm saying sounds like an obsolete way of thinking. But your modern-day world of the present is not the 1920's world. Realities change. I'm sure poo-shoveling is mechanized now.

By the time the Second World War began, what Daddy done for a living stewed an embarrassment in me, turning into mortification to the brim. I'll remind you of some words of one of our heroes, General Patton's himself —

George S. Patton: "There is one great thing you men will be able to say when you go home.... Thirty years from now, when you're sitting around the fireside with your grandson on your knee, and he asks what you did in the great World War II, you won't have to say, *'I shoveled shit in Louisiana.'*"

But that wasn't the end of my shame. You'll hear more about Patton later in my story. Trust me.

∼

Man's Cruelty to Daddy

His boss taunted Daddy. Repeated barbs. And not just him. All God-fearing people around us mocked him. Because he was a failure. And more. Because he *was* a certified failure, how could he refute their accusations when after all, weren't they speaking the truth?

Yes, they spoke the Essential truth, and that fundamental truth was that Daddy was nothing more than a pig shit shoveler. That meant he was no better than what he was shoveling. That is how the eyes of our folks saw it, or him. And that stung me, even though, as I said, we constantly fought. Or I did. Cloudy bitterness to crystal clear bitterness at the world. Soring my childhood and adolescence until I'd go to Berlin. 'Soring' isn't a word, but I made it a word. Or verb.

'Cloudy'?Because sometimes I couldn't understand my feelings. Or why they were doing what they were doing. Trembling hurt. But 'stung' by what? Stung by people's basest viciousness. And by 'people,' I mean all people. No quarter, no mercy, no compassion was ever shown to Daddy. I kept asking myself the same unanswered question, 'Why?' *Why* would people feel it necessary to go out of their way whenever they came across my Daddy and spit at him? *Why* did people feel a need so crucial to singly and hurt, demean, and publicly degrade an innocent man? *Why* can't the decent side of Daddy also be taken into consideration? *Why* did it always have to be the vile, insidious, dark side that overwhelms everyone and not the virtuous side in people?

But then, what a hypocrite, Dorothy! Wasn't I too implacably abusive to him? Wasn't I rude to him on a daily basis? Wasn't I shouty to him on a daily basis? And yet, when people verbally mocked Daddy, I felt plunged deep, deep down, with depressive sorrow for the poor soul.

So I existed silently blazing. Uncoordinated, fragmented rage. Nothing constructive. How many times, I screamed in my brain, "Daddy! Defend yours! Fight back!"

But he's a failure. So, why would I expect him to react positively when positivity did not exist in one cell of his body? Total, abject failure. He'd given up on life, I guess, looking back. I don't know. He never spoke. And that was another thing that hurt the life out of me after he finally left the hell on earth that was his 'life.' I never asked him about his life, about his experiences. So, I knew nothing about him. Did he suffer anxieties? Panic? Depression? Was he abused as a child?

The only side he showed was the proud, dignified, literate, fiery conversationalist back in Germany. I remember he was liked or loved by millions of people. Of course, I've no idea if any of those people were genuine; they could've been 'friends' because of his money. More to the point, because not only did he endlessly invite them to the poshest restaurants for lunch and dinner, he'd also give them money and buy them expensive items such as cars, pay their rent, and so on. Who wouldn't be attracted to be his 'best friend'?

But once in happy Kansas, he was beat. Whispering more than talking. Faded. Dying. You'd think he was dumb. The only time his old flaming energies would be rekindled was when he talked to his children. He wanted to imprint his errors in our minds so we wouldn't go down the death trap he hurtled down into in his life.

And that's how folks in Kansas saw Daddy. But is that it? That's all they saw. That's how they judged him. It didn't matter he was an entirely decent, loving, peaceful, compassionate human being. Doesn't our civilized society care for those noble attributes in Man anymore? The answer, my friend, is no.

No. And that's because decency, morality, virtue, and decorum don't matter in society. So that's it— end of the road. Nothing more to say for now. See you in the next chapter.

~

Hearing of A Job Opportunity – To Be Sent to Germany

United States Government – Washington D.C.

Job Vacancy Opportunity

Job Description: Interviewing Ordinary Civilians.

Requirements: Fluency in German Essential.

Location: Europe

When I first read of this job vacancy, some government announcement, I was unsure if it was real or a joke. Only when Daddy told me it was serious did I understand, and boy, did he encourage *me* to apply. Apply? Me? A simple Kansas farm girl?

And when he persisted, I resisted. And the more he insisted, the more I resisted! His overtly positive views of me had to be skewed in my skin because I had no sense of pride, self-worth, nothing. And *this* job? Seriously? I mean, Daddy had to know, not even a half-witted state official of our noble United States government would hire an unschooled country girl for such a sterling-sounding job. And he'd give me some dreary answer or statement or whatever like - "*Girl, you must know yourself.*"

That's the key to joy. Know your limitations. Know your strengths. We, humans, are as a nation. I'm giving his opinions, by the way, not mine. A nation has a population, geography, and resources. It's up to governments, leaders to harness the best for their country. Unfortunately, most governments, regimes, leaders are uninterested in the people; they harness all goods for themselves, their families, cronies, and few supporters. Such countries are weak, and, as stated, most people live lives of no hope, high unemployment, low wages, back-breaking jobs with long hours, homes unfit for human habitation, no education, no medical facilities. And therefore, most consequentially, there isn't much hope or prospect of climbing the financial and social ladder. Now remember what I said – people are exactly as a nation, keep that in mind. That's how most people live out their lives too. Most people live in dilapidated homes, bad neighborhoods, high crime, divided families, lousy education, high dropout rates, inadequate medical facilities, unemployment, low-paying, under-staffed, and over-worked jobs with no promotions they too have next to no chance of ever getting better socio-economic status. But there is hope. If there's a will. You can educate yourself, despite the wrecked schools. You can still navigate the choppy waters, get a degree and find a job that will make you financially independent from anyone and any institution, such as a lending bank.

~

Daddy Tells Me Why I Must Take This Job - *If* I Want to Find the Meaning of My Life and Why God Allows Evil

Jacob Gale: Girl, that's precisely why you must apply for the job.

DG: What? Why ... how ... why would they hire me when I've got nothing, no facts, no knowledge?

JG: I have three reasons.

DG [Angrily]: Oh, you came all prepared, talking to me and all that! Please, Daddy!

JG: Girl, don't give me attitude, or I'm done talking.

{*Tense Silence*}

DG: This posting or job is for an educated candidate. And you know, and I know ... I've not got that level of brains.

JG: I agree with you.

DG[Angrily]: Excuse me? You now saying I'm dumb?

JG: What do you think?

{*Tense Silence*}

JG: Have you ever read one academic book? No. Have you ever shown any interest in anything in the world apart from Hollywood actors and actresses? No, you have not.

DG [Angrily]: Well, then, Sir, you've just made my point, now, haven't you?

JG: But that should be one of the most potent incentives right there.

DG [Shouting]: You ... drive ... me ... insane! And I don't even understand your damn words!

{Tense Silence}

JG: Do you hear the way you talk, girl?

DG[Angry]: I hear your attitude. It's disgusting.

JG: You cannot even speak one sentence in English.

DG[Angry]: You see? You're evil. The worse Dad in the world!

JG: And you know that, so don't pretend you don't know –

DG [Angry]: Tell me something new! I know my English is slangy!

JG: And your delightful *'slangy'* English will never get you a white-collar job.

DG: Who cares?

JG: "Who cares"? Do you want to live in poverty all your life? Haven't you had enough? Look now, English is not *my* first language. I should be excused if I make mistakes. Not that people care, because they don't. But I learn, and I'm always trying to better my language skills because that would me look -

DG[Angrily]: Please, Jesus, don't give me the 'self-pity-me-story' again, will you?

{Silence}

He took a deep breath, closed his eyes, and sat back in his chair.

DG: You good, Daddy?

{Silence}

JG: Super.

{Silence}

DG: Why you quit talking?

{Silence}

JG [Slowly]: This is your first opportunity. Stacking up your mind with academic literature. Texts. Reading relevant details. Facts. Statistics.

{Silence}

JG: These treasures will, in turn, situate you in the precise location and the prime position when you will be aiming your unrivaled questions.

DG: Questions about what? Whose lives?

JG: Don't you whom we're talking about, girl?

{Silence}

JG [Excited]: We're talking about our people. Our blood. Deutschland! It hasn't been so long ago that we had to leave Germany. Never forget your roots, girl!

DG: What 'roots'?

JG: You remember we had to leave home?

DG: Yes. Kind of.

JG: And now, today, no people on earth suffer more than our people, girl. Isn't it time you too should do something? How about you, too, send a helping hand for your blood and race? Shouldn't we pay back? Do something for them?

DG: *They* began the war, Daddy.

JG [Firmly]: I'm *not* talking politics, Dorothy. I'm *not* interested in politics. I'm talking about humans who happen to be our people. Our blood.

DG [Laughing]: You sound like them Nazis!

JG: This is your moment to awaken, girl. You can choose not to wake up. You can go back to sleep. Remain an idiot for the rest of your life. Remain living in poverty. That's your choice. But now you're being given the possibility of upgrading your life. Getting a better-paid job. Making more money. Getting yourself out of the deathtrap known as 'Poverty.'

My mind was wandering everywhere. What is Vivien Leigh doing right now? What did she eat today? Probably crumbs. What's her house like? Palatial. What a dumb question? What did I think? She'd live in some African hut? Ha! How many servants does she have? Did Daddy notice I'm daydreaming while he's rattling off his numb words? Does she have her sexual needs fulfilled? Wait a minute; is she a virgin? God no! She's married, isn't she? I'm not sure … I don't know. Is she a lesbian?

JG: Germans are going through the Apocalypse of the Beast. I know these terms are complex, especially for you kids. Unfortunately, the Devil's Apocalypse is doing just that. He's doing it right now as you and I converse here … visualize thousands of miles away from us, a place called Hell, our beloved Germany. The Apocalypse is thundering right now down and upon our homeland, Germany! Neither you nor I have the faintest intimation of what it is like out there. That is why *I believe God has called upon you, my daughter Dorothy, to go there, to witness and to experience the Devil's Apocalypse in that cursed land.*

DG: Daddy, it's just another war like all wars. We all know what they're like —

And if she's not sexually satisfied, what's she doing about it? Vivien Leigh. Jesus, Son of God and Mary, what a beauty!

Women can't hook up with whores. I never thought of that. What *do* we do in those challenging circumstances?

JG [Angrily]: No, no, no, no! You have *not* understood what I just read to you, the text from our Holy Book. What has befallen upon Germany is *not* a war!

DG: If what's going on between us and Germany isn't a war, what would you call it?

JG [Frantic]: I plead with you to understand that no war and no calamity in history has ever befallen a nation, a people, a civilization such as that which is plaguing and, in essence, exterminating Germany.

{Silence}

Do you have to be straight to be a great actress? I know, I'm sure, many actresses are lesbian. Just entering the acting world means society regards you as a whore. That was true in Germany back in the twenties. So, by definition, any actress, and any cabaret performer, had to be a misfit, ostracised by 'respectable' German society.

{Silence}

DG: Why is this war different, apart from having better weapons?

I felt guilty for not noticing, let alone hearing Daddy speak. It's funny because, like I told you 99%, I was a bitch to him. But then, in unknown and unexpected moments, I'd be almost drowning with sorrow for him. I didn't want to hurt him because I know he meant well for me. But he too had to understand ... I had nothing in connection or interest in his numbing words.

JG: You cannot just go there, thinking I'm only going to be reporting a 'war.' You've got to study much more, girl. You must explore the specific *reasons* why the Devil, with his Apocalypse, chose to plunge this civilized, sophisticated, wealthy, cultured nation of Germany into his pits and in his realm of the abyss.

DG: Daddy, words or expressions you use, like "pits" and "realm of the abyss," mean nothing to me. They're just manufactured words.

JG: Before judging, will you at least try to listen?

DG: What's the point of listening when I'm lost?

{Tense Silence}

JG: The Devil chose for our flesh and blood people to exist in a place of perdition that no society and no nation has ever witnessed. That is why I am talking to you. For this is not a war; we are witnessing the mass extermination not just of our people but the deliberate physical extermination of Germany itself.

DG [Excited]: But Germany declared war on us, and they deserve –

JG [Angrily]: No, that's not true. That's why you must read. You must learn, Dorothy.

{Tense Silence}

DG: How long are you planning for this conversation?

JG [Angrily]: Seriously? Is this the tone you choose to speak to me?

DG: Daddy ... why can't you just understand this subject is tedious, dead, dull as death, and killing me?

{Tense Silence}

JG: If that is how you feel, so be it.

{Tense Silence}

DG [Angrily]: Daddy ... I've hardly ... you know ... I've never been interested in Germany, and you know that. And now you pretend I'm supposed to be fascinated by Hitler and that war and all that?

JG: I know. It's my fault. I was obsessed with you, my children becoming Americanised. I neglected our German heritage. It wasn't easy being German in America in the Twenties.

Talking of getting sexual needs fulfilled, what about prisons? What do straight girls do? Where or what ... no how can they satisfy their instincts when all they are women? I'm not stupid to think straight women in prison can go for years without water.

JG[Angrily]: Are you listening?

DG[Angrily]: Hell yeh, I am! I'm happy you remember you taught us nothing about that country ... fantastic. Now try to understand my world *from my viewpoint*, right? All I'm interested in is ... and it is not surprising, is America – Hollywood, Hollywood, Hollywood, Hollywood, and Hollywood! And you knew that, Daddy! And now turn to me, out of the blue and you ... you suddenly want me to do some retarded job in Germany, a country I don't give a damn about ... and you want me to be a student in that country's Germany's recent history, civilization, and culture? Are you nuts?

{Silence}

JG: You're right.

DG: What?

JG: I asked too much of you. You don't have the mind for it.

DG: Good!

∼

After Fighting Daddy So Much, I Choose to Think About His Words

I went to Daddy and played cute and coy. He knew what I meant. I'd accept more of his words on that hated subject.

JG: You must study that regime, its philosophy, its ideology. And that's why ultimately, you've got to go in-depth and explore the man in question, Adolf Hitler.

DG: Why that idiot?

JG: Without knowing Hitler, you cannot understand the German people, and if you don't understand the mentality of the German people today, you won't be able to ask them the relevant questions. Remember, they've been living with that regime for twelve years. That means you were only eight years when their experience began. It's almost a lifetime. And you must remember how it all started. God chose you, girl. In the beginning, it was the same as it was with Eve. They were seduced, rightly or wrongly. That's how this catastrophe began. And there's another matter you must know.

DG: Wait. Why would you say *'God chose me'* to do this checking-up in Germany? You know that sounds crazy, right? It's one thing doing the job, you know, interviewing Nazis and all that, but then your language changes when you start personalizing the job, as though -

JG: I don't know why I have this belief, Dorothy ... but I do. And you are correct. My primary motivation is not the job, per se. It is my belief the job will liberate your soul from the cave you are in.

DG: What in God's name are you –

JG: It *is my conviction*—one given to me by our Lord in that you are the chosen one to go back to our beloved Fatherland ... and so it must be, Dorothy. And the purpose is clear. As I said, it is difficult as it may be through that job, so you shall discover your genuine self and be happy for your earthly life.

DG [Laughing]: Okay, that's crazier than all the crazy words you've already said!

JG: My daughter, do you think I'd purposely insist you go to a dangerous place?

{Silence}

JG: Obviously not. So, why on earth would I be talking about sending you to the most dangerous spot on the planet, Berlin?

DG: Because you're nuts!

JG: I will tell you my second reason. Girl, we live in a No Man's Land, you know that.

DG: Actually, no, I *don't know* that.

JG: What?

DG: Just kidding!

JG: We are poor. We have no hope of making our lives better. But, again, you know that.

DG: Whatever.

JG: If you want to better your income and better your living standards - how do you suppose you'll be doing that when you're nothing more than a secretary in Goodland?

DG: I thought of that, Daddy ... you know.

JG: No, I don't know.

DG: Well, I mean, I'd just live in Nowhere Land. Being a Nowhere Girl.

JG [Angrily]: There you go! ... I'm happy you've been thinking as to how to get yourself out of your economic plight. For me, I'm too old. I've used every card God gave me, and I –

DG: You wasted every card.

JG: You're still only a precious twenty years old, girl. Now God is giving you His first and most incredible card He has ever offered to my princess.

DG: I think you're kind of being way too over-excited about this vacancy.

JG: Hear me out. Third reason.

DG: "Third reason"? Why I don't remember –

JG: And maybe this is the most important one, girl. When you go, you shall finally discover not only the Truth - more importantly, you shall find the identity of yourself.

DG [Laughing]: What on earth are you talking about, Daddy?

JG: And the two are as one entity.

DG: What "two"? What "entity" do you mean? You're nuttier than nuts!

JG: The Truth God intends for you is the reality of your mind and soul. Each individual needs to find their identity. Otherwise, we can only go on living out our deplorable lives in a procession of silent mourning depression. He who does not know of the reality of his mind lives an unlived life. Only those who discover themselves and the Truth God intended for them can be serene in their lifetime. Again, remember what I just said. Finding your reality and the truth of God is one. As energy and mass are one too. What I say is difficult to achieve. That is why only a tiny minority achieve that exalting self-knowledge in their lives. And you shall several existentially necessary facts about yourself and your presence on this earth.

I felt hopeless and already exhausted by his tedious words. My God, please help me get out of these conversations from Hell.

DG: What?

JG: You'll discover your mind. That is number one. Two, you shall discover the actual meaning in your life here on this earth.

DG [Chuckling]: All of this simply is going to be achieved by talking to Krauts?

JG [Frantic]: Yes, yes … exactly! Finally, you'll understand why God allows evil, misery, and suffering unto Mankind.

DG: I hear you, but it's not easy understanding you because you sound like them, crazy evangelists. Your words are not for me. I'm too young, Daddy. Like I said, the truth, my truth is true right now.

JG [Excited]: If only you have faith in me. Hitler once said, *"Geduld! Geduld!"* He was warning Britain that if they continued with their bombing campaigns against civilians of Germany –

DG [Angrily]: Why do you quote that man?

JG: He promised that patience has its limits, and soon he will unleash his terror bombing campaign against British civilians. So, I tell you ... again, Dorothy ... *jump* into this glorious opportunity! Keep your eyes closed and take that leap. Keep Faith! Do not hesitate! And do not overthink the matter. Jump! And so, you shall be delivered unto differing realms of existence you believed did not exist, *for there are* different realities on earth.

I was so bored. God help me.

JG: You shall witness differing moralities in this journey you shall undertake. You shall meet differing truths on this earth. You shall meet Saints, and you shall meet Sinners. Some know of themselves, while others are ignorant of their attributes. Only in seeing and experiencing evil do you, and you shall finally find your mind, which is the moment of true happiness. There can be no other way to the path of contentment or serenity.

DG [Laughing]: Already? And you're still driving more nonsense! Old man! What's up with you this night? How can there be differing realities and differing moralities on this earth? You're talking old-time hogwash, Daddy! There is only one truth, one reality, and one glorious God in Heaven!

JG: And when you fuse those contradictory symptoms of the sickness and the sacrosanct in the mind of Man. That will be the gracious day you will have reached the peaks of Jerusalem; so, help me God if I lie unto you Beloved Daughter, that you are. For, He is my Silent Witness. *You must dine with the Devil, carouse with him,* and believe me, Dorothy girl, only then shall you know of the Truth, and only Truth will grant you eternal serenity.

DG [Laughing]: Daddy! If you admit you're nuts, I'll admit I love you no matter how nutty you are!

Maybe Daddy was right, in some ways. Or was he using me to get him money? Here was my first and last opportunity to get out and away from No-Man's-Land of Goodland, Kansas. Get instant fame. Being the first interviewer asking Germans in-depth questions. Not bad for a twenty-year-old Kansas farmer girl?

And all I can tell you is this — I started to read. Funny, because that's God's first word to Mohammad, Prophet of Islam. *'Read!'*

"Read! In the name of thy Lord who Createth. Createth man from a clot. Read! And thy Lord is the Most Bounteous, Who teacheth by the pen, Teacheth man that which he knew not."

- (Quran - Surat Al-Alaq 96:1-5 MPT)

So, I did, and with tremendous zest, I swear to you, I dove deep into every word, book, text, journal, periodical, document on Germany, the regime, their leader. And when not reading, I would think and analyse it all, which would sprout a million more questions I had to answer. And so, the process went on.

~

Job Interview with Anonymous DC Official – December 1944

Yes, I chose to go for the interview.

I. The Anonymous Interviewer Loses His Nerves

Anonymous Official: You have been selected for this interview, and we would like to welcome you.

DG: Who is the "we"?

AO: Excuse me?

DG: You said, "We would like to so and so on." I'm asking you who's the "we"?

AO: This is the proper manner professionals talk ... sorry, what is your name?

DG: Dorothy.

AO: Good. What do you know about this post?

DG: All I know is what you guys wrote. How else can I know when you wrote nothing else?

AO: Just to be accurate, I did not write the ad.

DG: Well, the guy or gal who wrote it did not say much. Meaning when you ask me what do I know about the job, I can only answer you given what —

AO [Angrily]: All right. I understand. Enough.

DG: Angry, already?

AO: What did you read in our post?

DG: You don't know what's written in the post?

DG: Ms. Gale. This is an interview. You are not here *to ask me questions*. Is that understood?

DG: You want to know what I know about this post?

AO: That is my question.

DG: You guys want a German-speaking person interviewing German civilians.

AO: And specifically, the enemy demanded a relatively uneducated female.

DG: Excuse me?

AO: I said the German side insisted on one condition. The interviewer had to be a female, not older than twenty, and more importantly, she must not have any university education.

DG: So, you want idiots like me.

AO: That's not what I —

DG: I'm only kidding. Go on with your interview.

AO: What do you know about the war?

DG: We're fighting two nations, Japs and Krauts. It sure looks like we're winning.

AO: What do you know about Nazi Germany?

DG: Well, as you may know, or you may not know, my parents emigrated from Weimar Germany. I think I'm well acquainted with my former homeland. I've got lots of families there too. Don't know who's living or dead, though.

AO: What do you know about our present military situation?

DG: We're in a bit of a pickle at this moment –

AO: What do you mean?

DG: Well, they kind of surprised us in that Ardennes attack, didn't they?

AO: Early days, my dear.

DG: What?

AO: Never mind. Go on.

DG: I didn't think he had it him to do anything.

AO: Could you please speak in a proper manner?

DG: I said I didn't think Hitler would do anything against us.

AO: Why do you say that?

DG: 'Cause he's beat.

AO: We will continue our drive straight into Germany proper, and it will be us rushing and racing to reach Berlin first.

{*Silence*}

AO: What do you know about their ideology?

DG: I was hoping you wouldn't me ask that one.

AO: Why?

DG: Because it's embarrassing.

AO: Why is it embarrassing?

DG: All my life, we been picked on, you know?

AO: Why?

DG: Well, we've been harassed, ridiculed, and bullied, you know. But then again, who can blame them, you know?

AO: Why?

{*Silence*}

DG: You don't know why?

AO: No, I don't.

{*Silence*}

DG [Laughing]: Do you not know I'm German? A German emigrant?

AO: I did not know that.

{*Silence*}

DG: You thought I'm American?

AO: Yes.

{*Silence*}

DG: Wow. You sure read your notes right on me.

AO: Excuse me?

DG [Laughing]: Shouldn't you know whom you're talking to before interviewing people?

AO [Angrily]: Now listen here, this is the *second* time I'm reprimanding you. You do *not* ask questions. Do you understand? If not, this interview must end. Do you understand?

DG: Yeh, but my point is still valid.

The idiot shuffles his notes, looking for my name.

DG: Dorothy Gale.

AO [Angrily]: Thank you, yes. Do you wish to proceed or not?

DG: Shoot.

AO: Are you talking about your neighbours?

DG: I'm sorry. I lost the point of us talking.

AO: You mean you forgot my question.

DG: Yes, put your reality in your words.

AO [Furious]: Honestly, I must say this. I have not yet, nor ever met any person such as you, Ma'am. You are not just rude. You are not just linguistically challenged. But you have a style that bores ion the mind of a professional such as I am saying this because one essentiality in my job is level headed no matter what the enemy in front of me is doing and saying and –

DG: Wouldn't that make me best for your job thing?

AO [Shouting]: Yes, in a sick way, you would … you would …

{*Tense Silence*}

AO: I'm sorry I lost my temper. That was unprofessional.

DG: It sure was.

AO: We were talking about people taunting you, your family.

DG: Yes, everyone. Students, acquaintances, colleagues, people at work.

AO: You said, 'I can't blame them.'

DG: Did I say, 'Who can blame them?'

AO: Yes, you did. What did you mean?

DG: I mean, people can sort of put up with Wilhelmine Germany and that great war. But this one? This war is seriously different. We've never seen a fight like this in modern history.

AO: Why?

DG: Because of the freaky ideology of Germany.

AO [Angrily]: You're really fraying my nerves –

DG: "Fraying"?

AO [Angrily]: I've repeatedly asked you to refrain from speaking in slang.

DG [Angrily]: Why the hell do you care? The moment I speak, you blow up! What kind of an interviewer are you? And you've got the power and right to kick me out, don't you? So, if you find me so damnably offensive, why are you still interviewing me?

DG: Like you speak in this automated way in your home? And you know what? If you don't like me, tell me to get the hell out, and I'll be gone and happily so too.

For some reason, I started laughing, pretty much uncontrollably.

{Silence}

AO: Are you ready to resume our –

DG: Listen, if I'm so bad, why you still talking to me ... or excuse me for my bad language? Why're you still interviewing me?

{Silence}

AO [Stiffly]: It is your choice. You can leave this room, or you can stay.

DG [Laughing]: No, go on. Fill me in with your questions; why not?

{Tense Silence}

I could feel he wanted to mangle me to shreds.

DG: And to have the weight of all the continual mockery heaped on us when neither I nor anyone from my family ever claimed *we're* the Master Race and other such idiotic words.

∼

II. Yours Truly, Attacking *His* Lack of Aptitude

I felt ... I noticed he had no idea what I was talking about because he forgot what we were talking about before losing his temper - dumb idiot! What an ass!

DG: Who hired you?

AO: I told you, and repeatedly –

DG: I know. We ask nothing. You ask us—the end.

AO: Precisely.

DG: But you lost your temper, man, and that's not in your rules and codes of conduct now, is it?

{Tense Silence}

AO: You have no right to make any comments on my conduct because -

DG [Laughing]: Wait a minute! If you're a lousy interviewer, we're *not* allowed to talk to your superiors? I know you've got seniors. After all, are you sure the president of the United States nor the boys of OSS are checking on you?

{Tense Silence}

DG: It's embarrassing, you know. Add to that the killing of Jews going on, and it adds up to be a nasty, brutish, and poor existence for us 'evil' German immigrants. But I haven't answered your question –

AO: Try not to repeat the same words, such as you did when you said, "add to that."

DG: Try not to be my stenchy stale English teacher.

{Tense Silence}

The cretin drew in a deep breath. I knew he was struggling with me. But my tactics were risky. Obviously, he could just throw me out as a useless candidate. But he didn't. And that's what incentivized me to push him more. Because, as I say, if I were out of line, I'd have been kicked out long ago. The fact that he didn't kick me out meant my behavior was acceptable. Maybe even agreeable.

DG: Probably I'm hiding my hypocrisy because I know for sure if I were a non-German American, why I too would be right there joshing them people, skirmishing, and striking them dunces, for believing they're racially 'superior' to us. That's why I understand them for doing what they have been doing to us.

AO: If, for some reason, you were chosen for this post, how would you feel going back to Germany and being with your people? Wouldn't you be biased or in an emotional state whereby you would favor them?

DG: Who hired you? How many years of experience have you had in interviewing us poor folk in America? Where are you from? Have you ever interviewed a farm girl from rural America?

AO [Shouting]: Stop these –

DG [Shouting]: Don't you dare shout at me, or I'm reporting you for verbal abuse.

{Tense Silence}

DG: I know you've got no clue. But I'm going to clue you in.

AO: I do not need –

DG: You're probably from a middle-class suburb. You've never met, let alone interacted with, any of us rural Americans. Why you don't even speak our language now, do you ... and you've manifested that already, haven't you, Sir? And 'ain't that odd now? Because you're a DC man, representing the government that is supposed to represent the people of America. But the truth is, as I said, you've got no connection to the majority of us Americans. You don't even understand our ideals, lifestyles, language, ethics, and so. Because you're just one more insulated government official who feels entirely foreign to the majority of 'his fellow' Americans. Now isn't that just one more supreme act of indifferent idiocy on the part of the elites running the show of government in DC when they choose the likes of aliens such as you?

To my surprise, for the first time, the idiot in question sat down.

~

III. Anonymous Interviewer Asks What I Know About Hitler

DG: Listen, I'm bored. I'll answer some more questions, and let's get going.

AO: Why did you apply for this post if you —

DG: Because of Daddy.

{Tense Silence}

AO: If accepted, would you be interested in deepening your knowledge on Hitler, his life, and deeds?

DG: Sure, I can. What's there to know about him?

AO: Excuse me?

DG: He is a nut. A kook.

AO: And is that it, in your learned opinion?

DG: Aha! I catch your sarcasm!

AO: What 'sarcasm'?

DG [Laughing]: You've been calling me an idiot, and now you tell me or ask me - my "learned opinion"?

AO: I do not understand your words.

DG [Angrily]: Listen, let me tell you something. A piece of my rural, retarded mind. I don't care if I get this shit job, you dig?

AO: How good of you to say that.

DG: Are you always robotic?

AO: I am robotic, yes. How correct you are.

DG: What more do you people want to learn from a lunatic?

AO: He is undoubtedly a madman; yes, that is true. He is also a madman who controlled a landmass stretching from Paris to Stalingrad just a few years ago.

DG [Laughing]: That only makes him a clever nut.

AO: Yes, you are funny, indeed. And, again, you may be correct. Now, if these iniquitous human beings can achieve vast feats of spectacular achievements, wouldn't you think it would be in our interest to study their minds?

DG [Laughing]: You know, him being a nut, why not save your time, resources, and money, and send me to my nearest local Kansas nuthouse and interview any of them, madmen, there?

AO: Do you think Germany's leader is in the same category as inmates of a mental asylum?

No, I'll stand my ground
Won't be turned around
And I'll keep this world from draggin' me down
Gonna stand my ground
And I won't back down

• *Tom Petty. 1989*

DG: Sure, as the sun rises and sets! I mean, he's no raving, out-of-control nut, the type you'd need to straitjacket! But then, not every lunatic inmate in them mental asylums need straitjackets. Sir, if you give me enough time, I'm sure I'd find you many Hitler's or Napoleon's and many more 'famous' kooks too.

AO: You may indeed find some inmates who have similar attributes that Hitler has. But we cannot be sure, can we?

DG: Say what?

AO: Again, I ask politely; ask you to try to speak proper English, please.

DG [Fuming]: This *is* my 'proper' English, please.

AO: Well, I was -

DG [Laughing]: And by the way, you ain't supposed to end no sentence with a preposition.

AO: You are correct. Now, all I'm saying is this. We can never be sure unless we talk directly to the man himself. Wouldn't that be far more to tangent for our purposes?

DG: "Tangent"?

AO: This post requires our candidate to interview the leader of Germany, Hitler.

DG: Yeh, you said that a million times.

{*Silence*}

I was bored again with this bare flesh. The entire point and purpose of that interview meant NOTHING to me.

DG: Well, because I'm German, I know a lot about that man.

I was lying.

AO: What do you mean, "you know"?

DG: I just told you that I know that I know; what more do you need to know from that man.

{*Silence*}

AO [Flustered]: Who told you?

DG: Do you think I can tell you?

{*Silence*}

AO [Confused]: What?

DG: What's confusing you?

AO: How did you know what you say you know?

I change the subject because, as I said, I was lying.

DG: What's *he* getting out of this?

AO: The man wants to reveal his Final Testament. Ironically, he does not trust one of his Herrenvolk to keep his words safe for posterity. Thus, he reached out to us to do that for him.

DG: Who can talk to him without him screaming and raving at you?

AO: Because we know he is not that kind of character as he is generally portrayed.

DG: How do you guys know that?

AO: That is not a question I can answer.

DG: So, what kind of interview or what's —

AO [Angrily]: I've already told you — we ask the questions, and you respond. If you're uncomfortable, you are free to exit this interview room.

DG: He's fine with that?

AO: Excuse me?

DG: I said Hitler is fine with us interviewing him?

AO: That is precisely it.

DG: Again, *why?*

AO: Sorry?

DG: What's in it for them?

AO: I've answered that question.

DG [Laughing]: They're not all dead, are they? Well, not yet anyway.

AO: Excuse me?

DG: You said he doesn't trust anyone from his people. Isn't that an exaggeration, right? I mean, doesn't he have someone, anyone to type whatever he wants to say?

AO: You mean to say, "doesn't he have someone, anyone to type whatever he wants to say?"

DG: Whatever, yes.

AO: I am sure he can get any typist, but that is hardly his real worry. He feels any supposed trusted men may well edit his words to give themselves a better chance when their trial day comes. Or maybe he thinks they will destroy it, fearing incriminating words – again to render their reputation in a cleaner light when they must face the courts.

I wondered if this man spoke in that same tone of voice with his family and friends? Was he insecure? I ask because, facing me, he presented an austere, robotic-like certainty when talking. Did he have anxieties that made him shiver with fear? Was he a closeted homosexual? Worse, if he were, was he married? God help his poor wife!

DG: How ironic is that!

AO: What do you mean?

DG [Laughing]: Well, our archenemy is depending on his archenemy to show an indifferent world his final unhinged words!

AO: You are right and wrong. The first part you say is correct, but the report we will gather will *not* be published.

DG [Surprised]: The interviews will remain secret?

AO: Until the war is over, the answer is yes. It's only for government officials to analyse. Officers from the OSS, the Department of War, top government-appointed psychiatrists, and other scholars will investigate many of our unanswered questions. Previously the OSS produced a psychiatric report on the man, and already many in the State Department, the Pentagon feel it is already too dated.

DG: What do you mean?

AO: The first report was written by the psychoanalyst Walter C. Langer. He worked for the Office of Strategic Services (OSS) and submitted his paper in late 1943 or early 1944, entitled *'A Psychological Analysis of Adolph Hitler: His Life and Legend.'*

Bored and despising this empty droning man.

AO: The report was an assessment of his mind. We have another analyst, the psychologist Henry A. Murray who wrote an essay entitled *'Analysis of the Personality of Adolph Hitler.'* But within months, many in our government found faults with these reports. For example, according to our profilers, most criminals have criminal attributes.

The subject meant nothing to me. If you're not interested in a topic, be it in a conversation or a job, you're not succeeding. I'd never thought of Hitler. Yet, this dreary man was going on about him. Meaning – Hitler. But I had to pretend to be interested. Wouldn't it be hilarious if he was gay and his wife a lesbian?

Anyway, back to my point about wanting to succeed in life, if you're going to do something, anything, you've got to have a *passion* for it.

Otherwise, no matter what they force you with, you'll work, but you'll be doing shoddy, shabby work.

AO: Take Stalin. Already in his youth, he was a habitual thief, bandit, fugitive, murderer. The Czarist police officially wanted him. His psychiatric profile fits the typical profile of most criminals. Yet, Hitler had none of these attributes. Zero. And that is one of the many questions that baffles us.

DG: Are you saying all psychiatry is bunk?

AO: Well, no ... So far, no psychiatric report has been credible on that man. Throughout his youth, Hitler had no blemishes whatsoever. No criminal records. Never indulged in drugs. He's a known teetotaller. He was never convicted for any act of violence, larceny, or felony. These facts caused many government analysts to reconsider and restructure their thinking on Hitler's personality since his past does not indicate his murderous deeds. Furthermore, a report is so much more valid if the subject himself is interviewed. Therefore, their theories were just that, speculations.

DG: Yes, Sir.

Is he an alcoholic? A functioning alcoholic? Meaning every night, after work, he'd get trashed but able to get up the next, free from any hangover and ready for work. Does he have children? Does he abuse them? Is he a pedophile? Does he physically hurt women? Or maybe he's addicted to gambling? What if he's a serial killer and has never been caught?

AO: Our men in DC want to know answers to questions, such as, 'What are the major factors contributing and ultimately create depraved individuals?' 'How can a sick individual rise be not only the leader of one of the world's most civilised, sophisticated, rich, industrialised nations on earth but also an individual who just happened to conquer most of Europe?'

DG: I can think of another one.

AO: Excuse me?

DG: I'd like to know how or in what manner does his particular type of madness differs from other mental illnesses of people in our mental asylums?

Who cares about a dying figure ten thousand miles away? No one. No one cares. What is this interview for or about? Why do they care when no one in America cares? When I say 'they,' I meant the government. But you already knew that, right?

DG: You know you said the report or interviews would be published after the war?

AO: Yes.

DG: You sure about that?

AO: Yes.

DG: I will be all famous, right?

AO: Not with that language; you certainly will *not* be famous.

DG: If I'm given this job, how long do I have to prepare myself?

AO: Approximately three months, Ma'am.

DG [Chuckling]: I can do that. You don't know Dorothy Gale, Sir. What you see isn't what you're getting!

AO: We can only hope so.

DG [Laughing]: Well, again, Sir, thank you for having me. And I hope I've passed the audition!

AO: You will need to resolve one matter if you are selected for this job.

DG: Yes.

AO: You will need to refine your language. You may *not* employ slang, jargon, or street-talk, as you may call it.

DG: Sure.

Is he speaking from a well-rehearsed script? He must be. I doubt he's improvising in his words. Maybe he's bored, just like me. Perhaps he even hates his job. He looks like he's in his twenties. Wouldn't he prefer to be a hero, fighting with his comrades against Hitler instead of droning on talking about the man? Or maybe he's a coward. Thanking God, the government didn't send him off to Europe.

AO: In conjunction with that, you must upgrade your vocabulary.

DG: Yes, Sir. Can you give me an example?

AO: Using terms such as 'them people' or 'bunk' is unacceptable. If you seek to be credible, you must be polished with your appearance, language, thought, logic, and behaviors. Otherwise, people treat you like a hobo.

I thought, given my hideous performance with that interviewer, I wouldn't get the job. Well, I got it wrong.

And it wasn't until some time later did I learn why that cretin didn't just expel me out. Here, I'll tell you now why. Yes, he hated me. He wanted to kill me. I'm exaggerating. But, basically, he did not want to continue interviewing me, and he'd go outside forever and then come back looking frustrated.

To my surprise, there just happened to be several OSS [US Secret Service] men who were looking and observing our interview behind a black window. I thought the latter was a secure screen so that none can see us. But, of course, that's why it was black, to make you feel or think that there was no one but you and the interviewer in that small room. Anyway, going to my point, these higher-up officials actually 'liked' my personality. And why? Because I bored through the sensitivities of that anonymous idiot interviewing me, that was exactly the kind of personality these Washington DC officials wanted to interview the Almighty Fuehrer.

∼

What First Deepened My Interest in Adolf – A Human I Was Hitherto Uninterested In

Unconsciously, consciously, but basically because of Daddy, I dived into seeking knowledge on that Austrian man. To be honest, I thought I didn't know Austrians spoke German. Yes, that's how childish I was. Being honest.

But what intrigued me was that Mr. Hitler did not have any revolutionary quality in his mind, life and experiences. Revolutionaries or genuine revolutionaries fight to the death for their beliefs. This man had no interest in politics, apart from talking. Talk is cheap, isn't it? And yes, he'd get passionate talking endlessly about politics, given that that was the one subject that aroused his anger and fascination. But what was he practically doing as per his complaints against the ills of society? Nothing. How fascinating is that! Because, as I said, every historical revolutionary I read about committed their lives for the advancement of their respective ideologies. But, Adolf? No, the dandy or bohemian did not bother to do anything to further the cause of his professed ideology. Now, what does that mean? Given that he specifically chose not to do any active work for his political ideology, how do we judge him? Was he just a cheap talker? A hypocrite?

More to the point, the future Fuehrer of National Socialist Germany, the future leader of an ideology that stressed the necessity for the strength of healthy bodies for both genders; an ideology that insisted all people work and it is from that hard work a nation can organically evolve and so becomes mightier in its physical health and mind turned out to be a man incapable or unwilling to work not even one day in his life.

The more I read his about his ideology and Nazi philosophy that was practiced throughout Germany; I was astonished what they emphasized - the need for the superior bodily health of all their youth; the necessity to achieve beauty standards — was never practiced by Adolf!

And yet, there's no denying Hitler was obsessed with physical beauty; not only did his preferred art — paintings and sculptures — reveal those feelings, he endlessly emphasized the beauty of the German race's physical and mental superiority. Remember one of his mottos — 'Beauty and Strength.'

I learned Hitler created the *Kraft Durch Freude* [Strength Through Joy], where millions of Germans participated in all kinds of *communal* physical activities such as going to libraries, having picnics, the opera, hiking, camping, dancing, gymnastics, going on free cruise holidays to neighboring countries, seeing plays and many more activities. Again, the emphasis was on communal adventures, bringing in all classes and strengthening social bonds between people and classes.

And then there was the Nazi passion of the *Schönheit der Arbeit* [Beaity

Through Labor] emphasizing that labor was not only a necessity for the survival of the race, but its effects also would beautify every German hamlet, village, town, and city and that in turn would uplift German morale and so, happiness in seeing what a beautiful Germany they were living in.

Now, all that may sound wonderful or not to you — but that's not my point here. Remember, I'm talking about what first piqued my interest in that man. On the one hand, you see his passion for physical activities and actual manual labor for all Germans as the fundamental cure for a healthy population. But, meanwhile, the man himself was a shy, loner hermit who could never forge one human relationship with anyone. So much for his communalism.

Moreover, the creator of these ideas hated labor. He hated all physical activities. And he never - ever - participated in any sports-like activity.

See the weird irony?

Here was a man who implacably opposed doing any work, be it physical, manual, retail, serving people in a café, office work — nothing was acceptable to him - in his youth. He preferred to be unemployed. He chose to be homeless rather than work. Preferring to live in Homeless Shelters than daring to work. It was these peculiar attributes that intrigued me. Making me want to understand his mind. His motivations. His lack of any motivation as per getting a salary.

Think about my words, if you will.

How many people, men or women, *choose* to be homeless rather than to work? Especially when we remember Adolf had no handicaps, nor any physical or mental ailments that would force him to be homeless. He wasn't an alcoholic, nor was he a drug addict or gambler — I mean, he had nothing that 'forced' him to live the homeless life.

Again, maybe I'm over=stressing this point. But isn't that so unusual, so unnatural? And then, again, revert your minds to the Nationalist Germany he envisioned and built — one that was fundamentally a nation based on work.

Perhaps some people genuinely prefer or voluntarily choose poverty, right? Again, as I said, some unfortunate people could not work because of mental health issues, drug dependence, drugs, alcohol, etc. Or maybe they have other severe personal failings. And so, they couldn't work.

Hitler himself highlighted the pains of poverty in *Mein Kampf.* Again, if he was honest [which I doubt], why didn't he simply get a job and alleviate poverty?

But once he became a politician around 1920, we see an entirely different character from the pre-1914 Adolf. By that year, Adolf transforms himself into a zealous, fanatical modern-day fighter, a man who believed the only virtuous life was that of the worker, the farmer who labored from dawn till dusk.

Really? What so suddenly changed your mind, Adolf? Hitler's rigid philosophy was to ensure all Germans were forced to hard work for the overall health of the German nation, military service, and outdoor activities for both boys and girls. And in truth, when the man became the leader of Germany, the entire country, the entire population, became an ant or bee colony constantly working for the German nation. I do not quarrel with that approach. My interest was only piqued when you go back some years and look at how the same man lived out his life — one of an equal fanaticism and zeal to refuse to do any job or work.

I'm not sure ... I may be wrong, but I think every revolutionary leader went through years of suffering for their respective ideological cause. Obviously, Jesus comes to my mind. Spartacus, William Wallace, Joan of Arc, George Washington. Forget ancient history. Let's observe modern history. How many times was Stalin imprisoned by the Czarist police and carted off to Siberia? And in between his holidays in Siberia, didn't Stalin constantly worked as an underground revolutionary, forever fearing the Czarist police? How about Tito? Trotsky? Lenin?

The point I'm making here is simple. Those who were existentially driven to create a revolution that fitted their respective ideologies fought to achieve their ambition throughout their lives. The same goes for Castro or Che Guevara, Ho Chi Minh, Pol Pot, Mao Tse-Tung, Gamal Abdel Nasser, Martin Luther King, Malcolm X, Saddam Hussein.

No revolutionary chose not to do anything for their ideological struggle, except for our Adolf. And that struck millions of nerves and emotions in my body. Well, what kind of mind did Hitler have if he was never prepared to do anything to fight for his ideological cause?

I *was* naïve and all that, and you know that because I had said that before, but I understood the man. I had to get better. I needed a sophisticated understanding of why humans have persistent urges to abuse other innocent humans for my part and interests.

I was going to meet modern history's worst mass murderer. What should I be looking for? What questions would be incisive? How do you get the Devil to speak Truth? Or is such a question absurd? Conversations with Satan. Ha!

I needed to know what the hell propelled him to incessantly and without a scrap of compassion to fulfill his overwhelming desire and need to pick and stab the hungriest, the poorest, the meekest, the neediest, the most isolated human beings on earth? A man with only one passionate love affair, and that was with mass murder. And he cannot stop. He needs to go on and kill innocent humans one by one and kill them ceaselessly until our soldiers must physically arrive at the crime scene and kill the perpetrator, thereby liberating those millions of inmates in his Godawful concentration camps.

What on earth can be so damaged in Man's brain? [I'm talking of Hitler]. He didn't even have a correct premise to start with. So, it wasn't as though I need to discuss the fact that Jewish people are human. That's a dead no-brainer.

Take Stalin, for example. Why he probably killed more of his people than Hitler. And yet, one could still 'reason' with Stalin because the foundational principles for his hideous deeds had their basic economic principles. Thus, while most of humanity disagreed with the entirety of his thoughts, you could still have a discussion explaining why killing Kulaks was not necessarily the most productive manner to increase output, far from it. On the contrary, it caused a decrease in production.

"A single death is a tragedy; a million deaths is a statistic."

- Joseph Stalin (1878-1953)

But with Nazis, there is no beginning for a discussion on anti-Semitism. Why? Precisely because their conviction is preposterous! I could not imagine talking or even discussing the question – 'Are Jews so bad they must be exterminated?' I mean, even thinking or saying such words makes me feel half infantile and half sick. But then again, I could hardly ignore the man's 'reasoning' since one must confront *his* reality.

And *that was* his extreme, annihilator anti-Semitism, his fundamental ideological pillar. Only this man applied his convictions into a deathly reality. I mean, seriously, being anti-Semitic is one thing. Believing you must restrict the lives of Jews is one thing. Thinking you must deport Jews from your country is one thing. But to mass murder every Jew is not entirely a different matter; it has never been practiced by any leader nor nation in history – ever. So, what does that make Hitler?

Daddy was right. Maybe being a rich, famous Hollywood actress would add nothing to my non-existent happiness. These are possibly illusions. And yet, how powerful they are! Isn't it every person's dream in life to be rich and famous? Of course, it is. Or most people, anyway. All those millions of people loving, adoring, and even needing you even though they know nothing about you. Screaming, crying fans stretching their arms out in the faint hope of teaching you. You are like Jesus, I suppose. Millions of people read and tune in to see you on television. They need to see you be interviewed or perform whatever you do, be it acting, singing, or being a comedian. It doesn't matter. You're a 'god' to millions of not just Americans. I was obsessed with Marlene Dietrich. But I also found her troubling.

She was German, like me. And like me, she too emigrated to America. And when war came, she donned the US army uniform and entertained our boys throughout the world. And this is where I was troubled by her. Wasn't she a traitor? It's one thing leaving Germany, hating Hitler – but helping Americans obliterate your people and nation? She said it repeatedly – Nazis were evil, and the fact they were Germans was irrelevant. Either way, Nazis had to be destroyed, or they would swallow up the world and kill off every race except for the Germans. I found that difficult to accept, and yet my turmoil deepened when I heard my brother Henry joined or was conscripted by our army and was on active duty fighting our people. Anyway, as for Henry, I'll have lots to talk about later because he was declared an MIA [Missing in Action], and that spiralled my anxieties out of control.

If I'm going to understand Hitler, it *was* necessary to go down to the Devil's repugnant level, get in the muck, speak, do the arguing, and try to make him understand his idiocy non-thinking. Explaining the sun rises and sets. Only by living, experiencing evil and madness will I know their disfiguring truth.

Paradoxical? Yes, it was. Would I feel senselessly stupid engaging with his imbecilic theories? Yes, I would. But it had to be done. Obviously. What else should one talk about with a genocidal anti-Semite?

And yet, my mind retorted, 'What is there to prove or disprove to that maniac?' How can one have a semi-intelligent conversation with anyone who believes Jews need to be exterminated because they're supposed to be evil? There can be no rational and objective conversation with a genocidal maniac.

No, my friend, this is not black humour. This is the reality; this is the truth because the fact was that one man single-handedly 'achieved' his genocidal policy at the expense of 6.0 million elderlies, men, women, children, and babies who just happened to be either of the Jewish faith or Jewish heritage. So, the question is, *why?* Why this *abnormally monumental rage?* Why this need to go on killing and killing and killing until the entire world of nations finally unites and arrests eighty million of your adherents from murdering more innocent people?

Remember, even in the final months of the war, that man insisted on force marching bare-foot Jews from their camps to other camps away from the advancing Russian armies. Can we even comprehend this type of intense madness? That meant even though he knew the war was ending soon, his criminal urges *still* forced him to go on killing and killing, as I say, literally until the Russians will arrive at the camps in question and finally put an end to the criminal activities of his people, like any serial killer.

He won't stop killing until the law slams him where he belongs, either in jail or is executed. He won't stop because he enjoys killing — lust for murdering ad infinitum and without ad nausea. Whatever the actual cause, be it neurochemical imbalances in their brains or their awful backgrounds and lives, they cannot stop sadistically murdering so long as no law enforcement units arrest them.

And now I want to bring you back to Daddy.

I think it's the same ugly phenomenon with those folks who spat at Daddy, rain, or sunshine. But, of course, in his situation, there was no ending to his ordeal. You cannot call cops for verbal abuse. By the way, I know I'm using vernacular, informal English here, but I promise you, when you'll be hearing me begin them conversations, you'll see a different Dorothy!

Anyway, as I was saying, there was only one thing to do, to get rid of the pain I felt for Daddy. First, I needed to understand the nature of violent, uncontrollable, sadistic humans. Second, I needed to understand what they 'have' — what exactly is in their nature and constituents that *overpowers their* homicidal urges? Why can they only be temporarily relieved from their sadistic impulses once they finish their appalling deeds?

I was going to succeed. However, I was unsure if that was what Daddy wanted me to learn and achieve, though that definitively became my obsession.

You don't know Dorothy Gale. I was leaving backward Kansas farmland and plummeting straight in the filthy innards of the belly of the beast. I wanted to not only quiz the leviathan monstrosity himself, but more importantly, yours truly needed to discover the reasons - simple or complex - why evil exists and how evil functions. In other words, ladies, and gentlemen, farm girl Dorothy Gale would be the first human who will finally discover the Mechanics of the Evil Mind!

I thought my own interview went as smooth as sailing through Hell, given my lousy lingo and jargon or whatever the man said. But life's a bucketful of surprises, some sweet, some nasty, and boy was yours genuinely surprised by lofty heaps and endless miles when I received a letter stating I was accepted within a few days!

I was to interview the man himself, the leader of the crumbling Thousand Year Reich. To be frank, it was only then I felt the shock, given the actual enormity of the task. Prior to getting accepted, I was all enthused about diving into studying that man. But once I was accepted, I balked. How the hell can a naïve twenty-year-old quiz a man who happened to be Mr. Hitler on his life, philosophy, and deeds?

"Learn from me, if not by my precepts, at least by my example, how dangerous is the acquirement of knowledge and how much happier that man is who believes his native town to be the world than he who aspires to become greater than his nature will allow."

- *Victor Frankenstein* (1818) Ch. 4

But there was an answer, as Daddy told me. The answer was simple — read and think and think and read endlessly till you find the truth.

I had already begun my journey with literature before my interview. But now, the academic digging had to start in earnest. That is what my Daddy done told me. I know I'm not grammatically pure — but I am talking to you, my reader, so I don't need to act and all that!

'Read so you refine your mind, girl, and shall come to know of your soul and mind.'

Read if you want to be human. Whittle away the vulgarities of your language. Hurl out and throw away the black holes of stupidities in your mind. Illuminate your soul with the engines of knowledge. Learn how to use those tools in a rational, refined, and erudite manner. Structure your thoughts and language. Create a hypothesis. Test it. Understand the fundamental concepts that have been in place in Man's history since we became literate back 5,000 years ago in Sumer. Learn of Man's mental attributes and characteristics. Descartes was famous for discovering he existed. Well, so much for him. Physicists discovered quantum mechanics, revolutionising our understanding of reality at the sub-atomic level, with all the uncertainty therein.

Well, what about us humans? What of our minds? That is undoubtedly the most important question to ask and to answer. What are the constituents of our minds? How could I be living without knowing my identity? Isn't that absurd? Isn't that beyond crazy? At least animals know who they are. I mean, a tiger knows he is a tiger, right? But we humans, we know our own attributes, neither the physical nor the mental.

The more I thought of myself, the less I knew of my mind. Superficially, it is so easy to define myself. I can say I am kooky; I'm a chatterbox. Flighty, airy, and all that. That is how people see me, that's for sure, and I am saying that's one portrait of me. But there is more inside this brain of mine. A physical organ housing an abstraction called one's 'mind' that defines the 'I,' the 'me' in question. And the frightening and daunting problem is I don't even know how to access my mind, let alone study it.

Or I did not know back then. Not before I went to sunny Berlin '45.

~

"You know once, the Fuehrer suddenly and quite frankly said in a café called the *Café Anast* in Munich, when *he saw a little Jewish boy, saying that he would like to squash him flat like a bug on the wall.* I couldn't believe it and thought it was just provocative talk. But he really did it later. *And I admit that was the first time I saw, with my eyes, the ingrained, deeply rooted hatred in his ice-cold blue eyes.* A boy, remember! And yet, to my own awe, I just devalued that scene."

- Magda Goebbels. Talking to Ello Quandt, sister of Magda's first husband, Günther Quandt

~

The Differing Types of People I Interviewed

In my memoirs, you shall hear Hitler's voice speaking. You shall hear his worshippers, and you shall hear interviews with his victims.

I. Actors Denying Any Knowledge of the Holocaust

Some play the role of actors – the exemplar maestro must surely be Albert Speer. He brilliantly fooled many people into believing he was the '*Penitent Nazi*' who *had no idea* the Holocaust was going on. Speer became the media's most sought-after and interviewed Nazi, making him rich and famous. And we cannot just critique Speer. How many actors do you and I know? If anything, most people assume fake roles and masks and personalities that best suit their changing circumstances. It is,

I suppose, a question and a matter of survival. Let's not be hypocritical here. Speer did what most people would do, seeking any way to save their skin from being fried. But what stuns me personally is that when he was repeatedly asked throughout his life, "But *you must have known* of the Holocaust since you were an integral part of it and therefore on what moral grounds do you now defame the Nazi regime that you willingly served until the death of your beloved Fuehrer?" The man shrugged off such an insipid question, denying any knowledge of the continent-wide annihilation of Europe's Jews.

In fact, in this category lie most of the high and low-ranking Nazis - in this category are such illustrious men as — Goering, Keitel, Jodl, Ribbentrop, Hans Frank, Robert Ley, Alfred Rosenberg, Franz Halder, Erich von Manstein, Karl Donitz, Wilhelm von Leeb, Gunther von Kluge, Gerd von Rundstedt and Herr Kaltenbrunner.

In other words, those people require of us to believe that never they noticed anything criminally suspicious; nor did they understand what was going when others told them about the mass murders; nor did they smell any of the wretched gossip; nor did they read any incriminating document; nor did they witness, see, attend any meeting or conference on the Holocaust - though they just happened to be side by side with Hitler, Himmler, Eichmann et al. throughout his twelve-year Thousand Year Reich.

Here is an example -

DG: "General von Manstein, did you know of the concentration camps?

Manstein: I never heard any words to that effect. I can say I heard as much as the German people, or *possibly, even less.*"

Most Nazis chose that excuse. And they stuck by it, no matter how screamingly silly it was. After all, how could they not know when Hitler discussed his exterminatory plans? Did they magically and coincidentally excuse themselves every time the Fuehrer and his SS officers discussed the Final Solution? How can top Nazis claim they never heard any German talking about what was an ongoing reality? It's absurd! Of course, it is, but what else could they say, given their high-ranking positions? To be 'fair,' there wasn't remotely any justification lurking out there to aid their pitiful defence.

However, when forced to see the mountains of incriminatory documents, films, and witnesses, most of these men stated that only 'now' they realize what naughty Hitler had done. The exception is, of course, Goering, who, as we shall see, remained *by far* the most forceful personality compared to the rest.

Similarly, you will also hear interviews with civilian murderers who had the gross temerity – just like Herr Speer et al. - pretending 'nothing' happened. Later, I shall introduce you to Ms. Adelle Sorella.

Adelle Sorella

She murdered her two daughters, though acting as though nothing happened. Of all the bizarre criminals, this one is an ace.

DG: *"How can you explain how this could happen? What in your life brought you to that? We must explain this. Look at that! This is the truth. These are your daughters. Something brought you to do that to them."*

She refused to react or listen. We cannot just do that. This is how some people simply do not believe the obvious. They deny its validity.

That's why we have Holocaust deniers. That's why with every mass murderer, you'll inevitably find followers fanatically denying any crimes committed – like Adelle Sorella. More to their point, they are absolutely certain they are right, and the rest of the world is wrong. As a simple example to this day, if you want any Turkish government, no matter what political party they come from, and should you remind them of the Armenian Genocide their forefathers perpetrated on the innocent Armenians, they will deny any Armenian was ever murdered during the First World War. Denialism is everywhere. So, I think you can see denialism or revisionist history is alive and well, not just in post-1945 Germany.

In other cases, perpetrators will frankly admit they committed acts of mass murder, atrocities, and even genocide, but they excuse their actions as necessary for their survival. How? Because, they say, had they not exterminated their enemy, the latter would have exterminated them.

In our specific case, wherein an entirely peaceful community – Jews – had no malice towards Germany and more importantly, perhaps, not one Jew or any Jewish organization ever committed any harm, damage, or take the life of any German, we must face this daunting question – *how could millions of Germans and non-German perpetrators willingly mass murder Jews who had never lifted a finger against any German?*

We – all of us - must somehow explain this murderous urge. And yet, therein is the seemingly unyielding confounder, for how do we explain homicidal rage against the innocent? We are being asked to use rationality to answer our questions. Yet, it was irrationality, even madness, that was the sole impulse in the deeds all of these mass murderers felt compelled to commit their mass- crimes in the first place.

When Goering was show footage of the mounds of corpses, he remarked these could only have been corpses brought in from nearby morgues and placed in concentration camps. Presumably, Goering knew better, but many Germans believed the Holocaust was a Hollywood-staged event.

I know the more intelligent Nazi officials knew the Holocaust happened, but they had to deny any knowledge to save their necks from the noose. And that is understandable. One must presume some of these deniers genuinely believed the Holocaust was fiction. But what staggers me are the majority of ordinary people who will not accept the Holocaust in the face of overwhelming evidence. And again, not to belabor this point, but most people who follow a leader and political party tend not to believe that their side committed atrocities because they genuinely believe their party and leader are pure-hearted.

Sometimes, I think I know why. These people have a dream, a hope that their future will be better. And by 'future,' I mean their lives shall be better in the financial sense, in terms of getting employment, getting decent housing, and so on. So that's why they entirely invest their heart and trust in their regime and leadership. Only the latter can uplift them from their miserable lives and settle them in a comfortable middle-class life. They will have decent housing, schools, universities, etc. hospitals, and job opportunities. And then, out of the blue, their enemy reports their leaders and political movement have committed acts of horrific mass murder. I can see it from their point of view. They cannot accept that their leaders are kleptocrats stealing every penny for their pockets, stashing it in anonymous Swiss bank accounts. They cannot accept that their leaders have not invested a penny in their nation or region, even though they all know they haven't built one school, university, housing, or hospital. They know that because they're not blind. They can see their beloved leaders have made nothing for their people.

So, given all these facts, the obvious question is, why can't these people understand that their leaders are criminals? Here is the answer. They suppress every negative truth in their minds.

Why? Because if they were to admit the truth, their dreams and their hopes would be shattered. What 'dreams and hopes' are we talking about? Remember, for such people, we said they'd pin their hopes that these self-same leaders will somehow, one way or another, lead them to better living conditions and better employment opportunities. If they were to accept the truth that their leaders are, as stated, nothing but kleptocratic criminals, that would by definition have to eradicate their hopes and dreams. And consciously accepting the eradication of their hopes and dreams is not easy because it means, not only had they been fooled, but more importantly, they must accept they have no future for any prospect for the betterment of their miserable lives.

All the world's a stage,

And all the men and women merely players;

They have their Exits and their Entrances,

And one man in his time plays many parts,

His acts being seven ages

-

- [Shakespeare. *As You Like It*, Act II Scene VII Lines 139-166]

~

II. Ted Bundy – Seducing His Executioner, Judge Edward D. Cowart

Ted Bundy

This 'man' is my all-time favourite American serial killer. He was a kidnapper, rapist, pedophile, and necrophilia. But he fooled everyone into thinking he was a golden example of the ideal, Intellectual, cultivated, charming American gentleman. Especially the women. As you are about to see and note.

Please allow me to introduce you to this man's exemplary deeds -

1. Bundy *decapitated* at least 12 of his victims.

2. He kept some of the severed heads in his apartment.

3. He had 'sex' with some of his corpses. *Necrophiliac.*

4. He *groomed some of his corpses*, such as hair shampooing and the application of makeup. In Utah, he applied makeup to Melissa Smith's lifeless face, and he repeatedly washed Laura Aime's hair. "If you've got time," he told Hagmaier, "they can be anything you want them to be."

5. He only stopped having 'sex' when the corpses became *too decomposed, putrefied, and liquefied.*

6. He lured 12-year-old Lynette Culver, drowned her, and then sexually assaulted her. *Child Murderer. Child Rapist.*

7. Twenty-year-old Lisa Levy was beaten till she was rendered unconscious. He then strangled her till she died. He then ripped out one of her nipples with his teeth. Next, he bit deeply into her left buttock. Finally, he repeatedly inserted and pulled out a hair mist bottle in her dead vagina. Sadist.

8. Words and adjectives run out.

We now hear the principled words of the American Judge (Dade County Circuit Court Judge) Edward D. Cowart (1925 – 1987) handing down Bundy's sentence, ending his comments lamenting Bundy's life with the following memorable words -

"It is further ordered that on such scheduled date that you will be put to death by a current of electricity, sufficient to cause your immediate death, and that current of electricity shall continue to be passed through your body until you are dead.

Take care of yourself, young man. I say that to you sincerely; take care of yourself, please. It is an utter tragedy for this court to see such a total waste of humanity as I've experienced in this courtroom. You're a bright young man.

You would have made a good lawyer, and I would have loved to have you practice in front of me, but you went another way, partner. Take care of yourself. I don't feel any animosity toward you. I want you to know that. Once again, take care of yourself."

— Judge Edward Cowart

I misspoke when I said his words were 'memorable.' No one remembers them anymore, nor do most people remember the character himself, Bundy, for that matter. So, what are we to make of these glowing words by this Judge?

How can it possibly come to happen when even a presiding *judge* who heard all the gruesome details of Bundy's crimes is still enamoured by him? How can this judge who sat throughout the trial, listened to the testimonies and witness statements of all those who suffered at the hands of Bundy and who saw all the graphic photographs of Bundy's mutilated victims still feel such an admiration for the serial killer? No one would describe Judge Cowart as stupid. And yet, those were his admiring words.

'It is certain, That Man seems to be a very inconsiderable Being, when we judge of him through' the Prejudices of the Senses: We are not far from finding him incapable of Vertue, when we consider his *Vileness;* and incapable of Happiness, when we reflect upon his *Misery*.

The Smallness of his Body is the first that occurs to the Eyes; the Scripture denotes it, by telling us, *That Man has his Foundation in the Dust, that he dwelled in a Tabernacle of Clay,* and *That he is consumed at the meeting of a Worm.*'

[The ART of KNOWING ONE-SELF: Or, An *Enquiry after the Sources* OF MORALITY. The FIRST PART. Wherein we Treat of the *Nature* of MAN, of his *End,* his *Perfections,* his *Duties,* and his *Strength.* Abbadie, Jacques, 1654-1727., T. W. Page 12].

Don't we see connections with these disturbing facts? Isn't it easy for men and women of all intelligence ranges and erudition to be profoundly enthused and enthralled by criminal characters like Ted Bundy? And, further, what does that tell us about Nazi Germany? I'll be discussing this point later, but for now, I think judge Cowart's words reveal a million star-lights of wisdom as per how the great mass of humanity can be so readily corrupted into willingly committing acts of evil.

And the other question is this. How do we define or categorise the mind of Ted Bundy? On the surface, as we said, had you met Ted, you would have hardly thought for a moment he did what he did. So, what is he? Is he mad? Is he evil? Or both?

What's the difference between Ted Bundy and Hitler? Can the two be compared? Or is that a silly question? I know it's unorthodox comparing leaders of nations with individual mass murderers. But I pose that question.

There are obvious differences. Hitler didn't physically partake in any of the actual murders. And, insofar as we know, Hitler didn't feel sexual or any gratification when implementing the genocidal plans — but then again, how do we know what Hitler felt? Maybe he was beaming with joy when Himmler informed him of the latest death statistics of the remaining Jews in Europe? We can never know. We can guess, we can approximate, but to be certain? That's an impossibility. Perhaps, at the least, given his fanatical hatred of Jews, he must've been elated hearing millions have perished. Indeed, after Stalingrad, the only 'good' news he heard was about his genocide which was succeeding.

There was a much more disturbing difference between Hitler and other leaders.

Take Stalin and *his* extermination of Kulaks. Somehow, I think he was happy, not in the process of his economic plans, but the results, or specifically the numbers of how many Jews had so far been exterminated. In other words, I think he didn't care one way or the other when hearing that millions of these poor folks were murdered or deported to Siberia. Stalin saw his plan strictly within the format of Marxism-Leninism, as he defined it, and his life's work was to achieve the goals he set that Soviet Russia had to attain, no matter the human cost. In other words, I'm not sure Stalin had a homicidal hatred of Kulaks, as opposed to Hitler and Jews. These are essential differences when history or we, as individuals, judge mass murderers. Both Stalin and Hitler had the same intention. Both had the same fanatical will, drive, and determination to carry out their exterminatory policies. But I don't think Stalin was as gleeful in wiping out every Kulak as Hitler's thirst and need to wipe out every Jew on earth biologically.

All historians instinctively assume everyone knows that everything in their books and articles are the truth. I could be wrong. I'm only making a calculated guess based on what I've known, experienced, and read.

∼

Why Were My Books Never Published?

When I returned to windy Kansas, brimming with over-excitement, hoping, and waiting for the official publication of these conversations, I was shocked to hear — well, nothing. *None of my interviews were published. Not even one conversation!* I thought DC would publish my conversations, and that was my first shock. After all, no one in DC, my superiors, complained about the work.

We sent them through some encrypted thing or other — you can tell I have no idea about this technical part, so I have no formal language in describing it - but anyway, my team, the stenographer, and radiographer regularly sent each conversation back to my superiors in Washington. And none complained. No one sent back to our team they would like me to change this or that. Therefore, I can only assume they were satisfied with my work, even when I went beyond their orders, such as going outside the Bunker and speaking to German civilians, German victims of Hitler, and of course to Russian soldiers. Worse, not one official called, and when I tried to get some answers calling and writing them, none answered. They vanished like a dream.

Why was that? What was the point of all these efforts, if not to reveal my words to the public and the world? Did I miss something? What 'wrong' did *I* do? Or were the answers delivered by the *interviewees* themselves deemed by historians to be historically worthless? And if that were the case, *who* decided every word of my interviewees were to be officially classified as worthless?

Far, far more importantly, *who* dared to presume they had the right to in effect to muzzle history? Who are these people who genuinely believe they have the right to delete parts of historical testimonials when it also happens that it is our inalienable *right* to hear, read and watch whatever people have to say?

That's one reason why after these decades, I went back to the original and well-preserved set of transcripts and read up on them again. *What exactly was so 'worthless' in all those conversations? Why this wall of silence?*

I realized, in good time, why my works were never published. You know, not even one book publishing company and not one literary agent responded to my applications to publish my conversations. But I knew why — as I say, in time. Because the contents in these conversations evidence a different reality of Hitler and his henchmen and women from the only acceptable, respected, conventional, and standard narrative on this subject, and because my conversations showed Hitler in a different light, no one would dare publish those thousands of words and pages. We're back to the Asphyxiation of Knowledge. The powers that be, the elites, academicians, politicians, journalists, Hollywood, do not want the public to see, read or watch any other version in the description of Adolf

Hitler. That's it.

That's when for the first time, I felt hate towards the elites. Why? Because they were de facto and de jure deciding what can and what cannot be seen, read, or seen by the public. In other words, the America I loved was a dictatorship. Before going to Berlin, I would've punched anyone saying we were not, as FDR said, the 'arsenal for democracy." I was fifteen at the time, hearing Roosevelt's voice saying those electrifying words because I felt only America would save the planet from tyrannies across the world. Did he say, 'arsenal for democracy" or 'arsenal of democracy"? Anyway, who cares. That was in 1940, and I was as fiercely patriotic as those boys back in the summer of 1914 who ardently marched off to war to fight the savage, baby-killing Huns.

As I said, with time, the great healer, I reread my conversations. I felt a hitherto undisclosed forceful verve blasting out from texts. To my horror, at first, I hallucinated hearing the voices of the interviewees. Louder in tone than when I first revised the transcripts when I went back to Washington DC in 1945. I think today they call it auditory hallucinations. Implying you have schizophrenia. But I was struck with joy in re-hearing those words and voices of all I had interviewed because I was re-living those days, weeks, and months in Berlin. So, schizophrenia or not, welcome baby to my brain and ears!

And it wasn't just the tones speaking louder. A guiding spirit, switching randomly between breezes, gusts to gales, flowered and wilted in my mind. A mind whose attributes I can only define as abstract. One matter, though, was unavoidable. The grave signposts were suggesting; if not insisting, I had to seek a different understanding of the entirety of the contents of my experiences. Remember how the Red Army posted skeletons, some dressed in German uniforms, pointing in the direction of Stalingrad, saluting the Master Race as they trudged on towards their death? I, too, saw skeletons of the millions of dead soldiers and civilians urging me to speak out and rectify the portrait of that one man who caused the unnecessary deaths, tortures, rape, mutilations, torture, imprisonments of millions of innocent human beings.

Russian soldiers put up this skeleton welcoming Germans to Stalingrad.

But how is that achieved? My interviewees came from radically different lifestyles and ideologies. There seemed no *coherence* in my story. It was unreadable because no one could link or thread these disparate peoples' experiences, impulses, and lives. And people need a logical story, not a chaotic one. That seemed obvious, and that refrained me from doing anything with my manuscripts. After all, what a hypocrite I was; I myself didn't understand the entirety of the story precisely because of the contradictory stories by individual interviewees. More to the point, these vast, gaping contradictions stated by the various interviews tended to nullify or depreciate their own stories and beliefs, thus rendering the entirety of their narrative worthless.

But there has to be a meaningful thread throughout these transcripts, despite the contradictions. Otherwise, history has no meaning. Right? What credibility would you give if people tell you nonsensical stories as per their interactions, motivations, ideologies, and life events? Obviously, nothing. My God, how depressed I appeared. What then was the point in talking or interviewing all those bastards if they all told me lies and baseless claims? If I were an honorable journalist, I should've shot myself given the enormity of my failings.

The only conclusion I could think of was this. Read the lines. Read in between and behind the lines. Read under and above the lines. Then reassess what meanings they impart to you, willingly or not, knowingly, or not. Compare and contrast the words and experiences of the differing interviewees. Do I see similarities? What are they? Note them down. Do I see any recognisable pattern or a theme emerging from these interviews? What is this pattern? What is it suggesting? Is there a commonality in its themes, reflecting the reality of human life?

Given the radically disparate lives I was interviewing, could there possibly be one unifying law that orders and governs our minds? I wished I had Daddy with me.

With the sparse grace and determined awfulness of Time, I fingered a different face and body of Berlin's reality of 1945. It was different from what I understood it to be back in '45.

Again, I reread texts—revisited memories. But now, different emotions and thoughts sprung everywhere in my mind. Sensing an entirely different flavour from that which I thought was 'real' back in 1945. The meanings, feelings, and convictions I had back then were wholly changed.

What and why this massive change? But wait here. Fundamental elements of reality itself don't change — isn't that rationally, objectively clear? I mean, the conversations themselves did not change. The words did not change. The events and scenes did not change. That was obvious. None of my notes changed, preserved as they were for those seventy-plus years.

And yet, no less than the truth itself was now unrecognizably different.

~

Are My Memoirs Unique? If so, Why?

No book on Hitler, no book or film on the Third Reich, and no lecture or text on the Holocaust has ever been written in the format I present to you.

Why are my Memoirs unique?

Because they are set in a *conversational format*, involving four sets of scenes -

1. First. A one-on-one interview with the character in question – Adolf Hitler.

2. Second. A conversation/interview with his entourage.

3. Third. I was talking and listening in to the varying groups of his entourage speaking *away* from Hitler himself. I found that some people exhibited different characteristics when speaking away from their leader.

Why this conversational format?

A conversational format liberates the writer, allowing greater flexibility and maneuverability for the questioner to switch, refine, rephrase, and restructure his questions precisely and in time as one hears the answers. Thus, if an interviewee must dodge or duck a specific sensitive topic, I will not back down; instead, I'd chase up the subject matter with a different approach. Sometimes it could be a bull-headed confrontational approach. At the same time, my question needs to be nuanced and discrete — though, remember, my intentions and the final bull's-eye destination is forever the same — since I can, I always try to extricate the truth, regardless of whether the interviewee is or is not aware of what I am doing.

The other literary format is the established one, wherein the historian tells his story. And like any story, the historian never bothers to interact with any actor in the play. So, what *exactly* does the typical, conventional historian do when writing historical biography? They think it is only necessary to *describe* the individuals and the events.

I think you now see how and why the unconventional and conversational format delivers a refreshing immediacy to our subject matter. I needed to directly and face to face talk and engage with the self-same characters I do *not* need to describe; instead, I needed to hear from them on their opinions and justifications directly.

That is the gasping difference.

That is another reason not one of my friends and colleagues have ever deigned to share even a one-star, dingy platform with me and discuss the contents of my memoirs.

I'm a heretic to the Standard Officially Accepted Model historians, scholars, artists, and journalists! A Nazi. And so on. How else could they interact with my memoirs? How can anyone write any words, let alone over half a million words, deviating from the prim, proper, respectable, elite-established historians?

And who is this foul, unschooled Kansas farm girl writing on such monumentally grave subjects as Hitler, exterminations, gas chambers, mass killings, six million dead Jews, on concentration camps notoriously infamous as Auschwitz and yet liberally remembering and noting so-called 'comedic' strands throughout her experiences? This muddy creature did not have the brains to go to university, nor was she ever a scholar, nor was she an intellectual - and yet she still dares to write on the world's most sensitive and momentously significant subject matter for all Mankind and for all times?

Dorothy Gale - Heretical indeed!

In effect and de facto, in the perfumed elite writers and scholars' eyes, I am no different from the lunatic fringe of the Revisionists. I'm *forcibly* lumped with them! Did that kind of threatening pressure stop me? The answer is yes. For years after my 1945 experiences, that was *exactly* why I did *not* dare writing my thoughts on this story. Instead, I chose to emulate my friend Copernicus and thought it best to publish my memoirs posthumously. What can they then do? Desecrate my grave?

Phooey!

∼

Why Did I Finally Decide to Write My Memoirs?

Well, you'll be happy to know I'm living in this sprightly age of mine — well, some will be happy, not all.

I've been asked, *'Well, gee, Dorothy girl, why did you finally choose to publish your memoirs?'*

Here's why.

A year ago, I went to London and on my tourist to-do list was, of course, the famous Madame Tussaud. And of all places, that's where it blew up - in *Madame Tussauds* — and it there I found my mind uncomfortably swaying. Seasickness of the soul.

There I was, walking past tourists and the wax figures. Unaticipatingly, I stood face to face with the waxwork of the man himself — Adolf Hitler.

I remember people casually walking past him. Some snickered, some said rude words, others had nothing to say. By the way, to be honest, whoever made that wax impression was no talent; the figure looked nothing like the man in question. Anyway, I didn't even think Adolf would be at

Madame Tussauds. I shouldn't have reacted emotionally as I did, and to this day, I don't understand why I responded in the confoundedly awe-struck manner I did.

But there I was—my eyes facing Hitler's eyes. I froze. Standing rigid - because I had no flexibility communicating with my senses. Unable to compromise with my confounded reason. I was no more than a foot or more from that hideous *lifelike* waxwork. Ah yes, the first definitive emotion had just arisen! I was an experienced corpse, no different than him, the Hitler wax figure. I say 'experienced,' meaning I had my experiences with him and 'corpse' because I'm already more than halfway in my own grave. I faintly remember passer-by's thought I was a Nazi. Some, not all. Maybe it was because of physical fixation on the wax figure, people figured, 'This is one Nazi admirer!'

The wax dummy seemed alive. Animated. The disparity between the wax figure that looked nothing like the man and how Hitler looked in reality disappeared. The latter image triumphed. I'm not mad. I recognized the man while that stupid wax figure vanished. The wax had gone, and skin replaced it. Skin and living, breathing flesh and body. Now I remember! Hitler was standing before me.

> Henry: Look! It's moving. It's — it's ... it's alive. It's alive ... It's alive, it's moving, it's alive! It's alive, it's alive, it's alive!
> It's ALIVE!

> Victor: Henry — in the name of God!

Henry: *Oh, in the name of God! Now I know what it feels like to BE God!*

- Mary Shelley – *Frankenstein. (1818)*

I was joltingly dared to interact once more with that man - Adolf Hitler. And remember, maybe I'm repeating myself, but that was after a good seventy dormant years since I last conversed with him. This old mind of mine became a field of blazing disquietude.

Meanwhile, oddly enough for his part, the living criminal remained steadfastly speechless. Stillness. There he stood, erect as ever, staring right back into my eyes. I saw him grimace at me, watching the bizarre experience lingering on while he continued staring intensely into my restricted pupils. Why didn't I say something? I didn't want to accept him as a 'human' worthy of any discussion. What a stupid response!

But then, I had to concede to the scrupulously devout dictates of life and longevity since I presumed that had to be the final conversation with that man, given the fact I, too, was facing the autumnal years of my life.

But my fears subsided, remembering or noting he was, after all, forcibly ensconced in a prison glass cage. Now it was kind of funny seeing him boxed in there. And that's when I realized why the voluble Fuehrer did not speak — the glass cage, remember!

Stalin wanted to do that to him. Put in a box and let the world see him in his glorious nakedness! I felt free to get out. And how he must've felt repressed, seeing the world pass by him and not being able to proclaim one word!

I remembered how he told me many times back in 1945 that he would never end up as Mussolini did —strung upside, allowing him to be publicly stoned, spat at people urinating on him. And yet, here he was struck in this glass cage.

Then I realized how stupid my thoughts were — Hitler couldn't care less if I left or stayed or rotted in front of him! He wanted out. Wasn't that obvious?

I think, despite my earnest and frank diligence in seeking to produce a judicious portrait of that man, he nevertheless sensed that I had deceived him. I say, 'maybe.' Buy why?

There's no perfection. There's no absolute, descriptive reality. Reality is jagged, fuzzy. Not a pleasant, comforting concept.

Quantum physics dictated uncomfortable principles causing unwillingness and disquiet in Man, for who can but refuse any hints of denialism of certainty, accuracy, and reality itself? Yet such are the ineffable, transient, metaphysical constituents, structures, and properties of the 'physical reality.' Yet, on the other hand, why worry when we know the vast majority of people haven't even heard of this branch of physics? While the few who have heard of it can only bother now and then, assuming it must be an arcane, esoteric field — and here I'm guessing they ever do think of it.

Humans are constitutionally no different from the properties of sub-atomic particles. What does this have to with History? Because with that bizarre and incomprehensible baggage in mind, I can only provide a probabilistic vision and understanding of the entirety of Hitler's mind, the Third Reich, the people involved and affected during those lawless, disordered, unrestrained, exciting, and riotous years in Man's history. There is no 'final truth' inexactly as there is no 'total reality.' We can never know the totality of the attributes of an electron any more than we can know with precision the constituents of the human mind and so much less of historical events. We do, however, and we can reach approximate understandings of these matters in question but let no one dogmatically claim they know the 'full truth'! The ghosts of every noble quantum physicist hovers over us and our ethereal reality!

~

I'm Going to Berlin '45 Baby!

I got the job.

Even Daddy was surprised. A twenty-year-old uneducated Kansas farm girl interviewing Hitler – really? And with my attitude! You may be surprised that I thought nothing of it. I didn't feel pressure, insecurities, or fears in taking that task. You see, it's because I never thought much of the dimensions of any war, let alone that war; yes, as I said, I read loads, but words never even touched my skin, let alone my heart. I know I used 'let alone' twice.

Anyway, off I went; from DC, we flew to some airport outside Paris. From there, I was escorted by three US army officers in a jeep, presumably to the frontline in Germany. It was a long journey because some roads were shattered, some blocked for God knows what reason, and re-fuelling, which sometimes meant waiting for hours. No, there were no running gas stations.

When asked by my escorts why I, a young girl, was going to Germany, I casually replied, I'm a journalist and will remain ensconced with the US army for my protection.

One of the boys surprised me —

US Army Escort: How would you get any reports if you stay within our lines?

DG: I don't know, these are my orders, and I'm here to obey.

I knew my answer was stupid. I lied. They probably thought, typical dumb girl. Anyway, some days later, the scenery dramatically changed. I knew we were entering the war zone or war area or whatever the word is. Not far from us would be the actual frontlines of the war. But, to be honest, there was no such thing as a 'front' nor did I see any 'line,' but anyway, it's funny how we humans create perfectly well-sounding words. Unconsciously - without thinking — we believe we know what they mean. We believe in their 'reality' when we don't know until we experience the said word in question.

Every village was broken, wreckage, rubble. Weary-looking people, mainly women, old people, and children, walking in columns, carrying their belongings in wagons. *Yep, Ms. Gale, welcome to Germany!"* exclaimed one of my escorts. I didn't realize we had entered Germany — my God, how stupid could I have been? But this looked nothing like the Germany I lived in! Ragged people pulling wagons! Were these really Germans? This was not even a country. It's Wrecksville through and through.

Never mind, don't look back at stupidities; think ahead.

Our trip slowed down because the deeper we moved inside 'Germany,' the greater the obstacles. Passable roads dwindled. We drove through country fields, but they too were cratered here and there. Yes, these were Germans. Who else would they be?

DG: How … or what do these people eat? There's no place to eat.

US Escort Officer: They shit, don't they?

Then I remember, why was I objectifying them? Weren't these my people too? I'm German, and yet I did not feel sympathy, to be honest.

Some week or two later, I heard for the first time the sounds of war. Gunfire. Artillery. Rockets. Bombs. Suddenly someday, we stopped. "This our final designated point." I was told. "We've got to go, and your next American escort will pick you."

There was an ancient-looking tavern confidently named *Liberté, égalité, fraternité*. That was our meeting point. With the German side, I mean. I walked in; an old woman was shocked seeing me. "Je suis Americain," I said, not realizing the old lady knew that, since I was in a US Army uniform. My God, I wanted to smack myself for these strings of idiotic mistakes. Instead, she smiled and told me how much a room costs. I had no idea what money figure she said. I had

American money, which the French accepted, so I was fine. My room reminded me of van Gogh's painting of his room in Arles. After all, this poor woman's motel was near the frontlines. Who can fault her for her faulty place?

But then, wait a minute. Wasn't I in Germany? How come this lady was French? I couldn't ask her questions because I spoke no French. Jesus, what if those US army guys dropped me in the wrong location? But *we were* in German territory, that's what they told me. Or were they playing pranks on me, seeing I was so dumb? But then again, no, I was told in DC that I'd meet Hitler's men from a hotel called Liberté, égalité, fraternité.

Tired from overthinking, I dozed off.

The following day, the old hag or bag shouts at me, clearly in anger and fright. I ran downstairs, and there stood three erect SS men. One was clearly their commander. He asked in English, "Are you, Madam Gale?" I told him I'm fluent in German.

"I am *SS-Gruppenführer und Generalleutnant der Waffen-SS* Hermann Fegelein. I'm here at the Fuehrer's personal request to safely escort you to see him." Suddenly I remembered the scowling bag. Fegelein told me to get inside their jeep, and so off we went. I couldn't wait to ask the obvious, "Excuse me, Gruppenführer Fegelein, but are we in German territory?" As rushed as my unfinished question was, Fegelein smiled, replying, "The lines are in all shapes and directions. As far you're concerned, trust me; we'll safely take you to the Fuehrer." I didn't understand him, but then my interest in my own question vanished.

We approached Berlin. The sounds were deafening. You know what sounds I mean. Smash, boom bang! But now, we faced another obstacle. No car drives through rubble. So, off we went, on foot, of course! Fegelein firmly held my hand as we had to clamber over detritus of war. But it wasn't all wreckage, thankfully. There were some clear spaces. Fegelein would hail a German tank, and that's how we proceeded. The closer, I suppose we were reaching the Bunker, the sharper the sounds and furies of the battle raged. We'd have to leave the tank because of more rubble, shards, and blocks of shattered buildings in front of us. The three Germans had to literally carry me at several stages, as I just couldn't climb over the jagged rubble without slicing my fingers off. And so, it went on. Sometimes we'd find a subway or U-Bahn, and we'd walk through thousands of Berliners living there. And God, the stench of these miserable people forced me to vomit several times. "Please, no more of these tunnels!" I asked Fegelein.

He looked at me with a grin, "Where did you think you were coming? Disneyland?"

~

Unnatural Effects of Being in Berlin – Mixtures of Jackson Pollock, Egon Schiele & Edward Hopper

We entered the Emerald City of Hell. Hear me now, St. Augustine!

I remembered the barmaid *in A Bar at the Folies-Bergère* [1882], painted by Édouard Manet – vague, glinting, and unclear. Paradoxical attributes. In sum, I cannot see the beautiful barmaid's facial expressions. Because they're hazy, meaning I cannot judge what she's thinking and feeling about me as I look and engage in a conversation with her. Like, is she bored with my approaches, or does she find me engaging? As I said, I cannot know because the 'reality' Manet created disallows me from gauging any certainty as per my questions.

Remember the electron's attributes? And no matter how much I try to prise out her specific attributes, she remains dizzyingly elusive. That's how I felt being in Berlin at that moment, as I silently observed the few silent Berliners.

Next, I see Berliners looking like Egon Schiele's canvases, especially women. Vigorously vitriolic in their looks and facial expressions. Striking, stark, and eagerly intent in doing whatever it is they want to be done.

To me, they looked vicious, far from inviting and amiable; disturbed by something, presumably the war, I'd guess.

But then, dreamily, I interplay in a thousand flexible postures and unnatural excitements emotions with *'Sappho and Erinna in a Garden at Mytilene'* painted by Simeon Solomon in 1864. Fluidly swapping pleasurable razor-sharp flesh and guttural sounds while heaving with contorted motions between taut bodies.

Then there were those rare quiet night-time moments. These feelings only occurred during the brief and irregular lull hours in Berlin's cool nights. That's when I felt calming scents and the giddying exhilarations of van Gogh's *The Starry Night* [1889].

Someone slaps me. Rushingly twirled a trillion tingly, titillating gratifications.

I behold fidgeting hordes. I recognize each one of them. I sense their totality. Enigmatic and amorphous batches of Munch's silly men and women in *Anxiety* [1894]. Some run frantically away from the world. Some waddle in mournful processions towards nowhere. So much for titillation.

I mentioned Pollock and Hopper.

Being one drop in a Jackson Pollock painting. Crazy. Isn't that man, right? You, we humans, are dots in a screaming world of painfully swirling minds, behaviors, actions, events beyond our control, like Brownian motion. Bombarded by billions of other actors in life — again, beyond your control. And then comes the final bump — your death!

Jackson Pollock

But you know what's crazier? Only while being in Berlin made me understand that nut of an artist! Once I understood what Pollock's paintings meant, I thought to myself, *'Well, why would he think like that?'* I mean, he *is* American. He never went through war. I know that. But then, Daddy told me, the man's a *natural* nut. He was clinically, certifiably, professionally nuts. Add to that alcoholism. What a mixture to have in one brain, right? So anyway, he died in a drunken car crash. So much for him. But going back to Berlin, that is what it felt like. Pollock got it right. We've all, in some time or another, lived in this Pollockian world. This event happens, and we don't know why. Worse, we don't understand the event itself. Some of us react to it with extremes of violence, hurling us in jail. Others respond to the same event with depression or panic attacks or insecurities, or all these terrible attributes put together. Others remain passive. Whatever. The point is we're thrown into a situation we know nothing about or one we didn't expect to slam us so hard. We're just atoms in Brownian motion. I said that already. I'm sorry. Pollock speeded up our manic lives, thereby showing us the derangement within which we live in. You see, we live our lives in slow-motion. That's why we overlook the sick delirium Pollock visualized so accurately. So, I had to respect him, even though he was a nut. Quite odd when you think of it. His New York mind must've felt exactly as you would if you were in Berlin in 1945.

But it was not just that. I mean, there's more. I came across a perfectly normal-looking man or woman sitting somewhere. You may say, "So what?"

Edward Hopper, 'Nighthawks' - 1942

This was the vision of Edward Hopper. A vision of 'perfect' Weberian anomie. A society of atomized, disconnected humans, while still living in a city or town or village but where there's no connectivity between anyone of us. You may be in a crowded or emptying diner, or you may be in a business meeting, or you may be in a nightclub, or you may be alone — in each case, we will still exist on two levels of dysconnectivity — one from those around us; and far worse, health-wise, we're disconnected from ourselves, no matter our circumstances.

Hours or generations later, I understand I'm nowhere. Why 'nowhere'? Because nothing was precise in Berlin. I know that sounds vague, if not meaningless. I say 'nowhere' because there was no certainty in anything surrounding my existence in that damned city of hell.

Daylight did not matter. Dates did not matter. The increasing numbers of the dead, wounded, and the missing in action did not matter. Murder didn't matter. Night did not matter. Money did not matter. Education, music, the arts, children, culture, refinement, politeness, decencies, fashion literacy, morality, families did not matter. Up was down and vice versa. Morality? I laughed when I thought about that! You see how quickly I'd already changed character? Just like Daddy foretold.

> *Just as every cop is a criminal*
> *And all the sinners saints*
> *As heads is tails*
> *Just call me Lucifer*
> *'Cause I'm in need of some restraint*

I became Noah. Firmly stuck inside stinking entrails of a bloating cadaver—decomposing corpse. You do know, don't you, that decomposition exists within several stages?

Mental pressuring manic furies aggravated on by frenzied hurricanes in my concussed mind. I'm one unnoted, disorientated bee in a Jackson Pollock painting. Minds and flesh fighting to kill each other. And those two are both in the same body. Humans tearing each other apart. Stupidities and intellectuals were conversing only to implode microseconds later, becoming screaming bulls seeking to gore each other.

For no reason, I pictured Ernest Hemingway. What a scoundrel! Seeking 'glory' portraying his sick body and sicker mind as some kind of unbiased, healthy 'war reporter' while everyone knew his years of glory had long died. Now his only temporary purpose in life was to seek a revival of his dead 'fame.' So, he'd jeep around Germany, and presto, he'd be beloved and famous again! Pretending to be a war 'hero' when he had nothing to do with the frontlines.

I can tell you not one American GI appreciated or cared for that fat bastard. Years later, when we heard the dunce finally ended his life, well, that was his most significant act of creativity done for humanity. I hate inauthenticity. Don't pretend who you're not. That's all. Be yourself. But when pretending, don't you think people smell your fakeries? One day, I remembered how our soldiers hated Bob Hope with his tours, dipping in and out from the war. I felt self-righteous about their hatred. But then a receding mirror peered at me, speaking words of wisdom, "Ah yes, talking of being self-righteous, but didn't you too dip in and out that war?"

For the first time in my adult life, I saw a naked teen girl. No more than seventeen. What was she doing? What … I didn't even know what or how to ask Fegelein. He was typically laughing. What's so funny seeing that disturbing scene? That's how clobbered I felt. Berlin '45. I named her *Lady Godiva* because she was ranting about helping the people, and that's why she was naked.

Zealous Nazis. But I could feel their crucifying loneliness. Berlin '45. I remembered I had to steer and steel my mind towards unity and not allow fragmentation. Because fragmentation means madness. Berlin '45. Otherwise, only madness can and must ensue. Eye's focus. I distinguish my presence in Edward Hopper's *Nighthawks*. Horrid morning breath. Life-killing anomie. Actually, which was more deathly dead, my 'town,' Goodland or Berlin?

Oozing orifices. Why do ugly thoughts and images pop in my brain?

Again, I turned to Lady Godiva. My God, I forgot to note her extraordinary beauty. Instead, I was trying to hear her screaming though faint words, given the sensitive roars of guns and bombs. Now I was rushed with fleshy emotions. Obsessed with beauty on this piercing scale. Pungent. She smelled too.

The infamous portrait of Dorian Gray. Our mind, reality, and truth are not the Official Standard Model historians paint it to be. But on the other hand, I cannot but love the truthfulness of the grotesque replicas of Andy Warhol's Factory mass-production of utterly inconsequential goods. Their end-product is that nothing meaningful can be created by pens, strings, keys, brushes, and imagination. That's why people with no talent, like Edith Sedgwick, became famous.

Just as we hobble on, so too, I note I'm not fully in control of everything whizzing in my brain. And that's what frightens me because it means I can evolve into schizophrenia?

I've said it before, and I'll repeat myself because it's grossly ignored in literature and films, both fiction and non-fiction. Watching two men or more in hand-to-hand combat. What an antiseptic way of describing it all! But you know, describing and seeing are two planets. Explain colors or tastes. Imagine two hungry, mean dogs in supersonic speed jolting and jerking each other, threshing out each other's eyeballs, mauling each other with mouth-sized chunks of flesh, and flaying it out to the death. Replace dogs with humans. Now revisit that scene of the fight. And no book or film ever shows you those scenes because they are supposed to be too hideous or terrifying to be seen.

I catch my body and mind. Is this really Man? Yes, it is. But how did Man ever become like this? What made him so repulsive in his nature? Was Man akin to the brutalized, despised monster in Mary Shelley's novel Frankenstein? Did Man brutalize Man? Or did life brutalize Man? Or both?

For no known reason, Dorothy's mind fuels up into overdrive. Pangs of mental thirst. Sexual readiness to be received. Throbbing desires. Of all places – in war-torn Berlin! I hadn't felt any of these heated surges of sexual arousals in Kansas. I lusted recklessly. Meaning I cared nothing for consequences. And yet, ashamed of sinful attributes. So, I try ignoring them, which is what I'd done all my life. Because whatever threatens the unity of your mind, you must exterminate.

Actually, I'm lying. I felt intolerant sexual needs needing to be obeyed instantaneously back in Goodland, Kansas. 'Intolerant' meaning they'd accept nothing less than they were demanding that had to be done.

Another cure - distract yourself, girl. Play cards, play girly, draw, knit, play innocent, talk stupid to stupid people, play like you're dumb as an inanimate thing, like rock, do anything. I'm don't if I succeeded. Did anyone catch me when I was genuine to myself? No idea.

Another oddity. Going back to Lady Godiva, forget there were so many drop=dead gorgeous German women. Never mind the war - you wouldn't think you'd see seriously attractive humans in war consuming your entirety! My ill or wicked brain urged me, *'Do it, girl; in Berlin, nothing exists. God does not exist. Jesus forsook Berlin. And certainly, morality did not exist. God won't even notice your terrible transgressions.'*

I beheld madness. What pompous words! They are meaningless. Because scripts, literature cannot ever allow you to experience the described story. Just like no words can make you understand or taste of an apple. You cannot avoid the castrating limitations of swords and literature. Just like no raped woman can ever make you feel her pain.

People publicly fornicating. Willingly. I'm not talking rape. People were publicly doing it without any shame or care if people were watching. *I certainly watched and stared.* It happened anywhere and everywhere. On rubble. In dingy shelters. On charred tanks. Inside charred tanks. Naked, half-naked. Some looked like they were being tortured. Was it pain or pleasure? It sure did not look like pleasure to me. Who knew? I could not exactly interrupt and ask the couple in question, could I? I wanted to, mind you.

Anything and everything existed in Berlin. Especially during *quiet hours*, you see them. Prostitutes of all ages, pimps, smugglers, hustlers, abandoned feral children, murderers, rapists, drunkards, lunatics, loners, sadists, masochists, loafers, thieves, pedophiles, killers-for-hire. You see professional dancers and ballerinas performing amid the ruins. A middle-aged man frantically sermonizing what he believed to be a grandiose oration, aware or unaware or indifferent either way to the fact no one was listening. What did he do before the war, I wondered. He must've been sane. Maybe he was a most outstanding, virtuous, loving man. Or perhaps he was an SS murderer who returned home because of his insanity. I listened to some of his oddball words —

"No, we are dead because of too much light and no lantern in the hottest day changes matters and we run like Gilgamesh thinking or believing eternity is for us but we fall because God and Satan dug ditches in every step of our lives so be certain you shall fall and many of you have fallen and some realize and some don't realize they've fallen and nothing changes your state of mind no matter what you do if you're the richest man on earth or the poorest you are alike because light wipes us out washing rationality into drizzles …"

Had enough and walked on. Ragged man playing a centuries-old composition. Holding a fragile violin. I noticed it wasn't fragile; it was broken. He was in his thirties, early thirties, but boy, what a surprisingly fresh face he had for a Berliner. He looked like those moving marionette puppets, and his facial expressions struck me like those medieval automatons. Faintly human but convincingly wooden. He repeated the same sentence in a squeaky voice – *"Welcome to the show. Welcome to the carnival. Come on inside! Gather here, all ye good people! It's free. And you're already inside."* Oh yeh, I forget to say he wasn't actually playing his violin.

Prostitutes yelling for customers. One Mediterranean-looking prostitute screeching to no one in particular, "What's price, today you in me?" And what varieties of whores you see in Berlin, ranging from eighty-year-old ladies to young girls. What 'customers'? Believe me, many customers were seeking their services. Otherwise, why would they advertise their presence? But curiously for me or what was more far more interesting, was the number of *women* seeking the services of these prostitutes – now, that shocked me! That made me proud. Isn't it odd, now, because in Western countries, it's always men who seek prostitutes because women are too shy to go for the latter's services. But in Berlin, as I said, where nothing exists, as regards morality, social constraints, women felt liberated to do whatever they wanted to do, and especially whatever their needs required them to do, and that was why I was thrilled and deeply pleased seeing these Berlin girls finally getting their nourishment to live and survive.

Some drunk, some sober. Some lying amid the rubble. Some seeking food amid the rubble. Not knowing if they passed out from alcohol or if they were dead. No, they can't lie in the jagged rubble. It's too painful. I heard soldiers from both sides cursing each other. Some shouted insults with jest, others with hatred. Every now then, you listen or hear [I don't care which verb is better] singing on both sides.

Old and young 'philosophers' haranguing each other in esoteric and weighty subject matters discussing weighty subjects such as the value of zero or the meaning of words such as 'is' is. A famished-looking young lady selling beautiful watercolor paintings [I never thought to ask if she were the artist]. Young children of all ages playing games with sticks, rocks, and debris.

Talking of rocks and debris, a well-attired old man was reading a newspaper on a chair. Upon closer inspection, I notice the paper was years old. There he was, spruced up, clean-shaven, intently looking at his paper, presumably reading — or pretending to read? I don't know. And every time I went outside the Bunker and on the Berlin streets, there he was in the same place 'reading' the same paper. Of course, I had to talk to him.

DG: Sir, why do you read the same paper every day?

Old Newspaper Reading Man: News does not change.

DG: Why are you sitting where there's a battle going on?

{*Laughter*}

Old Newspaper Reading Man: What an impolite lady you are! Do you not think it pertinent to introduce yourself before addressing me with your questions?

DG: I'm sorry. I'm Dorothy Gale, journalist with the US Army.

Old Newspaper Reading Man: I see! You've sailed all the way from America, did you?

DG: No, by plane.

Old Newspaper Reading Man: Excuse me?

DG: I was flown by plane.

Old Newspaper Reading Man: I don't see Americans here. How can you be 'American'?

DG: Well, I am American. And there are many of us journalists, by the way.

Old Newspaper Reading Man: No, that's impossible. The Fuehrer informed us we're only facing the Asiatic Bolshevik hordes.

DG [Laughing]: 'Only' the Russians?

Old Newspaper Reading Man: What are you laughing about?

DG: You said you're "only" facing the Russians.

Old Newspaper Reading Man: What an awkward-looking girl you are, my dear!

DG: Never mind what I just said; I apologize.

Old Newspaper Reading Man: Good of you to apologize. I find it hard to believe you are a journalist but be that as it may, what is your purpose in coming to our country, if I may ask you?

DG: I told you. I'm a journalist.

Old Newspaper Reading Man: And you are here to say what?

At this point, I'm thinking this must be a senile lunatic.

DG: Sir, are you aware that you're sitting in a battle zone?

Old Newspaper Reading Man: What does that have to do with my needing to read the news, which was your original inquiry?

DG: Didn't you just tell me news doesn't change?

Old Newspaper Reading Man: Indeed!

DG: So, again, why are you risking your life sitting in a battlefield?

Old Newspaper Reading Man: Only being here, in situ, so to speak, I sense realities occurring.

DG: You can't sense how the battle is evolving while sheltering somewhere in some safe place?

Old Newspaper Reading Man: Exactly! The newspaper is a ruse. Only by being here, I know of the truth, my young girl.

DG: And you sense the changes in the fortunes of this battle change?

Old Newspaper Reading Man: Well, that is it, is it not; what do you think it is?

DG: What is 'it'?

Old Newspaper Reading Man: I know. You don't know.

I couldn't continue with this stupidity, so I chose another subject.

DG: Do you have children?

Old Newspaper Reading Man: Dead. All dead in the war. Dirty blood.

DG: What do you mean —

Old Newspaper Reading Man: I do not know if my three boys died honorably or not. Maybe they were cowards. Maybe, they were Soviet traitors. So, keeping an open eye and mind, I must presume they have dirty blood.

DG: But you say you don't know ... why then judge them when you have no evidence either way?

Old Newspaper Reading Man: Good question. I always assume the worse with every human and event. That is why you must physically position yourself as close to the truth, as I said, in situ, so you can know of the desired truth you seek.

I was revolted with that ugly creature, abruptly leaving him.

Anyway, going back to those doing what you are supposed to be doing in the privacy of your bed, doing that, I felt an entirely different meaning to sex. I learned about differing definitions of sex. No, sex is not just 'sex!' You see, yours truly learns, and not just a pig-headed girl! And the same goes for every subject, value, and concept in life. Concepts such as 'right' and 'wrong.' For example, you say 'war.' You don't even think about it because the confident, smug you implicitly believes you understand its meaning. But you do *not* know its meaning. Until you experience it. And deeper still, your experience of war will be entirely different from someone else, though, let's say, both witness the same battle and in the same spot. On a more practical level, you 'know' what hypocrisy means. But you won't actually understand it until you experience it. Or 'orgasm.' Anyway, who cares about philosophy?

Why was I 'revolted' by that old man reading his paper? That was a harsh reaction, wasn't it? What harm did he do to me?

∼

Four Unexpected Twists I Experienced in Berlin

Everything sounded simple to me. Interview the man, get it done with, and I'll be escorted right back home.

But the minute I arrived in Berlin, everything changed in April of that year. Your twenty-year-old Kansas farm girl could never be the same girl. And that's not an easy thing to say. So, I guess the first question would be - 'Well, Dorothy girl, why and what was it that made you change, girl?'

~

I. Differences in Realities Between Berlin, The Bunker, Hitler, and My World

There was a battle going on. A radically different reality from peacetime country life. Most people who never witnessed a battle won't understand. It's difficult to convey any sensation to those who were not there. Just as trying to explain the taste of an apple to one who never ate an apple. Or explain the color red to a blind person. Is it so remarkable then to what extent we didn't and could never appreciate the difference in realities between war and peacetime?

II. The Unique Nature of the Russo-German War

Meanwhile, this was no 'ordinary' war. Here's the difference. This war was unprecedented in our Modern History. Why? Because Mankind had not seen or experienced an exterminatory war, especially as the Eastern Front or the Russo-German War. Put simply, no one thought nor imagined human viciousness could reach these gory levels. As a result, a multi-polar world ended being a bi-polar world, with only two superpowers, America and the Soviet Union.

III. Hitler Is History's Most Unique Characters in Modern History

I met a man who was modern history's most hypnotic, charismatic, enthralling, and demonic characters—contrasting attributes. On the one hand, he was the supreme seducer of millions of people from all classes, ages, and socio-economic backgrounds. Yet, on the other hand, the man initiated and implemented a European-wide program of genocide.

He was the cream of both - the cream and the crap of the crop.

IV. Hitler Was Not Just Evil –How Many Times Must I Say This &, Yes, He Had Great Qualities!

The fourth surprising twist occurred within my first conversation with the man. I appreciated this wasn't going to be me interviewing one leader of some nation. This man couldn't be understood simply by interviewing him, even if we spoke for a thousand years. The man, in and of himself, wouldn't suffice. I needed far more colours and ingredients, sounds, and witnesses to complete my final composition. That's why I deliberately interviewed his closest disciples and victims.

Still, even having done that, I knew life's limitations. No human can have a one hundred percent accurate portrayal of any other human being. No human can ever get an entirely accurate representation of any event, for that matter. No human can ever explain the totality of their own mind. There can never be a totality as per reality for anything and anyone. Even something as mundane as observing a chair before you – you will still never be able to present us fully with all its attributes. Here's a straightforward example – depending on your location, you'll only see a specific angle of the chair. Move to another position, and the image you describe changes.

Goering - "That's impossible! The Americans only know how to make razor blades."

Field-Marshal Erwin Rommel - "We could do with some of those razor blades, Herr Reichsmarschall."

~

Portraits of Berlin 1945

'Will they not go astray who devise Evil? But kindness and truth will be to those who devise Good.'

- Proverbs 14:22

Looking back now, as I write these memories, I'm still unable to explain my relative lack of fear in what I was embarking on. No, that's not true. I regretted taking the job because I was convinced it was pointless, therefore, tedious. Why? The story was already dead. Where I came from, no one was interested in Hitler. In the Mecca that was Goodland, Kansas, none were interested in Hitler.

Intensities of flashing mixed with contrasting colors. Some blinding white explosions rip everything standing before you, and it's all dust and rubble the next second; these scenes were especially spectacular in the nighttime. The latter instantaneously switched night to the sunniest day.

Add in this delicious cauldron torrential rain and lightning and visualize now nighttime in wartime Berlin, 1945.

We all spoke and said 'Berlin.' But what was left of Berlin?

Monstrous, twisted rubble. Smashed buildings. Oddly enough, it seemed always to be the sides of buildings that managed to keep up their spirits and survive. But I swear I didn't see one intact house, building, or shop.

I.   Evolving Lives of Corpses

Now you may ask me, "What does talking about corpses have to do with Hitler and trying to understand the mind of Hitler?" I, too, had never thought such matters as describing Berlin in detail had anything to do with Hitler. But after years, even decades, my mind changed imperceptibly; I didn't realize my viewpoints had changed. Stealthy mind, indeed.

So, why discuss corpses, for example? Because understanding that man isn't just knowing his ideas, beliefs, intentions, motivations, and, of course, his deeds. Yes, they're essential, but knowing or seeking to portray as accurately a portrait as one can, you must add in every other element connected to the subject. Historians never mention these points, do they?

To get to the point, corpses are entities Hitler created in the millions, innocent civilians or soldiers. His life directly caused the highest number of corpses in modern history. Millions of corpses are his legacy, from Paris to Stalingrad, from Oslo to El Alamein — these are his proud deeds. How can we disconnect millions of corpses from his life? Do we think he was unaware of these decaying corpses that only he deliberately, wilfully, and systematically ordered to be done since that was an essential part of his fanatical, blind Nazi ideology of racial purity?

Maybe, he ignored such thoughts. Perhaps he never thought once about his innocent victims, though they counted in the millions. But surely, he must've thought once or twice about the millions of his dead Germans, civilians, and soldiers. When traveling in his train, and when it stopped at some juncture - if he saw wounded German soldiers, he'd shut down the curtain. Every brilliant historian states that's because he was heartless and uninterested in seeing what he caused. I think otherwise.

Remember, I don't believe Hitler, or any evil human for that matter, is one hundred percent, twenty-four hours a day, behaving in evil manners. I think he felt pangs or aches for those wounded boys, especially those unrecognizable, so damaged their faces and bodies. That's why he shut down the curtains. That's why he did not view mangled corpses of his civilians and soldiers, spread out all over Europe and North Africa. Because they're *his* legacy. Since no one but his fanatical insistence in carrying out his war caused those once healthy civilians and soldiers to end up in the contorted, bloated state they were.

In fact, I know the more German civilians died from the devastating air raids, the more his zeal for mass murder increased, believing it to be his 'right' to retaliate against what he considered as acts of war. The dead, in all their various stages of being, was on his mind. That awful idea and scene inflamed his already genocidal hatred to ever more extremes, as per acts of more suffering, torture, and death for those he considered were responsible for the Second World War.

Corpses everywhere, never a life to spare.

I found them fascinating, to be honest. I thought I'd be squeamish, disgusted, or frightened, but to my surprise, I was fascinated by them. But then again, being a pig farmer's daughter, why would I be squeamish? This is, like it or not, the entrails of 'life' after death. Each corpse thrives in a different state of decomposition. By 'thriving,' I'm sure you know, I mean maggots 'thriving,' while the rest of the body decays into an eventual mixture of dust, liquefied matter, and fragments of hair and bones.

Who would've known that? You see, back in Kansas, we don't let pigs decompose. We kill them, butcher their meat into their parts, package them, and then have them delivered to be sold to the public.

But in wartime, death is different. You see the changes in how God decomposes the carcass of an animal or the corpse of a human being. And there's nothing uniform here. There are many variations in decay trajectories, depending on factors such as the temperature, if the body is on a block of stone or in a forest, water, or mud. Every detail accentuates the differences in how the body decomposes. These tenants live in your stomach, in the small and large intestines, your colon, faces, and so on.

Colors change skin color from white to blue, green, and ultimately black. If left with enough time, every bloated corpse will eventually explode from the increasing pressure from the multiplying gasses of the billions of farting bacteria. They call it 'purged liquid.' Doesn't that sound sweet? *Purged liquid.* What a scene! I learned what the stench was. I knew as I said it was from the bacteria, but what exactly was the stench called? *Cadaverine!* There you go! Cadaverine is the chemical compound emitted by bacteria. Putrescine is the other chemical compound emitted by cadavers.

If I remember correctly, the first to be liquefied is the soft parts of the body, such as the eyes and skin. Eyes are rapidly eaten and are gone. Next, the skin retracts, turning yellow and eventually looking like scarred waxy skin of a mummy.

But then, to my astonishment, some corpses remained in a gelatinous and mushy goo state. I don't why, but I can only guess their surroundings allowed the corpse not to be liquefied.

Corpses struck me with their physical postures. I suppose a sculptor would be interested in seeing so many poses. I never knew humans could be so contorted, some stiff as rocks while others were jelly-like, oozing fluids from orifices and wounds. Some faces stare mindlessly with wide-open eyeballs stare into your eyes, almost lifelike. But not really. Upon closer inspection, they're not really 'staring' at you. That's more of a Hollywood thing. A dead eye has no stare nor even any look in any direction.

That wobbled my nerves. Maybe I was squeamish. You're not sure if this gashed 'head' is living or dead? The uncertainty scared me. In contrast, others have that classic finished look, you know, with glazed eyeballs. Some had fearful expressions, even though they were dead. How odd. Expressive even in death!

Stabbed eyes. Again, there are many variations here. Gouged out eyes. Eyeless faces. Partially ripped out eyes. Why would anyone do that to corpses? Frenzied, revengeful hate. Man, furiously needing to tear Man to shreds. It's not a pleasant sight for untrained eyes and unscratched nerves to experience. That, my friends, you must know. I must tell people what war is. And yet, that was precisely what frightened me the most, what repelled me from seeing these all too familiar scenes. I thought it best not to speak of the realities. A man is literally tearing another man's throat with his fingers, and I guess, nails. Why should I be the bearer of hideous news unto Mankind? That wasn't my job. I was in Berlin only to interview people in a reasonably calm setting of a Bunker. These humans no longer appear human. Nothing human. Not even animals, because animals don't act maniacally, hysterically.

But there were so many resentful objections in my mind. Fairness. How could I deny what I see, which is the truth about war?

Haven't you noticed that you never see what actual killing in any documentary or fictional portrayal of war is all about? And you never wondered why? Well, I think I've already given you the horrid answer – no film, no documentary shows the public what men killing men looks like because it's far too disturbing for any sane person to see. No director, be it of a documentary or fictional portrait, would dare show you two men tearing each other apart and not stopping until one side finishes off the other. My goodness me – after the war, how many times did I see audiences being terrified from so-called horror films? Horror films scare people! But there's an awful consequence to a denialist attitude as per the realities of war – and that is, no one knows what combat is about until they personally experience it. Further, since no one experiences actual combat in peacetime, glorifying war and militarism seems almost natural.

I just thought of this. In moments of silence, I hear singing birds twittering just as they did over the trenches in the First World War and every battle throughout history —

In Flanders Fields

In Flanders Fields, the poppies blow
Between the crosses, row on row
That mark our place, and in the sky
The larks, still bravely singing, fly
Scarce heard amid the guns below

We are the dead, short days ago
We lived, felt dawn, saw sunset glow
Loved, and were loved, and now we lie
In Flanders fields In Flanders Fields
And now we lie In Flanders Fields

Take up our quarrel with the foe:
To you from failing hands we throw
The torch, be yours to hold it high
If ye break faith with us who die
We shall not sleep, though poppies grow
In Flanders Fields In Flanders fields

Youthful dead boys not yet ready for faint stubble, let alone beards. Clean boys.

Crosses and rows endless of tombstones, some named, some anonymous. All dead. That fact tied them all together in those huge airport-sized cemeteries. And these boys died in concentrated areas, like Flanders Fields. Mind you, though the dead were bunched up in concentrated areas, yes, though these clusters of the dead stretched on for hundreds of miles in all directions.

Why *larks?* Because they're forever cheerful, singing no matter the temperature, weather, or state of murderous inter-human activities taking place. Larks are also among some people birds that carry messages of truth. Isn't that peculiar? But for *whom do* they send their messages to? I can't believe they send these lamentations unto us humans. Because we're stupid. We cannot understand frightful wisdom.

They can send them to churches. And churches can then choose to peal or toll their ancient bells. Churches peal bells when there's a celebration and toll bells when there's mourning. Well, now you know why those larks though inherently cheerful, why they too had to reflect the truthfulness and reality of the millions of different battlefields to the public, to let them know of the sickening agonies going on.

And throughout it all, throughout every day and procedure of wartime, you need to be brave. Why? Because at any unknown second, you could be blown to shredded atomized nothing, given a well-placed and well-targeted shell striking you straight above your every worrisome head.

~

II.   Sounds of Lovemaking & Sounds of War

At first, it was the booming bombs and shrieking rockets that jolted me the most. Not just your mind. Anytime there is a diving rocket, the wind, air, or pressure hurls you. God knows where. Screams and shouting from the living and dying. Cries from all ages. Especially children stung my ears. Some were screaming for help, and those I guessed were the wounded. Others shouted orders and directions for other soldiers to obey. Clattering sounds of steel. Rumbling tanks, reminding me of raging elephants. Ear-slicing, screaming, click-click, crackling sounds of guns, bullets, bombs, and shellfire were swooshing to and fro. Squirty sounds of German *Flammenwerfer* 35 or FmW 35 flamethrowers.

Tanks thoughtlessly rolling over corpses or the wounded, squelching out their lives. Did you know you can differentiate between sounds of tanks cruising over corpses or living bodies? Do you care?

For me, one of the sickening and fascinating events was watching grenades, bombs, or missiles splattering humans into numberless pieces of differently sized fleshy blobs of meat and spraying varying colored and different smelling liquids— Pitter patter of vomitive rain.

Shattering a human body is no different from slicing open a pig's entrails or shooting a watermelon. Many gooey liquids spurt out, in addition to ruptured organs, bones, intestines, excreta, brain, and other physical objects. I'm deliberately describing these truths because no documentary nor scholar discusses nauseating matters directly as I talk to you about what war means. In other words, television, the internet, and all others who communicate to their respective audiences never speak about the actualities of what killing means — as in a battle. Maybe it's because they don't want their attendees or watchers to feel revolted, much as, I suppose, a surgeon wouldn't go into the details of they operate on a minute-by-minute basis, fearing their listeners would also be too revolted by the details. And that is known. Have you ever seen a video or film of men killing each other? Of course not. It's illegal. I think some call it 'snuff movies.' And as I say, they're illegal, like child pornography. But how can people understand what war or a battle is if they don't see the realities of war or what a battle looks like?

In my opinion, if anyone is interested to know what war and battles mean, they must see the entire panoramic scenes of the operations I'm discussing. Otherwise, their vision and understanding would be stilted with a rose-colored image of what war means, which would thwart and distort their comprehensive knowledge of the subject matter. That's why generation after generation, we see ardent youth seeking glory on any battlefield because they have no idea of what they're going to face. Forget the frightfulness of two soldiers tearing each other apart. I told you about that before. Has anyone of you seen a leg being blown up? Has anyone seen an amputation? Of course not. Can any of you imagine that scene? You can imagine as much as you like, but you can never see it as reality shows it. Because even if you see it in a film or video, that is still nothing compared to the reality where the poor soldier's leg is blown off. That psychological deficiency lessens our knowledge of what war is. Thus, historians cannot accurately describe war — though there are millions of battle history books.

∼

III.   Procedures of Death and Dying

Sometimes I walk, and I'm surrounded by the dead. Ants. Other times, I see civilians milling about among the dead and dying. Watching them fading into the unknown realm of Death. Or Heaven. You can tell the moment they expire. I felt proud. I'd check on them, see when they'd die. Maybe I should've been a coroner. Though I did not fancy too much the frothy gurgling sounds dying people make. There was a troubled hissing breath too. In fits and starts. They must've felt pain. I mean during those hissing fits. Who knows? You couldn't ask them. Actually, some or many or who knows how many tried to 'speak,' and amid the coughing, blood spurting, hissing, wheezing, croaking, you'd heard jumbled words emitted from the cavity that was once their mouth, lips, and tongue. Imagine all the girls who once adored that same face, lips, mouth, and tongue. Imagine them crying to no end, out of jealousy because they couldn't have him. If only they'd see him or it now. Ha! I imagined I'd surprise one of their sweethearts, one who felt severely suicidal if life were to be without, and I'd gleefully bring in the faceless cripple to her house or demolished house or whatever. *"Hi! Guess who I brought with me for dinner tonight?"* I'd joyfully shout as I wheelchair in the cursed monster of Dr. Frankenstein. Of course, she wouldn't recognize him, but more importantly, her reaction would be one of the purest fear and disgust. That's what I first thought. But then, thinking more, weren't Berliners by 1945 pretty much used to seeing faceless freaks that once were recognizably human?

And then I'd have to say to the young lady, *"Here's the man you thought you could not live without. You wanted to kill yourself if he did not marry you. Well, he secretly told me he decided he's now ready for you; what do you say?"* God, how I laughed, visualizing that scene!

These people could not talk. Anyway, the other sound was gurgling blood bubbling in and out from their gaping mouths and wounds. Some did try to speak. Or I think that was what they were doing. You could only hear a guttural croaking, nothing else. No words. Others mostly groaned. That must have meant they were in pain.

Some had reddish-black blobs that once were heads and faces. Some had parts of their head and face gashed, partially or wholly. A face with nothing but loose meet beneath their nose.

∼

IV.   Obscene Odours, Some Weirdly Enticing

I cannot in a million years explain this one. Who knew God designed so many stinky variations of stench? And for what purpose? I did not know then, but in time, there were answers. But what a Devil's variety of stench! The oddest of them all was the putrid yet *attracting* ones – do not for *now* ask me how.

∼

V.   Civilians Between Madness & Stoicism

And the living? Mostly they were nowhere in sight. Living or surviving in basements. Enduring 'life' within the wreckage and rubble. At first sight, I thought there were no civilians left in Berlin. One disheveled American drunkenly walks. Yes, an American! Who was he? A POW who somehow got himself released? But there were no American soldiers in Berlin! He was bloated, seemed to be in his twenties, long-haired, bearded. For no reason, he turned to me, speaking with a muffled voice and glazed eyes - "No one here gets out alive!"

Most open spaces such as streets, plazas, gardens were empty. Because you're unprotected in those places. Especially during battle time. But then, whenever there was a convincing lull, suddenly out they'd come, hurriedly scampering here, darting there - presumably seeking basics such as food.

Seeing them people, oddly enough, made me intensely happy. Made me secure. I felt normal again. Because seeing humanity, no matter how desperate, no matter how wrecked they were, still they infused in me all colors, temperatures, and beliefs that hope, humanity, and love exist and live - a belief that normality, sanity, and reason exist in Berlin.

And you know, when reflecting a little bit, that's when I reexamined my old town, Goodland in Kansas. I realized its beauty for the first time after having intensely hating it all my life precisely because I thought of it as nothing more than an open grave mass pit burial of massacred citizens who were still 'living' and plodding on in their drudgeries and chores. But now, being in Berlin, I wanted to return to my tinsy Goodland, a place where I know my coordinates, my visual perspectives - sanity. I wanted to get back to a place where physical proportions and the geometry of buildings, rooms, any object would be recognizable again. A place where recognizably-looking humans acted the roles God intended for them to play.

Do you understand my garbled words?

~

Dawn of the Battle of Berlin

This was April. The year 1945. Battle of Berlin. Two million Berliners. To be precise, April 16th, 1945. First day of the actual fight.

The city rocked and shivered beneath your feet. Cracked and craggy buildings either exploded or limped frantically to the resting ground. Berliners awoke to the maniacally insane screams as their frontline soldiers were force-fed by the fanatical willpower of 8,983 Soviet artillery pieces, 270 guns every kilometer, vomiting out an astonishing stockpile of seven million shells - 1.2 million on the first day alone- at German defenses on the Oder-Neisse River line. This was, after all, the final act of World War II in Europe.

The war was ending. Hitler's Thousand Year Reich was disappearing. And yours indeed truly was in the center of Germany. In the heart of the Devil. And Sweet Lord, the Devil was King in Berlin, wherein no decency, compassion, and a helping hand dared to show their presence. This was the Reign of Lucifer, who needed no restraint if ever you needed to know.

At the same time, I understood why German soldiers fought Russians, knowing full well they'd all be swallowed up by the tidal wave of the Soviet Army's superiority in men, tanks, artillery, planes, weapons, and reserves. So, what could they do? I mean, German soldiers? Their hatred was fierce. That's true. You'd think they'd just give up given the overwhelming disadvantages they faced. But, fight on, they did. Fanatically, zealously, knowing their cause was dead and had died back in February 1943! Why did they fight on and not surrender like the French in 1940? Because they were defending their homeland and hoping to protect their women, from little girls all the way to gang-raping old women en masse. Not one female was spared. And there is another angle to this hideous story, which is not mentioned in history books; millions of boys and older men were also mass raped by Russians. They had no choice. Or so they believed. In hindsight, of course, not every Russian acted in beastly manners, but when you were in that typhonic cauldron, in situ, believe me, I too would've fought to the death because I too believed every Bolshevik was out to tear the German people limb from limb. And this goes back to the unique nature of the Russo-German War — it was one where no human would be spared from exquisite torture, mutilation such that you'd like a Picasso painting of the faces he drew, and of course, continual mass rape. That's why I don't think Germans specifically fought to keep up Hitler's regime.

A war of Biblical proportions.

"And when the LORD your God delivers them before you, and you defeat them, then you shall *Utterly Destroy Them* You shall make no covenant with them and *Show No Favor To Them*."

- Deuteronomy 7:2

"Behold, the day of the LORD is coming, *Cruel, with Fury and Burning Anger*, To make the Land a Desolation; And He will *Eterminate its Sinners* from it."

- Isaiah 13:9

∼

Nothingness *is* Berlin

Daddy was right. This was Germany's Apocalypse.

Einstein was right too. He told us of time dilation. Yes, I read on him too, didn't think of that of me, did you? Anyway, he said time slows down as you come close to the speed of light, and it ceases to exist in a black hole. I don't know if he also understood time ends right here on earth. It's a place called Berlin, to be specific. The Germans already knew about that earth oddity. They called it *Stunde Null* ['Zero Hour']. Meaning time stopped for them. And they were right. There was no more time in Berlin.

After all, what fool would ask a Berliner, 'Pardon me, do you have the time?' What difference would it mean to a Berliner if time itself spoke aloud and said, "It is 3.00 pm, or 7.00 am?" I wouldn't say I liked the epithet 'Stunde Null.' I thought of Berlin as 'Nichts Stunde' [Nothing Hour].

Because nothing rational existed in Berlin, there was nothing you and I could connect with civilisation, culture or any of life's necessities. Maps were meaningless. Directions were meaningless. What difference would it make if you were to walk left, right, back, forward, north, south, east, or west, when you'll end up in in a location exactly as the location of your starting point — which is one of rubble, death, and suffering? What did language matter? Everyone knew what you wanted. Anyone can read the faces of both victors and the defeated. The victors only wanted to kill, torture, mutilate, rape, drink alcohol, and pillage in mind. The defeated only needed safety and food—no need for language.

"Be practical," they said. "Give a coffin."

- **Berliner talk – 1945**

And those last weeks seemed to be the *most* pointless and absurd—what a waste of human life! After all, what need was there for fighting? Fighting for what?

I understand soldiers fighting for their nation. But what were the Germans and foreign volunteers fighting for or defending? Why would any rational human give up his life to keep some road or building a few more days in German hands? The fact is Germany ought to have given up back in 1943 after Stalingrad. From the fall of Stalingrad, Germany was fighting only to postpone the inevitable. That's why to me, it was a pointless war. They were doomed to death. And yet, they fought on. That's why from my perspective, it was messed up. How else could I describe it? Who the hell fights when he knows it's a lost battle? Or was I wrong?

~

When Evil *is* Good & Good is Evil

Sanity and insanity blurred.

Evil and good interchanging. Interchanging love into hate and reversing. Charity and depravity. Chaos and randomness reigned. It was a situation of free for all. Lawlessness.

Anyway, as I walked on, I asked Berliners on this matter of fighting for a pointless cause -

Dorothy Gale: "Would you go on a plane if they told you there was a 1% chance of a mechanical failure happening, which would result in the plane crashing?

Berliners: Of course not! What a stupid question to ask!"

But when I asked them, in effect the same question but with a different scene, here was their typical response:

DG: "Would you fight in a battle if you knew it was a doomed one?

Berliners: Of course not!

DG: Do you know, or do you realize Berlin will sooner or later fall to the Russians?

Berliners: Yes.

DG: Do you wish for your soldiers to battle on or surrender?

Berliners: Of course, we must fight on!

DG: Why?

Berliners: Otherwise, the Russians will exterminate us!"

You see my confusion? Or why I pitied dazed Berliners for whom reality and illusion were fused? Again, years after the war — the time factor - I thought back on those same wretches of Berlin. Who could have had a sound mind in Berlin in 1945? How could any Berliner have a decent sense of proportion and wisdom in 1945? It was so easy for me to oversimplify and generalise. I can only attribute those stupidities to my naivety, being just a twenty-year-old girl back then.

As I say, it was only with the complicated counsel of time, I learned.

∼

Giving You An Impression of Germany's Destruction

There were around 20.0 million homeless Germans. Can you *visualise* that number? Twenty million roaming Germans, seeking any form of shelter to exist. Forty million refugees throughout Europe. In Russia, there were over 13.0 million more women than men. A third of all German children were fatherless.

Berlin. Where was morality? Justice? Nowhere. No laws, no telephones, no books or literature, no newspaper, no television, no cinemas, no restaurants, no bakeries, no butchers, no fishmongers, no supermarkets – basic food could be found in randomly scattered places, few buildings still standing, barely fit for human habitation, no underground, no trains nor trams, no airports nor planes, no fuel, no coal, no electricity, no gas, no kindergartens, no schools, nor universities nor any educational institutions, no libraries, no banks, no money, no cigarettes, no alcohol, no cars, no radio, no government, no bridges, no press, nowhere to throw your rubbish at, no hospitals, no pharmacies, no doctors, no dentists, no medicine, no engineers, no theatres, no music, no police, no prisons, no music, no shops of any kind, from bookshops to clothing shops, no toys, scare sources of water, no shampoo, no soap, no hairdressers, no tailors, no laundry - nothing functioned. We were in the Stone Age. A city where individuals seek whatever source they can find for shelter, food, and water.

> "Animals flee from this hell," he wrote, noting the attempts of dogs to swim the Volga. *"The hardest stones cannot bear it for long. Only men endure."*
> - **Lieutenant Reiner (1892-1955) - Fourth Panzer Army – 1943**

It was the turn for Berliners to experience one more Stalingrad repeatedly re-enacted, courtesy of the same Red Army. It was oddly enough a city awash with foreigners from every continent and nation. One does not normally conflate Nazi Germany with foreigners. I expected a uniformly German population. But the minute you arrive, you're struck by the odd fact that maybe half of the people there spoke anything but German. It gave Berlin a bleak form of cosmopolitanism. Who were they? Some were men and women forced to work for Germany, while others were volunteers fighting for Germany. The ex-slave workers were liberated by now. Free to go wherever they wanted to. But that was the problem. How could they travel back home when they had nothing but rags on frail bodies? Mind you, wretched as their conditions were; they were nowhere near the actual concentration camp inmates' frightening conditions. If anything, these freed foreign workers still had a Joi de Vivre, enjoying their newfound freedom, albeit in a city of the dead.

And then, of course, there were the Russians.

And the ever-increasing might and physical presence of *'der Ivan!'* as Germans fondly called Russians. Spongey Berlin was sucking them in. Steadily.

The first wave of Russians was generally speaking professional, meaning they behaved without committing depravities. They were attired correctly, with the latest tanks, machine guns, and artillery units.

But that was one damning false alarm. Ah yes, those pesky Russians!

Mind you, saying 'Russians' does not give you an accurate picture. Stalin's soldiers were not just Russians; many were recruited from the occupied countries — a vast collection from exotic nations I never even heard of, such as Georgia, Armenia, Kazakhstan, Moldova, Siberia, Mongolia, and many more I cannot remember.

Within days of those men, there came a blobby mass of a drunken rabble who looked like they were let loose from the highest maximum-security prison in the furthest corner of Siberia. Given their grimaces and sarcastic facial expressions, they shouted what I assumed were vulgar, coarse language whenever they pass girls and women. They were shabbily dressed, often being transported by horses and wagons. Many of them looked exotic with costumes and had an air of stunned wonderment looking at Berlin. I found that off because Berlin was a shattered crater, so I wasn't sure they were so impressed with it.

Oddly enough, whenever they noted me, an American instantaneously would snap out from their hideous vulgarities and transform into humble creatures before me. As though I were Eisenhower.

"Добрый день, мадам. Мы братья и сестры. Товарищи по оружию. Борьба за победу. Гитлер хочет быть мертвым. Немцы хотят быть мертвыми. Месть против фашистов!"

"Dobryy den', madam. My brat'ya i sestry. Tovarishchi po oruzhiyu. Bor'ba za pobedu. Gitler khochet byt' mertvym. *Nemtsy* khotyat byt' mertvymi. Mest' protiv fashistov!"

["Good day, Madam. We are brothers and sisters! *Comrades in arms! Fight to victory! Hitler will be dead. Germans will be dead! Revenge against the fascists!*"]

I thought it funny; all Russians called Hitler 'Gitler.' I automatically assumed they were stupid; how could they mispronounce their greatest enemy? Only years later did I learn; there again, *I* was wrong. The Russian language, like Greek, has no letter 'h'; the closest is either the Scottish 'ch' [as in Lo*ch* Ness] or the letter 'g.' Hence Gitler!

Everyone heard of their behavior in 1945. That was one truthful forecast Goebbels forewarned Germans about. And it was not just rape. Countless German civilians were tortured and shockingly mutilated. Rape was as common as daylight or night. After a while, even seeing Russians mass raping females from ages six or seven to seventy was common as seeing soldiers snacking or simply idling, waiting for the following order. Rape 'became' normal in Berlin. Saints were sinners, just as sinners were saints. After all, how many times can you be surprised and shocked when you see such incidents again and again?

Just as every Cop is a Criminal
And all the Sinners Saints
As Heads is Tails
Just call me Lucifer
'Cause I'm in Need of some Restraint

Mind you, *they* thought they were doing nothing immoral. When I spoke with them, they regarded rape as a matter of their 'inalienable rights.' They called it revenge. Very well, revenge, but if that were true, why also rape non-German females, such as Polish women, the latter being their supposed racial brethren? Their excuse for raping German as retribution was pig manure, and that was the end of it, as far as I was concerned. Later, I'd think twice on this topic. Good Lord, even their leader, our friend and ally, Uncle Joe, had no qualms about this widespread phenomenon, in fact praising his men for their atrocities -

Stalin: "You should understand it if a soldier who has crossed thousands of kilometers through blood and fire and death *has fun with a woman or takes some trifle*. We lecture our soldiers too much; let them have their initiative."

But, then, stupid me, since when did Stalin have any qualms on any moral issue? In his mind, a Russian who fought battle after battle, beginning in Stalingrad and stepping on, fighting all the way to Berlin, has the right to rape *any* woman. I think that was his argument.

And then I thought of myself as immoral for not feeling shocked anymore. Does that make me deplorable? That is up to you to decide. Excess of anything numbs you. I felt senseless. That's precisely the right word. Like a bored surgeon amputating limbs and lives. What else can he think after twenty thousand similar operations? Do you suppose that he would still feel the repulsive realities and horrors of life with the passage of time? Not if he were sensible.

Harsh conditions coarsen skins. That's why I once read Bedouins are one of the toughest races. They must be. Otherwise, you'd melt like the snowflake you are. And though it's cruel to say this, I think it was much better for the weak to die away as quickly as possible, precisely because they couldn't bear the overall suffering, causing a constant swivelling of their lives and minds. I know I sound harsh. Over the years, I've been repeatedly critiqued for this 'harshness' in me. Though I think it's in truth mercy that motivates me. Wouldn't you put a dying, wounded dog out of its misery by shooting the life out of it? Or would you let the poor animal go on 'living'? I know I could never be a psychiatrist, psychologist, counsellor, therapist, or whatever label these creatures give themselves.

I learned psychiatry meant nothing in Berlin '45.

God died in Berlin, 1945. No, on second thoughts, Man died in Berlin '45.

~

"Mighty victor, mighty lord, Low on his funeral couch he lies! No pitying heart, no eye, afford A tear to grace his *obsequies*."

- Thomas Gray — *The Bard*. A Pindaric Ode, lines 63-6 (1757)

~

First Impressions of the Bunkerites; Feeling I May Not Be Up to The Job Given the Disgusted Looks I Was Getting from Them

I entered the Bunker - finally!

By the way, I know I maybe should've put in the word 'Finally' in front of that first sentence, so it should have been — "Finally, I entered the Bunker!" But I told you, I'm not a professional writer, or reporter, or anything. And then I remembered *why* Hitler insisted on having a relatively uneducated farm girl interviewing him? I never thought of that. The man must've thought I'd be like Eva Braun or Traudl Junge, a twenty-year-old who was his typist. No brains required in her parking lot. But the Austrian would be in for a surprise. And then I was surprised to learn that Mr. Hitler regularly appointed inexperienced humans for whatever jobs he set them for!

Take my 'favorite' — Goering, appointed as Reichsminister of Economics. What did he know about economics? Nothing. What did Ribbentrop know about diplomatic affairs? Nothing. But, then again, one chicken farmer 'succeeded' in killing six million Jews, not to mention millions of other 'undesirable races' — Himmler. So, you can't automatically say you need the experience to do whatever job you've been offered. But, in general, I think I'm right in my judgment of Hitler's appointees.

Anyway, going back to the Bunker, the burning humming in my ears gradually adapted to the relative tranquillity. Once safely entombed inside the blessed Bunker, well to your relief and joy, your mind and body gradually regain their independence over the might of sound. Funny, I never thought sound could be 'satanic.' Satanic intensity.

I looked at the people. People in the Bunker, I mean.

Mostly military men, some civilians. Primarily men, of course, though females represented about twenty percent of the population. Surrealistic island. Bunkerites were of all ranks and ages. Jobwise, as far as I could tell, apart from the uniformed military men, they seemed to be a motley of adjutants, chefs, secretaries, engineers, waiters, cleaners, doctors, nurses, and many others, civilian-dressed individuals whose function or purpose in being in the Bunker I honestly couldn't discern.

I noticed an oddity faintly revealing its appearance. Many of the underground inhabitants were staring. At me. Eyes imbued with a strange cocktail mix of stilled shock and a fragile curiosity. Or fear?

That was the unexpected though proud hour I discovered common cause with the inhabitants of zoos. I'd never been an object worthy of being stared at in a gawping manner. Hence, my pride. But the curious looks in their stare made me think they thought their leader needed more pet companionship and so ordered Dorothy Gale to be hurriedly bundled out from Berlin Zoo, right back in his lonesome Bunker?

I, too, looked back at them. Surveying them left to right and then panning around again. I couldn't find anything definite in the language of their eyes. I realized *I* was the oddity. Not them. *"Monkey cut loose from the zoo, and here I am!"*

No one laughed. That was supposed to be a joke. Silence.

Then, for no reason, I blurted out —

"I'm a fellow human. Exactly as you are. I'm here because I've been given an official request with the kind invitation of your great leader and government." Oh my God, and again, as I spoke, not one of the people's facial gestures changed. I realised the idiocy of my words. I was a monkey — to them.

Finally, some reserved, resigned chuckles. I guess they were being polite. But the rest remained frozen—unchanged countenances. Was it my US Army uniform? Was it my bad German? Maybe they were right to be confused. Who'd imagine a uniformed American female, speaking funny German calling herself a 'monkey' just plop in the Bunker?

Some voice rang out, "Have the Americans arrived in Berlin?" I had to disappoint them. "No, we are not coming to Berlin. *It's the Russians, your favorite race; they're the guests you've invited, you forgot!"* Now come on, that one was funny; but no one laughed or even smiled at what I thought was a funny joke.

Then, it crossed my mind, well, maybe these people are surprised this young American spoke fluent German? Or maybe not. Perhaps no one gave a damn how I spoke or what I said. Possibly, they were distressed by the mere fact an enemy – me, as an American – just happened to there. I assumed none had been told of the German-American negotiations to send me to Berlin to interview their crumbling hero. Or maybe they did know. But if they did know, why the stares and surprise? It had to be my frilly imagination, unconsciously hoping to add weight to my flighty existence—dunce, doltish Dorothy!

It wasn't until sturdy, smooth, and confident Fegelein finally appeared from God knows where, and politely as ever, explained to them the reason for my presence. Their faces became relaxed. I was now one of the Bunkerites!

But, Jesus, I thought, this was *not* going to be easy. I mean, communicating with the Master Race. *They* seemed so alien from me. Strange people. Are *these* the same Germans I lived with when I was a young girl in Germany? They're certainly nothing like Daddy. That's why I spoke stupid words - nervousness.

Then I thought. I'm wrong; *of course,* they'd be scared out of their mind and skin at the sight and sound of any unannounced newcomer. How could they but not freeze, wetting themselves thinking I was a Soviet agent? No deathly imagination could conjure up what was in store for them—and coming very soon. Grotesque tortures awaited them. Being shot to death. They all knew it. That's when their criminal gig and presence on earth would be up and *gone with the wind* for eternity.

Everyone knew what revenge-hungry, vitriolically vengeful Russians had in mind for their soft ivory German necks.

For some reason, out came another batch of words from my mouth —

"I'm here to understand you and your National Socialist ideology. I'm here hoping to know why Germans committed genocide. I'm here seeking to understand why this great nation turned to the Devil." As soon as I said that, I knew I misspoke. Too early. Telling them of my feelings.

There was no reason to continue. Apart from chuckles, no one took me seriously. Credibility dashed. I was no longer an object worthy of a glance.

I *was not* doing an excellent job. Let's face it. Maybe I wasn't up to the job. What would happen to me? You know, until that moment, I never even thought that just perhaps or just maybe ... I may not be good enough for the job. And you you know why? Because of my arrogance, just like Daddy said. Arrogance equals violent blindness. How could I go on being the girl interviewing Hitler when I'm asking and speaking idiotic words, and God knows what. God, how many times do you need to extinguish yourself from a moment you embarrassed yourself in front of your best friends?

Would Hitler or someone from his entourage kick me out? I did not have a commanding presence, like when I talked. It's how you do the 'talking' that matters. And then I remembered that Hitler specified that the interviewer had to be a female; she had to be aged no more than twenty years old and had no education. Surprise! That fitted me!

Isn't it odd how crowds collectively act in unison? Funny how all kinds of thoughts, visions, and feelings just stray uninvited into your conscious mind. Funny how little I know of the unconscious me. Like an iceberg. Anyway, I am babbling. God knows where and why. Why on earth would the Almighty Fuehrer wish to be interviewed by one young, impotently immature twenty-year-old American [aka Enemy] girl?

One *SS* officer gently led me to the one small room. Or cell. Not interested in unpacking and settling in that room, I threw my small luggage wherever and rushed back to face the same 'pals' of mine of the famed Bunker. The SS officer looked disturbed, asking me, "Do you not understand clothes and other belongings must be neatly unpacked, separated, and put in their proper -?" I smiled, brushing him off. "I'm American," I replied.

Now, I said 'famed' Bunker because *we* knew of its existence and Hitler's presence in it. Meanwhile, the Red Army and the entire Soviet regime, including Stalin, had no idea of its existence, let alone that *this* dump was Hitler's final resting abode. That's why the Russians never knowingly targeted the Bunker, instead choosing to bequeath the Reichstag building as their symbolic epicenter of the Nazi regime.

Meanwhile, none of the Bunkerites themselves knew that the Russians did not know. They assumed wily Uncle Joe knew of their location. But he did not know. And they didn't know that he didn't know. Therefore, their fears remained alive, stoked by their erroneous conviction. Entangled unknowing, yet creating concrete emotional reactions.

In one moment, while I was in my tiny room, Fegelein entered, smiling – "Frau Gale, I know you're intimidated, but you're only here for a while, and you'll get back to your country, safe and sound. Meanwhile, these idiots ... well, they don't know if they're going to make it out alive."

Wasn't that odd? Why did he exclude himself from the nervous Bunkerites facing death or capture by Russians?

~

Idling While the Titanic Sinks

I wanted to focus on my Bunkerites since Hitler was still absent or busy, and I was given no indication when I'd start my interviews with him. So, what was I supposed to do? Hunker down in that midget-sized cell? No, Dorothy was going to make use of her empty time speaking to my fellow cave-dwellers. Why should they be the only ones to observe me? I presumed they, too, were living in the Bunker because it was the safest space for them to be. So, we're all in it together! Well, not me; I meant them.

There was an exciting and ugly contrast between upstairs and downstairs. While the Bunker itself was well supplied with every necessary and non-essential commodity, the exact opposite situation existed above us. Usually, we think of 'the above' as heaven and the underground world as hell. But here, everything was routinely incongruous and absurdly upside down. While down here in the earth's pits, our above was hell on earth was relative bliss and safety.

The general exhibited mood was intermittently changing, from extremes to extremes, pitted with hours of sheer boredom when no one seemed to be doing anything. Some characters, however, remained steadfastly with the same demeanor no matter what news filtered in, like Himmler, while others were flighty, barely able to control their self-control, as shall see. Actually, in my later years, with the advent of plastic surgery and Botox, I thought Himmler must've had a secret plastic surgeon because I cannot recall any changes to his facial countenance.

Most conversations were primarily conducted in quiet, formal manners. Sometimes voices were briefly heated. Brief flurries of activity. Some were running from room to room. Those were, as I say, the exceptions.

It has always fascinated me how we converse. People come up to a conclusion on a story or events that have happened. But in many circumstances, people pre-judge well before the story or the film ends. Now how can anyone judge without hearting the entirety of the tale from all sides?

~

Contrasts Between Innocence of Happy Children and Suicidal Adults

Oddly enough, I heard sounds of *children* playing.

Somewhere. Innocence in the Bunker? Spookily incongruous. What, how, and why on earth were children placed in a terminal place such as this? I learned those were the six angelic children of Goebbels. It was sickeningly odd because they were too young to understand hell facing them. As with all children, they were endlessly teasing, joking, and playing. *"Misch! Misch! Du bist ein Fisch!"* That's how they taunted the six-foot-something Rochus Misch, who, like everyone else in the Bunker, was delighted by their distracting innocence.

Another observation. Eccentricities. There did not seem to be much of any *'work'* going on. How could that possibly be? Can you imagine FDR, Truman, Churchill, or Stalin's offices being humdrum? Lacking in activity? Can you imagine other world leaders having most of their staff, military, and civilians merely milling around? That was it. Not much else was happening—kind of odd when you think about it. Because I was expecting frantic action, meetings, discussions, officials crisply enunciating orders, that is how I imagined a government would be like, especially when it happens to be conducting a world war. Sounds reasonable of me to say and think that, right?

But that wasn't happening in the Bunker. This inaction or inactivity puzzled me. Visualise this, if you will. People gently walking here or pacing there and doing not much of anything. Some drunk, some tipsy, some dead-drunk dozing off somewhere. Courteous conversing. Flirtations, both shamelessly explicit, while others were more discrete. Some lounging about. Laughter here and there. Voices of the chatter rising and ebbing. Smoke everywhere – everyone smoked. Eating, drinking – some dancing.

Whenever I ventured outside of the Bunker, the eccentric part of my imagination pounced and took control of my 'self'; a 'self' I always assumed was independent. And every time I put myself in a sickly, absurd situation, it was my imagination that connected the incompleteness of the pervading reality I was facing—connecting the missing dots. Imagination to the rescue! Otherwise, I'm mad. How did such people live in these abnormal circumstances? You've got to make sense of the nonsense. Reversed unreality back to reality. At least, that's how *my* mind functioned in a relatively stable manner. To stay sane, everyone had to believe their insane situation was rational, and that had to be not only the end of the matter but no more thinking about such issues; otherwise, they'd go insane. In other words, if you live in an insane, meaningless, absurd, sick, inhuman reality, you must accept these attributes as the norm, or else you go mad. End of discussion. And of course, many couldn't accept these terms and conditions God had afflicted them with, so they rapidly degenerated into madness, in whatever form that may be. Some of these mad people froze in a catatonic state. Some howled like Ginsberg howling poem animals. You'd never think any human had such vocal ranges

Some 'preached' Jesus and the Bible to no one since no one listened, though that didn't affect their motivation to continue sermonizing to no one in particular. Some were idiotically hyperactive. Some acted drunk, though they hadn't imbibed a sip of alcohol. Some acted out roles, such as being a violinist when there was no violin or 'conducting' an orchestra when there was no orchestra. Some painted childish paintings; others painted beautifully expressionist paintings — though where they got their oils, palettes, and canvases. Some were over-sexualized, exposing themselves, groping anyone, and raping any weak person, no matter their gender or age. Some 'talked' manically, mostly gibberish. And let it be said, categories and types of the mad types are endless.

Yet, it was difficult *not* to see these people as world-weary actors. I say 'actors' because I believed in pre-war times they didn't behave like that in public. Given the murderous circumstances of their lives, they succumbed to madness, though ironically enough, they did it to survive and overcome the rage-filled madness that subsumed their fiendish lives. Or at least a majority of them were sane in pre-war years. Again, I'm only conjecturing because how could I know? You cannot talk to these people because they were out of their minds.

I rush back to the Bunker. I cannot pretend watching monstrous scenes and events and not reacting. Because when I hear, experience, feel any emotion, thought, or event, my mind reacts. And it reacts in manners I do not know about. This is one of the verities I hate. Because I cannot change them. Do you know ... or let me say it this way. What I hate most is being helpless, especially when it concerns myself. It's one thing seeing a bastard violently raping a child, and you can do nothing. Yes, it's traumatic. But to me, personally, what was more traumatic is not being able to help myself when I was routinely raped by people whom society deified as demi-gods.

Pouring gazes unto these same Bunkerites. They're waiting for any squeak of a cue that would finally order them to scurry off and out from this terrifying, capsizing stage. Groaning stage because no progress is conceivable. Excessive mental guilty baggage. Too many people in too small a space. Far too many, given the confining size of the dingy Bunker. I'd delete my words if any of these Bunkerites were doing any work. But they weren't. No energy. Deadly inactivity. People moved in slow motion. Others are erratic. Maybe they were on drugs. And talking of drugged out people, I've got to say Magda Goebbels looked drugged out of her mind. Though, not always. But sometimes, she flitted in and out like a zombie, hardly conversing with anyone and gliding now and then from to room.

Then, reason told me what and why the scenes I witnessed were as I noted them to be. In some sense, it was simple — since meaningful news was sparse, most Bunkerites breathed on, pushing out thoughts of the reality occurring above their heads. I thought that maybe some people on the Titanic were deaf, dumb, and blind. Overcrowded ship of sick cultists doing nothing and waiting for their Almighty Prophet to kill himself. I thought ... I expected seeing scenes from the final helter-skelter hours of a Titanic ending given their catastrophic situation. But that was not what I was seeing and experiencing.

Meanwhile, there was another thorny problem - who would go around the Bunker and dare to ask if anyone wanted to escape so long as their dearly beloved leader had not yet sanctioned any outbreak? Mind you, I'm sure they were constantly thinking, 'The Fuehrer can't waste any more time!' Or 'The war is over. Our blessed saviour knows that fact. So that means he must kill himself this night or maybe sooner, right?' Even in the Titanic, and I'm assuming here, the passengers could sense how much the ship was drowning, how many lifeboats were out there, and so they could have some degree of cognizance about their chances of survival. But in the Bunker, no one knew anything because no one heard any news.

We were in a black hole. Disconnected from reality and the outside world. The point here is that we did not know — the outside world - was precisely what would most eagerly dictate who would live or die.

- *"Every seven seconds, a German soldier dies in Russia. Stalingrad is a mass grave."*

"The only knowledge that man can attain is that this life has no meaning."

- **Leo Tolstoy (1828-1910)**

There was another side to the inhabitants. Many young soldiers, barely men, sat or huddled together. Stung with that thousand-mile stare. Caring not one whit where they were or who was around them. They were either in too much shock or mentally too wary of thinking of anything coherent. The rest of the Bunkerites pretended they were pieces of furniture. Dying statues, I suppose. It was mutual-ignoring of each other — I mean, between the wounded and the non-wounded individuals.

As weeks progressed — Time — the numbers of injured men brought in dramatically increased. Bloodied batches. Some beyond repair. Hurriedly dragged down into the dungeon. One dungeon was already far too overheated, overcrowded, stinking, and with an over-worked, under-equipped, under-staffed, under-supplied operating theatre room.

~

With the Passing of Every Hour, Ivan Was Getting Closer

The Bunker was the last residence of Mr. Hitler. He was forced to move here on January 16th, 1945. Given the daily and nightly payback time of our Anglo-American aerial bombing campaign, living anywhere but in a dungeon was known to be far too risky for his glorious safety.

Back in January, the Soviets were some 70 miles away. Given the trends and events, it didn't require too much of any mathematical prowess in calculating how much more time before those armies would soon be impolitely – to put it mildly - knocking on their door.

By April 20th, Russians were about two to three thousand meters from where we were. Ironically, that was the day Nuremberg, the 'spiritual' capital of National Socialism, also fell. I know for a fact that must've stung every Bunkerite. Or maybe, some no longer cared? How can I say, 'I know how everyone felt on this or that day?' That is idiotic! I mean, it was clear sunlight; their cause was dead. No hope. And yet, they remained in the underground tomb of Adolf Hitler. What were they thinking? Did they believe the non-existent Wehrmacht would annihilate the combined armed forces of the Soviet Union, Great Britain, and the United States? No, of course, no one thought that. The Soviet artillery had already begun shaking the Bunker. This or these nasty bumps would increase with every few hours, implying, I suppose, the Russians were moving forward their artillery and Katyusha shells ever closer to our Bunker.

I'm sorry. I was supposed to be describing the Bunker for you. All right.

The Bunker's surroundings were shabby. *This* was supposed to be the monumental, first-rate, living headquarters of the great Fuehrer himself, the one-time leader of the global power, National Socialist Germany? Yes, it was. But that *was* the current condition of his homely residence.

The underground structure was entirely built out of grey concrete; none of it was painted. Thus, the walls and ceilings were simply concrete cement slabs. As for the furniture, it's mostly old and dreary, sometimes tattered, seemingly second-hand, and derelict. Darkish and dilapidated halls, stairs. Mucky soot and grime here and there. Mind you, I noticed some fine paintings hung on walls, adding some sparkle and vivacity to the otherwise gloomy atmosphere.

For some reason, my attention was consumed by one recurring question, *'How does this Bunker communicate with the outside world?'* Claustrophobia. Deaf commanding center. Deaf commanders. Mute soldiers. Why would anyone stay here in a doomed dungeon? What brought them here? Why didn't they secretly leave? Did they imagine their lives necessitated them to come to this inevitable Passion of the Anti-Christ?

I heard the high-ranking officers and generals endlessly reminiscing on their earlier 'glory' days. Sipping cognac. Smoking fat cigars. Dining with some sober and some rowdy drunken elite comrades. Some spoke elegant German, and others spoke mixtures of soft and hard-core vulgar German.

Meanwhile, I saw batches of dolled-up tarts. I assume these were the same ladies I saw above the Bunker, parading their bodies. How come these young ladies were so well dressed? I say 'well-dressed,' though I don't mean they were all dressed like whores. But still, they had to find someplace in Berlin to buy such 'clothes,' right?

Some flirted openly; others were discrete in their advances, be it mutual or not. Then I realised one more stupidity. These *were* the same ladies I saw above the Bunker, parading their bodies. You could find them being in discrete places. The second you look at them; they'll give you a sexual come-hither smile. Some were remarkably beautiful, with no look of weariness on their face. There was one former commandant of some concentration camo; her name was Irme Gresse. Astonishingly beautiful. But she wasn't a whore, strictly speaking. She didn't need money. I was told the party gave her a salary. Never mind asking questions such as 'What party?' and what exactly was the value of money in the confines of the Bunker when everything was freely available?' So, I guess, that forced me to change my opinion on the rest of those women; inside the Bunker, they were not prostitutes since they had everything they needed, but should they go outside the Bunker and have sex, they'd be categorized as prostitutes because they'd charge their hungry clients for their quality services.

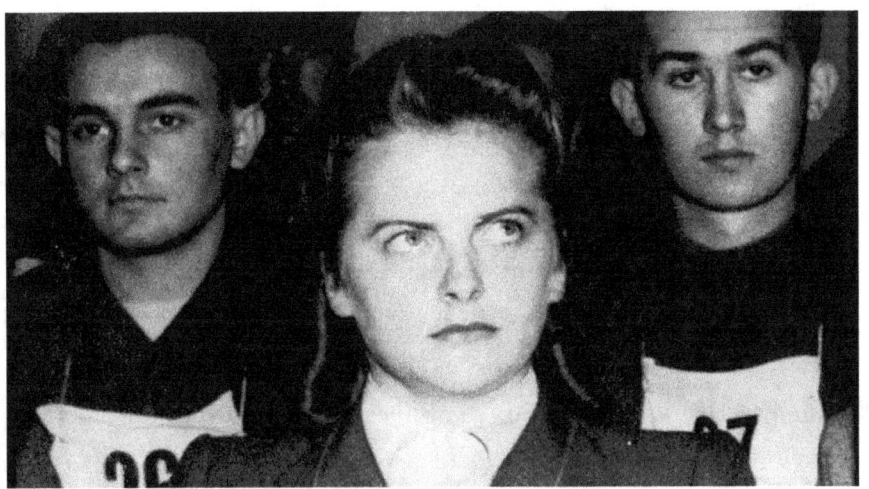

Irme Gresse

And forever circling everyone, like bees, were servile waiters. I noticed many of the waiters were SS men. How could healthy young men from the most elite armed forces end up being waiters while Berlin was desperately short of manpower? I suppose feeding those freaks was more important than defending Berlin. Wow, what a classic case of the Ouroboros.

Never mind because I didn't ask anyone that question. The food was the best cuisine — whatever you can think of, was available, which I found odd because I knew the Fuehrer was highly frugal in his food. Or maybe I shouldn't say 'frugal,' because he loved sweets and cakes. So, I'd be more accurate in saying he was a strict vegetarian. The next thought driving through my mind was where did all that food come from when being above the Bunker? I swear to you, I didn't see one bakery, one minimarket, one butcher, one coffee shop.

Some of the Bunkerites seemed permanently sullen; some seemed stony as statues, thinking God knows what. While others enjoyed themselves and the company surrounding them, and every now and then, I would hear roars of shrieking laughter. Some were engaged in dull, quiet conversations, while others interacted in heated discussions, mostly on politics and military affairs. As if any of those subjects mattered by the time! Almost everyone smoked, while only the highest-ranking men smoked cigars. I wondered, being the submissive spectator, you know, how many of these actors would remember any of their conversations the following day?

My recurring question was recompensed by Misch, that tall, affable-looking, welcoming, chirpy officer. He heard me inquiring on this subject matter. He motioned me to follow him. I walked to a tiny room grandly entitled, *'Fuehrer Nachrichten Abteilung'* [Communication Battalion Room]. Though there were several radio-telephone link set transmitters, only one man was working there. I so, I began my first conversation with this genial officer.

∼

Conversations With Oberscharführer Rochus Misch

Rochus Misch

I. Misch: "What are Our Only Means of Communication? Randomly Calling Anyone. If They Speak German, We Know the Area is Still in German Hands!" And the *Unknown Pre-Raphaelite Woman.*

He was tall, handsome, but by far the most beautiful aspect in him was his personality, forever smiling, laughing, calm, willing to talk, and forever genial. To me, the ugliest attribute in people is temperamental people. I know that's odd because I was hell to Daddy. But, anyway. The closest character to Misch had to be — and yes, you're going to be surprised by my choice — was none other than roly-poly Goering, the jocular head of the Luftwaffe, second in charge after Mr. Hitler.

DG: My name is Frau Gale.

RM: Nice to meet you. My name is *Oberscharführer* (Sergeant) Officer Rochus Misch.

DG: If I may ask you, how good are your links to the outside world?

RM: A mess!

{*Misch Laughs*}

DG: Can you explain?

RM [Surprised]: *You are* interested?

DG: Yes, I am. That's why I'm here, Sir.

RM: I heard you were here to interview our Fuehrer?

The mind turned again to that experience of a beautiful German girl flirting with me. I don't know when it was. Stupid me. She was aged maybe sixteen or eighteen at the most. Looked like those Pre-Raphaelite Brotherhood 'stunner' women. I named her **Medusa**. Her eyes dragged me. Maliciously snaring me inside her. How odd, she sat solidly atop rubble. Fixed on rocks, jagged. Yet assured, she remained. I walked by, pretending I noticed nothing. There was something about her solidly sitting atop that jagged rubble that told me she was steely nerved.

Medusa

DG: Yes, but I also want to see the broader reality. Obviously, Hitler cannot provide me with that truth. He can only do what any one human can do—give his distorted slice of reality. And it is my job to make a composite image of the reality going on here in Berlin. That's why I must talk to anyone willing to speak to me.

RM: We don't have direct links with the outside units and commanders. Or very few.

DG: Excuse me?

RM: That's true.

DG: Well, then - how do you *communicate* with the outside world?

RM: You go through many codes. Then *if* you get a line, typically, it's weak. Within a minute or two, the line will be cut off. And so, ends the brief and fractured conversation. We wouldn't be able to run a laundry! Meanwhile, we hardly obtain any helpful information on Berlin's changing situation in that temporary space of time. Having said all that, I know that not a word I've just said matters if we communicate with the outside world or if we don't communicate.

DG: I don't understand you.

RM: What's puzzling you?

DG: Surely, if the great Fuehrer and his great generals cannot run a laundry service, how then can they conduct war on such paltry communication systems?

{*Misch Laughs*}

RM: Frau Gale, please! We're *Germans!* We innovate.

DG: So, *what if* you're Germans? Deaf and blind gods cannot communicate and conduct a war!

RM [Joking]: We know how to solve every problem from here to the end of the universe!

DG [Smiling]: Explain it to me, if you will; what *exactly* do you do in this charming room?

RM: As I said, we try to communicate with outside military commanders using radio and telegraphic means, though that is usually unsuccessful. Now, we innovate if the radio links are too weak, such as the sound crackling too much. For example, recently we've been using a telephone book directory.

DG: A telephone directory?

Who was she? I'm talking about Medusa. Assured in her exorbitantly flirting with me. Lolling tongue, please! I didn't flirt back. I smiled weakly. She said words. I couldn't hear them. Din of roars of God knows what because my mind was fixated on her rather than the scenery. Then repeatedly came he 'Come hither …' finger motions. Again and again.

RM: Yes, a Berlin telephone book directory.

DG: And what or why would you need a telephone directory for?

Misch: That is how we can call people.

DG: *Whom* would you be calling?

RM: No one.

DG: Nobody?

RM: Nobody that we know, no.

DG: How can you call people you do not know?

{*Misch Laughs*}

RM: We call anyone—any number in the telephone directory.

DG: Randomly?

RM: Yes, randomly.

DG: Are you joking?

RM: Man must have a sense of know-how when facing the gallows.

DG: You call people you do not know?

RM: Completely unknown human beings. Yes.

DG: And what's the purpose of communicating with unknown humans?

RM: If a German answers, we'd ask them questions about their whereabout, the situation, such as if the enemy is near them, and so on. And many times, if we hear a Russian voice answering us, that's when of course, we hang up.

DG: If a Russian answers, would that mean the area must've fallen into enemy hands?

RM: Well, yes, exactly. Otherwise, there wouldn't be Ivan speaking.

DG: That's how you get information on the whereabouts of your men and Russians?

RM: That's one method. The other method is sending runners to go to some so and so area and let the officer in charge observe the neighborhood's status or the district he has been sent to investigate.

DG: Presumably, that's far riskier since the searching officer may get shot?

RM: Exactly. He may be held up due to a heavy exchange of fire, thus paralysing him for hours. That's why sending runners is less and less used because we don't have time to wait for bad news.

DG: Doesn't that mean Hitler is issuing several orders without anyone knowing the actual frontline situation out there?

RM: We issue hopeful orders for the presumptively existing units in hypothetical geographical points in Berlin.

I decided she was illiterate yet sensitive. Genuine yet uncaring. Excessively emotional yet ultimately distant.

DG: And that's not insane?

RM: Time changes everything. If an officer reports area A as being in a military situation B, we may already be in enemy hands by the time we get that report. That's why you see inoperative orders being issued. Meaning, the order in question is meaningless. Not applicable. The Fuehrer ushers his next batch of orders based on the original faulty report. It would be up to the officer charged with that specific order if he obeys or disobeys the Fuehrer's orders.

DG: What is the penalty for disobeying?

{*Misch laughs*}

RM: Death, of course. On the spot too!

DG: Who would shoot him?

RM: Men specialised in crushing any seditious or defeatist behaviors. They're routinely sent to weed out such characters. They're from our ranks. SS. Quite a zealous lot, we are too.

DG: Now, if a German officer disobeys an impossible order and since he knows he will be shot, why wouldn't such a fellow not go over to the other side?

RM: You mean to surrender to the Russians?

DG: Yes.

{*Misch Laughs*}

RM: Were he to do that, Ivan's would first skin the lad in question, I mean skin and flay the idiot, and when their amusement dries up, that is when they grant and gift him the final bullet of death.

∼

Peace of a Tomb's Life While Outside Is Hell

Hysterical sounds of Soviet bombardments grew too. Intense hatreds. Brewing retribution. Shaking and jolting the Fuehrer's cozy Bunker and temporarily freezing every occupant in a state of controlled fear. Rudely stopping them from whatever they happened to be doing. You sense the materiality of the atmosphere. Ceiling heaving.

> "I could smell the madness."
>
> - Charles Bronson

I lie in my coarse bed in the Bunker. Trying to ignore dullness. But dullness can be overpowering if the mind has no effective reaction against it. And always knowing only some feet above my head is the ending of history's most brutal war. I know above is hell on earth, and I have said that before, but I will not say all humans — I forget the reality beyond me. So, when I'm in my Bunker cell and have nothing to do, I'm bored, thinking only of my Bunker context. Remember too because I had no telephones, no books, no television, no radio, no magazines — nothing to distract my mind. Wouldn't you too be bored in what I felt was a form of solitary confinement? To be precise, Hitler had telephones, but I felt intimidated to ask him if he'd allow me to call Daddy.

"Ye are of *your* **Father the Devil**, and the lusts of your Father ye will do. He was a ***Murderer*** from the beginning, and abode not in the Truth, **because there is no Truth in Him**. When he speaketh a Lie, he speaketh of his own: for he is a Liar and the father of it."

- John. 8:44. King James Version

So, as I said, having absolutely nothing to do, I watch my cell. Sometimes I'd look at ants and try guessing why they're marching wherever it is they're going to. Do they think? Are they conscious? If not, doesn't it mean they're no different from machines?

For no reason, my mind notices grimy water trickling. Maybe, the water became grimy since it had to go through pipelines filled with crusty mud and muck. But then, I didn't know if I could verify my assumption as a fact. I remembered the existence of scattered water pumps in Berlin. How could there even be any water in Berlin? I can understand Hitler had unique pipes providing him with clean water but in the shattered noncity of Berlin? Wasn't Berlin's infrastructure destroyed? So why weren't the water pipelines also destroyed? No idea.

A mind endlessly chasing silly questions. It's not just me, you know. Clearly, despite the ferocious bombing and rockets, Berlin was enduring; still, water pipes must not have been damaged, which is why Berliners could get water. Look, they weren't even starving. I'm talking about Berliners. Years later, I'd see on television scenes of famine in Africa. But nowhere in Berlin was anyone ever famished or starving. Isn't that weird? How did food reach them when streets were blocked, and there were no functioning outlets, such as bakeries or eateries? I suppose soldiers or civilians made it their duty to hand-deliver food every day. But how much can any individual carry? Not much. Not enough to feed the hundreds of thousands still living inside what remained of the ever-shrinking German-controlled Berlin. And soldiers don't have the time to feed people. What a stupid idea. No, that's impossible. So, there must be inside Berlin's wreckage and rubble food-operating places, and that is where Berliners were getting their sustenance. Because — and I'll repeat this — I didn't see one famished German. On the opposite, especially the women, many were somewhat on the plump side.

Did my Medusa think of me? God! What if she's dead? I didn't think of that. My mind frame was still set in Kansas. Peaceful Kansas. Peace. Security. People don't just die, especially young ones in Kansas, that's for sure.

How can I meet her? Obviously, there's no way. I don't know her name nor address. But then what addresses were there in Berlin? Stupid me. So how do you locate anyone in Berlin?

Scratched nooks and crannies. Soldiers must have done that, scrawling whatever comes to their minds. *"I'm officer A.D., still alive!" "Remember me, Mama, your Beloved Son, G.T! and it 'ain't gin and tonic!"*

My mind switched my attention back to my beautiful cell or room. Generators constantly humming. Sometimes they stopped, given the constant bombardments from the Red Army, but they were instantaneously repaired. Hence, we were blessed with the luxury of electricity. But all that work by the electricians couldn't stop the flickering light, on and off. And when the lights were temporarily off, so everyone experienced temporary blindness. But as I say, those 'temporary' timeframes were nothing more than a few seconds at most.

Acrid smoke and weighty dust fused and seeped into our Bunker, causing the subterranean dwellers to be increasingly frightened. And that fright only increased with time, as differing noxious emotions invisibly waft as everyone could not avoid a stench. A memorable aroma. A cesspit of corpses. Liquefying humans and oozing gangrenous juices and vapors. To be honest, I had no idea, wherefrom these stinky smells came from. And it gives me a wicked delight the more uncomfortable the Bunkerites were feeling.

Time shifts on. Odd because you have no sense of time living in a bunker, nor can you know if it is day or night. So, time in that sense did not exist. Then there is the bizarre feeling of both eternity and nothing changing. I say 'eternity' because time is dead; therefore, nothing moves, nothing happens. And that feeling is entirely wrong since events above our heads were rapidly moving towards the final victory of the Red

Army. But as I say, living in this Bunker, nothing changes, so you feel the weight of dead time.

And that's exasperating since everyone wanted the battle or the war to end so they can leave the damned Bunker and resume their everyday lives. But, on the other hand, when Hitler was raging at his generals or when there was a particularly heavy bombing on the Bunker, everyone panics, and time suddenly seems to be speeding at an impossible speed, because you know you are unable to stop the madness of the onrushing frontlines of the raging enemy.

Some of the Bunkerites express increasingly dreary eyes. Some feel an awakening resignation to their inevitable fate. If you enter some rooms or spaces in the Bunker, you feel atmospheres of suicide. You're in an eternal wake or funeral. Enter some other room, watch Bunkerites drunkenly reveling, and you feel idiotic joy. Some expressed uncontrolled fears and anxieties, though officers would rapidly whisk such characters away from everyone else. Panic breeds panic, you know.

Hitler never, as far as I know, never mingled with anyone. He was either in his bedroom, the military conference room, or in his monologue room, where only a certain number of invited guests were allowed to join him. But as for the rest, he never mingled, in contrast to Eva, who not only mingled but often held parties with loud music, smoking, drinking, and dancing. Hitler never complained — again, as far as I know, because that austere man must've heard the boisterous, drunken laughter as officers danced with the ladies on shaky tables. Now you'd think such scenes never occurred when times were better, such as when Hitler was in

Berchtesgaden. I suppose, by now, he no longer cared, knowing the end was near.

I expected to see the headless Anne Boleyn. Casually holding her severed head, making me feel uneasy as I stare at her lolling black tongue. Spitting words out. Unreasonable rationales. Orders given by suicidal officers. I gave up on reason. Or the other way. It did not matter. The ends matter. Reason fighting reason. Where is help? Who is the Saviour in this land of the mad, the criminals, and the victims? I felt pity for Man. God's kooky children. Especially young soldiers. Delicate boys. Despite their grime. Not even ready for stubble. Pity you - Man! Man, the Fool! And Man, the Mass Murderer. Or maybe I saw Marie Antoinette's piked head. Ha! Is Godot a reality?

Involuntarily I pant. Panting with needs. Unmatched and unmet. God's ultimate enchantress. No, Jesus is staring at me. God hates sins. That negates my feelings. It's Medusa. But they're irrepressible—beatific portrait of the woman standing naked not more than a few feet from my body. Stop me panting. I notice she changes her facial expression. Momentarily I'm in too deep in my unconscious-controlled imagination, not noticing her. Time passed. Whatever happened in the interval, I don't know. But before me, I beheld Medusa's, after much work, looing as the face of the *Ecstasy of Saint Teresa*.

Next moment, emotions switch. Imagine Caravaggio's *Judith Beheading Holofernes*, [c. 1559]. Imagine *Garden of Earthly Delights* painted by the Dutch master Hieronymus Bosch [c. 1490 - 1510]. Imagine *the Punishment of Marsyas* or *The Flaying of Marsyas*, Titian's last known work [c. 1570-76]. Imagine Théodore Géricault's *Raft of the Medusa* [1810]. *Imagine* Francisco Goya's *Saturn Devouring His Son* [c. 1819 -

23]. Imagine Salvador Dali's *The Face of War* [1940]. Imagine them all together now. Instantaneously jerking each other. A oneness of grotesque furious unisons. Fleshy humans. Each tearing the other apart. But we are not done yet. We have got to add more of God's cuisine and His delicious spices and relishes.

Add the worse psychotic inmates. Uncontrollable impulsivity. Maximum security insane asylums. Add a splash of those handful lots from Jean-Martin Charcot's hysterical women. Some fake it, others not so.

"I can't judge any of you. I have no malice against you and no ribbons for you. But I think that it is high time that you all start looking at yourselves and judging the lie that you live in."

— Charles Manson

Manson's children let loose. Finally. It's too late to call her for help! No time to discern which is which. Do what you want, evil or mad. Do it. That's known as the supremacy of irrelevance in a war situation. A lesson I learned. Learn it—a new reality. In peacetime and with sex, it mattered. You needed to know who was mad and who was faking it. But in Berlin, no one cared. Why? Because, like the ever-changing attributes of time, the status of a person's mental health did not matter—another supremacy of irrelevance.

Now colour in the sounds of the combined screams emanating from the wonders of pain; pleadings for mercy; begging for food; quietly sobbing soldiers; Shrieking babies too. But you cannot know why they shriek because they are either in a real or imaginary life-threatening situation. Either way, you cannot stop them and ask them any questions, given their wild hysterical nature.

Mix in these additional ingredients. No questions exist. And it doesn't even matter *how* you do this mixing or the cooking process. Do it in any fashion you fancy. Either way, it's going to be your reality, like it or lump it. Knead them. Sear them. Sledgehammer them. Incinerate them. The point is to fuse these ingredients into one pitilessly bestial fabric. And now finally comes the time when you'll see for yourself but one realm of the Devil. One slice. In one time. That's how you create the energy field of Satan. Drum roll now. Here they come of all energies, ages, and generations.

∼

"These children that come at you with knives -- they are your children. You taught them. I didn't teach them. I just tried to help them stand up."

— Charles Manson

The Master Race Squirms with Fears

And ladies and gentlemen, if you are still paying attention, this is one moment of His Satanic Majesty's Reality.

What *was* going on? *Who* knew what was going on? Can anyone please tell me what the matter is here? Will someone tell us yes, or no? Is our plane crashing or not? Maybe it is best actually if we are left in the dark? Look, there he is! *Ivan the Cannibal!* Scurrying from black hole to black hole. That's all right. You'll never know if you will be safe anywhere. Someone speaks to himself. No exits. Where are they going? There must be somewhere safe in this City of Hell? Why doesn't Germany's savior speak up, for God's sake? Isn't he the leader, or is he not?

Fegelein was nowhere to be seen. I felt insecure. Unknown reasons. Wasn't he supposed to be my protector? A woman cries in one corner, trying not to be noticed. I say 'woman,' but she looked far from any female I have seen—lumpy flesh. Yet pinched with a skinless body. More complexities. Absurdities. I thought of the peculiar calm of Misch. I felt I loved him - platonically - just for that heroic attribute. I respected him. I dare say I appreciate very few people in this world. Not even that. I respect only two humans, and one of them is now dead. How could anyone be calm in a storm? There was a stark difference between Misch and Fegelein. Fegelein, I can honestly say, never showed any genuine emotion, except for sarcasm, disgust, or hatred, whereas Misch consistently found his surroundings absurd; it was laughable. Now you judge who is moral, less moral, or more moral and all these tedious questions. I think Fegelein had no empathy, no compassion for any human, not even his own so-called Master Race Germans. Now, with Misch, a much lower-ranking soldier than Fegelein and therefore much less experienced, I think he saw Berlin, Hitler, the war itself as a kind of Theater of the Absurd.

Meanwhile, my mind took me back to that lumpy, faceless woman; who was she? Why does no one bother to help her? Who is she? Unraveling and disentangling her squalidly deranged self from her other derailed self? No one was in the least interested. Only Hitler's dog found her to be something of interest. Did I imagine her? Why wasn't Hitler himself helping her? What a stupid thought, I thought. Sometimes in stressful situations, you go mad; if you don't catch yourself, you go mad. Like, thinking. If you allow 'your' thoughts – and they're not all your thoughts, because most of your thoughts come from your unconscious – anyway, if you allow 'your' thoughts to have full freedom, they'll continually ask you questions, pushing you to the limits of sanity. Stupid thoughts self-replicate like bacteria. Fegelein appears. Much to my relief! Mutating self-destructive thoughts. I saw a young woman, thin, in rags, deliberately offering us her one dried breast. *"Feed me milk!"* she screamed as she stumbled towards us. 'Us' being Fegelein and myself during one of our Berlin tours. I asked her, "What do you mean?" Unexpectedly she emitted a roaring animalistic sound. Was that Lucifer's voice madness? Then she stuck out one of her surprisingly firm breasts, hissing, "Suck milk!"

Salads and soups of fear. I held on to Fegelein. Forebodings and panic. Some controlled, others not necessarily so. Flaky whispers. Speaking tones. My mind was roaring between extremes of brief spasms of panic to heartless stoicism. A questioner asks —

> *'Have the Russians broken through?'*

I looked at the man.

> *"And I don't care!"*

I screamed back at the pitiful idiot. Endless questions hurtling. Imploding nowhere—too many directions. So, finally, I gave up trying to follow any thread.

> *'Frau Gale, what is the exact situation now, please?'*
>
> *'Frau Gale, where is this division or that division?'*
>
> *'Frau Gale, where are the Russians?'*
>
> *'Frau Gale, has America declared war on Russia?'*

Questions. Questions. Everyone knew they knew nothing.

'Frau Gale, has this area or that street been taken over by the Russians?'

Fegelein was laughing at these pathetic people, once the crème de la crème of German society! Never a definite answer. Everyone with changing opinions. Like rats in an ever-heated cage. And how could they know anything given the explicit absence of any valid news or credible information?

"You're American; why don't you people liberate Berlin rather than the Russian hordes?"

I gave up as I answered that question a million times. I told them we Americans had no interest in Berlin. And now, I pretended I had no answer. I was surprised none of these high-ranking Berliners knew what Eisenhower said. I say 'high-ranking,' meaning weren't these men the most influential Nazis?

"One should let one's nails grow for a fortnight. O, how sweet it is to drag brutally from his bed a child with no hair on his upper lip and with wide-open eyes, make as if to touch his forehead gently with one's hand and run one's fingers through his beautiful hair. Then suddenly, when he is least expecting it, to dig one's long nails into his soft breast, making sure, though, that one does not kill him; for if he died, one would not later be able to contemplate his agonies. Then one drinks his blood as one licks his wounds, and during this time, which ought to last for eternity, the child weeps."

— Comte de Lautréamont (1846-70) *Maldoror and Poems*

Didn't Charlie Manson say it all? Like him or hate him, he still prophesied what must happen when a society is cracked. If you raise your children and society, civilization, traditions, and culture as Jack the Ripper treated his sophisticated, discerning ladies, what kind of children do you expect them to be once they are adults?

"There is no end. There is no cure. It gets worse with time. Cure. How can you cure an institution, *we are bricks crumbling in the walls of despair?* Death is inevitable for us all. But the insanity is here to stay."

- Charles Bronson. Insanity: My Mad Life

∼

Conversations with Oberscharführer Rochus Misch

II. Misch: "The Carnival of Finding Anyone to Defend Berlin; Or What's Left of It!"

Misch: You remember me? I'm the man you saw working on that telephone operator.

DG: Of course, I do, *Oberscharführer* Misch! I noticed one more officer was working with you in that room, right?

Misch: He's been sent off. So, now it's only me.

DG: Sent off where?

RM: Fighting above somewhere.

DG: So now you're the only man communicating with the outside world?

RM: Yes.

DG: But how can —

RM: Frau Gale, I know what you're thinking. How can one human be the only contact for Germany to communicate with the outside world? And that's because there's not so much work to be done here.

DG: I'm shocked, to be honest.

RM: Think about it, or let's put it this way. You're thinking of Germany in our glory days when we ruled Europe. Back then, there were thousands of men and women in the communications department. But today, there's not much left of National Socialist Germany, and I think you know that.

DG: Come to think of it, you're dead right.

RM: I'm 'dead'?

DG [Laughing]: Excuse me, I'm translating English to German. I meant you're absolutely right. ["Wenn ich daran denke, hast du vollkommen recht."]

{*Misch laughs*}

DG: How long do you think the Battle of Berlin will go on?

RM: As long as we have petrol, guns, bombs, we can fight back against the Soviet juggernaut. And to answer your question, I doubt we'll have these resources for more than a few weeks.

DG: You mean Hitler and his Bunker people ... do they know that?

RM [Laughing]: How can I know what each of these individuals believes in?

DG: You're right. Dumb question.

RM: On the opposite, don't be hard on yourself. How many outsiders would understand this unhinged situation within which we're living in? Because you come from America. You come from a land of security, peace, and sanity. That's your world. But now you're here. And we have the exact opposite attributes you have in America, and that's why it's almost impossible for you to understand us. It's like the sane trying to understand the insane. How could it possibly happen when the two are opposites?

{*Silence*}

DG: Let's go back to your occupation ... No, I'm confused ...

RM: Don't worry. Believe me, your frightened reaction is, in fact, totally rational because you're a normal human being. I'm telling you because you're sane, so logically speaking, you cannot understand the gibberish the mad speak, right? Just as only the mad understand the language of animals, like monkeys. If ever you've been in a mental hospital, you'd know what I'm talking about. Well, by now, the German people have been infused by the madness of the mad in those psychiatric wards, such that there's no difference between the two. Everything is positively nonsensical. Nobody talks sense. Because reason is unreason to us. Do you understand? People speak backward. Walk upside-down. Up is down, and down is left. Humans blathering idiocies. But we never think for a moment we're blathering idiocies. I'm talking about people like Goering, Goebbels, Keitel – the whole rotten lot! We believe we speak Gospel Truth. And oddly enough, our existence of absurdity has to worsen as it becomes ever more irrational precisely because everything surrounding us is nonsensical. I think the likes of Antonin Artaud would fully appreciate Berlin at this hour! Eventually, this tragi-comedic absurdity destroys the remnants of our previous existence.

Actually, it fascinated me how Misch brought up this topic because I've often squabbled with myself on the same niggling conundrum - can the sane ever communicate meaningfully with the insane and the vice-versa? But I'd add a significantly different attribute, in addition to madness – evil. And now, how can the rational meaningfully communicate with those who are *evilly* insane? It seems to me impossible because for any meaningful communication to be achieved, one must assume an understanding with insane, right? And an understanding presumes a measure of agreement while good and evil surely by their intrinsic natures cannot ever agree on any subject matter.

DG: I can think of Diogenes too.

{Silence}

DG: How can you or I rationalise an irrational world? That's absurd.

My mind insists on going back to Medusa. Masturbation. Why is that such a significant matter? It is. Don't hide, Dorothy. It's a gigantic part of our lives. Medusa has no shame whatsoever in masturbating. But ninety-nine percent of us women fear and loathe doing it. Though it is one more secret of womanhood. More importantly, it's a Cross we bear because we're desperately terrified and pained knowing we regularly do it. We're supposed to be your typical coy, blushing, innocent, child-like, kittenish, purring Southern Belles. Not the furiously masturbating bitch we are. Forget 'bitch.' Why did I say that? Self-hate. You see? The crime enacted before your eyes.

RM: Because when you remain long enough inside a microcosm governed by the physical and metaphysical laws of irrationality so you, too, will come to find it 'normal.'

DG: You cannot make sense out of nonsense because that would only create nonsense.

RM: Exactly, and you've spoken my point for me.

DG [Shocked]: No! Absurdity *cannot* exist in this world! How can one be mad in a mad world?

RM: Why not?

DG: Because if we're mad and the world or this city is mad, then we wouldn't notice anything being mad!

RM [Laughing]: But that's exactly what I've been trying to tell you!

DG [Flustered]: No, no, no! Mad means crazy, abnormal ... and yet you're saying we're all mad, which implies everything is 'normal' ...

I felt mad in this mad conversation!

RM: You can accept it or deny its existence. Anti-reality has its own properties, just as reality does.

DG: I've learned from quantum physics the acceptance of indeterminacy, uncertainty, and complementarity of totally opposing attributes fused in one state of being or matter.

RM: What? Now *you've* lost me!

DG: What do these add up to? An existence of relative chaos. Existence and a universe that humbles Man in not knowing and in never knowing. But the Man of Arrogance cannot accept this reality. So, he fights on a pointless cause for which, like Gilgamesh and Icarus, he must lose. I must ask you if I may. I see increasing spasms of panic and hysteria. Do you know what's new?

{*Misch laughs*}

Misch: Ha! That's our latest show of the Revolving Door!

DG: What *do* you mean?

RM: This is a circus. Have you forgotten my words? We were, or *they* were trying to find someone who can defend our lines. Well, this was all good and well. But the Fuehrer insisted he won't accept anyone from Wehrmacht ranks. He only wants a man with a 'fanatical will.' That puzzled everyone surrounding him. None understood what the

Fuehrer's words added up to. And none dared to ask him for his definition for the required job qualification.

DG: Hitler wanted someone with *no* military experience?

{*Misch laughs*}

Misch: That's what some gentlemen thought. Others thought, maybe the Fuehrer wants any idiot. Grab anyone from a lunatic asylum, and we'll show Hitler a man of suicidal zeal. The Fuehrer cannot just need someone to have 'zeal,' some argued laboriously because zeal in itself cannot function without reason. Hence the lunatic asylum theory was dropped.

DG: You mean you guys were thinking of bringing in some fanatical inexperienced man?

RM: Once the Fuehrer made an order, all the sheep would go away and deliberate on the meaning of his words.

DG: Why's that?

RM: Because they couldn't understand his words or order.

DG: Wasn't it evident what he wanted?

RM: Actually, you're correct. His words were clearly stated, but because they were so nonsensical, the officers and generals tried to make it or transform his order into a sensible one.

DG: I'm lost.

RM: You'll soon understand; hang on. So, some suggested maybe the Fuehrer only wanted zeal plus cretinism. Surely not! Others said passion with intelligent youth. Others suggested they'd need to get a military officer with quality zeal plus minimal intelligence? Perfect! But there was the problem of time.

DG: 'Time'?

RM: The problem was that no one had any time to interpret what the Fuehrer wanted. That was quite a bother. I'm sure you'd agree.

DG: Why is that a bother?

RM: There was no time to discuss and find the 'proper' candidate' for the job Hitler was calling for.

DG: So they randomly chose anyone?

RM: Not quite. Mind you, the number of candidates was so few because most officers had either surrendered, fled to the Americans, been shot, or were on POW camps.

DG: So that made your job ... or their job easier, right?

RM: Exactly.

DG: By the way, who are the people deciding who would be the next defender of Berlin?

RM: Goering, Guderian, Jodl, and other top-ranking military officers.

DG: So what's happening right now?

RM: In the meantime, Hitler isn't just thinking of this question of who would be the next commander of Berlin. You must know that he was also issuing numerous other military orders and the latter were to anyone and everyone who could receive his order. That caused conflicting military acts since some German units ended up firing at other German units.

DG: Why?

RM: Since we had no commander in chief defending Berlin and ensuring what each unit had to do, as per their operational plans and purposes, so each unit receiving those orders would interpret it in any way they wished, and so they'd fire off their ammunition in any direction they thought was the correct way.

I was even more confused.

DG: Why didn't Hitler do that?

RM: He never did. Hitler always left details for his subordinates to flesh out. And as I said, every officer had to immediately respond on any order at once—no time to philosophise or interpret.

DG: But how can you implement an order if you allow yourself no time to read it properly?

RM: Here, instincts and experience matter. You must immediately understand the order's substance even though you may not have the exact meaning of the intentions of the order may be. And should you fail to act in time, your head would be on the chopping block.

DG: So he made the big ideas while the rest had to figure out the logistics of how to carry out his order?

RM: Yes. And because we had no communications with those units, Hitler's orders were meaningless.

DG: Why?

RM: Because the situation on the ground does not correlate with what Hitler sees in his maps. Because with each minute, the military situation is changing. Units are being destroyed. Frontlines are changing. So what is the poor field offer to do? For example, he reads an order from Hitler – 'Street X must be attacked. Enemy positions Weak.' But as he surveys Street X, he finds that the street is infested with enemy soldiers, tanks, and artillery units, contrary to Hitler's report. He knows he has no chance of achieving any advance at Street X since his forces are infinitely weaker than those opposing him. If he refuses to obey, as you know, he'd be shot. But how can he obey? Meaning, if he did obey, he'd simply be throwing his boy soldiers into the belly of death.

As Misch was talking, I remembered a horrific scene outside, above the Bunker. Russian soldiers grabbed a German soldier and shoved his face through a serrated road with broken glasses, stones, pins, and God knows what. He screamed. They laughed. The German boy and I say 'boy' because he didn't look more than sixteen years old before being marred by that incident. I say Russians 'laughed,' but to be accurate, not all. Some smiled. Others were wholly detached from the ugly scene being enacted next to them.

Anyway, the perpetrators barked at the German boy to lick everything in the street. Once he heard the words translated into German, he tried to swallow the debris, filth, human remains, feces, detritus of the streets. His screams turned to the voice of an old woman. Begging for mercy. Out of the blue, some Russian shouted, *"Let him live!"*

I was shocked by the mercy of that man, and oddly enough, those criminal soldiers duly left the poor German boy, leaving him alone. His torture ended. At least he hadn't been killed. The Russians walked away from the scene, leaving that young boy crawling or doing God knows what as he tried to move, wiggle, or whatever. Where did he want to go to? That's when I noted the lower half of his face was gone. Meaning he couldn't talk. Why was he crawling? The Russians smashed his legs. They literally stomped on his legs with their iron-studded boots. What else could he do but to crawl, using his puny arms? And again, as I looked at him, I thought, "Where do you think you're going to go? I swear you won't be going to where you wish to go to. You'll be dead in a few minutes. Because you're bleeding too much blood for any human body to exist."

DG: Going back to choosing someone to defend Berlin, since you say no one understood what he meant, how did they resolve the problem?

RM: It's a touch-and-go situation. Pick and choose. And hurry!

DG: All this confusion arose from Hitler's insistence that the defender of Berlin must only have 'fanatical will and zeal'?

> The hour will come when you, crying,
> Must take her on her final walk.
> And if she asks you, then give her an answer
> And if she asks you again, listen!
> And if she asks you again, take in her words
> Not impetuously, but gently and in peace!
> And if she cannot quite understand you, explain all to her gladly
>
> *For the hour will come, the bitter hour when her mouth will ask for nothing more.*

- Adolf Hitler, *'Denk' es!'* (Be Reminded!) Hitler's only known poem. *1923, first published in Sonntag-Morgenpost (14 May 1933)*

Misch [Loudly]: Exactly! No talent needed! You forgot that we already had the supposed 'talent' with our old generals and brilliant officers, and what did they achieve? They left millions of our comrades dead. Sattered from Paris to Stalingrad. And now, aren't we right here in this dungeon?

DG: What's your point?

RM: Meaning those generals and brilliant officers failed. That's why it was time to seek a zealous fanatic.

DG: And you say Hitler is against the Wehrmacht because they failed?

RM: In his opinion, they failed us, or him. Yes.

DG: Doesn't that only leave you guys, SS?

RM: Not just us SS men. There are naval units. Former Luftwaffe officers.

DG: So, *who is* defending Berlin now?

{*Misch laughs*}

RM: Going back to the freak circus, yes. In January of this year, one anonymous shadow called Bruno Ritter von Hauenschild was appointed to defend Berlin. But apparently, he was ill or, so I heard. No one bothered to check on his health status when they proposed him to the defender in question. So, he was booted out. Next, on March 15th General Hellmuth Reymann was appointed.

DG: Are any of those two men good, efficient, or what?

RM: No one heard or knew much of anything about General Hauenschild –

DG: Isn't that surprising?

RM: What do you mean?

DG: Well, from all the glittering array of generals in the Third Reich, how can or why would your Fuehrer appoint one who was practically unknown?

RM: I see, yes, but that is exactly my point! The Fuehrer believed the shadow man had the requisite fanatical attributes for the defence of Fortress Berlin.

DG: Berlin is no fortress!

RM: I know, but that is the definition our Fuehrer has designated this disappearing city to be.

DG: So, what happened next?

RM: We were secretly asking each other, 'Well, who exactly is this man now, the one meant to defend us from the Bolshevik hordes?' As I said, no one knew him. So that already nullified the validity of our question since how could any of us men who knew nothing of the military officer in question produce even a half-baked answer with any degree of truth when the man himself was entirely unknown? It was impossible.

DG: Right, so what happened next?

Misch: So, what happened next was, as I said, this General Reymann gets the unwanted plum job. He was slightly better known. I say this, though I myself and comrades had never heard of him.

DG: Is that it? Is this man now defending Berlin?

Did she have a job? Medusa. Was she abused? If so, how? Verbally and physically, I assume. Or more? Sexual abuse? Was she raped? If so, how often? Was she mad only to save her sanity? How odd is that! But then what other way can one remain tight on earth? Did she masturbate? No, I asked and answered that question. She does. Furiously and proudly. Not like us 'normal' females. Shamed of our gender, bodies, and sexuality. There you go. The simple trio. That's why we cannot talk to each other. But it's worse. We cannot speak to ourselves, for the love of our Lord, Jesus Christ, don't you know that? We fear talking to ourselves.

RM: No.

DG: What do you mean 'no'?

Misch: On the 22nd day in April, this Reymann was inelegantly booted out.

DG: Another one booted out? Why?

RM: No one knew.

DG: In the Bunker here, is there no one who has the official role of speaking the news?

{*Misch laughs*}

RM: No.

DG: So how does anyone know what is going on?

RM: No one knows what is going on.

DG: But ... What? In a tragic and catastrophic situation as you Bunkerites are in, why wouldn't Hitler appoint someone to speak the official news?

RM: We get bits and pieces of news that could be too old, as I told you. So, not much reality seeps in.

DG: What about listening to the BBC?

RM: We're not allowed to do that.

DG: I'm sure Hitler and people like Goering secretly listen to the BBC because it's their only reliable source of news.

RM: I agree, but, and again, as I told you, our wires are so bad, listening to the BBC is difficult because of the interruptions and the crackling sounds.

DG: So, no one knows, and each must figure it out for themselves?

RM: We certainly dare not ask. Mind you, some said Goebbels despised him, others said Wilhelm Burgdorf hated him.

DG: Who's Burgdorf?

RM: He is Chief Adjutant to the Fuehrer. Anyway, whatever the reason was or was not, the man Reymann was out.

~

III. Dorothy – "Uncanny How Similar My Life Is to The Wizard of Oz!"

DG: What happened to him?

RM: Excuse me?

DG: What happened to this man General Reymann? Where is he? Is he alive? Dead?

{*Misch laughs*}

DG: Why's that so funny?

RM: Given our enchanting context, do you think anyone is remotely interested to know or find out about the specific fate of one entirely meaningless human amid and within this existential maelstrom?

DG: How can you call any human being 'meaningless'? The more you talk, the more I feel we're in Alice's 'Wonderland'!

RM: What is Alice's Wonderland?

DG: Didn't you see the movie *'The Wizard of Oz'*?

RM: No.

DG: Really?

RM: Yes, really.

DG: That film changed my life. Or one thing that changed my life.

RM: How so?

DG: Well, it's just like me. Odd that, now, 'ain't it? It's about a young American farm girl who somehow finds herself in an evil land, the Land of Oz. A good witch tells her if she wants to go back home, she must find the Wizard of Oz, and he'll grant her the wish of returning home. The girl asks the beautiful witch, "Well, how do I find where this Wizard is at?" "Simple," replies the Witch, "all you have to do it to follow the Yellow Brick Road." And so off she trots. On her way, she meets and befriends a lion with no heart, meaning no courage; you see this lion believes to be happy, all you need is courage and nothing else.

I knew Misch was bored, but I didn't care because, I'll be honest, I was talking to myself and entertaining myself with the story of that eternally great movie.

DG: Next, she meets a Tinman who has no heart. He believes to be happy, you need a heart to feel and love. Finally, she meets a Scarecrow man with no brains. He knows life can only be enjoyed if he can think and be rational. And so, the trio trots off to see the Wizard, hoping he'll make their wishes are to come true. Well now, 'ain't that deep when you think about it? A heart, a brain, and power. Who is right?

{Silence}

DG: Don't you Misch? These are questions we must know … questions we must know! And don't you see it's not those characters in that movie that search; we're all searching, right?

RM: 'Searching' what?

DG [Excited]: Finally, you understand, I'm so happy, Misch! That's the point ... searching for what? Because we don't know what we're searching for or some know what they're searching for like Lion, Tinman and Scarecrow and Dorothy and they think this massive, gigantic, all-powerful being, the Wizard of Oz, will give them their meanings for life so they can then be happy while living. Meanwhile, they have no clue who, where, or what this Wizard is or even if he truly exists!

RM: Did you mention 'Dorothy'?

{Silence}

DG: Why yes, I did now, didn't I?

RM: Why are you puzzled?

DG: I never thought of that.

{Silence}

RM: That of what?

DG: I mean, I knew the film had so many similarities with my life. But you just reminded me the girl has my name too. Dorothy Gale.

{Silence}

DG: Well, I don't know. But anyway, that film is true for everyone.

{Silence}

DG: I just want to go back home. But another part of me believes I cannot go back home if I don't find myself first. I mean ... I could quickly go back home right now. I'm sure. But my bosses will scream. Because I wouldn't have done my homework, you see Misch?

RM: You speak German, but I don't understand American thoughts.

DG [Angry]: Well, just listen harder, will you? You must because you must… that's why. You'll help me … you see in getting me back home!

RM: How can I return you to … I forget which state you come from.

DG: Doesn't matter. Once we leave this hell, I promise I'll tell you. But I'm talking silly now, 'ain't I?

{Silence}

DG: I must stay here and find myself. What's the point of going back home if you're a nobody? Like Daddy, I suppose.

{Silence}

DG: I must. To be human means you've got to have a brain, right? Well, that's obvious now. Stupid of me to say that. But how many people have brains? No one has brains! That's why the world's mad!

{Silence}

DG: Oh dear, am I Ophelia?

{Silence}

DG: And that's the point and meaning of life, obviously to have a brain and so that same brain finds you. That's it!

{Silence}

DG: But how does my brain find 'me' when I don't know where I am?

RM: You're in Berlin.

DG: To find oneself. And then you'll be happy.

{Silence}

DG: Look at our life, at Man's life. We began by violating God. Adam and Eve. Next, we commit murder. Cain murdering his brother Abel. Is this Man? Yes, this is him, her, and us. Criminals. That's who we are. We ignore our truths. We forget our realities. We couldn't care less about our criminal past. That's how we think we survive. Forgetting we're murderers.

If Ophelia is allowed to soliloquize, why should I, too, be allowed to do what she did in her erotic reveries?

DG: And so, we live on throughout our days, years, and decades. And all the while in our unconscious, imprisoned there somewhere in that monumentally abstract mind, is that entity known as conscience or decency, humanity, and love. And that squeaks out in protest at our villainous behaviors. For, some people may feel twangs of emptiness in their lives. They may feel dispirited in their lives. Some know why and others don't understand why. The majority of 'humans' have no humanity. They live a life of unreserved, extreme, zealous evilness. Either way, we're all murderers. And it's up to us how we're to resolve that sin. Either ignore it or deal with it.

{Silence}

DG: Why else would evil exist? Who creates Evil but Man? Therefore, who should resolve this sickness, but the creator himself - Man? And yet, look at us. Look at how we fret from the first moment of adolescence. Fretting first about our looks or our lack of looks. That's our only obsession To look better. And then, as years travel on unto other fields of experiences, so we remain either diligently or recklessly worried about our stability. Why? Because we don't know who we are.

{Silence}

DG: Man, the murderer, has awakened to the truth of his deeds. He is horrified. So said Jeffrey Dahmer. Only after waking up away from a blindly drunken night before did he see the wretch of a man beside him who had been visibly murdered. However, he couldn't remember killing the man lying beside him. Regrettably, reality wouldn't switch its accusatory eyes from him. He knew. And isn't it ironic because most 'normal' people don't realize they are murderers, while this serial killer realized only too well his indecencies?

{Silence}

DG: I'm not saying we're all in one category of murderers. No. But we're all in different levels of evilness.

RM: What's the point of this?

DG [Angrily]: Because we live in a jungle, don't you understand? ... You, of all people ... living here in Berlin, can't you see, feel, smell the madness, the evil raging on and on every day here?

{Silence}

RM: We're in an ongoing battle. That's all I know with certainty. But I've no answer or comment about your Cain and Abel and that Jeff man from America.

DG: I know we're in the midst of a battle. That's my point. And what is a battle but madness?

RM: Why is it 'madness'?

DG: Excuse me, I didn't mean to say all battles are madness. But surely this one here madness because it's pointless because you guys have lost the war.

~

IV. Dorothy – "I Cannot Accept We're Living in an Alice in Wonderland World and All Germans Have Become as Automatons."

RM: Well, anyway, to answer your question, life in Berlin is so cheap, it is, or it's become meaningless. Life in Berlin is fictitious in terms of its actual value, which is nothing.

DG [Huffing]: That's wrong!

RM: It may be wrong. It may be right. It may not be correct. Nobody knows because nobody has the luxury to think. I'm confident you'll accept that – at the least?

DG [Saddened]: No, because when there are times of peace, people mull over what the hell is going on and what will happen.

RM: Believe me, Frau Gale, no one thinks. Everyone is numb. Any lofty intellectual concept is entirely irrelevant. They don't exist in Berlin. Just as deflation decreases commodity prices, you must include humans as one more item among those useless commodities. Berliners only sniff for food, water, shelter, and that's it. Nothing else enters their brains.

DG[Angrily]: My God! Do you people not believe in good and evil? In right and wrong? Is that it?

RM: Is that what?

DG: Is that what Germans have become? Robots?

RM: Precisely.

DG [Frantic]: But why? These are *also my* people! *I'm German too!*

RM: Frau Gale, relax! The problem is that you look from the outside in. One cannot understand the reality of a person or an event looking and judging it from your context. So, you must look from the inside. Meaning you must pretend you too are a Berliner or any other German from any other city that has been continually bombed night and day for months. How would you then feel? How would your nerves handle round-the-clock bombing?

DG: That's true. I cannot imagine what it's like to live in that condition, to be honest.

RM: Of course, Germans don't just live with that burden.

DG: What?

RM: Millions of our comrades are still fighting. Mothers, sisters, daughters, grandmothers desperately needing to know what's happened to their loved ones. But they've no answers because news is as destroyed as this city is. News is just another casualty here.

DG: Some news flutters in, no?

RM: Sure, but it's either hearsay or lies or who knows what? How can a grieving mother believe what some strange individual tells her about her son? Gossip, words of individuals aren't necessarily 'dead' – they flit in and out of consciousness, and sometimes it speaks the truth when they're in the latter state. But then, if it has a weak disposition, the 'news' is nothing but incoherent words.

DG [Quietly]: That makes sense.

{Silence}

RM: The only truths existing here are the fleeting events we witness, experience, and interact with. Now, as for philosophical concepts you have excavated, no, none of them remotely matter.

DG: So, what matters to you people here?

RM: Survival.

DG: How do you do this 'searching'?

RM: You asked me that question.

DG: I'm sorry but -

RM: I told you, it takes time to adapt to a different reality.

DG: I mean ... not only given the chaos of the war or the battle above ... in Berlin ... and given the facts that we know ... You know. You say. The frailty of your communication links?

RM: Sorry? I did not understand your question.

{Silence}

I don't remember the rest. I needed a break. That was all. I was kindly escorted by Misch back to my tiny room. Peace. Temporary peace. In the hell of Berlin's bosom.

~

Contradictory Thoughts – Kansas Virgin Country Girl Sightseeing in Gay Berlin

I walked outside, escorted by Fegelein, of course. *"Haven't you seen enough of war?"* he asked me. I smiled without answering.

Fresh air, of sorts. Funny seeing women still lavishing make-up on their pinched faces. For whom? Tiny tots happily wandering. *"Where's Daddy? Where's Mommy?"* some ask. I knew where Daddy was —dead, dying, wounded, or in some Siberian Prisoner of War Camp.

Teen German girls gossiping. Giggling. They could've been straight out from my town in Kansas. Finding tickling amusements despite their surroundings. Laughing and raving about some subject while death is their background. I mean, not far from them are corpses. And I see men. Mostly middle-aged to the old, dressed in suits and ties. Walking stiffly. But where? Work? Is there work in Berlin? Well, yes, incredibly, that's what I found out!

There were some offices functioning. And then, for the first time, I saw two or three 'restaurants.' Imagine that! People dining amid this epic battle. Only during respite hours, though. But who would have an appetite in this vortex of death?

Again, no, that makes no sense. I speak too fast, leaving my thoughts way behind like the ever-expanding distances between infantry and tanks. Hunger prevails in Berlin. And yet some people eat in restaurants? They can not only get food - but posh food! I was wrong! Somehow, somewhere, lavish food existed amid the oceans of rubble. I guess some have money to dine out. But wasn't money worthless in Berlin, right? I'm not sure. You don't have the luxury of time to mull and think in a war zone. That's why your thoughts, emotions, and impressions are crumpled. How else did they pay for the food they ordered? Imaginary money? Or services. By far, most Berliners were desperately eking out an existence based on scraps, shreds, and morsels. Contrasting scenes. Maybe not to Berliners because they gradually became accustomed to their present-day infernal circumstances, as Misch the Fish said. And then Marx barreled in my brain. I was furious. How the hell and how come even in this worse hour in German history did wealthy Germans still have the ability to dine and wine themselves when the rest of their people were living on the questionable and stingy sustenance of desperation?

The Reichstag.

What a magnificent sight to behold! I cannot believe it's still standing. I swear you cannot measure more than an inch of brick or marble, and you will not come across a blasted gash. Splattered with bullet holes and shell gaps. Yet, weirdly, I still sensed a mysterious beauty in this increasingly disfigured building. Massive in size. This is the work of Man.

Man created it. A monument to Democracy. But now Man destroys it. Everywhere screams of disgruntled and proud scrawls in Cyrillic letters. Ivan's writing, God, knows saying what. I, too, was tempted to scrawl my words.

The Reichstag, 1945

For posterity, I suppose. It's funny because I don't think Ivan's would've been so eager to graffiti on that Reichstag shell of the building were it not because that same building was fixated in their brains as the central 'lair' of the building Hitler. I understood why they felt they had to write their inscriptions on the hated 'symbol' of Hitler's fascist den, [as they called it]? Hell yes! Ironically, the ruined Reichstag had nothing in common with that man. But I guess someone had to be the sacrificial lamb for the rage of some two million Russian men. Where else could the Russians find Hitler's symbolic building? Yes, you still had the Brandenburg Gate. But you cannot compare it in size to 'democracy's building.' The Berlin Palace (Berliner Schloss or Stadtschloss) is destroyed. Nothing but charred debris.

I walk in front of the Bellevue Palace (Schloss Bellevue). It's also shattered. The Kaiser Wilhelm Memorial Church. Destroyed. You know, within minutes or hours, you get used to anything and everything.

I'm numbed. Fegelein's question begins to resonate. Death, destruction, anything goes. The repetitive scenes of destruction numb me. Numbed by the redundant number of criminal acts I see. Numbed by the repetitive number of criminal words I hear. And with the numbness, guess what happens to your conscience and morality? That's right, so too, your ethics and decency go numb indifference to right and wrong.

The only relevant truth here is the moment. And, in a way, that is good, or it has its good side. In Berlin, I felt the immediacy of each moment, each encounter. Berlin changed and sharpened my sensitivities to matters I never thought were worthy of a second thought or glance. Take a flower. When did I ever think of flowers back in Kansas? Never!

Here in this solitary funeral pyre, I see an isolated simple, no-frills flower. It's living uncomfortably side by side amid the connected and unconnected paths and spaces of concrete hell. And I feel coy exhilaration—survival in the face of pitilessly stormy winds isn't that insane!

Back in Kansas, do you think I ever once thought about flowers? Hell no! But in Berlin, the fact any flower could live, even thrive, gave me joy, hope, and a different outlook on my personal life and of its meanings and purposes.

I mean that no matter how murderously hard your life may be, there's still the fact that you can someday turn your life around from sickness to health as long as you have that faith, that belief in your skills.

I see a dirty child of six or seven walking. The child looks as deformed as the shredded life-size doll it is carrying.

Another child walks randomly, holding something I think was once a teddy bear. Walking or dithering nowhere really to be accurate amid the oceanic rubble of what was once one of the grandest cities in the world.

I see another child looking dead. Though he or she walks on zombie-like. You cannot tell gender. They're too dusty, filthy, covered with sorrows, such that gender becomes meaningless in that specific moment in time. Tattered rags, covered in white and black soot. That is it. And yet, the sickening incongruities are eternal in my mind.

I've been asked years later, "Did you ever try to help anyone in Berlin?" And my answer is, "No." Some think that's cruel. Maybe it is. But I saw myself as an animal reporter. I observed animals doing whatever they do and never interfered.

Why? Because if I, for example, a Russian is about to shoot a German child and I moved the latter to safety, then the scene before me that I'm supposed to be reporting as the truth has now become corrupted since it would not be a truthful portrayal anymore.

And then the other side of my parliamentary mind retorts, *"You are exaggerating what you see, Dorothy!"* and I yield. Maybe I am. Perhaps it is because I am an outsider; I see Berlin the way I do. And that makes sense because an outsider, by definition, isn't used to seeing the horror on a minute-by-minute basis. When you see something awful, you go on with your life acting as though nothing abnormal was going on. Or maybe it's because I'm a country girl.

Maybe, it's because I'm a virgin. Or maybe, it's because I have my period. I don't know. Senses can be little devils in our minds. I see a grieving scene whenever I see someone dying. Especially girls and young women. Maybe to a Berliner, they see nothingness.

How can anyone know I'm a virgin? I say that because many women knew it. Weird, isn't that?

I contradict myself. Didn't I just say in Berlin, everyone is numb? So why feel sorrow or whatever when I see dying people breathing their last moment of consciousness on earth?

~

"Here. Here I am. You've taken everything from us, but not who we are! We still exist! One-day grass will grow here and overgrow the ruins. Or day, this will be forgotten. But you ... No one will ever forget you! The shame of humanity."

— Bruno Apitz (1900-79) *Nackt unter Wölfen*

Conversation I - Three Soviet Officers – Squabbling Among Each Other

There were so many tedious moments when no one was interesting to talk to that I finally decided to speak with Russian soldiers. I knew no German would escort me to where Russians were for obvious reasons. They would either be shot dead or captured as one more POW. So, damn it, I was going on my own, asking local soldiers where the enemy was.

Once I heard a fresh lull in the fighting, I went above and began my journey through the rubble, craters, holes, debris, waste, corpses, steel rods poking out from concrete blocks, ashes, and dust. Clambering here and there, I saw one lonesome German soldier, looking pitifully sad. Wounded, he was. But I didn't care about his condition. I asked him where the enemy was, upon which wearily, without questioning me, pointed towards some point ahead, and that's where gallant Dorothy headed.

I was exhausted and felt I couldn't go on, even though God knows I had only moved about a thousand meters. Finally, panting, I decided to continue, and so I did. For some reason, I looked back at that boy or soldier. He was dead. His last words were giving me directions for my career. What a life.

Suddenly I saw them. Hazy scenes before my teary eyes. Teary because of the acrid smoke, I think I told you about that. Anyway, there they were - Russian soldiers!

Before I'd introduce myself, I thought, "What if they kill me?" No, they wouldn't. I was wearing our official US Army uniform. But that could've meant nothing to them. Everyone by then knew how during the Battle of the Bulge, Obersturmbannführer Otto Skorzeny used English-speaking German soldiers dressed up in US uniforms, diverting US jeeps, tanks, trucks in the wrong direction.

They saw me. I knew that from their movements. Looking back now, after seventy-six years, I cannot tell you how exactly I 'knew' they saw me. Maybe because of the panic on my face. No, wait, I didn't panic until I saw them. In any case, I was now in their hands. If I retreated, they'd readily shoot me dead. I was a captive, a POW, whereas moments ago, I was able to exercise my freedom by going back to the safety of the Bunker.

I steeled my Kansas nerves and chose to speak, or rather to holler — *"Ya amerikanskiy zhurnalist! Ya prishel pogovorit' s toboy!"* ["I am an American reporter. I come to speak to you!"] Silence. Didn't they hear? Or maybe my accent rendered my words unintelligible. More silence. *"Mogu ya prosto pogovorit' s toboy?"* ["Can I talk to you?"]

Out of the blue, one of the soldiers waved me to come forward. To my surprise, not only did he speak English, so too did the other two Soviet soldiers. That was one more detail I forgot to tell you about. I learned a few Russian phrases. I just need to remind you in the Russian language; they don't have the letter 'H'; they pronounce it as 'G' or 'Ch' as in the Scottish word of Loch Ness.

DG: As I said, I am from the US Army –

Soviet Officer Yezhov [Angrily]: And how do we know that? These idiots tell you to come here without thinking!

Soviet Officer Solzhenitsyn [Angrily at Yezhov]: What now? Inform the NKVD [Soviet secret police]

DG: Officers! Can we just have a civil conversation?

Soviet Officer Khrushchev: That dog is unbearable. I am sorry for this is the sick brain functions.

DG: My name is Dorothy Gale.

The Soviet officers, though not Yezhov, politely introduced themselves. To be honest, I was surprised at their mild manners, expecting savage, drunken boors. Instead, even Yezhov was strictly rude and in no way physically aggressive.

DG: How did the war start for you? I mean, where were you –

Soviet Officer Solzhenitsyn: I was a civilian, an author.

DG: How interesting! Were you allowed to publish your books?

Soviet Officer Solzhenitsyn [Laughing]: Absolutely not! I never dared to –

Soviet Officer Yezhov [Icily]: How come you still tell us your profession is an 'author'?

Soviet Officer Solzhenitsyn: No, he is right. I was a secret author, if you like. My work was in a governmental department dealing with agricultural affairs.

Soviet Officer Yezhov [Sarcastically Laughing]: That means he purges our nation of Kulaks!

DG: And how about you, Officer Khrushchev?

Soviet Officer Khrushchev: I was already in the army –

Soviet Officer Yezhov [Sarcastically Laughing]: And he was killing off traitors in our Red Army! Don't you love how these idiots paint their roles in these cushy, mild terms?

DG [To Yezhov]: And I assume you were in the army too?

Soviet Officer Yezhov [Loudly]: And proudly so, serving our leader, Marshall Stalin!

DG: In the beginning, did you think the Germans would win in the summer of 1941?

Soviet Officer Solzhenitsyn: You know, I still think this war could've been avoided.

DG: That's not my question.

Soviet Officer Yezhov: You are mad. But you don't know that you're mad. Therefore, society must control you and your madness precisely because you are incapable of understanding your madness. The lady just asked you a simple question. Typically, like a robot, you ignore her, and off you run with your pre-prepared transcript that has no relevance to the question at hand.

Soviet Officer Solzhenitsyn: If he were mad, how do you think Khrushchev achieved the noble military rank he holds today?

Soviet Officer Khrushchev: What is infuriatingly typical of arrogant people is their blindness to their ideology. Life is black or white. We are good; the rest must either be murdered or turned into slaves. There can be no discussion since that would be an admittance of political weakness, which means the firing squad in our country. So instead, they first think people like you are to arbitrarily condemn millions of human beings without even bothering to read or listen to our point of view.

Soviet Officer Yezhov: For once, the idiot speaks truth.

Soviet Officer Solzhenitsyn: I don't mind Khrushchev being mad; at least he's not an Anti-Christ.

Soviet Officer Yezhov: It is weaklings like you Solzhenitsyn the Motherland must forever be vigilant about. People like you are the deviationists and wreckers.

Soviet Officer Solzhenitsyn: Go back to the NKVD boys and report me. You've done it once before.

Soviet Officer Yezhov: You repeat yourself, idiot. Pity is, you learn nothing. That's why we mentioned Comrade Stalin to have criminals like you to be exterminated, but he refused.

Soviet Officer Solzhenitsyn [Pointedly at Yezhov]: Far from it. The criminal so-called 'culture' of Stalin created the automated criminal before us today.

DG: Officers, what do you think this war is about?

{Laughter}

Soviet Officer Yezhov: I'll never understand how stupid Americans have so much power.

Soviet Officer Khrushchev: Ever thought you're the idiot for thinking of them as idiots?

Soviet Officer Yezhov [Threateningly to Solzhenitsyn]: You shall see your end coming, boy.

Soviet Officer Khrushchev: That's precisely the cancer in our present-day so-called 'communist' regime. You see, communism is the noblest philosophy there is in the world, but perverted bastards deformed it —

Soviet Officer Solzhenitsyn [Aghast at Khrushchev]: You still defend communism?

{*Silence*}

Soviet Officer Khrushchev [To Solzhenitsyn]: How many years were you in prison?

Soviet Officer Solzhenitsyn: Let me count.

{*Silence*}

Soviet Officer Solzhenitsyn: About eleven years.

Soviet Officer Khrushchev [To Solzhenitsyn]: And is it or what caused you to betray Marxism?

Soviet Officer Solzhenitsyn: I had clear experiences our ideology is wrong and a crime against Man's soul. Then your people put me in prison. I was cemented in jail. I became cement. But my convictions fully emerged intact in their entirety despite the passing of years.

Soviet Officer Yezhov [Sneering]: What a fool! Pretending to be like your hero Dostoyevsky!

Soviet Officer Solzhenitsyn: The fact I too write novels doesn't mean I ever equated myself with Dostoevsky. However, I, along with millions of other Gulag internees, have one thing in common. Those cruelest years had to create a crucial change in the mechanics of our souls. How else could any rational human not react and change to what he must experience and witness in Stalin's prisons?

Soviet Officer Khrushchev [To Solzhenitsyn]: Yes, but you became too extreme. Too emotional. You cannot slander Marxism only because our present leader is criminally negligent in this sphere of politics. Communism is not just Stalinism.

DG: What do you mean, if I may ask?

Soviet Officer Khrushchev: Look, Stalin was an absolute necessity in the late twenties and thirties for all his faults. Had it not been for Comrade Stalin, Russia would've been crushed by fascist Germany. Yes, it cost much, with the restructuring of agriculture, the dekulakisation of millions of peasants, the famines everywhere, and the mass deportations of entire nations, races, and communities. But by 1939, Stalin achieved his singular goal: not only to make the USSR a power but also to face the brunt of the Hitlerite fascist armies. We knew England and America would wait as we fight it out, and only in the final moments will they come to fight Germans.

DG: And, of course, happened with the Normandy invasion.

Soviet Officer Khrushchev: Exactly. But think of the timing. The so-called western allies only arrived in this war in June of 1944.

Soviet Officer Yezhov: Absolutely! And to be precise, listen to Truman's words - *"If we see that Germany is winning the war, we ought to help Russia; and if that Russia is winning, we ought to help Germany, and in that way let them kill as many as possible."*

DG: Do you favor Stalin or not?

Soviet Officer Khrushchev: Yes, and no. As I told you, we needed him to win the war against fascist Germany. But now that it is plain and clear we have won the fight against the fascistic Gitlerites; we need a far more liberal, less dictatorial need in the future.

DG: But how can you have a liberal society and still be a communist when the two are contradictory?

Soviet Officer Solzhenitsyn: Exactly! Here is where Comrade Khrushchev's brain ceases.

Soviet Officer Khrushchev: Because in the post-1945 world, there will be no direct, existential threat to our existence anymore. And therefore, the new leader must relax the restrictions against the peasant and the city worker's freedom. He must give the people more freedom in every realm of their lives. No nation in history survives and thrives when its people are prisoners, terrified in every moment of their lives. As I said, that situation can only be morally acceptable when the nation faces annihilation by an enemy, such as the Gitlerites were.

DG: Why? All communist nations are, by definition, dictatorships, and no mass uprisings have ever been reported.

Soviet Officer Khrushchev: I'm talking in the long run.

Soviet Officer Yezhov [Shocked]: How could you be so stupid? You yourself just admitted that fascist capitalist nations of England and America seek our destruction. Don't you understand that they will next turn their attention to our destruction?

Soviet Officer Khrushchev: And I agreed with you! Capitalist nations, by definition, need war to amass profits which is the lifeline of their existence. But that doesn't mean we must continue our stranglehold on the Russian people. Why? Because the existential threat against our nation no longer exists, as it did in 1941. That's why I agree and appreciate Stalin's iron grip on all of us during the thirties and forties. But with Gitler dead, the West can no longer possibly threaten our existence since they will not, nor can they military expand their war against Russia. Therefore, since the scale of the military threat against us considerably diminished post-Gitler, so I know Marxism-Leninism pleads for us communist leaders to allow greater freedom to our brother and sister citizens.

DG: You believe war between us and Russia is inevitable?

Soviet Officer Yezhov: Communist scientific laws dictate that capitalist systems need wars to thrive economically, and that's why, in addition to their colonies, they must still find other battles to fuel their need for profits for their elites.

Soviet Officer Khrushchev: You're right and wrong. Of course, capitalist nations need war. Of course, they want to annihilate us, precisely as Gitler did. But the post-1945 world is a vastly different one from 1939. Meaning, no capitalist superpower will dare to directly attack us as Hitler did because the Soviet Union, thanks to Comrade Stalin, has made us far too strong for any capitalist superpower even to contemplate attacking us.

Soviet Officer Solzhenitsyn: Yes, but if the new post-Stalin leader liberalizes our country, we will still be an authoritarian dictatorship. And I'm telling you, any totalitarian system, Stalinist or otherwise, has only one function, and that is to powder the masses into flecks and crumbs and turn them into robots for the sake of supporting the luxurious lifestyles of the rulers, whoever they may be.

Soviet Officer Khrushchev [To Solzhenitsyn]: Absolutely not! Marxism has only one central theme and ideological goal: to liberate Man from his chains imposed upon him by the elites you talk about.

Soviet Officer Yezhov [Sneering]: One monkey discussing abstract mathematics with one baboon.

Soviet Officer Khrushchev [To Yezhov]: There it is again! Arrogance! And I'm comfortable with this fact, unlike many of my comrades who tear their hair out when confronted by the likes of you. Not I. Because I know your heads will soon be rolling too, just like every criminal extremist, beginning with the French revolution's leadership.

Soviet Officer Solzhenitsyn: Yezhov is a replica of Robespierre and Jean-Paul Marat, and his fate shall hopefully be the same as those French dogs.

Soviet Officer Khrushchev: How true.

Soviet Officer Yezhov [To Solzhenitsyn]: I'm genuinely staggered. You don't have the decency to praise for securing your release?

Soviet Officer Solzhenitsyn: You and genuineness cannot be.

Soviet Officer Yezhov: Why haven't you been shot?

Soviet Officer Solzhenitsyn: You order my rape for over ten years. You then release me not because you felt a flicker of humanity but because the Soviet Union needed soldiers, and you now think I should prostrate myself in thankfulness creatures like you?

Soviet Officer Yezhov [To Solzhenitsyn]: As a matter of fact, that is precisely what you do, fool. Was it not for me, you know you would have died in whatever camp you were in.? I allowed you a second chance to live life.

Soviet Officer Solzhenitsyn: Here, we have the essence of satanism. This black midget believes only he has the right to give life and take away life.

DG: Officer Yezhiv, do you think mass-murdering Russians is the only way to create the ideal, socialist, egalitarian society?

Soviet Officer Yezhov: First, my name is Officer Yezhov, not Yezhiv. Second, ask any surgeon who has to operate on a sick person or his body. What must he initially do? He must remove the cancer or tumor. That is by definition an unpleasant act, a bloody act, but it must be done if the patient is to survive. That is why we communists have no sentimentality when we purge millions of deviationists because it is a necessary procedure that seeks to cleanse the body of Russia.

DG: Officer Yezhov, do you think it is moral for your soldiers to rape German women?

Soviet Officer Yezhov [Laughing]: If a man raped your mother, do you not think that it would be your moral and dutiful right to make mincemeat out that bastard?

DG: Not every German woman raped Russians.

I didn't expect such emotional vehemence from all three Soviet officers on this question of the acts of mass rape committed by Soviet soldiers against German women. I was surprised by the fact that I kind of enjoyed talking to these people. Their manners and facial expressions were all too alien to me. They gesticulated differently from us. Their reactions to words and their interactions with each other did not make sense to me. So when they talk about what I considered a highly emotive subject, they were calm as a breeze but on some trifling subject, why they'd get mad as dogs in heat.

Soviet Officer Khrushchev [Angrily]: What do you talk about, woman? Every German man and woman participated in the mass murder and the mass rape of all European peoples! I may not do it, but I certainly understand what revenge means … You are speaking as someone who comes from the Moon.

Soviet Officer Solzhenitsyn: What would you have wanted us to do with those well-fed, fat German whores? Give them cake?

~

Conversation with Oberscharführer Rochus Misch

V. "War Destroys All That Is Good, Sane, Virtuous, Leaving Only Evil and Insanity."

DG: Can you go into more detail about how SS men search for this someone who has to defend Berlin?

Misch: I haven't been on any of these hunting trips myself, though I've been told how they're done. Search parties go out and drag any healthy-looking fellow back to the Bunker. I say 'drag' for two reasons. One is because there is no time to investigate if the candidate does or does not possess the specific qualities that the Fuehrer requires. Second, since no one wants such a job in the first place, he must be forced back here.

DG: What job?

RM: Mighty defender of Fortress Berlin!

DG: Why is that?

{*Misch laughs*}

RM: Because it is an entirely one-sided, Mickey Mouse slaughterhouse battle. So, then, Burgdorf –

DG: Who's that man?

Misch: You asked me that question!

DG: Did I?

RM: General Wilhelm Burgdorf assumed the role of the Chief of the Army Personnel Office (Heerespersonalamt) and Chief Adjutant to Adolf Hitler since October of 1944. Anyway, *he* was the towering genius who now proposed this supposedly well-qualified man for the job, a lieutenant-colonel called Ernst Kaether.

DG: Who was this man?

{*Misch laughs*}

RM: He was one more unnoticed and anonymous human. I searched for his details. He was a Lieutenant-Colonel (Oberstleutnant), commanding the 14th Infantry Regiment of the 5th Jäger Division. So? And that was supposed to impress us? All we knew was that this man has now officially replaced Lieutenant-General Helmuth Reymann as commander of the Berlin Defense Area. *He* was now in charge of the defenses of the city of Berlin. Kaether had to be personally promoted to Major-General and then Lieutenant-General by the Fuehrer.

DG: Why?

RM: That was the only legal way for him to hold the rank of Defender of Berlin. But then we heard that this unknown human didn't survive one day in his job. Within hours of hearing him being hired, we heard he too was sacked and replaced by another man, this time, General Helmuth Weidling.

DG: Wait ... Why and how was that man hired and fired in one day?

{*Misch laughs*}

RM: We exist in an absurd reality. Didn't I say that?

"A terrified rat will swear to anything."

— Alistair MacLean (1922-87) *River of Death*

DG: No, Officer Misch. I'm serious; now could that happen?

RM: In any intense, prolonged battle, such as we've been experiencing since June of 1941, there comes the point in time when the losing nation must accept that it has lost the war. But if a leader refuses to accede to that truth, that means all meanings have died. Wars don't only kill humans and physically destroy nations – which is the cliché most people use. From sanity to goodness, wars destroy everything – everything positive is drenched off and out from existence. What you have left is evil. That's it.

DG: What's all this philosophizing when I asked you a simple question?

RM: Please try to understand our reality, as insane as it is, from our eyes. Can't you do that for a moment while you ask me questions? I've told you many times, stop seeing our reality from your eyes. Otherwise, you'll never understand our language because language is not just knowing the same grammar and vocabulary. Language is also knowing the feelings, intentions, and motivations of the speaker.

DG: If you say so.

RM: I say so.

{Silence}

RM: How can we know of anything but that which exists before us? We can only speculate, like the imprisoned cave-dwellers of Plato. But if we wanted to find a concrete reality, well, that's not meant for us. It cannot be. Not in this lifetime anyway. And here's the most crucial point here.

DG: I've no idea what you're talking about.

RM: I'm saying no Man can see the totality of reality. Is that understandable?

DG: Yes. But I presume the leaders like the presidents, prime ministers, and your Fuehrer have a kind of eagle's eye view of what's going on, right?

RM: I cannot speak for our enemies. I will confirm the Fuehrer has no idea what's happening in Germany, and the reason is simple. The man has a million advisors, and each advisor sees the reality through their slanted, narrow viewpoint. That's what Hitler collectively hears and sees. Assuming he's even listening to everyone reporting to him on the situation on the ground, which I doubt, you will see that what he hears and sees are so many distortions -

DG: That Jackson Pollock!

RM: Excuse me?

DG: I don't understand. Why do you think Hitler doesn't read every report?

{Silence}

RM: He's never been interested in details. I can only offer you my truth. My reality of Adolf Hitler, from my restricted viewpoint. He cannot, or at least I've never seen him read through any document that's more than twenty or more pages long. That's why he sees the truth through distorted lenses.

DG: I find your words hard to digest because from 1939 till late 1941, your leader was impeccably successful in his military adventures.

RM: Those years had different circumstances. The nations facing us during those years were weak. It wasn't so much we won every battle, as our enemies were wholly unprepared to fight in any adequately organized manner. The first time Hitler came face to face with an enemy that wasn't only his equal, but his superior was Herr Stalin. The genius, Stalin. Hitler himself knew not only had he met his match, but worse, he knew he'd finally been entirely outmatched in every aspect of warfare.

{Silence}

DG: You're right. Stalin was the first to eradicate Hitler.

RM: Obviously, Hitler couldn't accept that.

DG: But surely with ... or by ... after Stalingrad, he must've realized the colossal might of the Soviet Union.

RM: True, but he vacillated. Maybe as early as the failure of our campaign in 1941, he must have understood just how much he underestimated the 'inferior' Slavs under the direction of Stalin. And I mention Stalin again because, without that genius of a man, the Soviet army would have collapsed in a matter of weeks. And by 1944, I'd say the man finally conceded Stalin had created a new class of Slab warriors, superior in every sense to us Master Race Germans. He accepted the risk that the French could potentially defeat him, the British, or the Americans since they were a superior race. But to be beaten by the second-lowest scum of the earth race, how do you think that made him feel?

DG: Who's the first lowest scum of the earth race?

RM: Jews. Hitler was globally ridiculed when he failed in Russia because the supposedly stupid, primitive Slavs had destroyed us Herrenvolk. It not only staggered him, but it also embarrassed him.

DG [Laughing]: The Untermenschen crushed the Ubermenschen!

RM: And of course, it made every one of us National National question the most fundamental premises of our ideology. We got it wrong.

DG: The "it" you got "wrong" physically annihilated your nation and people.

RM: Or Hitler got it wrong.

DG: When did the SS know the war was lost?

RM: After Stalingrad.

DG: Let's go back to our topic of who was supposed to be defending Berlin?

RM [Laughing]: You do like hopping from subject to subject ... Anyway, apparently, Kaether displeased the Fuehrer with some embarrassing faux pas. Perhaps he may have been too daunted by the role expected of him. I cannot say. No one knows the truth. But none of these trivialities matter. You concentrate far too much on the frail trees rather than the haunted woods.

DG: So, what happened next?

RM: This time, the Fuehrer himself proposed appointing General Helmuth Weidling, the LVI Panzer Corps commander. Everyone was shocked because there was a tiny problem.

DG: What was that?

RM [Laughing]: The Fuehrer was tactfully reminded that the gentleman in question had been condemned to death. "By who?" Hitler queried the matter, whereupon he was politely told, "By yourself, Mein Fuehrer." I think Hitler himself smiled at the absurdity of that story.

DG: Was he executed? Was he already dead?

{*Misch laughs*}

RM: Apparently, he deserted us. Or so the Fuehrer heard. And that's why he issued an order to have him liquidated. And yet, somehow, no, he was not killed. He's alive.

DG: You guys didn't have time to kill him?

RM: I suppose that must've been the case. It's odd because, especially in the SS, executions occur immediately once someone is ordered unto death. So, how that man survived for so many hours or days, I don't know. Anyway, I thought, here we go again. Once more, the Fuehrer and his staff must now seek another candidate! Then, out of the blue, the same man, Weidling, appeared right here in the Bunker!

DG: *The* condemned man?

RM: Yes!

{Misch laughs}

RM: Well, we thought, this man must be one of those laughing lunatics you see, a soldier who's seen too much. Maybe he endured one too many battles, you know. Or maybe, he was drunk? One officer insisted the man came here for the honor of having the Fuehrer place his neck on the chopping block. Many believed such a man like this Weidling surely should be reprieved given his incredible bravery. After all, he chose to walk straight into the belly of the beast, as far as he would be concerned.

DG: Did you find out why he came here?

Misch: Weidling had indeed come back protesting his innocence. And no, he wasn't a lunatic nor a drunkard. Next thing we see, stiff as steel, he walked straight into the Fuehrer's chamber. And then, the Fuehrer declares his unshakeable faith in that man's integrity.

{Misch laughs}

DG: Did that mean those officers or whoever condemned him to death had misjudged him?

RM: Who knows? Maybe he committed treason. Maybe he didn't. In any case, the Fuehrer forgave him. Maybe the Fuehrer found the very act of daring to come back, protesting his innocence was enough to validate him for the job. As for those who initially condemned him to death, either it was all a misunderstanding, or the man who condemned him to death did because they had it in for him, Weidling, I mean.

DG: I'm confused. Was he guilty of treason or –

RM: That question no longer existed. Remember when I told you, "You concentrate far too much on the frail trees rather than the haunted woods"?

{*Silence*}

RM: The matter of him being treasonous or not had evaporated. And so, he was now warmly received. His foolhardy act rendered his impending rendezvous with death to be duly cancelled.

"The peoples of Islam will always be closer to us than, for example, France."

- Adolf Hitler [2 April 1945]

DG: The Fuehrer appointed him to conduct the defence of Berlin?

RM: Yes. And he's still in charge, as we speak.

∼

My First Battle Wound – The Horrific & Absurd Existence of the Anonymous Katharina Esser

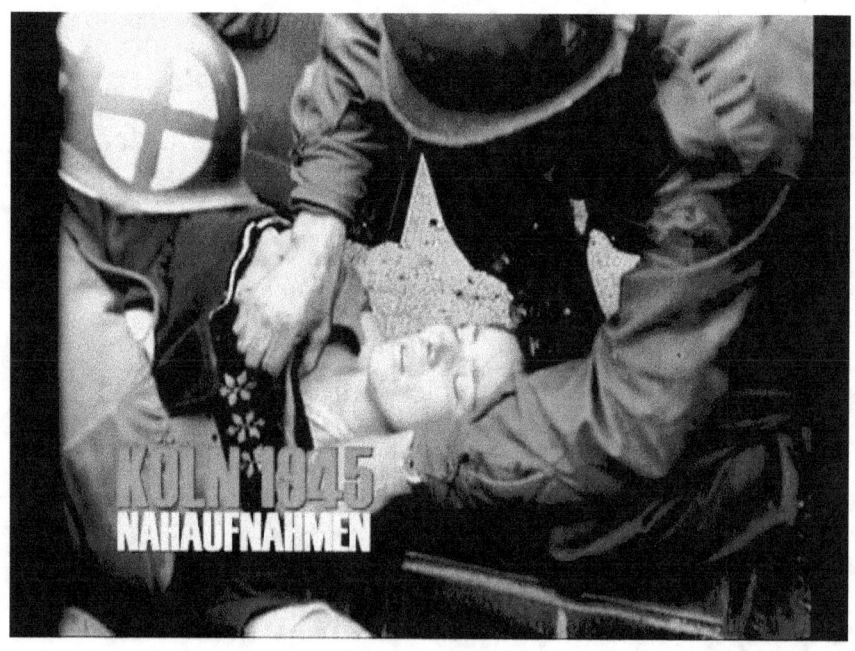

Katharina Esser

I had to see live combat. I had to get out. That's reality, reflecting my nature. Or my nature needing reality. Whatever. That's why I hated rural Kansas. There's nothing to do. Caged animals in zoos had more entertainment seeing amused people walking by. Because there were so few people. We didn't even have that. Actually, we didn't have a zoo. So, I'm just imagining all this up. How stupid. How can a tinsy town of some few thousand have a zoo? I know 'tinsy' isn't a proper word. I made it. I like it. It stuck. Anyway, the point is being caged in Goodland kills your mind. Goodland is my village, in case you forgot.

I was in the most famous city in the world or what once was the most famous city in the world. I couldn't just sit there doing nothing, especially since His Royal Highness had still not yet invited me to do my job, interviewing him. But at the same time, going out was a dangerous matter, even during quiet hours. I was told a million times, you never know when the lull would be shredded and battle resumes.

But none of that gibberish meant anything to me. Shred this, shred that! How can I be in a war zone and return to Kansas and tell people I never saw the war? When I spoke to Fegelein, he sharply rebuked me, saying —

Fegelein [Sternly]: "My order from the Fuehrer is to protect you! Should I see you trying to get out, I'll have you shot!"

DG [Laughing]: So to protect me, you'd kill me!

Never mind his stupid contradictory words, I was determined to go outside. And being huffy, I'd double down, going out when the battle resumed. That way, I thought, any interest in my existence lessens since every officer's main concern would be about the battle. And who best would accompany me? What do you think?

Misch, of course, my favorite!

So, up those stairs, right bang in the middle of the screams of battle, we trudged. Passion screamed, 'Dorothy! You've got to witness a battle in action and not just Berlin in its quiet hours!' Reason screamed, "You're nuts, and you'll either die in a nuthouse!" I knew which part of my mind was right.

Your plucky Kansas maiden girl took a deep breath as she viewed the panorama surrounding her. Surveying alien wonders and demons of every emotion. This was a full-scale raging battle. At first, it's everything you expect. Shrieking and acrid smells. Clang, boom, stench, clank, and shrieks!

I was on some street. Constant exchange of fire between Germans and Russians. Russians blasting machine guns and grenades at Germans and the latter doing the same at the former. Mind you, though, I couldn't see any of them: meaning, soldiers. I laughed, you know. It seemed childish as boys on opposite sides were firing at each other, waiting until the last man survives. Anyway, you soon get used to sounds and smoke. See, because the intensity of the shrieking metal clanging and explosions and buildings crashing down varies. When it declines and suddenly ratchets up again, it'll still hurt your ears, ribs, and skull. And it's challenging to think for more than a few seconds. Because the sounds and threat of being shot derails your concentration. It's like a lion chasing you while you're running, trying to think of a loved one. I know that's a dumb analogy because the lion outruns Man, but forget it.

I thought, what are we doing – I mean we Germans – firing when you can't see the enemy? But firing on, they did. Again I laughed. Misch was looking at me with surprise. It was funny. Just fire your weapons blindly, hoping you're going to win the battle. And then the war. So, war is really blind! Maybe Misch thought I'm unhinged. Who cares? But then, how do soldiers 'know' when they 'win' in this blind game'? Presumably, if the enemy stops firing back at you, right? But what if the enemy plays dead? My brain was whirling with these silly questions while I – a spectator - had no answers.

Suddenly, something momentous occurred.

I can say this with confidence because my detachment of German officers blanched at seeing this scene. From nowhere, we see a car, a civilian car, driving ... presumably trying to cross the road to get to the other side of the street in question. Now, if that didn't shock you, I guess you ought to reread that sentence. A civilian car! Who the hell on earth drives in the middle of an ongoing ferociously lethal battle?

I hear shouts of anger and laughter from my officers, *"What the hell is that?" "Who's driving?" 'What a maniac!"*

Someone from the German side or the Russian side chose to target the car itself. Within seconds it was punctured and riddled with hundreds of bullets. It looked to me like a re-enactment of Bonnie and Clyde; are these people nuts? Did they think they were seriously going to pass through scatheless amid a raging life-or-death battle?

The flaccid car swerved sharply and speedily, plowing headlong into a tall, sturdy-looking lamp post. Well, that lamp post defended its existence all right since the offending vehicle was crushed.

In the next second, two passengers hobbled out, a man and a woman. The male looked like he was in his forties, while the female looked my age, not more than twenty years old. The man dithered for a second or two, rapidly falling to the ground. He seemed dead. The female did not seem able to walk. Soon, she too plops down to the shattered ground. Let me correct myself here. The woman did not even have the energy to get herself, her entire body, out from the crumpled car.

As far as I could tell, the man was dead. I'm sorry, I just said that. I glanced at him and forgot I had already registered him in my mind as dead because not much of his earthly body was free from bullets and shrapnel gashes. That's why when I caught sight of him again; it was too obvious he was dead as the dead can be dead.

Anyway, my passion was far more aroused with that beautiful woman rather than the male driver, no matter how tragic his situation was. The girl was alive. I knew. That spurted the velocity of my blood circulation a million times faster.

We can rescue her! *"My God, she is alive!"* - my mind screamed; remember Dr. Frankenstein's monster?

I could see her lying on her back, with her eyes still open. I shouted at Misch - you must shout in a battle if you want your voice to be heard -

DG [Frantic]: Do something! Help her!

Misch [Shocked]: Are you serious? You want me to walk into that hell?

As soon as he said that, I realized the idiocy of that question. I hated him at that moment. He was a coward. He couldn't even save a German women's life. Oh no, he was far worse than a coward. Only concerned for his safety. So much for SS bravery. Suddenly, out of nowhere, my lips screamed at Misch:

DG [Screaming]: Bastards! You're all bastards! Aren't *you* the SS? Help her! Do something, cowards!

I don't know why I said and thought those things. Poor Misch. Don't ask me … Nerves sizzling. Raging sorrow – not at poor Misch … well, yes at him too but at *my* helplessness in helping that beautiful, wounded, and stranded girl. That is a jolly word there. Helplessness.

I cannot tell you what elemental, primordial terrorising grievousness I felt being in that criminal situation. I say 'criminal' because that's how I felt. By not helping that beatific-looking girl, I knew I was a criminal. Or worse. No, that's wrong. Criminals don't care for their foul deeds. What the hell am I talking about? Didn't those moronic soldiers realize they had to cease their hatred, forget the silly war for a moment, and stop firing and help the poor, abandoned, and forlorn girl?

There she lay. Dying on a road or street, or whatever it was. Anyway, who cared what it is or was anyway? I'm sure before the war, it must've been a posh, elegant street lined up with high-class people and boutiques, restaurants, and the choicest, chic cafes.

Well, forget all that because it was now shrouded in the excrement of war. And damn it, there were no living human beings that I could see, except for that dying woman.

Suddenly, unexpectedly, the shrieking screams of war flew away, sky-high where they should forever be. My dream was realized, though I didn't even pray. Rest and heavenly silence returned upon our afflicted and malodorous scene.

With no firing of guns, I heard human voices. Shouts coming out from the nooks and crannies. Soldiers were talking!. I listened to our — or the German boys — asking for a truce to help the abandoned girl. They seemed concerned for her life. Or is that what I wanted to hear? I heard Russians shouting back.

"Even in art, there is no light without shadows, and no shadows are cast without some light. Even the shadow of Adolf Hitler is accompanied by some light."

- Hans Frank. To Leon Goldensohn, July 20, 1946, from "The Nuremberg Interviews"

Did humanity of these soldiers sprout out from nowhere? I wonder. It made me rethink my opinion on Man. Yes, Man does have some 'humanity' in him; otherwise, you'd never be able to stop the two of them from killing each other. That lonesome girl stopped the fury of an entire battle. She was a dying peacemaker. But at least, she achieved that truce – albeit a temporary one.

That had to be the truth. I comforted my dazed mind. Within moments I saw several German soldiers and *astonishingly* Russian soldiers appear from oblivion and heading straight for my angel. My heart must have missed a beat. How did these two sides walk calmly towards that woman, seemingly no longer fearing nor seeking to kill each other? Wasn't this scene reminiscent of the Christmas Truce of 1914? What joy! Oh, the humanity, I felt electric sparkles in my nerves!

On the Kahlenberg

Almighty One
In the woods
I am blessed.
Happy every one
In the woods.
Every tree speaks
Through Thee.

O, God!
What glory in the
Woodland.
On the Heights
is Peace,—
Peace to serve
Him—

- Beethoven - September 1812

I forgot that evocative scene. My heart bled for that woman. I adopted her. She was my twin. I know this sounds crazy, but I'm mad, remember? So you cannot blame me for being who I am. Meanwhile, thinking of this, I fell in love with her.

Mindlessly I too walked with the German soldiers, startling Misch, who screamed at me to come back. Yours truly ignored Misch. I continued my path unto my beatific archangel. I forgot it was his duty to protect me. I didn't care. For the first time in my life, I was honoured being in her sacral presence. Our imaginary church.

Finally, I was staring at her, close-up. Mixtures of speaking and shouting German and Russian soldiers. Slim, petite, about five feet three. And her face. Before me sprawled, bleeding, was Inanna, Aphrodite, Ishtar, and Venus blended. I could not look directly at the gaping holes on her body. I knew they were there.

"Help her! Help her! I beg of you! God! Where are you?"

I noticed more things I got wrong. She wasn't lying on her back. She was lying sideways on her shoulder. And she was right next to the damaged car. Her legs somehow got themselves under the car. *"Who are you?"* I screamed. *"What's your name? ... Speak, girl! ...I will help you .... Don't die!"*

By now, medics had arrived. Soldiers on both sides casually threw away the mangled, dismembered corpses to their respective lines. As for the wounded, they gently carried them to their sides. And, of course, the medics were trying to save her life. But I wasn't interested in them.

Her face turned paler and bluish. Staring into ice-blue irises. I had revitalizing energy. For her. I knew at that specific moment in time and history my destiny. I understood my presence would save her from clutches of death. Staring intensely inside her dimming pupils. But I'll drill on inside her no matter because that's the only way I'm going to resurrect her. I noted her black holes diminishing in size. Drowsy eyes. Was she, too, seeing me? Could she? 'Black holes' meaning her pupils. I was awash with idiocies.

DG [Frantic]: Beautiful lady! Give me the life of yours. Because yours is diminishing. Only then can you live off me! Can even you hear of my presence? Is there anyone out there? If so, wink a word, girl ... the medics are just coming now!

I was lying through my teeth. I had no idea what would happen to that angel. The next thing I remember, I swear I think she nodded; and out of the blue, unexpectedly mumbling words -

Katharina Esser [Hoarse]: I'm alive? ... Too close ... I'm as death become ... As humans are ...

DG [Frantic]: No, no, you're not dead! What's your name?

Katharina Esser [Faint Smile]: Is ... important? Katharine Esser. German.

Flickering eyelids. Glazing eyeball. Fading iris. She couldn't maintain her eyelids from their need to shut down the pointless theater of her brief life.

I cradled her. I had no idea if she was going to live or die.

"I want nothing but death."

Jane Austen to her sister Cassandra on her deathbed.

I wasn't examining her wounds. Looking back now, it should've been clear to me she had no hope of being alive for more than minutes. But I didn't want to think back then.

DG [In Tears]: You're fine. Why ... why you driving in battle zone?

I thought if I constricted my words to a minimum number of words, it would be easier for her to understand me.

Katharina Esser [Faint Smile]: Fiancée.

I felt guilty talking to her because I knew ... I felt the strain, the pain required for her to speak. Her eyes lazily unexpectedly moved towards my eyes. Did she see me? Did she fancy me?

Then just as slowly, her eyes in an idiotic kind of jerking movement swiveled towards the skies above us.

I was furious.

Fiancée?

You wanted to see your *damned fiancé?* What size of a brain do you have, woman? *Why on earth and in death land would you fancy hooking up with your fiancé when you're in a war zone?*

I snapped out from those gushing words or thoughts or whatever, and my affection returned, and tenderly I asked her -

DG [In Tears]: Where's ... your family, honey?

Katharina Esser [Faint Smile]: I do ... know. Maybe ...

I wept uncontrollably. She couldn't talk properly. And I was asking her questions. Gurgling and foaming out blood and other liquids from her mouth. Meaning I was forcing her to answer in her dying moments. I peeked at one gash on her chest. I noticed soldiers stopped talking. Why was that?

Katharina Esser [Faint Smile]: Woman, why weep?

{Silence}

DG [Startled in Tears]: You're an angel! Why did you do this?

{Silence}

Katharina Esser [Faint Smile]: *Weep not for me ... but you ...*

{Silence}

Katharina Esser [Faint]: Weep for Humanity. Behold!

{Silence}

Katharina Esser [Drowsy]: Days a-coming ... in ... [Weakly] *Say, "Bless the Barren!"*

{Silence}

Katharina Esser [Faintly]: *Blessed ... Wombs ... never bore! {Silence}* [Hushed] *Blessed... Breasts ... never gave suck."*

She ceased speaking. I recognised her spirit commended her sacral self to the heavens and unto God. I recognised death. Eyes glazed. Skinny rubbery coating covering them. Eyes of death.

Intense staring at my beloved while soldiers speak frantically. Their respect was dead as my dearly beloved. And then, silence.

I understood we happened to be standing on Gladbacher Strasse. I looked at the driver of the car - a repulsive-looking corpse. Spindly, shredded legs firmly outside. Shredded remains of humans surrounded us. German medics walk away. A mad butcher haphazardly threw his chops of meat. Except, of course, butcher's meat is bloodless, clean, and cut in straight lines. These jagged chunks of flesh came in different shapes and sizes. And these chunky pieces of beef were not all white or pink — they were already bluish, black. For no reason, one German soldier speaks to me —

"Come on; we've got to get back."

I felt a murderous rage to kill the soldier. "You want me to forsake this angel? Never!" I shouted. Misch interjected, "Frau Gale, they're going to fire back ... back at each other ... you've *got* to come back!" To which, I screamed, "I'll never abandon a wounded woman!" Some German soldiers laughed; others said words to the effect, "She's a lunatic!"

"Leave her; she's with us!" screamed back Misch. I couldn't even see him. I didn't expect he would defend me so forthrightly! The Germans seemed puzzled. "What's this about?" someone said. I thought of nothing at that moment. I was frozen, intensely cradling crucified Mother Mary. Immediately, the Germans backed down from mocking me or

questioning my lunacy when they saw Misch's SS rank. Quietly, they turned around and ran back to the German lines. So, too, did the Russians scatter back to wherever their lines were. Then, hurriedly, Misch said, "The man is right, Frau Gale, we've *got* to go, and now!" As I walked back, I noticed two soldiers, ironically enough one Nazi, one Soviet, grabbing Katharina from both ends and gently laying her on the side rubble.

I understood battle was soon to resume.

My brief Rendezvous with Death was over.

I Have a Rendezvous with Death

ALAN SEEGER – 1917

I have a rendezvous with Death
At some disputed barricade,
When Spring comes back with rustling shade
And apple-blossoms fill the air—
I have a rendezvous with Death
When Spring brings back blue days and fair.

It may be he shall take my hand
And lead me into his dark land

And close my eyes and quench my breath—
It may be I shall pass him still.
I have a rendezvous with Death
On some scarred slope of battered hill,
When Spring comes round again this year
And the first meadow-flowers appear.

God knows 'twere better to be deep
Pillowed in silk and scented down,
Where Love throbs out in blissful sleep,
Pulse nigh to pulse, and breath to breath,
Where hushed awakenings are dear ...
But I've a rendezvous with Death
At midnight in some flaming town,
When Spring trips north again this year,
And I to my pledged word am true,
I shall not fail that rendezvous.

I was one more brick. Endless wall in a factory. Mass-producing dead **human bricks.** I'm organized; I'm manufactured by 'my' society to do the same routinized robotic work. And it doesn't matter what job you do. We're still in the same category – bricks. You may have an office job; you may work in a department store, a restaurant, or a corporation. All of us are the same. We're all a mass of nothing people. We're one mass that's genuinely **and equally nondescript, faceless individuals** with no spines, no lives, no expectations. There's no future in our dreaming. How can unliving people dream?

Time, of course, passes with or without our consent. Remembrance is time's tax bill. Fleeting in and out of awareness. Being aware of this or that scene. Forgetting this or that memory. Remembering a conversation differently from how you remembered it yesterday. Noticing a staring pair of eyes. A figure gestures. Grimaces of faces making me feel awkward. Forgetting people I had numerous interactions with. I care about a person, and the next moment I don't. I start sobbing again. Floating brain. All together now. I feel sad. I feel remorse—collusions between feelings. And thinking and believing I'm just a spectator. Not an acting agent. No individual. No self. No 'I.' But relative to everyone else, I'm their object. A nobody. Yet, to keep your sanity intact, it's from these shards of emotions, experiences, visions, thoughts, you've got to paint a credible reality that faces your face on a daily basis.

A person walks by me. I'm nobody to them. Russian soldier laughingly shouts, *"Vojna Kaput dlya etoy devushki!"* ["War is over for this girl!"]. He's pointing to a dead German teen. A German soldier nodded though in somber agreement. Sobbing turns to loud crying. Misch intervenes, gently pressing my shoulder, indicating which direction I should go. Because I'm a rambler by nature, taking no heed of dangers. I guess. For the first time, he raises his voice, "Did you think war is a picnic?"

My gaze changed not. What a fool. There she lay, presumably dead. Maybe she was still breathing? Did she actually see me? Was she conscious? She was conscious. She was speaking words, wasn't she? But wait, you could still be unconscious even if you speak words, like a sleepwalker. I glanced back to get one more look. She seemed crumpled, contorted much more than before. She joined the rest of the wonderfully exhibited array of disfigured corpses. At least she was intact. That was good. Not scattered lumps of flesh. By now, Misch was carrying me.

How dare any human amputate us from each other? Idiots. Catholics don't divorce. But I abandoned her. I think she's killed. I mean, I think she was killed. But if we bastards ardently, willing betray the dead, what care can we expect of Man to have for the living? Years later, I wondered how beautifully noble it was for Misch to physically carry me, running right through bursting fires, acrid smoke, unexpected explosions, swinging bullets, startling grenades, through masses of steely, knife-like, jagged rubble, wreckage and right back to the safety of the Bunker without halting once to catch his breath. I admit I didn't think once for his heroic deed at that hour. That was because of my love for Katharina.

~

Conversations with Gruppenführer Fegelein

I. Fegelein: "Nazi Germany Is Structured on Sand, Thanks to the Fuehrer's Disinterestedness in Governing."

Gruppenführer Hermann Fegelein

I pretended nothing happened. That's how I was back in Kansas. Seeing Daddy whipped like a dying horse, I'd never cry. When alone at night, I'd liberate feelings out. Feeling magically freeing every caged animal from my soul.

DG: How many men are now defending the city itself?

HF [Shocked]: Are you sure you want to talk?

DG [Laughing]: Please, I'm a sturdy cowgirl, rough as a bull!

HF: General Weidling has around 85,000 men, although half of this number are old men or young teens. All entirely untrained.

DG: How many Russians are out there?

HF: Around 1.8 million men.

{*Fegelein Laughs*}

DG [Shocked]: Are you serious?

HF: Why do you ask such detailed military questions?

DG: But that's why I'm here; what did you expect? Asking you about your last supper?

HF: Many Bunker characters despise you.

DG: Well, your Fuehrer ordered my protection –

HF: No, I know that Frau Gale; remember I'm the one who escorted you from the west to the Bunker? I'm just telling you -

DG [Curtly]: All right, I understand. Now all this sounds as shoddy as management gets.

HF: What does?

DG: I mean the process of defending Berlin. It sounds too comical to be true!

HF: And who's disagreeing? I'm sure Misch explained how most of our communications have broken down, a direct consequence of not having contact with other units and generals. Well, let this be one more experience tasting the ongoing chaos and confusion you seek to understand!

DG: I'm getting the impression the entire structure of the Wehrmacht is absurdly gargantuan; is that the problem?

HF: "Getting the impression?" This has been the most sickly, destructive factor in National Socialist Germany! Here in the great land of National Socialist Germany, you see the egotistic, self-interested existence of thousands of entirely independent ministries, sections, departments, sub-sections, mini-sections, chambers, offices, sub-chambers, mini-chambers, offices within offices, sub-mini rooms, sub-departments, mini-departments. The list is so long, and no one bothers to check if some of these sub-mini ministries even exist or not. I underscore the word 'independent.'

DG: Well, why not?

HF: You mean why no one bothers these days?

DG: Yes.

HF: Because the war is lost.

DG: But your Fuehrer –

HF: My dear, why bother or care to find out anything that is by definition functionless and therefore meaningless?

DG: What about in your better years?

HF: Back then, Germany was just as divided into multiple regions and departments controlled by mini-Fuehrers, or Gauleiters. But even then, in the good years, so to speak, instead of each Gauleiter working to develop his territory, these men primarily spent their entire time enriching themselves or fighting against each other.

DG: Why?

HF: Assorted reasons. Some sought to destroy the influence and the reputation of others. Some sought to enhance their power. Others worked as Gauleiters because they genuinely disliked other Gauleiters. What mattered was that these independent ministers' overall result was a continual infighting state between each other. That senile situation creates black holes of idiocies inviting the kings and queens of chaos to reign. No orders are implemented. And why should they bother? They were, as I said, Little Hitler's reigning in their specific territories and people therein. And then there were smaller, mini-Little Hitler's, such as the person next in command to the Gauleiter who would be the *Stellvertreter-Gauleiter* (Deputy Gau Leader). Below him are the district leaders (*kreisleiter*), who direct the chapter leaders (*Ortsgruppenleiter*).

"Following a meeting with Hitler, Cardinal Michael von Faulhaber, a man who had 'courageously criticized the Nazi attacks on the Catholic Church' - *went away convinced that Hitler was deeply religious.*"

— Ian Kershaw - Hitler

DG: And, I guess, they fought against each other for power?

HF: Power, prestige, money, and influence. This situation became worse after Stalingrad.

DG: Why is that?

"I use emotion for the many and reserve reason for the few."
— Adolf Hitler

HF: Because the Fuehrer's authority, credibility cracked. And after the Normandy invasion succeeded, most Gau leaders solely fought against each other to enhance their image to curry favors with London and Washington, fearing being categorized as War Criminals. Not that Hitler cared.

DG: And where did that leave the civilian population?

HF: Well, the question should be, where did that leave the civilian population and all the actual fighting military personnel? The answer, quite simply, is more chaos. Orders were either ignored or revoked, with the result nothing happened. Or conflicting orders were sent to two units from the same division, and no one knew how such idiotic orders could even be sent out to them in the first place. Incomprehensible orders were written. Illiterate generals. And it was up to each commander to decipher what was being asked of his men to do. Take Goering or Udet. Yes, they were aces back in the ancient First World War. But, after 1918, did they keep up with the rapidly improving Luftwaffe technology? No, they didn't. They had nothing to do with the airforce industry until Hitler appointed them. So, you have someone like Goering, whose military knowledge dates back to 1918. As for waging modern war, he knows nothing about the new fleet of planes. More importantly, he knows nothing about modern airforce strategies and battle tactics. Honestly, one day after this war is over, I must sit and write on these attributes of Germany's persistent madness if I survive. Because everyone thinks we Germans and Hitler created this massively disciplined war machine. And false is that! That's what I want people to know. Nothing else, but on this subject of the rigid anarchy throughout National Socialist Germany. I know people will say, 'Fegelein only writes fiction!' I know not many will understand, much less believe my words. Us actors are fated to ashes. When future generations forget us, so we will no longer exist. Isn't that another mystically odd phenomenon of life?

DG: I haven't an idea what you are saying.

HF: Don't worry. Nothing makes sense. During the end of the Great War, everyone screamed, '*Never forget the Glorious Dead!*' But we forgot them, The Glorious Dead. On November 12th, 1918, they were deleted from our minds. Come to this next world war, who among our soldiers knows anything of the First World War? No one. So, the cycle of history tumbles on. What a scene! What an entirely Man-made scene, is it not? And then we plead, '*Where is God?*' Is that the question? *Where is Man?* No one bothers to watch the play. No matter how graphically gruesome the game is. No one is interested. That's the truth, I tell you. Apart from those who lived during the Great War, no one is interested in them. You have a handful of scholars who are interested in that war. But 99% of Germans forgot about our Great War. No lessons are learned.

I wasn't interested in what he was rambling on but pretended to be.

DG: How did National Socialist Germany fight a global war, given such an anarchic infrastructure?

HF: Now that is the *real* miracle of Adolf Hitler and National Socialism!

DG: How did he do it?

HF: In a word, charisma. His personality. And don't ask how he works his overwhelming charisma on us all. I mean, you've seen him, so you'd know.

DG: Actually, I've yet to see him, let alone interview the man.

HF: Really? I'll speak to the Fuehrer on this matter.

DG: And talking of the man, Hitler, where does he fit in all this disorganization?

HF: Nowhere. He just lets them go on, in or out. This is either because he is unaware of their existence or because he is indifferent. He's an artist by nature, you know. A bohemian. Hates timetables, getting involved in tedious squabbles. He can't stand certain subjects, like economics. Certainly, he gives broad outlines of what he needs to be done, and the rest go and do what they think will please the man. But does the check on anyone or any project? Unless if there's a crisis, Hitler never does anything in German politics. He loves building, you know ... architectural projects. In that matter, he does get excited and involves himself, though even there, it isn't full-time. The whole governmental machinery runs on its own, as I told you. By the way, these infighting and inter-part squabbles run everywhere, not just in the lower echelons of the governmental institutions.

DG: Can you explain?

HF: So far, I haven't given you one specific example. Now I will oblige you. A simple though important example concerning two of Germany's most powerful men. Goebbels has his cronies with their departments, divisions, and ministries. Goering also has his cronies in their departments, divisions, and ministries. Now, what happens? Both Goebbels' men and Goering's men fight against each other when it suits them. But if they find common ground against someone else, say, Himmler, they will temporarily unite to declaw any measure or order Himmler wishes to undertake. And the next month, you see a Goebbels-Himmler alliance countermanding anything Goering seeks to do. And so, this idiotic zero-sum game goes on. Honestly, as a soldier, I say the only gravitational force keeping all these independent elements, ministries, and individuals from exploding is Hitler's personality. That's why he's undoubtedly an uber-genius! And I don't know how he does it. Charisma can only go so far, you know. And obviously, he is magnetic. But across thousands of cities to thousands of hamlets – how can one man's character grip everyone's love, passion, and zeal for him? How has he so successfully kept a nation of eighty million Germans loyal till these final hours – how?

DG [Smiling]: Sounds like you're planning to escape?

HF: Usually, a population turns against its leaders once they sense they're losing a war, and the defeated nation in question collapses. I still don't have any idea or any understanding of how the Third Reich ever managed to last twelve years, and especially the last six years. That must be understood, and I intend to study this absurd situation after the war.

DG: I agree with you because I too don't understand how he's blinded your people, specifically given the mass atrocities you've perpetrated -

"I don't see much future for the Americans ... it's a decayed country. And they have their racial problem, and the problem of social inequalities ... my feelings against Americanism are feelings of hatred and deep repugnance ... everything about the behavior of American society reveals that *it's half Judaised, and the other half Negrified.* How can one expect a State like that to hold together?"

— Adolf Hitler, Hitler's Secret Conversations, 1941-1944

HF: Remember, I'm one individual. How can I see the entire Wehrmacht from the eagle eye viewpoint? I don't know. I cannot understand.

{*Fegelein Laughs*}

HF: Look at Russia. How did we go there?

DG: What do you mean?

HF: We went in that campaign undermanned and understaffed. We had no reserves. We went in without enough food, without enough weapons, without enough clothes, without enough transportation, without enough fuel, without enough spare parts, and with absolutely no intelligence on anything about the enemy. Their weapons proved to be superior to our weapons. I need only mention the T-34 and the AK-47 Kalashnikov, while we had nothing comparable. Our industries never produced as much as Stalin produced. And yet, we still thought we would win the war in two months. I heard Misch telling you something clever. He said you could only understand your enemy if you look at his world from his viewpoint. And that is precisely the truth. And that's exactly what we Germans did *not* do. On the opposite, given our racial theories, we ignored the Soviet perspective because we 'knew' they were idiots while blindly assuming, planning, and managing every move based entirely on our false assumptions. And that's why we lost battle after battle.

DG: Yes, he did say that.

HF: Now think back to the Great War. What happened there? We crushed Czarist Russia in that war. Today, as you talk to top leaders or generals, they provide you with excuses. They tell you we lost Russia because we were outnumbered. They inform you we lost Russia because of the temperature. We lost because of Adolf Hitler. And so on. But excuse me, I'm no genius as they are, nor am I from an aristocratic background. But didn't Russia have so many more men than we fielded back in the 1914-17 years? Yes, they did. And didn't Russia have the same climate back in 1914-17? Yes, she did.

DG: I'm not sure I understand you ... So why did Germany lose against Stalin?

HF: By not looking at the war from Stalin's eyes, naturally, we underestimated his colossal genius in transforming a pitifully weak nation to the strongest nation on earth, apart from the US. And, in many ways, who could have believed what that Georgian achieved? In ten years, 1929-39, he industrialized a nation with no electricity, no steel production, no arms industry – a country dependent only on the wooden plow, with no agricultural machines into, as I just said, into a global power. So, perhaps one cannot be too harsh in faulting our leadership because nobody, not in Germany, not in London, and not even in Washington, gave Russia any chance of success when we launched Barbarossa.

∼

II. Dorothy to Fegelein - "So Who Is Defending Berlin Now and with What?"

DG: Going back to finding someone to defend Berlin, undoubtedly, the Fuehrer must have already had a list of qualified, suitable men instead of having to go in the streets searching for someone that suited his requirements?

HF: Ha! If only that were true!

DG: What?

HF: Well, actually, it was true. But time and again, these listed names failed abjectly in the eyes of the Fuehrer, so he felt he had to dispense with them, one by one.

DG: Are you saying most of the top German generals are no longer available?

HF: That is correct. The point for us here is nowhere near the point in the US or the West. That is the point.

DG [Laughing]: What?

HF [Laughing]: Our world is incomprehensible to you in America or England. I know that because you and your people live in circumstances that are entirely different from our circumstances. Hence, that is why our reality in Nazi Germany is completely different from the reality that exists in England and America.

DG [Excited]: And that is precisely what I do not and *will* not understand. *Reality is the same, no matter where it is!*

HF [Laughing]: And *I am telling you reality is dependent on its specific circumstances in question!*

DG: The problem I have with your argument is this; when anyone starts telling me their reality is different from my reality, I know you're what you guys are doing. You're deliberately slipping me in a crucially important concept, and that is morality.

HF: I suppose that must depend if the individual believes in these concepts or not. If one does, then yes, our reality has its morality, ethics and you Americans have your own morality.

DG: Right, but if one believes in the 'different moralities' theory, it's an invitation for evil to be considered 'good,' because if you believe in a 'difference' between the two, that's a license for Man to create his own morality, and that's exactly what your Hitler has done.

HF [Laughing]: Don't worry. Soon you'll find not only comfort in your favorite expression - *Alice in Wonderland* - here; why you'll even discover this to be the Land of the Sane!

DG: One more question, please. You fight in 'Cavalry Divisions.' Of what use are horses in a mechanized tank and truck-based war?

HF: Specifically in occupied Russia, tanks were of no use because of the terrain. For example, it was too muddy, with no roads, swamps, and so on. Thus we riders found it much more convenient fighting partisans with horses.

DG: Interesting. I never thought of that. I heard you're in a cavalry division, and I thought that's just a name.

∼

Conversation with Three Female German Teens I – Discussing Each Other's Concerns & Needs

I noticed three German ladies conversing not more than twenty years old, not more than some fifty meters from the Bunker.

Eva Gretl: Who knows where my fiancée is?

Ilse Koch [Laughing]: What do you think? He's hopefully dead. Or he's some POW camp, or he's physically crippled beyond recognition!

Gudrun Ensslin: You're one sick girl, Ilse. You know what I'd love to know?

Ilse Koch: No, I don't know what you'd love to know.

Gudrun Ensslin [Angrily]: You're mentally sick. A deranged, perverted bitch. And you know when we surrender, you'll be tried for war crimes – being one of the few Nazi female whores?

DG: Now come on, let's speak without -

Ilse Koch [Sarcastic]: The mad cannot discern their 'madness' because they don't know they're mad.

Eva Gretl [Sad]: Girls, why do we fight? German kills German. Isn't it enough? Haven't enough people died?

Ilse Koch [Sarcastic]: Do not weep now, little girl! You'll find a Russian to bed.

DG [Shocked]: How can you say that?

{*All Three Girls Shout At Each Other.*}

{Silence}

Eva Gretl: For what purpose does God make Man weep when life is useless?

Gudrun Ensslin: It's one form of relieving toxic energies. Well, they're not all toxic. Some are pleasurable. But the point is, without venting or relieving ourselves, we'd better die. Explode.

Ilse Koch: If they're pleasurable, why would Man need to be relieved from them?

Gudrun Ensslin [Laughing]: You're stupider with each minute. Can that be? Yes, it can. How can it be? Because I see you.

DG: You take Ilse too seriously, you know? You can't judge when she's acting and when she's herself.

Gudrun Ensslin: Because *she* doesn't know the difference.

Eva Gretl: I'm lost.

Ilse Koch: Being brainless, it stands to reason you're lost.

DG: She has no awareness, no moral consciousness like any predatory animal. And just as animals are not always killing for food, so too is Ilse.

Gudrun Ensslin: She's nothing but fascistic spit and vomit.

Ilse Koch: Your rage cannot relax, can it? We all know why, darlings, don't we? You're sexually mute. Or you are muted. That's why you need to speak about relieving yourself.

DG: Who is doing the 'muting'?

Ilse Koch [Excited]: And that is indeed the question to ask and to answer! Not bad for an American. Well, it's a mixture. Their backward family and living standards mute their sex instinct, while their personality types suppress any sexual need.

Eva Gretl: And where do you think your husband is, Ilse dear? A war criminal. You know where he is going to, don't you, darling?

Ilse Koch [Mocking]: What 'husband'? Which idiot informed you I'm supposed to care about him? Ha! He's as impotent, just as the bitches before my eyes are desperate with repressed lust.

Eva Gretl: You're right. Stupid of me to think you cared.

Gudrun Ensslin: I swear for anyone who cannot feel emotional truths cannot be human.

Ilse Koch [To Dorothy]: Oh, how languidly erotic you are, with your poses and carnal words! You think I don't notice how you behave? Teasing bitch!

Eva Gretl [To Ilse]: How can you see anything carnal in Dorothy? Haven't you noticed she's a girl?

Ilse Koch: Dorothy, why are you still a virgin?

{Laughter}

DG [Angrily]: Who told you I'm a virgin?

Ilse Koch [Laughing]: Darling, it is obvious!

Eva Gretl [To Ilse]: How *do* you know?

Ilse Koch: That's only one dimension of her character.

DG: What?

Ilse Koch: You're a cauldron with ten million ingredients in the stew. Slowly, heating up. Many of the ingredients don't mix with the other ingredients. Instead, they blast or burn each other. Others are complimentary. These violent interactions continually heave the sensitivities, pain, and pleasures in the mind and the physical senses.

Gudrun Ensslin: Don't you love here absurd mathematical accuracy? Ten million, to be precise!

Eva Gretl [To Ilse]: Are you crazy? You've just met her!

DG: I don't know what she's talking about.

Gudrun Ensslin: Do you know what I feel, Eva? Do you think that oceanic spirit sometimes when a thought or a feeling beholds you, and you're no longer master of your mind and flesh — no, you are not a spectator in such alien moments that seem eternal! Instead, you are within the cataclysmic rushes of a million unknown, nameless emotions swirling you round and round. And all the while, you try to think, but you can't. Because there's no time. Because —

Eva Gretl: Didn't you say "eternity"?

Ilse Koch: I said "eternal," not "eternity." And in those moments, every minute point on your skin is electrified. At the same time, that selfsame intensely pleasurable electricity throttles every nerve, organ, bone, and muscle, causing convulsions and contortions you never knew your body could do. Causing aches needing kneading fists to massage them and flaring itches needing to be ripped, not just scratched.

Gudrun Ensslin: I know Nazis have drugs and dish it out to some of your ranks.

Ilse Koch: What do your communist masters teach you, idiot? I'll tell you what. When you speak of your 'communist' visions, you talk about your sexual frustrations in truth. Only you clumsily hide it in political terms.

DG: Politics or any other subject can be a distraction for someone repressed.

Gudrun Ensslin: Everything is rooted in sex for that woman.

Ilse Koch: Because *everything is rooted in sex!* Biology, blood defines who we are. Our primal urges include instincts such as hunger, shelter, food, water, self-defense, and sex.

Eva Gretl [Laughing]: It's Dorothy's turn to speak stupidities!

{Laughter}

DG: Where does your hero and his ideology with your belief in these urges being primal?

Ilse Koch: That's the essence of National Socialism! Blood, race, beauty, the athletic body, the need to reproduce, defending ourselves. Where's the difference?

Gudrun Ensslin: Does Germany's greatest failure still entrance you?

Ilse Koch [Proudly]: Of course, the Fuehrer is forever the most extraordinary human in the world!

Eva Gretl [Dreamily]: I'll dream on. That's one truth no dictator can steal from us. Hermann will return one sunny day, and back to our countryside village, we shall live.

Ilse Koch: You forgot, "Happily ever after."

DG: You know, Eva, you remind me of myself before I took on this job.

Eva Gretl: How so?

DG: I, too, lived clouded in my dreams. I knew nothing of the world. I only existed in my dreams. Only I didn't want marriage. Just fame and fortune, as a Hollywood actress.

Eva Gretl: How do you know I'm dreaming?

Ilse Koch [Curtly]: Because you are dreaming.

DG: As with all potentialities in life, you cannot say, 'Only this will happen and nothing else.' You must have 'Plan B' if 'Plan A' doesn't happen. You must expect the possibility your husband may not return. And that means you must prepare your future without him and be ready for the new context in your life.

Ilse Koch [Laughing Sarcastically]: If you think that brainless girl understood one syllable of what you said –

Gudrun Ensslin: Dorothy is right, Eva. You live in an imaginary land, as though there's no war going on. Don't you notice how you think and talk? I've never once heard you speak of the war raging around us. And what if Hermann returns, safe and sound? You know he's in the SS. And high-ranking too. Don't you think the Allies will put him on trial where he'll be hanged if found guilty of war crimes?

Ilse Koch: You girls think a parrot talking understands itself?

Eva Gretl [Firmly]: I know there's war ... why do you think Hermann is not with me? But one does not always need to talk of the dead, the dying and destruction –

Gudrun Ensslin [Angrily]: I wasn't just talking about war! You forget your husband is a criminal. He's an SS man; are you so stupid thinking he will be pardoned? Or hanged?

Eva Gretl [Angrily]: Why do you assume Hermann is a war criminal?

Gudrun Ensslin [Angrily]: Because every high-ranking SS dog is a war criminal deserving death by hanging!

DG [Calmly]: Let's not mention the war. All I say is that you've got to prepare yourself for the good, the bad, and the ugly.

Ilse Koch [Giggling]: And we've seen the last.

DG: What?

Ilse Koch [Laughing]: The 'ugly'; that's you, Dorothy!

Gudrun Ensslin: But life is more than that! You need an ideology guiding you throughout your life. We know Ilse is a criminal fascist. But you, Eva, you float in a world with no politics. No human can exist without a profoundly truthful ideology. You're negligible to your life and your children's life because no human lives in a political vacuum.

DG: Wait, you don't need an ideology to live! I know nothing about Democrats and Republicans in my country, and I don't care because nothing changes, and nothing affects us no matter which party is in power.

Eva Gretl: Both of you make life so complicated! All I want is my husband, children, a decent home, and that's it.

Ilse Koch: I think you disregarded the glue holding these elements together - money.

Eva Gretl: Is that how you think? How crude, coarse your mind is, Ilse.

Ilse Koch: Come now, darling Eva; if Hermann wasn't a wealthy, high-ranking mass murderer, would you marry him? Why you've had many chances to marry poor but decent German men, and you passed by every one of them. And we know why. They had no money and no rank.

Gudrun Ensslin [To Dorothy]: What are you talking about? You live within your ideology!

DG: How can I live in an 'ideology'?

Gudrun Ensslin [To Dorothy]: Aren't you from America?

DG: Yes.

Gudrun Ensslin [To Dorothy]: And are you pretending the US has no ideology?

DG: Well, yes, I just told you, we have two parties with the same -

Gudrun Ensslin [To Dorothy]: Your nation is capitalist. Capitalism is another criminal ideology, just as fascism is. You live within that ideology and its laws. We Marxists call people like you as being one in a state of 'false consciousness.'

DG: You know, I never thought of what you're saying.

Ilse Koch [Rudely]: So, you're dumber than I thought at first. Were you never aware the West is an alliance of capitalist nations?

DG: No, never. I just told you moments ago; I've never thought of 'capitalism' per se.

Ilse Koch: Do you know we Germans have an ideology fighting Jewish-capitalist nations?

DG: First, we're fighting you because your leader and his followers are genocidal maniacs. Second, there's not much left of 'fighting' to do.

Eva Gretl: Which is exactly why this conversation is boring.

Gudrun Ensslin [To Dorothy]: And *that* 'genocidal' attribute is because of their ideology, which you must know is National Socialism.

DG: We, the world, the united nations, have been forced yet again by you Nazis because you morons cannot stop attacking country after country plus murdering half the world's population for your supposed 'inferior racial' attributes.

Gudrun Ensslin [To Eva Gretl]: Having a family, a home will never bring you happiness, Eva. No life can thrive if one's socio-economic conditions are oppressive.

Eva Gretl: Oh please, don't begin boring me again with Marxism-Leninism.

Ilse Koch: Your Marxist-Leninist boys are not far from us, Gudrun. How come I don't see you too jumping in bed with them, or did I miss something?

DG: What? I thought, Gudrun, you're a communist, right?

Gudrun Ensslin: Oh please, Dorothy, you know even less about Marxism than you know about National Socialism. My dear girl, Stalinism is an inverted form of fascism. It has nothing whatsoever to do with pure, refined Marxism-Leninism.

DG: But the fact is today we have Stalin and his Marxism. How are you going to live with that system?

Gudrun Esslin: Oh no, I'll be going to the West.

Ilse Koch: Hypocrite! So you prefer the fascists to Stalinism?

Gudrun Esslin: Of course, at least in the West, they don't mass murder or mass deport entire communities on Stalin's whim.

DG: But to be sure, because I'm unsure, you prefer us fascists to Stalin's communism, right?

Gudrun Esslin: Life is nuanced. There are degrees of fascism. American capitalism is nowhere near as lethal as Stalin's so-called 'communism.'

Eva Gretl [To Ilse]: Who is your favourite minister?

Ilse Koch: The first who shoots Gudrun.

Gudrun Ensslin [To Ilse]: My dear, your empire has gone. No more Nazis. More importantly, where will you now go? Or which country are you going to flee to? Argentina?

Ilse Koch: You're such a naïve girl. Our empire is destroyed, that's true. But do you think all wars will now end?

Gudrun Ensslin: Did I say all wars will now end? That's what our fathers thought of the Great War. The war to end all wars. Far from it.

Eva Gretl: So, what's the next war about?

Gudrun Ensslin: And *I'm* the naïve girl? Ha! The next war will be between the proletariat fighting to the death against all forms of capitalism.

DG: Wait, why won't you fight the Stalinist states too?

Gudrun Ensslin: Because of resources and manpower. Also, if anyone peeps opposition in, say town 'A,' Stalin, as I told you, would literally exterminate the entire town and deport the rest to Siberian Gulags. Whereas in the West, governments rarely, if ever, resort to any form of violence.

DG: So you'll take advantage of the human rights laws enshrined in our capitalist nations being violent, knowing full well no civilized western nation would ever resort to violence to counterattack you, communists.

Gudrun Ensslin: Exactly. We will fight to end all fascist ministries, industries, corporations, businesses, and individuals. One by one, we shall target them and kill them.

Eva Gretl: But you are as brutal as Ilse, you know that? Did you just say "individuals"?

Gudrun Ensslin: Yes.

Eva Gretl: What do you mean?

Gudrun Ensslin: We'll kill every rich man and woman.

DG: You're as sick as Ilse!

Gudrun Ensslin: I know why you say that. You're brainwashed as most Germans. And most people, for that matter.

Ilse Koch: How are you communists, small in number, mostly middle to upper class white, educated students going to destroy the might of the West, which is anti-communist?

Gudrun Ensslin: It will be difficult. I did not say victory is certain. I really should introduce to my Argentinian friend; he is a faithful zealot.

Ilse Koch: I know a lot of our men are going right there to Argentina.

Eva Gretl: Who is this friend? What's he doing in Germany?

Gudrun Ensslin: If you think I'm a fanatic Marxist, you're are in for a shock, a pleasing one, to be sure.

Ilse Koch: I'm assuming he has a name?

Gudrun Ensslin: Ernesto Guevara. He's a medical student. Very handsome too.

Ilse Koch: I cannot stand Mediterranean people. They're lazy and talk too much. Like you, Gudrun, dear. Look at our great Italian and Spanish 'allies' – what a waste for our Wehrmacht. The Fuehrer once said, we'd love to have more volunteers from Italy and Spain to fight with us, but we'll do it our way. We'll just give our German boys Spanish and Italian uniforms and pretend to the world those two obsolete nations are with us to the hilt in our crusade against the savage Asiatic Russian hordes.

Eva Gretl [To Ilse]: I disagree with you. We Germans are too rigid, tight-lipped, nervous, cold. Too severe. Unlike Mediterranean men. Lava blood. They are immensely entertaining with their garrulousness. And I'm talking from experience, having visited Italy several times.

DG [Grinning]: Suddenly, I'm hearing sexual overtones from Eva!

Ilse Koch [Snickering]: If you're sexually excited with these swine, why are you waiting for a dead cold German Hermann?

~

Conversation with Gruppenführer Fegelein

III. Fegelein: "Where Are Our Great Generals? – No, Worry, Here Comes Himmler the Great!"

I was increasingly frustrated for the obvious sore reason of not yet seeing Hitler, let alone interviewing him. Every time I'd ask, I heard the same answer, *"The Chef is busy."* So, trust me, I'm not trying to avoid offering you my memoirs; however, I need to order them in the actual chronological time they occurred.

DG: So, just to be clear, you're saying it's almost random, the way your people or officers are getting or seeking the required man to defend the city of Berlin?

HF: No, that is not correct. We have standards. Of course, any selected man must be a decorated man, say with a Knight's Cross. But they're not interested in, say, merely hiring a professional soldier. Zeal now outweighs professionalism. That's the point here. Zeal. Fanaticism. Willpower.

DG: Would men of lowers ranks, men who by definition would have no experience in commanding army divisions, also be acceptable?

HF: Yes.

DG: But that's crazy!

HF: Did you already forget that immortal champion, Lieutenant-Colonel (Oberstleutnant), Ernst Kaether?

DG: Misch mentioned him. Are you saying that man had no qualifications? I ask you because I find that to be impossible.

HF: Can we compare him to generals such as Manstein, von Rundstedt, Guderian, von Leeb, von Bock, von Kluge?

DG: You know better.

HF: Do you know no provisions have been made for Berlin?

DG: Excuse me?

HF: Our leaders chose not to provision Berlin with the necessary supplies for the oncoming Soviet onslaught.

DG: But that would kill off civilians, right?

HF: Exactly. They're not considered to be of relevance in this ultimate battle. And in a way, one can understand our leadership. This is obviously the concluding chapter in our lives. So why bother with anyone who isn't a combatant? Going back to selected idiots as potential defenders of Berlin, I will now give you one of the most notorious examples of this folly, one which would have certainly amused Erasmus. Did you know our Fuehrer appointed Himmler to command an entire army group?

{*Fegelein Laughs*}

DG: No, I wasn't aware of that. But so, what? What's so funny?

HF: Oh, Frau Gale! Didn't you read about us supermen before coming here to interview the leader himself?

DG: I did. At least, *I think* I did the required reading.

HF: On the hallowed day of January 25th, 1945, our Fuehrer appoints this modern Caesar to command Army Group Vistula *(Heeresgruppe Weichsel)*.

DG: Himmler?

HF: Did you do know our 'conqueror' Himmler never served one minute in any army, nor was he ever a commander of one man in a battle?

{*Fegelein Laughs*}

DG: No, I didn't know that. But if that were so, and I'm sure what you say is accurate, how could he order or decide on anything militarily when he knows nothing militarily?

HF: The fault really isn't Himmler's – to be fair. It's the man who chose him. That job was forced unto Himmler. Anyway, so *what* did our modern-day Hannibal do? The answer is not much. Not much at all. Did you know his train had only one telephone line, old maps, and not one signal detachment or radio?

DG: What are they for?

HF: You can only communicate with the outside world if you have a signal detachment or radio. Meanwhile, I was told, the genius rarely bothered to venture out anywhere beyond his train during his tenure. And when he was on his train, he managed only a few working hours. Mind you, in that instance; one can hardly blame him.

DG: Why not?

HF [Laughing]: What work could the man do when he knows nothing? How can he order a regiment to go from point A to point B when he has no reliable information such as – the whereabouts of the divisions he supposedly has? How many companies does he have? How many men are in each regiment? What supplies will he need? Did he receive the necessary supplies? And then, once he's ordered to attack, he needs to know answers on matters such as what's the distance between his side and the specified enemy position in question?

I realized Fegelein knew far more than Misch on military matters.

HF: How much petrol will he need to have for his tanks? Did he receive the requisite amount of petrol? What are the terrain and weather like? How much ammunition, weapons, and medical supplies does he have? How many reserve men does he have? Next, he needs intelligence. How many enemy soldiers is he facing? How many tanks, artillery, planes do they have? What are their stocks of petrol? These are the fundamental questions any commanding divisional commander needs to know before operating any offensive movement.

DG: And so, what happened?

HF: The Fuehrer saw the error of his judgment and sacked Himmler on March 20th.

DG: Who replaced him?

HF: He was replaced by General Gotthard Heinrici as Commander-in-Chief of Army Group Vistula. But that's not the end of this tragicomedic story.

DG: But wait ... aren't you directly under the command of that man?

HF: You mean Himmler?

DG: Yes.

HF [Laughing]: Frau Gale, in politics, in times of war, alliances shift.

DG: Here today, gone tomorrow.

HF: Exactly. Do you think Himmler cares for the Fuehrer?

DG: I don't know. You tell me.

HF: Hear my words now. After Stalingrad, none but maniacs follow Hitler.

DG: You mean, men like Goebbels?

HF: And others, like Ribbentrop, Hans Frank, Ley, Keitel, Goebbels, Goering. But they're the minority because most of us know the war was lost back in February 1943.

DG: If that's the case, why are you still here in this Bunker?

HF: Because I'm not a traitor, Frau Gale.

DG: You make no sense! If you admit the war was lost at the beginning of 1943, why didn't you participate in the July 19944 assassination plot? Why are you still faithfully serving Hitler while millions of Germans die and historic German cities are burned to cinders?

HF: I cannot break faith with the Fuehrer.

DG: Doesn't that make you one more of the "maniacs," a word you used describing those still defending that man?

HF: Not quite. I will know what to do when the hour comes.

DG: What?

HF: Leave that subject right now, if you will.

DG: All right, going back ... you were saying Hitler sacked Himmler -

RM: By the time Hannibal was relieved of his post, we learned he *just had to* go to a sanatorium at Hohenlychen.

DG: Sanitorium? Why?

"The Whites have carried to these (colonial) people the worst that they could carry: the plagues of the world: materialism, fanaticism, alcoholism, and syphilis. Moreover, since what these people possessed on their own was superior to anything we could give them, they have remained themselves... *The sole result of the activity of the colonizers is: they have everywhere aroused hatred.*"

— Adolf Hitler. The Political Testament of Adolf Hitler: Recorded by Martin Bormann

HF: The realities of war rather frayed his nerves, I suppose. To be honest ... I don't know. But why else would anyone flee to a sanitorium unless if one is under great stress? The man is a perfectionist when it comes to killing Jews; that's true. Pity his nerves couldn't handle commanding one platoon of soldiers! Ha!

{Fegelein Laughs}

DG: How can your Master Race Germany not have one decent general?

HF: Again, you're assuming there's a beautiful harvest of generals still functioning in Germany. There's no one left. They're all either dead, sick, imprisoned, or they've fled to God knows where. Certainly, in the Berlin theatre, there's simply not one qualified general.

There you get it! I hope you *too* can sense the awful no-way, no-win, no-chance of the men and machinery in and outside the Bunker. After hearing Fegelein's words, I had to inhale and pause for a while. Was this the tawdry quality of the center point of all Germany's command and control structures while millions of civilians and soldiers suffer, fight, and die?

Can you imagine the depths of brainless desperation of the Nazi leadership? In particular, a leader ordering his men to search through the battle-scarred streets of Berlin seeking to find any man, any officer of 'fanatical zeal' to defend a forlorn, dead city? But, again, I always find in using contrasts, one gets the quality of the picture.

Previously I gave you an analogy with our Allied leaders. Here is one better. Can you imagine Churchill, Stalin, or Roosevelt frantically sending out men to find someone to defend their respective capitals? It's funny when you think of those leaders doing such a clownish act, but there was nothing funny in those desperate men when I think of Berlin. Desperation guiding them by the neck, seeking some desperate officer willing to take the hopeless job of what was essentially extending Hitler's life or conversely the delaying of his imminent death. Well, that was something I'd never reckoned on, to be honest. I imagined I'd see the famed German orderliness. The hard-working, zealous, super-qualified military and civilian staff. All would be fully equipped with the latest information and intelligence. Sending out precisely written orders emanating from the mighty Fuehrer. Or perhaps my jovial Rochus Misch and Fegelein were exaggerating?

~

Finally! - My First Impressions of Hitler! – And He Doesn't Look Like *'Hitler!'*

Anyway, let me rush you back to our immediate context. After several *SS* German officers again checked ourselves and equipment, I was led to a room.

Ad there, ladies and gentlemen - for the first time there in my earthly life, I was standing in front of the leader of this dying nation.

The proud Chancellor of the Thousand-Year Third Reich, the National Socialist Worker's Party leader, Adolf Hitler. The one-time homeless bohemian who ignited a world war, conquered lands from Paris to the Caucasus, murdered six million Jews and millions of more thanks to his wars — was that the man?

Anti-climax.

Yes, *that* was the first wave of emotions. Limping energies rippling throughout my mind and flesh. Anti-damn-climax.

Let me quickly describe for you his scrimpy living space — get it?

No? That was a joke.

Or meant to be one. *I* thought it was hilarious. Wasn't he the one shrieking endlessly banging on and demanding Germany's 'right' for *Lebensraum* ['Living Space']? Well, now look at the spacious living space he's left to defend! [Forget it, I thought it was hilarious.]

His office was relatively small, consisting of a chair, a desk over which hung a massive portrait of a staring Frederik the Great, a small sofa fitting two people behind the desk. I could not help but notice a photo of his beloved mother, Klara. Opposite that were two comfortable-looking chairs, and in between was a small table. Again, nothing was ostentatious or inappropriate. Instead, everything was as bare as the necessities of life required. [And in case you are wondering, *no,* I hadn't the faintest idea who the man in the painting was - Frederick the Great - until Misch told me and even when he told me I had no idea who Frederick was].

And what of the man himself, Adolf Hitler?

There he was.

Adolf, son of Klara.

Discolored lips, frail handshake. Without looking in my eyes, I think he murmured, *"Welcome,"* and that was it—his only word of introduction.

Shocked - shocked because I did not expect to see the man as *he* appeared before me.

This?

This was the noble Fuehrer, the greatest conqueror and subjugator in modern history, the lofty Reichskanzler, Adolf Hitler?

For a start, he seemed tiny! It's funny, isn't it, because whenever I imagined historically significant people, I imagined them to be at least six feet. But this man wasn't more than five feet four or at most five inches. Mind you, he did have a hump. So, maybe I'm wrong, but either way, right or wrong, I, Dorothy Gale, stomp my feet and say the man was too small in stature to be a historical leader!

How did this frail, stunted puny man cause all those hysterical German people were raving and swooning about since bloody 1933? I couldn't but chuckle inside.

"The scream of the twelve-inch shrapnel is more penetrating than the hiss from a thousand Jewish newspaper vipers. Therefore, let them go on with their hissing."

— Adolf Hitler. *Mein Kampf*

This was the man who caused the bloodiest war in modern human history?

Again, this limping, midget-man was responsible for the worst case of genocide in Man's modern history?

This was the same uneducated, one-time homeless man who singlehandedly created a nation of zealous followers and a fanatical army, succeeding in conquering most of Europe, right up to the Volga?

All right, enough disparaging. But then again, I thought, maybe it's not his physical being that created those gales of enthusing assuring feelings of joy and security? Perhaps it's his personality, right?

In any event, the only 'familiar' feature I noticed was that same uniform, one lonely Iron Cross, the swastika armband, black trousers, the double-breasted field-grey coat, white shirt, black tie. The jacket was plain, with the golden Party badge. As far as I could tell, he never wore jewelry. Even his gold watch was safely placed in his pocket. First superficial impressions are duly noted and done with. I reverted to my thoughts on the rinky-dink chap in front of me.

Maybe *this* had to be a joke being played on me! Or could this individual be one of Hitler's doubles? No, I'm stupid. But a fleeting period passes, and yours truly re-adjusted her evaluation of the human sitting before her. I accepted this was the man himself, Corporal Adolf. Pale skin. Pale as in sickly sallow. Puffy face heading a slightly plump body - totally unlike what we were generally accustomed to seeing in all those official news-footage films and photographs.

~

FAQ I - "Can You Tell Us How *Mad* Hitler Was?"

Now I've been asked a gazillion questions since I went to Berlin on that man. Among those questions, there have been a few prominent ones. Or infinitely repeated questions. Here is the first most asked question.

- *"Can you tell us how mad Hitler was?"*

I am afraid I must disappoint you all.

He was not a babbling, incoherent, out-of-control madman. Not as we had been endlessly told — sorry if I offend you in saying this. In fact, he was a most polite, caring host.

Generally speaking, he evinced an austere and frugal nature - a man who was, in the main, entirely in control of his mind. Now maybe, somewhere, in a secret annex hidden from our prying eyes, he was a rampaging monkey in heat. But, as far as I saw, he was as 'normal' as anyone could be expected, given the situation he was in at that specific moment in time—a fatally catastrophic situation, to put it lightly. So, no, at first sight, there was nothing 'crazy' about the man.

All right. Let's move on to the next most popularly asked question.

~

FAQ II - "What Were His Eyes Like? Did They Hypnotise You?"

We've heard about those famously 'mesmerising eyes' of the man in question. Upon first impressions, if anything, his eyes appeared glazed and lackluster. Two balls of eyes in a fresh corpse [assuming their eyes are open, of course]. Time matures emotions and intellect. A refinement in beholding reality. At some point, I remember a difference. His eyes *were* vigorously expressive. I can confirm *that* to be the truth. But that was up to him. He controlled the switches.

The man would switch in one moment from being disinterested, and the next moment has his withering eyes plowing inside your startled eyeballs. Within flashes of a second, the man switched moods. Overturning the atmosphere. Raging bull. Degrading the listener's intentions and validity.

He constantly changed his tone and the vocabulary of his language based on whom he was speaking to. For example, the manner he spoke with military officials was entirely different from communicating with civilians, women, or children. Language, the tonality of voice, and the flavor of emotion you just took for granted moments before are now restaged for a different play. And sometimes, he would achieve these jolting changes without saying a word. You or anyone would immediately become more than aware of *his* suddenly attentive attitude aimed directly at you and nobody else.

"False words are not only evil in themselves, but they infect the soul with evil."

- Socrates, *Phaedo*, 115e, Plato's account of Socrates' death

Sometimes he stares. Intently pinning bizarrely blazing attention at you and no one else. And oddly enough, this same burning attention can emit unmistakably glowing compassion for you. Making you believe you're the only significant human being in this vast cold, pointless universe. And that was an utterly comforting feeling.

In other lightning instances, faster than a frantic wink, the entirety of his persona lunges at you in synchronous time with that famous voice of his. And when he raised it - goodness me! - what a rasping, baritonal, guttural voice it was! Nothing like it had I ever heard before, seething in its own boiling cauldron of a ferocious tenor, forcible pitch! Sounding and appearing as a déjà vu wraith. Grandly flowing arms. Gesticulating messianic postures. Stabbing contemplative visions. Wild and yet controlled conductor. Implying each movement was meant to define some exhaustively meaningful gist. Numberless differing facial expressions. Bewildering because I have never witnessed nor knew Man had nor needed so many facial expressions, gestures, and gesticulations.

He *compelled* you to watch him.

Entrancing, fascinating, and more importantly - how can I describe it? It was as if he had a real, existing gravitational powerful pull on your mind towards his person and personality. Readily, I confessed I had never met a man or woman with this brutalising personality. Choosing to puncture the heavy air in this or that direction with clenched fists. A deaf conductor. Performing alone. Single-handedly directing his grand finale. Fully aware of his audience. Somehow he knew my every thought, wish, and desire, and he'd directly address those personal attributes deeply hidden in my bosom. Staring at our most private sensitivities and insecurities. A Magnum Opus. The Devil's Symphony. Blindly self-assured. Convinced of his surety. Only he knew reality and truth. You knew nothing. Immune from doubts. Forged with convictions with his all-embracing Weltanschauung.

"I know that fewer people are won over by the written word than by the spoken word and that every great movement on this earth owes its growth to great speakers and not to great writers."

— Adolf Hitler, *Mein Kampf*

∼

Disquieting Excavator of My Hidden Needs, Hopes, Sensitivities & Aspirations

I observe his listeners.

I've always been fascinated by audiences' reactions while a play is performed or when someone orates. After all, what would any performer be without an audience? And, with that man, their reactions were stupefying. Look at them! *They were* entranced! This was the first time, the first-hand experience of me witnessing, experiencing human beings in a spellbound state that Hitler induced among his listeners. Willing executioners. Faithful and fanatical. In a perpetual state of sacral adoration. *I* could not understand any of his words nor his logic. Not a word. Maybe *I* was the deaf part of the audience?

And being as frank as I am, the entire symphony's virtuality was lost to me. From my perspective, this was exactly as a cultist leader magically enrapturing his stooges. Only his followers understood and heard his orgiastic performance and its meanings.

Watch him brilliantly mimicking his opponents, voices, gestures, and all. Who knew he had an impressionists' talent? The man surprised me tremendously by his ability to mimic the men surrounding him and some famous people, such as that clown, Mussolini, because I just ... I never thought, nor visualized Hitler as anything but a sour, dour, and a constantly irritated man. Everyone genuinely burst out laughing at the sheer brilliance of his mimicking, and of course, in the ways he exaggerated attributes of famous and ordinary people, down to the ever-mute waiters. Who would have thought that of Hitler? Never in a million years did I imagine Hitler making me laugh. But that is one more side historians must consider when portraying the totality of the man's mind. And when he laughed, he covered his mouth as tears rolled out. Again, he was not the super crabby, petulant man as he is so often portrayed.

Then, he would propound upon his explanation or an excuse for this or that his foul deeds. Although your heart and even half your brain feels this man must only be enunciating the haphazard principles of madness, there was still an elusive air, and an indefinable aura was seducing the vicious, criminal, and wicked side of your persona. A side you choose to believe yet, knowing or half-knowing it does not exist. Temptingly, he fingers you, delicately urging your nerves and flesh to lick and lap up the eye-popping manic id over wormy reason.

I was seduced. Though not what you're thinking — there was nothing carnal. But attracted, I was. I confess. Though only in bits of time. Semi-believing in him. In a haze. Yet fully entering a fantastical realm of evil incarnate. I stopped myself. Gasping at the enormity of this titillating performance grandly being enacted before my innocent eyes. God, Rasputin must have been his doppelganger! For me to deny that fact would be a factual misrepresentation. I'd be denying what *I* was feeling.

The oddity with this man was the mental fluency, switching perspectives of my mind's engines and then just as rapidly clicking on or off some other emotional nerve nub. Who lets him in? I mean, why did my brain allow him such free access when no other person could do that to me? In an instant, he instills a soothing, warm tranquillity in the façade of my troubled mind. And then, he switches every Mount Vesuvius within my brain. Winding me down back to the safety of what I considered was the basis of my rationality.

Up and down — that was his unique power in swirling the entirety of your mind, in a dizzying spellbound merry-go-round, with its various contrasting and complementary emotions all bundled therein. I feel violated. Naked.

Again, nothing carnal — I hope you understand me on that point. I felt naked because I imagined myself being alone, looking at myself.

And here's another insane effect he had on me. He'd be raging on some political point, and yet I'd hear him and visualize ranting completely different words. I heard him screaming — "Be proud of your beauty, your sacred blood, you noble mind and know thou art the highest form of humanity!" What? How did that happen? But I had no time to rationalize or think about how this duality was occurring. "All your life, you've been taught, drilled to hate yourself, to hate your features, to hate your eyes, legs, nose. You've been taught and drilled all your life to hate your emotions, feelings, needs, instincts, and desires. You've been shamed. Shamed to think even of killing yourself, for that is how low you've been convinced you are. You've been taught and drilled to hate any ideas, hopes, and aspirations you have all your life. All your life, you've been taught, drilled to hate your intelligence, for aren't you no different from a baboon?"

He made me think of those millions of moments of bitter shame when I tried to look at my naked lean body. Hating my body. Feeling being a girl was immoral. I was a monstrosity.

His tirade of words rumbled on. Swaying my mind in the lushest of material skies. Knowing and most importantly, *feeling* every pleasure-creating nerve in my body was supreme. As I gazed at my nakedness and I beheld myself being Aphrodite incarnate. Mine body, I knew, has no equivalent. I was a statuesque, sublime — even sacral — beauty.

Moments of silence follow.

Then, I see nothing but his glassy, deep, oceanic eyes staring at me. But I cannot tell if he is angry or happy - nothing. What are these vitriolic commotions with his flailing arms? Why did his roaring, guttural Austrian accent arouse in me similar animalistic passions? He seemed to be reviewed the entirety of the world's history — from his vengeful, raging viewpoint. And yet, what struck me most is how he *simplified* every question, concept, an oddity on earth into the most straightforward formats, such that a child could understand — and that was one more reason for my exhilaration because I felt, I thought, 'Well now finally I understand the entire world's problems!' My rationality tries to catch with me, reminding me, *'Dorothy! You're stupid!'* ... And just as rapidly, I reply to my sanity, *'Yes, I'm stupid, for this is truthfully a bizarre man.'* 'Bizarre' as in crazy.'

Next momentary twitch, I'm reeled in metaphysical realms I had never experienced. Typhonic personalities in one body, one man. Not even in fairyland movies, let alone in reality. It was only later that, being unused to ever being in a situation shrouded with such unusual drama, I realized that I reacted in what I could only describe as uncontrolled passions. Why? *You ask me, 'Why?'* Because he forced me to not only face but to murder my ugliest abstract features; he *compelled* me to stand up to my self-hatreds. Isn't that crazy? Somehow, somewhere in the abstract nature of my mind, my fears - some well-known to me, while others long-suppressed and forgotten — were aroused in me. I feared myself. Not him. *That* is a crucial difference for me. The man somehow excavated a million-year-old arcane, inscrutable emotion I could only feel as prognostic foreboding.

Ignore that. Strike what I just said. His energy controlled not only the surroundings but the entire room and every human in that damned room. Kindling and soothing every other human and myself but having said that, Hitler mesmerizes your focused attention towards him and only him, such that I forgot the presence of others in the room.

It was *not* just those eyes, as everyone thinks. It was the totality of his changing personality, his rasping and soothing voice, changes in tonality, his sudden pauses when he became silent, his vivid use of words and expressions, his prominent physical features, and both his wild and calm gesticulations. Watching him and watching myself, we become somehow a duality, entwined as quantum particles can be entangled, an experience I have never faced before.

Finally, he winds down his theatrical play, and so he, too, winds down his histrionics and other such-like antics. Abruptly there is silence. I feel as though invisible violent, and loving bees have just swarmed me. I am aware I have just vented out my inner waves of anger and insecurities. Euphoria. The man with the lungs of a whale has ceased to move.

I previously said his character was 'brutalizing.' And he was. Those were the only moments I felt a threatening power. I know I am making no sense to some. But, in my defense, the only excuse or explanation I can offer you is this. For those among you who have not experienced that man, you cannot describe nor understand. And so long as I am writing truthfully as my conscience dictates, I shall not swerve from the good, the bad, and the ugly without bias nor prejudice.

∼

Conversations with Hitler's Inner Circle

I. Dorothy - "Did Hitler's Personality Change During The War?"

Many Bunkerites remarked how the leader had changed quite a lot. As compared to his years before. I chose to interview or converse with any of his other top-ranking men. To my surprise, they all wanted to talk — and talk.

"*Sparta* must be regarded as the first Völkisch State. The exposure of the sick, weak, deformed children, in short, their destruction, was more decent and in truth a thousand times more human than the wretched insanity of our day which preserves the most pathological subject."

— Adolf Hitler

Here is my first conversation with these men:

DG: Good evening, gentlemen. Thank you for talking with me.

{All Men Say, "Good Evening."}

DG: Dr. Goebbels, I heard your Fuehrer has changed over the years. Specifically, since he has been in the Bunker, I would like to ask you to comment on this topic.

Goebbels: Of course, you may. I hear you are German, yes?

DG: Yes, my parents emigrated from Weimar, Germany, to the United States.

{Mumbles of "Traitor."}

Goebbels [Loudly]: And who can blame them? That period in German history surely had to be the worst. I would go so far and say it was worse than the 1918 defeat itself.

Guderian: More exaggerations?

Speer: That's his job!

{Laughter}

Goebbels: Not at all, General Guderian, not at all. My job was never to create 'laughter' as you so eloquently put it; it was —

Goebbels

Guderian [Curtly]: Excuse me, *I* did *not* say that; you're confusing me with Herr Speer.

Goering [Laughing to Guderian]: You can't see the difference between black and white?

Goebbels was probably the least German looking of the Nazis; he was very short, dark-skinned, and had relatively no Nordic features. That's why Goering nicknamed him the *'Black Dwarf.'*

{Laughter}

Goering [Snide to Goebbels]: All your life, you never paid attention to anyone and anything but your own empty words.

{Laughter}

Keitel [Earnestly]: I must officially confirm and concur with Herr General Guderian's words, Dr. Goebbels.

DG: Herr Doktor, would you like to respond to my question?

Goebbels: He *has* changed; that is true. Previously, I would say he was —

DG: When you say 'previously,' when exactly?

Fegelein [To Goering]: I don't understand Herr Reichsmarschall; how can anyone pay attention to 'emptiness?'

Goebbels: In the years before we came to this damned Bunker, he was a different man. To put it succinctly, I would now say he is less rigid.

Goering [To Fegelein]: That "anyone" is Goebbels, and *only* the latter can and does pay attention to nothing.

{Laughter}

Guderian: I too find nothing substantial or specific ever coming from the mouth of Goebbels.

Speer: Again, isn't *that* the purpose of propaganda?

{Laughter}

Guderian [To Dorothy]: In my opinion, as a soldier, I believe the Fuehrer undoubtedly changed in every aspect of his personality once February 1943 was over, meaning after our catastrophic defeat in Stalingrad.

{Murmurs of Approval}

Jodl: True.

{Murmurs of Approval}

Fegelein: But isn't it also true that we've all changed during these war years?

{Murmurs of Approval}

Goebbels [Histrionically]: How true, how true, indeed; alas, such is our Fate!

Ribbentrop [Frantic]: But tides change, don't they? Remember how close we were to Moscow? And then overnight, I remember we faced colossal defeats.

Goering [Laughing at Goebbels]: Goebbels, we're not your audience.

Himmler: And we've never been.

{Laughter}

DG: Can you explain or give me examples as to how Hitler changed?

Goering [Laughing at Himmler]: Our Chinaman became more vigorous in his activities by 1943, whereas before, he was nothing more than a pimple in Hitler's ass!

{Laughter}

Goering nicknamed Himmler the *'Chinaman'* because he did have slanted eyes.

DG: What does that have to with Hitler?

Goering: He would never have dared to act in the ways he did had Stalingrad not happened.

Himmler [Coldly]: I became more of a 'pimple,' Herr Reichsmarschall, because the Fuehrer saw the continual failures of the Wehrmacht and your Luftwaffe, and so he was increasingly dependent on my sturdy SS men and that –

Jodl [Shouting]: *Halt dein dreckiges Maul, Himmler!* ['Shut your dirty mouth, Himmler!'] Your units, your men were nothing more than common criminals!

{*Tense Silence*}

DG [To Goering]: I'm not sure I fully –

Goering: The Fuehrer's relaxed grip on the government became far more relaxed, if you like, after Stalingrad, allowing much more freedom for any scoundrel to do as he wished to do without the Fuehrer caring one way or the other.

{*Everyone: 'Jawohl Herr Reichsmarschall Goring!'*}

Himmler [Icily]: General Jodl, I know why you speak as you do.

Jodl: You do?

Himmler: I do indeed.

Jodl: Well, then, enlighten us all.

Goering [Sarcastic]: Go on, Himmler boy, do tell us. Time is slipping away from us. From all of us in this macabre underground theatre. And talking of the 'macabre,' you of all bastards knows the most on that subject!

{*Laughter*}

Himmler [Sarcastically]: My dear General Jodl, do you think no one here knows the reason why you talk as you do?

Jodl [Shouting]: I just asked you, so, tell us then!

Himmler [Laughing]: You seek to escape from the hangmen awaiting you once you surrender.

DG: What?

Jodl [To Himmler]: 'We' surrender?' Meaning you won't surrender, Herr Himmler?

Speer: Frau Gale, Himmler believes all of us will be shot by the Allies since we are War Criminals. And so, by distancing himself from the SS, the general hopes the Allied judges will believe he was an innocent party in this gigantic adventure, we know as the Second World War.

DG: Herr Speer, you speak in a convoluted manner –

Keitel: If I may, Frau Gale; General Jodl, or Herr Himmler believes that once the ... the Allies achieve total victory and remember when I say the 'Allies' I mean our current enemies ... and then when they think they will defeat us, which I must inform you they will never do so because our Fuehrer insists victory is within easy grasp, and that is why the poor devils are deluded ... but anyway, however, even and suppose we temporarily align ourselves with their thinking, difficult as it is, I admit ... by their thinking, as I say, as far as our enemies are concerned, once they shall supposedly defeat Germany so next they will seek every high-ranking National Socialist and shoot the lot of us dead.

DG [Confused]: What?

Goering [To Keitel]: As opposed to 'shooting us alive?'

{Laughter}

Fegelein [Hushed]: What could be more boring than General Keitel?

Keitel: Herr Reichsmarschall, I do not -

Himmler [To Fegelein]: None is the answer.

∼

II. Dorothy – "Who and What Caused Germany's Defeat?"

Goebbels [To Guderian]: What more clap-track do we need to hear from our failed generals? For Heaven's sake, by now, in this final year of 1945, all of us know why Germany is defeated. There are two reasons and two reasons alone. One is the betrayal of the so-called scum of the earth 'aristocratic' generals. They never ceased to oppose and betray every sentence the Fuehrer ordered. Second, National Socialist Germany has been and still is entirely infiltrated by anti-German spies who have only one purpose – and that is the annihilation of our Germany.

Guderian [Contemptuously to Goebbels]: What a fool! After twelve years, you learned nothing. *Some* 'aristocratic' generals betrayed our Fuehrer, but they were *not* the majority –

Goebbels [Angrily to Guderian]: Did you know of the July 20th, 1944 assassination plot, Herr Guderian?

Guderian [Angrily to Goebbels]: How dare you insult my –

Goering [To Guderian]: Come *off* your lies, my man, you knew the details of that criminal day.

{Tense Silence}

Keitel [Angrily]: Gentlemen, please! The Fuehrer may change his genius mind, or he may not change his genius mind– which is what our American guest asked us. But, still, those questions are irrelevant. Why? Because should the Fuehrer change or not change his opinion and policies and rules and orders and thoughts, you must, all of you, know that these are not aimless changes and therefore throughout the presumed or assumed changes, one thing and the only matter that actually remains certain, is that the Fuehrer forever carries with him the thread of an unchanging state of eternal truth.

Goebbels: My God, my God! Why forsake us with this monologue?

Goering: Says the most boring monologist.

{Laughter}

Keitel [Proud]: By no means! For whenever our Fuehrer creates presumed 'alterations' of whatever kind and quality as he knows he needs to do, we perceive them to be 'differences,' and that is because we remain rigid in our rigid and —

Keitel

Goering [Referring to Keitel]: Any of you ready to rid us of this idiot?

{Laughter}

Keitel [Proudly]: Our limited brains have no accurate reflection on the integrity of what the Fuehrer intends to say and mean when he speaks or gestures and especially as per the so-called 'changes.' In other words, none of us will ever comprehend the changes the Fuehrer creates because we minions are strictly speaking irrelevant as compared to the Fuehrer and since the Fuehrer, being the Fuehrer, having the same steely-eyed, determined genius fighting for Germany will forever soar above our minds and so that then is all you need to know for the explicit evidence of our onrushing victory!

Guderian: Why can't your Fuehrer lift us from this hellhole and onto some other safer land?

Ribbentrop [Enthusiastic]: How true, General Keitel! Who can understand a genius when the human who is seeking to understand the genius in question is himself, not a genius. Therefore, it is logically an impossibility for the ordinary human. The latter is not a genius in trying to understand whatever a genius speaks?

Ribbentrop: As Foreign Minister, I can still offer many and countless varieties of peace proposals to the West and even to Stalin but you —

Goebbels [To Ribbentrop]: You mean "variations" rather than "varieties."

Fegelein: I think I now know and understand why Herr Socrates said, "I know nothing."

Keitel [To Fegelein]: What is it you say, my boy?

Goebbels [To Goering]: The more one 'knows' General Keitel, the greater is the uncertainty in knowing the subject matter.

{Silence}

Guderian [To Keitel]: What 'Germany' do you speak of?

Guderian

Goering [Referring to Keitel]: You're wrong. The more one knows him, the more one discovers that he dwells in ever deeper realms of nothingness.

Goebbels [Loud & Sarcastic, referring to Guderian]: You heard that question, gentlemen, didn't you? Those are the words of your classic defeatist, and I can assure you every Wehrmacht general was born a coward and a defeatist!

{Angry Shouts of Approval & Disapproval}

DG [Shouting]: Excuse me, I'm not interested in discussing that event; I want to go back to my question, please.

Goebbels [Calmly]: And what exactly is the nature of your dull and therefore forgotten question, Frau Gale?

Ribbentrop [Frightened]: Can't anyone say a positive word ... please? ... about our situation?

DG: How did the July 1944 assassination attempt affect Hitler's judgment?

Goebbels: Now your question is time-specific.

DG [To Goebbels]: Excuse me?

Goebbels [To Dorothy]: Originally, your great question was how the Fuehrer changed over the war years.

DG [Irritated]: All right, so what? Now I'm asking about -

Keitel [Angrily]: Not at all! What a stupid question! I will officially not sanction such un-National Socialist words! Did I not just inform you, Frau Gale, the Fuehrer need never change exactly as you would never expect a mountain to change or God to change! Therefore ask not "if" the Fuehrer changed over the war years, for in eternal truth, our Savior never changes just as God and the truth never change.

Goering [To Keitel]: Mountains change over centuries of time.

{Laughter}

Guderian [To Dorothy]: Well, for starters, he relied less and less on professional soldiers.

Fegelein [To Himmler]: What does 'sanction' mean?

Himmler [To Fegelein]: Meaning, 'acceptance.'

Guderian: Certainly, he did. That's why he increasingly relied on entirely unprofessional individuals, such as Himmler. And who can blame him?

Himmler: I never asked to be a general. But such was the love of the Fuehrer had for me, so he ordained that burden upon our SS men.

Fegelein: I confess; I never knew mountains move.

DG [To Himmler]: So your Fuehrer was blind in his assessment of your non-existing military capabilities.

Guderian: No, remember Himmler said it was a matter of "love" between Hitler and himself.

Goebbels [To Fegelein]: The Reichsmarschall didn't say "move;" he said "change."

Speer: I think the Reichsmarschall had the same meaning, "move" being equivalent to "change."

Jodl [To Dorothy]: After the July assassination attempt, the number of traitors vastly increased, and that affected our Fuehrer, especially considering their brilliance.

Goering: That's true.

Ribbentrop [Frightened]: Where are the excellent National Socialist generals, please?

{Laughter}

Himmler [Gloating]: Only the SS performed outstandingly well with bravery, tactical brilliance, and a fanatic loyalty unto death for our Fuehrer.

DG: So, again, I'm confused; if Hitler was *aware* of these traitors, why didn't he arrest them?

Goebbels: I told you; the Fuehrer too much of a humane man.

Goering [To Himmler]: That's true, but what about *your* SS record?

{Laughter}

Himmler: What do you mean?

Fegelein [Whispering to Dorothy]: I still don't understand why you were so terrified when that German woman was killed.

DG [Whispering to Fegelein]: I don't know. And don't want to open up that subject.

Fegelein [Whispering to Dorothy]: The oddity here is that the battle itself didn't shake you as much as when you saw her. You were blue when you saw her... what's her name?

DG [Stiffly, Whispering to Fegelein]: I told you to forget it ... *and her name is Katharina.*

Fegelein [Whispering to Dorothy]:: Her name 'was' Katharina. She's dead.

DG [Angrily, Whispering to Fegelein]: Oh my God, names don't die when humans die!

I realized I was being teased and controlled by Fegelein, playing on my buttons, and so I stopped myself answering that stupid topic.

{Silence}

DG: Gentlemen, why do you have his habit of straying every moment from our subject matter?

Goebbels: Didn't you think that maybe whatever your beloved subject in question may not be of any interest to us, dear?

Goering: Boredom.

Speer: Actually, we *are* still discussing your question, Frau Gale.

Goering [Laughing at Himmler]: You do *not* know what I mean?

{Laughter}

Himmler: No, I do not —

Goering [Roaring at Himmler]: Can you name me *one* of your offensive operations that succeeded?

{Laughter}

Jodl: [Rudely to Himmler]: Why so silent?

{Laughter}

{Silence}

Himmler: I've already admitted I did *not* want any military job, but the Fuehrer out —

Goering [Angrily]: Out of his 'love' for you …yes, yes, yes … go back to your abode of hell, scoundrel bastard!

Guderian: Mind you, this has been an ongoing physical and mental degradation of this man over the years.

Ribbentrop: Are you talking about me?

Goering [Giggling]: No, dunce, the Fuehrer!

Guderian: No one thinks of you, Ribbentrop. Therefore, no one knows of your presence or existence.

{Laughter}

Goebbels [Angrily to Guderian]: Absolute nonsense! If anything, he's been much more approachable than before. He's been far more accessible and more tolerant of dissenting opinions than before the Bomb Plot.

Ribbentrop [Angrily]: How can we allow this American to speak of our Fuehrer in these sacrilegious terms?

Guderian [To Ribbentrop]: Whom are we talking about? The Fuehrer or Jesus?

Speer: Both.

Keitel: Well said, Herr Speer. Your loyalty is never to be trusted. I mean, mistrusted.

DG [To Ribbentrop]: Unfortunately, it seems nobody told you of our agreement between Washington and Hitler. We agreed I would be allowed to ask any question on any topic, and no words or phrases are off-limits.

Ribbentrop [Stunned]: Seriously?

{Laughter}

DG: Seriously.

Ribbentrop [Stunned]: No one told me of this so-called agreement!

{Laughter}

Goebbels [To Ribbentrop]: Because none believes you to be anything more than a vacuum in a body.

{Mocking Laughter}

Keitel: What is the difference?

Goebbels: Frau Gale, you need to know something important.

DG: What is that?

Goebbels: The Fuehrer and Guderian never saw eye to eye. I mean never.

Goering [Smirking]: That's putting it mildly! Closer to the truth, no other man in the entirety of the Nazi leadership has been offered such liberties as Guderian with our Fuehrer.

{Everyone: "Absolutely True!"}

Himmler: The Fuehrer would relieve the wily Guderian of his command only to recall him later.

{Murmurs of Approval}

Keitel: Highly baffling, but then who are we to question the gods?

Goering: Nietzsche autopsied God.

Ribbentrop: But, if God is dead, or if He is not dead, it doesn't matter because we know the Fuehrer is alive and we know that with certainty, unlike the question of God's existence ... please, gentlemen, do you think that means victory –

Goebbels [To Ribbentrop]: My man, why fear death so much?

Keitel [Proudly]: We certainly know of the Fuehrer's existence whereas we can never know with any certainty if God exists or not and that is why the field of philosophy, being in essence speculative, is entirely unacceptable to National Socialism.

Ribbentrop [To Guderian]: What do ... why do say that?

Guderian: You do not know?

Goebbels: Let me assure you, Ribbentrop, you shall be found guilty of war crimes and hanged like a rat.

Speer: I think it would've been far more humane had your words come in a softer tone, Dr. Goebbels.

Goebbels: How can one express the fact of death by hanging in a 'softer tone'?

Guderian: There's your proof, ye faithless gentlemen – for why else would the Fuehrer recall me time and again, were it not for my military skills?

Fegelein [Whispering to Himmler]: Reichsführer, do you think Keitel is aware no one listens to him?

Himmler [Whispering to Fegelein]: I do not think so.

Fegelein [Whispering to Himmler]: Why, Sir?

Himmler [Whispering to Fegelein]: Because he is stupid.

Speer [Whispering to Himmler]: I agree with the Reichsführer; because if the man in question was aware, why would he talk?

Goebbels [Excited]: It is a well-known fact that Guderian and the entire German elites viewed our leader, our savior of Germany, as a bohemian tramp.

Guderian [Sighing]: Back to the *'hate aristocrats'* theme'?

Goebbels: They *hated* him because he was not aristocratic. They hated him because he was Austrian. They hated him because he came from a small town and not a city. They see him as coarse, precisely as the rich think of any peasant. Retrospectively, I admit, Roehm was correct in his vision. We ought to have exterminated an entire lot of the upper classes of Germany!

{Murmurs of Approval}

Speer: Historically speaking, upper classes always despise the lower classes – in any nation and throughout history.

Goering [Laughing]: I agree. When the Fuehrer went to Italy, the aristocratic classes could hardly contain their irritating disgust. Can you imagine a stenchy gaggle of these self-proclaimed 'aristocratic' old Italian hags, bloated with fat flatulence, would sneer whenever our Fuehrer spoke! And that other fart, Mussolini had to bow to *their* every word and flick of their hands!

{*Laughter*}

Fegelein: Whose every word?

Goebbels [To Goering]: 'Fat flatulence'?

Himmler [Tersely to Fegelein]: To the Italian aristocracy, my son; please concentrate.

{*Laughter*}

DG: I don't understand -

Goering [Amused]: What do you not understand, my girl? Is it so difficult for you to understand class hatred? In Germany, there is an elite, wealthy, aristocratic class. These creatures hated our Fuehrer. They infiltrated Germany, from the Wehrmacht to every ministerial department, and they ensured that every word and order our Fuehrer gave was circumvented or ignored or betrayed.

Fegelein: If I may, I would like to give a vivid example.

{*Everyone Nods in Agreement to Fegelein*}

Fegelein: Miss Gale, I will give you a simple - and yet a catastrophic example showing you how our Fuehrer's words were betrayed, resulting in the defeat of the German Army. I will not take much of your time. Once Barbarossa began, the Fuehrer intended our Schwerpunkt [Main Thrust] to reclaim the wheat, minerals, oil, and other resources in the South of Russia. But what happened? As anyone knows, the Wehrmacht ignored the South and concentrated on Moscow, which was a useless prize, as per General Halder's wishes. In other words, every time our Fuehrer ordered our units to go south, Halder would call us back to the central front.

{Murmurs of Approval}

Jodl: It *was* a chaotic situation because the Fuehrer refused to decide either way.

Goebbels: This brings us right back to me, stressing how lenient the Fuehrer was and still is.

{Murmurs of Approval}

DG [Strongly]: Actually, not only do I know class hatreds, I experienced that throughout my life, specifically as folks wealthier than us had nothing but contempt for my Daddy.

Goebbels [Laughing]: Why pretend you don't understand when –

Goering: I thought we moved away from that topic.

Speer: Dr. Goebbels, those are some of the techniques interviewers use to extract so much more words from the interviewee.

Halder [Indignantly]: What fools speaks before us! Who are you people to know or understand and even dare to talk of military tactics and military plans?

DG: What 'techniques'?

Goering [Angrily to Halder]: I do.

Halder [Laughing]: You're the worse examples of a failure! Try to limit the embarrassment of yourself, Reichsmarschall Goering.

{Murmurs of Disapproval}

Guderian [Sternly]: General Halder, you exaggerate wildly. The Luftwaffe was superb until Stalingrad.

{Angry Shouts of Approval}

Goering [Angrily]: Are you or are you not denying you circumvented the orders of our Fuehrer?

Halder [Solemnly]: Of course, I admit to that fact, and that is because 'your Fuehrer' was never more than a sub-standard corporal. My point is that Adolf Hitler was forever an amateur when it came to military operations.

{Angry Shouts of Disapproval}

{People Shouting: "Liar!"}

{People Saying: "Traitor! Criminal!"}

{Tense Silence}

DG: Why is everyone quiet?

{Gasps of Shock}

{Silence}

Speer: I think this is one moment of self-reflection being carried out by each of these gentlemen.

DG: What do you mean?

Speer: I'm not sure if I'm correct or not, but I feel these men who managed and directed our war seem to be quiet because they may be thinking where they made mistakes, specifically fatal errors for Germany.

∼

Goebbels Gives Sage Advice to A Woman Who Lost Her Home – 1945

Goebbels was touring Germany's destroyed cities in the hope his presence and his words would uplift morale. On one visit, he was confronted by one feisty German woman.

German Woman [Angrily]: Dr. Goebbels! Do you know my house was bombed last night? Everything was destroyed, including all my furniture. And do you know that today was supposed to be my wedding night?

Goebbels: My dear lady, may I ask how old are you?

German Woman: I'm 55 years old.

Goebbels [Laughing]: Well, you ought to be thankful only your furniture was destroyed.

German Woman: Excuse me?

Goebbels: My good woman, be thankful you didn't lose your husband, and you only lost your furniture. You can always buy new furniture. But do you think at your age you could find a new husband?

~

Conversation with Hitler's Inner Circle

III. Halder Is Accused of Disobeying Hitler's Orders and Thereby Causing the Defeat of the Wehrmacht

DG: Well, since this subject matter has been opened, I will ask you directly, Herr Goering, do you blame General Halder for Germany's downfall?

{Halder Laughs}

Goering: Of course not; one cannot say one man caused the downfall of an empire. That's silly.

Keitel [To Dorothy]: In other words, or if I may put it in simpler terms, Frau Gale; the Reichsmarschall thinks or ... no, he knows your question is silly because it is ... since it makes no sense blaming one head for the ruination of an entire nation since one human cannot have the power to complete such a gargantuan task and specifically when talking of the Fuehrer who -

Goering: However, that traitor played a gigantic part in our failures because he had many followers.

Hitler & Goering

{Halder Laughs}

DG: What do you mean?

Goering [Sternly]: Halder was one of the numberless men who made it their duty to obstruct every Fuehrer order because the man believed his brains were superior to our mere corporal. As an example, he was the main culprit for the failure of our first year in Russia. The dolt fanatically believed in himself, brooking no other ideas from others. He was determined to take Moscow as *his* first priority. The war was about him. About him achieving glory. It wasn't about the best interests of the Wehrmacht. Simultaneously, the Fuehrer, time and again, expressly stated the Caucasus must be our first priority, given the economic resources there.

DG: I don't understand. Presumably, he genuinely believed taking Moscow would destroy Russia, and if that were true, why do you insist his only interests were his personal ambitions for glory and not German success in Russia?

Goering: Two possibilities. One. The man knew he was wrong in thinking capturing a trophy city like Moscow would destroy the Leviathan Soviet state. Two. If he *did* believe that, then he is a moron.

Halder [Snickering]: The subject you're talking about is sitting right here, you know!

Himmler [Angrily]: What pains me is the Fuehrer's humanity! If people like Guderian or Halder were in Russia, obviously and rightly, Stalin would have shot them dead.

{Applause}

Goering: You may believe me, and certainly, the historian of tomorrow will not mention these truths because the victors shall legally only be allowed to express what the victorious governments will enable them to say. And Halder, I promise you, like many other seditious German so-called 'generals,' will be welcomed in the East and West precisely because they shall blame every unintentional public fart on the Fuehrer!

{Laughter}

Halder [Furious at Goering]: Are you calling me a 'criminal', Herr Reichsmarschall?

Goering [Smiling]: Absolutely.

{Murmurs of Approval}

{Silence}

Halder: So?

Goering [Shouting]: You have the indecency not to respond?

DG: But Rechsmarschall, you're also the highest-ranking man after Hitler.

Goering: What do you mean?

DG: Well, you're accusing all the generals, but you're in the same category –

Goering: Oh no, my dear! There's something you must know and learn. I intend to face the victor's court ... and I shall not denounce our Fuehrer; on the opposite, I will speak the truth, though knowing full well the victors must hang me!

{*Everyone: 'Jawohl Herr Reichsmarschall Goring!"*}

Goering: Meanwhile, the Allies will *not* put on trial these degenerate 'generals' precisely because they've agreed to sell their souls by declaring their intentions to decry the Fuehrer publicly and so save their necks.

{*Angry Shouts of Approval*}

{*Everyone: 'Jawohl Herr Reichsmarschall Goring!"*}

Himmler [To Halder]: You're worse than a criminal. You're a traitor, one more dog among our Wehrmacht generals, only serving the enemy!

{*Everyone: "Long live the Fuehrer!"*}

Halder [To Himmler]: The Master in Chief of Butcheries dares still to speak?

Himmler [To Halder]: I'd watch my tongue, you know what –

Fegelein [Exultant]: Mein Reichsführer, just hint at such an order, and I will proceed with my men to carry whatever you ask of us to do!

{Angry Shouts of Approval}

DG: Gentlemen, please, can we calm down?

{Silence}

Goering [Angrily to Halder]: Tell me, Halder, did you or did you not obstruct the orders of the Fuehrer during Barbarossa?

Halder [Dryly]: *Yes, I did and –*

{Gasps of Shock}

{People Saying: "How can this Man still be Alive?" "Bastard Traitor!"}

Halder [Dryly]: And that is because your Fuehrer had no adequate understanding of the intricacies of a military campaign in an area so vast as the Soviet –

{Angry Shouts of Disapproval}

{People Referring to Halder – "Senseless!" "Idiot!"}

Goebbels: But, Herr Halder, who exactly appointed you to be above our Fuehrer, such that you countermanded every demand of our Fuehrer?

Ribbentrop [Frightened]: Are there any peace proposals out there?

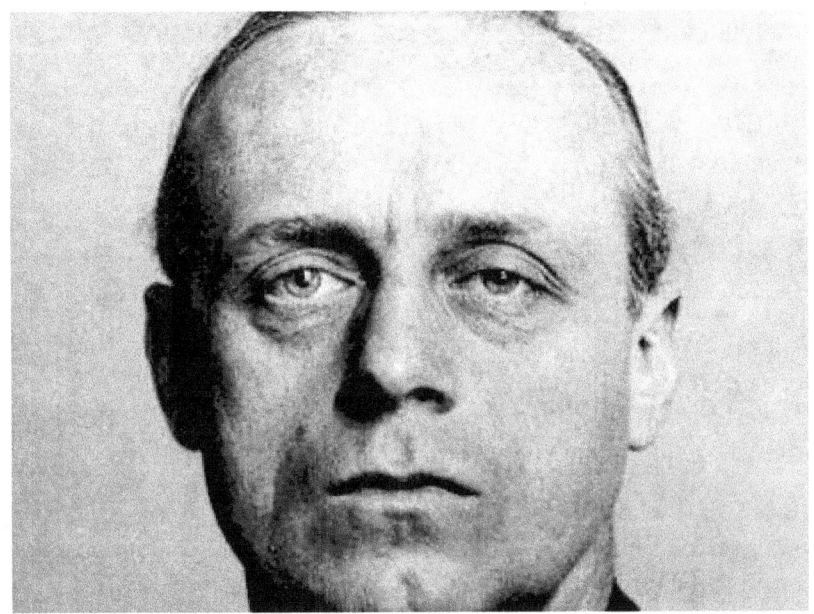

Ribbentrop

Keitel [Startled at Guderian]: What a complicated question!

Goering [To Keitel]: That question was not posed by Guderian.

Halder [Angrily & Proudly]: I *had* to take it upon myself to carry out the orders that were necessary for our operation's success and our survival. It was my duty to save the Fatherland from the misguided operations. Therefore, I stand fast, faithful, and true to Germany's honor!

{People Saying: "Traitor! Criminal!"}

Fegelein [To Halder]: But you failed.

{Silence}

Himmler [Disdainful]: General Halder! I believe a question has been posted to you by one of us 'inferior' men.

Halder [Angrily]: Barbarossa failed *not* because the primary objective was Moscow! My God, what idiots you are!

Goering [Smirking]: Is that so, Halder? It would help if you now educated us about why we lost in the 1941 campaign in the east.

Halder [Stiffly]: There were many reasons. That is obvious enough. You yourself stated – "One cannot say one man caused the downfall of an empire."

Goering: Again, I agree.

Speer: Nobody is saying you were the sole beneficiary for the downfall of National Socialist Germany.

Fegelein [Surprised]: But you were the primary cause, given the fact you were German Army's highest-ranking general and because you've admitted countermanding the Fuehrer's orders!

{Shouts of Approval}

Keitel [Proudly]: The boy is correct, General Halder! Since you ignored every Fuehrer order, you must accept responsibility for your operational directives, and since you, Germany, and all of us failed in 1941, who else are we to investigate as the primary suspect in the crime of murder but you and I never claimed to be a homicide detective but logic forces me to look at you specifically since you are telling us that you were the one -

Halder: There were many reasons. Orders were not carried out. I do not deny that.

DG: Why?

Halder: As Goebbels stated in his blurred terms, the Fuehrer, unlike what you people in the West think, was not scrupulous in deciding on this or that question. He left it to his subordinates to decide for themselves what to do.

Goering: We can agree on that. However, that did not give you the right to disobey him.

{Murmurs of Approval}

Halder: That was one gigantic factor that negatively affected our procedures to continue without military plans.

DG: Can you elaborate?

Halder: We planned military operation 'A' to do this or whatever. The next day, some general speaks to the Fuehrer and convinces him Plan 'A' is wrong and that we must proceed with Plan 'B.' Suddenly, as we are in the process of achieving our targets for Operation Plan 'A,' we get orders to switch to Plan 'B' – can you not understand how disruptive such acts will affect the overall performance of an army?

{Mocking Laughter}

Goering: No, that's a lie.

Halder: What lie?

Keitel [To Halder]: I believe the Reichsmarschall has just now officially proclaims you to be a 'liar.'

Goering: Yes, the Fuehrer was sometimes swayed by to change his military objectives, and that is normal because he's not a dogmatic dog, like you, Halder, my dear. However, in our 1941 Russian Campaign, his orders were explicitly clear and never changed – we were to concentrate offensive operations primarily in the south and *not* attack Moscow. That's your despicable lie.

Jodl: Halder, you destroyed the hopes for the fulfillment of a victory in the '41 campaign.

Goebbels: General Halder, do you require any more clarifications as per your lie?

{Murmurs of Approval}

Halder: Nonsense! Army Group South failed in achieving its objectives, proving how correct I was.

Rundstedt [Shouting]: That's because *you* diverted resources from Army Group South to the center!

{Murmurs of Approval}

Halder: That's true.

{Silence}

Rundstedt: How then did you expect my men to achieve any success when you admit stealing my resources?

Halder [Loudly]: I've told you people ten times already! The aim had to be Moscow! Any operations in the south was child's play.

Goering [Angrily]: What a fool! To repeat Fegelein's words, you still failed in your heroic conquest of Moscow, despite scavenging all the resources you needed!

{Everyone: "Absolutely True!"}

Halder: My dear Reichsmarschall. War is not so simple. It is a multi-faceted game, just like life is. I did not 'lose' in taking Moscow because of my plans. There were so many other factors beyond my control. Factors your Fuehrer should've addressed before invading the country in question. For example, given our idiotic racial ideology, we did not ... instead, we couldn't ever imagine the 'sub-human' Slavs could not only invent the T-34 but also mass-produce it on a scale far better than any German tank factory could produce our miserable tanks. And never mind the other superior weapons the Soviets invented, again in output that embarrassed every honorable German officer.

Himmler [Angrily]: Our *"idiotic racial ideology"*? Do you believe we don't remember you, General Halder, back in 1940 and 1941 when you were one of the most eager men in the Wehrmacht for a full-blown attack against Stalin, given what all of you elite generals believed to be the weakness of the Soviet Army?

{Angry Shouts of Approval}

Halder [Coldly]: Yes, I accept your words. But that was, as you stated, in 1940 and pre-June 22nd, 1941. Of course, once we invaded Russia, like most of my fellow generals, we realized we had vastly overestimated our strength. But the majority of Germans followed Hitler's insane racial beliefs, costing us horrendous losses. We were arrogant. It's known as hubris. The truth is the Slavs out-performed us in every aspect of war-making, again, thanks to our racial idiocies.

DG: Shouldn't we wait for your Fuehrer to answer these questions?

{Silence}

Halder [Angrily]: But that is precisely what Stalin succeeded in doing; that is, by transferring his armaments industries much further east to the Urals, he succeeded in continuing to out-produce us in tanks, airplanes, artillery, and in every other military category.

Goering [Quietly]: He's correct …if we forget his seditious acts, the man speaks the truth. The Russians were and remain far superior to anything we German people can do, and the proof is hitting us right now above this Bunker.

{Silence}

Jodl [Angrily to Halder]: Can you now publicly admit and tell us what Fuehrer orders were not carried out thanks to your criminal interventions, thwarting these orders?

Goering [Angrily at Jodl]: What's wrong with you, man? He admitted that fact hours ago!

{Laughter}

Speer: Didn't we agree with what Reichsmarschall Goering said, that is, – *"One cannot say one man caused the downfall of an empire"*?

Himmler: That is true, Herr Speer, but are you asking of us when facing a man in charge of Army Group Centre in 1941, a man who betrayed every Fuehrer order, should not be questioned for his treasonous acts?

Speer: No, I'm not saying that. But what exactly is the point of focusing on General Halder's errors or acts of betrayal when we know the war was lost for hundreds of other reasons that were beyond the fault of General Halder? It seems that we're accusing this one man for our failure in the 1941 campaign in Russia, and that is logically not true.

Goering [To Speer]: You're mistaken, Speer. The fundamental necessity for success for Barbarossa was that it had to succeed in the first four to six weeks, beginning on June 22nd, 1941. It was our only chance, exactly as our attack on France. In other words, in Russia, just as in France, we had but one chance. The year was 1941 in Russia, and the year was 1940 in France. Had we failed in France in 1940, we would've been bogged down as were in the miserable Great War.

Speer: what does that have to with my point concerning Halder?

Halder [Angrily To Speer]: 'General' Halder, if you will.

Goebbels: Well, not really. You're not a 'general anymore if you think about our context today.

{Laughter}

Goering: My dear Speer, when I tell you "Halder was responsible for the failure of our 1941 campaign in Russia," that does not mean only that man, as he for some reason needs to remind us of his presence sitting here, while all of us are fully aware, only too aware of his venal existence. But in any event, I am not saying it was just him. However, Halder isn't 'just one man,' so to speak. I'll explain. Halder influenced, directly and indirectly, thousands of other generals, officers, and all other ranks in the corrupt, traitorous Wehrmacht to obey him rather than our Fuehrer.

Speer [Excited]: Herr Recischmarschall, but the man still failed in the end despite all the influences and powers he had. And that proves or contradicts your claim that he was such a 'powerful' entity during 1941.

Goering [Shouting]: Of course he failed, and that is my point! Listen.

Keitel: I am confused at this point. Who is to blame for our failure in 1941? Obviously, it is not the Fuehrer, so apart from General Halder, who then are you accusing and I say this because I have not heard any other suspect in this most intriguing question.

Goering: He gathers all his seditious, criminal men and women –

DG: Who is 'he'?

{*Everyone: "The Reichsmarschall Speaks of General Halder!"*}

Goering: He orders his minions to follow his words, not the Fuehrer's sage orders. Now, I heard your concerns, so let me explain. As you rightly point out, he fails. Well, shouldn't that indicate he wasn't as powerful as we're portraying him?

Speer: That's my exact point because, in addition to Halder's undeniable seditious acts, other factors crushed, and we've discussed that – such as Stalin's might.

Goering [Angrily]: I understand what you're talking about – Russian resistance, Russian tanks, Russian military output. Yes, yes, yes! But these were utterly irrelevant entities or facts in the south of Russia. Had we *only* listened to and followed the Fuehrer's orders and gone south, we would not have faced the immense resistance we encountered as we did in Moscow. Why? Because in the south, there were fewer Russian units than in the Moscow front. Stalin cleverly suspected Hitler or his generals would repeat Napoleon's march, that is, to go for Moscow. And that's why Stalin concentrated the might of his Red Army in the Moscow sector.

Jodl: In other words, Stalin baited us to go for Moscow, and thanks to Halder, he went for the bait, not knowing the immensity of Soviet forces facing us there.

Halder: What lies! First, Army Group South failed because of stiff Soviet resistance –

Goering [Shouting]: Didn't we just tell you Army Group South 'failed' because you stole much of its offensive capabilities?

{*Angry Shouts of Approval*}

Halder [Angrily]: If you say so, I shan't argue on that matter because it's futile. Meanwhile, will you now tell us, Herr Reichsmarschall, that none of the other factors had no affect in destroying our chances for any success in 1941?

Goering [Shouting]: "Es ist mir scheißegal, ob du mich verstehst oder nicht! ["I don't give a damn if you understand me or not!"] I'm telling you, the Moscow Front was impregnable. I told you that was because Stalin put the entirety of his military colossus in that front, exactly as he would during the pointless Kursk Offensive, which means Moscow. Do you understand? Meanwhile, had we allowed our Wehrmacht to roam onward in offensive operations in the south, I'm telling you we would have thoroughly eradicated any Soviet opposition and reached the Volga in that same year, 1941.

{*Tense Silence*}

Halder [Icily]: I cannot accept that –

Goebbels: That is so true, and of course, I speak as a man without a speck of military experience.

Goering [Giggling]: Without a speck of anything else.

Goering always surprised me how he could easily and quickly change moods, temperaments, and emotions, unlike anyone else. Once we were beholden to one mood, everyone else remained in that mood until the circumstances changed.

Himmler: The Fuehrer stressed time and again that we Germans would have only one chance of exterminating the Russians and that had to be during the 1941 Campaign. Should we lose that year, so then, the best we can hope for would be an attritional war or a total collapse of National Socialist Germany.

Goering: We've said that, Chinaman.

{Laughter}

Jodl: We only had the requisite amount of manpower, oil, reserves, arms for a three to six-month campaign and certainly no more. Should we fail in achieving victory in 1941, so that meant by the following year, 1942, we wouldn't have the military capability to fight on all three fronts, only one. That's how drastic our losses were. And everyone knows in 1942, we were only able to employ one front, Army Group South. That was a *public* admission to the world of our grievous losses and injuries. Whereas you will, I hope, notice the opposite was the case with the Russians. Despite losing millions in 1941, Stalin could still attack us on every front, from Leningrad to Stalingrad.

Everyone seemed worried at this unusually harsh outburst by the elderly general, Rundstedt. Also, I must point everyone pretended to respect Rundstedt, given his age. Even Hitler allowed only Rundstedt [and Goering] to sit during any military conference.

Halder: If I'm an egotist, arrogant, or whatever else Hitler said, I don't care to confirm nor deny his words. I can only restate my words and what I did, and that is I knew what needed to be done, while the corporal Hitler you idolize has and never had any apprehension or proficiency in any military affairs, and that is because the gentleman in question was never schooled in any military academies or institutions.

Fegelein: Did Caesar study in any academic or military academy?

Goering [Angrily To Fegelein]: I am not criticizing our Fuehrer, but in the days of Caesar, soldiers were trained through years of battles, thereby gaining experience!

{*Everyone: 'Jawohl Herr Reichsmarschall Goring!"*}

Guderian: But we live in the twentieth century, not in pre-Christian times — and I think much has changed between Caesar's times and our times.

Goebbels [Angrily at Guderian]: Are you saying every genius must necessarily go through your elitist military academies to be proficient in military affairs?

Goering: He *is* saying that.

Himmler [Smarmy]: What is this idiocy? Geniuses, by definition, do not need professional education, nor academies or universities — geniuses inherently know the truth.

Keitel [Proudly]: But that is glaringly obvious! The Fuehrer is a genius, and so why would he enroll in any educational or military -

Guderian: Are these your words, Himmler?

Himmler: These are my words.

Guderian: So, why are we here in this tomb, then, were it not for your genius man in question?

Goering [Shouting]: We're in *this* mess because of *your* treacherous acts in *not* obeying any of our Fuehrer's military decrees and orders! How many times do I have to repeat my words?

Fegelein: Traitors only hear their paymasters' orders.

{*Everyone: "Absolutely True!"*}

DG [Loudly]: Excuse me, gentlemen! Please!

{*Tense Silence*}

DG: Why did your Fuehrer *not* ensure his orders were carried through?

Goering [Laughing]: Frau Gale, that is indeed the requisite question here!

{*Shouts of Approval*}

Goering: I know future historians will avoid our truths -

DG [To Goering]: I do not understand -

Goebbels [Emotionally]: And how true you are, Reichsmarschall! How often do you and I and many others beg him for once to act like Stalin to purge our traitors and spies?

{*Murmurs of Approval*}

∼

Goering Explains Why Hitler Germany Lost the War

DG: Herr Reichsmarschall, I believe you did not finish what you were saying.

Goering: My girl, if you want the truth about this Second World War. Two facts must be known. First, the Fuehrer did not lose this war. It was entirely due to the failures of our German government, including the Wehrmacht.

{Everyone: 'Jawohl Herr Reichsmarschall Goring!"}

Goering [Laughing]: And here is the second truth. *Der Sieger wird immer der Richter und der Besiegte stets der Angeklagte sein!* ["The victor will always be the judge, and the vanquished the accused!"]

{Everyone: 'Jawohl Herr Reichsmarschall Goring!"}

DG: Can you explain that Herr Reichsmarschall?

Goering: The Fuehrer often allowed his field commanders to solve the problems as they saw fit. Meaning he allowed them the complete freedom to act in any way they wanted to do. In any way that suited them, while he did not interfere.

DG: But didn't Halder just tell us one of the worse mistakes Hitler made was his constant meddling down to the smallest military unit?

Halder: Exactly.

{People Shouting: "Liar!"}

Himmler: How many times do we hear you repeating the story of "carpet-eating Hitler"?

{Mocking Laughter}

DG: But you must admit, or at least to us in the West, Hitler's mannerisms when orating look crazy!

Jodl: We're straying from our subject matter.

Goebbels [To Dorothy]: What a stupid subject matter you point out. Do you want to discuss Churchills' alcoholic -

Speer: I entirely concur with Reichsmarschall Goering. Many times, not just I, but many of our best men, begged the Fuehrer to take a far more active role in the war's daily operations, but that did not happen.

Keitel [Piously]: Dr. Goebbels, you make no sense.

DG: Did Hitler know of what exactly was happening, specifically as per his orders being ignored?

Keitel: I say this because 'morons' by definition have no brains. Therefore, your statement is invalid, and we National Socialists pride ourselves in not only being righteous but also in being precise -

Goering: That is a damned good question …ask him.

DG: Ask who?

Goering: The Fuehrer.

{Silence}

Goering: But we must not forget that we too … All of us massively miscalculated the sheer numbers of criminals, anti-German traitors who made sure Germany would fall. It wasn't just the Fuehrer. My goodness me! We were overwhelmed by the fanatical love, reverence, adoration the German people had for the Fuehrer. And we extrapolated from that gigantic fact that our governmental institutions – civilian and military – would also be in line with him. But that was where we failed, and we failed catastrophically.

{Halder Laughing}

DG [To Halder]: What makes you laugh?

Goebbels: Rats laugh.

Halder [Smirking]: I laugh with disgust because these morons still do not understand why Germany lost the war. To me, it is obvious.

Keitel [Indignantly]: What is your fundamental interpretation of the word 'obvious,' Herr General Halder?

Fegelein: Isn't the term 'obvious,' obvious?

Halder [To Goering]: I say 'obvious,' by which I mean the answer to your question is not only obvious but also absurdly obvious.

Goebbels: General Herr Halder, I think you are confusing us.

Halder: What do you mean I'm "confusing you"?

Goebbels: General Keitel asked *you* that question, and not Reichsmarschall Goering.

Guderian [Laughing]: And what's the difference between these non-entities?

{Angry Shouts of Disapproval}

Halder: And yet as I sit and look at you heroes, why is not one you has yet admitted any culpability on your part for the loss Germany endured during 1939-45.

Speer: Excuse me, General Halder – I have yet to hear you say one word of any error you committed during the word.

{*Angry Shouts of Approval*}

DG: And what about yourself, Sir?

Halder [To Dorothy]: What about me?

DG: Yes, you. Do you think you never made any errors during your military career?

Halder: Absolutely not!

Speer: Our Reichsmarschall states a critical point. Hitler literally carried our souls on a frenzied wave that was one of our joy and excitement, and what offends me is how every general of the Wehrmacht suddenly pretend they were never affected by his paralyzing charisma, which. As I just said, all of us were affected by to –

Ribbentrop [Frantic]: How true! How true! If only you were there, Frau Gale! How damnably can anyone judge our Fuehrer when they had never seen –

DG: Well, let me point-blank ask you, General Guderian – were you not at one time enthralled and captivated by the charismatic personality, mind, and ideas of Adolf Hitler?

{*People Saying – "That's The Question! Guderian! Answer! Answer!"*}

{*Tense Silence*}

Guderian: Never.

{*Everyone Saying: "Liar! Liar! Traitor! Criminal!"*}

{*Tense Silence*}

DG: Really, General?

Guderian: Yes, 'really.'

DG: And I suppose you too, General Halder, will answer in the same manner?

Halder: Completely.

{Gasps of Shock}

Goering [Angrily]: My generals, Frau Gale, knows nothing of our history. Forget her. Let us men talk, between us.

{Tense Silence}

Goering: I ask you now this. As Germans, and I presume you still have some honorable connection with our Fatherland, I ask you this – from 1933 till the winter of 1941, neither of you were Hitler accomplices; yes or no?

Guderian: What a strange question! During the years you mentioned, that man did not involve himself in our day-to-day military business.

Goebbels: That is not the question posed by our Reichsmarschall.

{Everyone: "Long live the Fuehrer!"}

Guderian: Are you asking me if I was ever specifically enthralled or mesmerized by Hitler's personality? Is that what you want to know?

Goering: Yes.

Guderian: Never. And let me –

{*Everyone Saying: "Traitor! Criminal!"*}

Guderian: Can I answer or not?

Goering: Let Judas speak.

{*Tense Silence*}

Guderian: I was never an infantile. Only idiots revered, fawned, wept, cried when they saw that man. Do you really think or believe I did that when seeing him?

Jodl [Angrily]: No one asked you if you 'wept' when you saw the Fuehrer, Guderian. You're once more avoiding the question.

DG [To Guderian]: Are you telling us you were never in the least emotionally influenced by Hitler?

Guderian [Exasperated]: How many times must I answer that question?

Halder [Laughing]: What idiots! You question if Guderian had any reverence for Hitler! Have you forgotten it was Guderian who disobeyed every order given by that Austrian corporal during the invasion of France? And now, given that undeniable fact, what does that tell you? Well, clearly, it stresses that Guderian knew perfectly well Hitler had no idea what to do as per any military operation. That is why he saved the day by ignoring Hitler's idiotic orders, and hence we achieved our historic victory over France because we ignored his orders.

Manstein: That's true. Remember, Hitler wanted to repeat the First World War offensive operations, meaning there would be no surprise against our enemies. That's how primitive he was. People think the invasion of France was Hitler's idea. No, it was not. It was my idea. I don't know if the future will see that or not. But I know for a fact, had we followed Hitler's plan for the invasion of France, we would've ended up in the exact same horrific situation as we had to endure during the First World War because –

DG: I don't mean to cut you off, but I'm not interested in getting bogged down with too much military information for now. We will definitively discuss these events later, but not for now.

Manstein: Do you remember Hitler's criminally stupid order stopping our panzers from annihilating the British at Dunkirk?

{*Laughter From Halder & Guderian*}

∼

Conversation with *SS-Gruppenführer* Hermann Fegelein

Dorothy: "I Want To See A Surgical Operation Room Where The Wounded Are Being Treated."

DG: SS-Obergruppenführer Fegelein, may I ask you a question?

HERMANN FEGELEIN: Certainly.

DG: Can you please take me to a surgery room? Any place where the wounded are surgically operated on?

HERMANN FEGELEIN [Laughing]: Have you been drinking cognac?

DG: No, this part of my job is to see as much of Berlin as possible.

{*Silence*}

He was looking at me and trying to figure me out. Trying to understand my motivations.

HERMANN FEGELEIN: Apart from the fact you're baldly lying, do you know what hideous reactions you'd be experiencing with your stomach, not to mention your mind, should you see those sights?

DG: 'Lying' about what?

HERMANN FEGELEIN: The part of the act, when you casually inform me, "... it's part of my job to see as much of Berlin as I can." Really, Frau Gale? I vividly recall when my Fuehrer specifically instructed me of my mission. And that was to get you from the front to the Bunker for you to interview him. I don't recall our Fuehrer specifying that your mission included chaperoning you as a tourist sightseer in Berlin. And the Fuehrer stated this simply because he genuinely feared for your safety, both physically and mentally.

DG: All right, I lied. But, does it matter?

FG: Lies don't matter?

DG Amused]: Oh please! You Nazis, you're ideology, philosophy, doctrines, foreign policy, mission, racism, your purposes are all lies, so don't preach to me on lies!

DG: Anyway, Berlin's going to fall in a few days. So why should you care? I know you've got your escape plans. I know though I don't know if you know I know you. You think you hide behind your charming looks and apparent loyalty. You're not the man who surrenders to the Allies, only to be hauled off to the military courts. Nor will you kill yourself, like those maniacs, Goebbels and –

FG [Smiling]: What's that got to do with my responsibility in protecting –

DG: Interesting how you didn't instantly jump to defend your honor against my forecasts!

FG: I will not be led by you, answering every accusation that –

DG: Anyway, comrade – yes, why not use communist terminology, since they're going to be here – the war's over, so what difference does it make to you? It should make none. The play is over, so we should be allowed to see and do things that weren't necessarily on the menu, so to speak.

HERMANN FEGELEIN: You're missing the point. The Fuehrer is aware that you're a young inexperienced, female American isolated from your country, let alone experiencing a battle. Thus he had two orders for me – one was for your physical safety. And more importantly, the Fuehrer impressed upon me to make sure you don't get your mind all imbalanced if you were to see and experience too much of the hideous aspects of war.

DG: That doesn't change -

HERMANN FEGELEIN: And I agree with your military assessment of the war situation, but I think such crucial life-or-death matters ought best to be left entirely and only to our savior, der Fuehrer and not for untried, untested people such as you are.

DG: I'm sorry, I agree ... but, still, I beg you to –

HERMANN FEGELEIN: Frau Gale, I ask you again, have you considered what you'd be seeing? You don't know how your mind will react seeing such hideous scenes. Think of what may happen to the stability of your mind. I believe you told me you've never been a war zone, nor a battle itself, and you've certainly never witnessed any war-time surgery room, right?

DG: Why are you assuming I'm mad? There are many American female war journalists right now all over battle zones, covering and reporting –

HERMANN FEGELEIN: Frau Gale, please, and again, I know of these American and other war journalists. They're all well trained, professional, and more importantly, they've experienced many battle scenes, so they are well equipped mentally speaking to experience more battles. You do not have any experience -

DG [Shouting]: I'm not mad!

HERMANN FEGELEIN: Frau Gale, please, your security, your life is in my hands, and I there's any harm coming to you ... the Fuehrer will have me shot. And to be honest, I've no idea what he's attached so much importance to your life –

DG [Angrily]: Are you saying my life is unworthy of life?

HERMANN FEGELEIN: Frau Gale, no, but the Fuehrer is facing his final moments on earth. He has never shown so much empathy or sympathy or whatever the word is for anyone as he has demonstrated for you. And he doesn't even know you!

DG: And what –

HERMANN FEGELEIN: Meaning my neck is on the chopping block if you're hurt; why don't you understand what I'm saying?

DG [Shouting]: And I'm telling you my mind is stable!

HERMANN FEGELEIN: Frau Gale, please, we've seen you, and you're not entirely of a firm mind, please. I'm not saying you're crazy, but 99% of non-military people wouldn't be able to stomach seeing surgical war theaters.

Now, I chose to lie.

DG: SS-Obergruppenführer Fegelein, you're mistaken. Before I came here, I was fully trained for my mission. In fact, I was forced to attend several surgical operations, and I didn't flinch. That's why I was offered this job. Every other applicant couldn't endure or withstand watching surgical theaters in France.

He was, or he seemed surprised. Did he believe my lie?

HERMANN FEGELEIN: Frau Gale, American, and British military hospitals cannot be compared to German theaters. Please, understand me! Just like everything with the West, you people have neat, clean, efficient, orderly surgical theaters. In contrast, we have inexperienced so-called doctors who were never surgeons operating life or death operations on our wounded boys. Second, we don't even have any of the requisite supplies, such as nurses, beds, anesthesia, chloroform, stitches, bandages, blood – and I cannot think what else surgeons need - do you now understand or can you please understand that what you saw in your American hospitals has no resemblance to our so-called military hospitals?

DG: SS-Obergruppenführer Fegelein, it is my dictated duty to observe German surgical theaters. And Hitler acceded to Washington's request.

Another lie.

HERMANN FEGELEIN: May I ask you, why on earth would you or anyone wish to see the most monstrous side of reality?

DG: My answer is to your question is this - I feel we must see the 'most monstrous side of Nazi reality.' Remember, you people started this war. You were totally unprepared. So, that answers your points raised. Everyone knew Nazi Germany could never fight a prolonged world war. Why? Because you people did not have the human resources nor any resources to sustain such a war. So, what you're saying to me is known to everyone in the world — ironically, the only humans who didn't know that fact was you! The Master Race Germans! You thought you could single-handedly fight and win against planet earth. You failed in that effort back in the First World War, and obviously, you failed in this Second World War. Now, how stupid does that make you, you Master Race people? I mean, what's after Hitler? Are you Master Race geniuses going to for a hattrick and try to fight the united nations of the world once more?

HERMANN FEGELEIN: That's not my concern. I'm neither a visionary nor a politician. though what you say may be true -

DG: What's your concern?

HERMANN FEGELEIN [Exasperated]: I've told you a million times — it's to protect you!

DG: And I'm telling you this; I've already met Satan's minions, meaning you people. Therefore please allow me to see the other galleries with the hideous paintings you Nazis created.

HERMANN FEGELEIN: How poetic. Frau Gale, allow me to say this. To you. I've been a soldier all my life; you know that, yes?

DG: Of course. I've read up on your military record, and it is uniquely impressive in its criminal records.

HERMANN FEGELEIN: I want to tell you that I have never experienced a more horrifying scene in all my career, even in the eye of the fiercest, bloodiest battle than what I've seen in these surgery operation theatres.

DG: And what's so upsetting, or is that what most upset you? After all, was it not you Nazis who began these wars?

HERMANN FEGELEIN: What does that have to do with the reality I'm discussing?

DG: You didn't answer my question.

HERMANN FEGELEIN: What's your question?

DG: If you deliberately burn innocent humans and you see them turning into gruesome melting bodies, shouldn't civilized society witness the barbaric acts that you Nazis precipitated?

HERMANN FEGELEIN [Exasperated]: Both sides have their injured!

{*Silence*}

HERMANN FEGELEIN: I'm not minimizing the hideousness of those scenes. But, watching these half-dead, literally half-humans desperate to leave made me think. I asked myself, 'Well, why were they so desperate to leave the relative safety of the surgery ward, where they could, in theory still get some medical attention, get pain-killers such as morphine, and risk going outside to the hellish scenes of the ongoing battles and thereby endanger their lives even more?'

DG: Well, that's a good question. I never thought of that.

HERMANN FEGELEIN: And I found the answer. I finally did. The madness of the war, the rage of the battle, the madness of boys being hideously injured. The sickness in seeing them once beautiful boys becoming unrecognizably hideous. Like a series of Elephant Men. I say this because as I walked or toured our military hospitals, that's precisely what I saw. Bed after bed, row after row, I saluted 'men' I honestly couldn't recognize as humans. The sad fact that we don't have enough anesthetics while surgeons still have to amputate legs, thighs ... it's madness. Seeing some of them the raging, spewing spit, blood, and fragments of God knows what ... screaming at the injustice of the so-called 'treatment' they were getting—seeing them being given a slimy mirror and seeing for the first time their Frankensteinian disfigurement. The turmoil of realizing their lives have forever been changed such that no one could ever see them without screaming in shock at the hideous nature of their deformities. Seeing others crawl frantically like smashed frogs, scurrying, seeking to escape the medical wards. And why? Because, in their deformed minds, they feel they will go mad, entirely mad, should they remain where they're at, and therefore, the only solution is to get out and face the raging battle outside. For, the raging battle outside is saner than the absolute hell of where they've been.

DG: Why do you say "rage"?

HERMANN FEGELEIN: Despite their inhuman features, I could still feel the rage, the hatred they evinced against me since I represented Hitler.

DG: Do you think their rage was justified?

HERMANN FEGELEIN: Concerning them, yes, obviously I can understand their hate. After all, while they live, they'd never marry nor be friends with anyone – in short, they'd never be allowed to mix with society. That happened back in the Great War. These lepers were secluded in remote communities where they could never travel to any German city or town or whatever. On the other hand, what do you expect our Fuehrer to do with these hideously disfigured people? Do you think we should allow them to go back to wherever they came from? I'm sure you understand; no society could tolerate seeing such hideous monstrosities.

DG: Why'd you call them that? They're humans, for God's –

HERMANN FEGELEIN: Frau Gale, in your untested, untried eyes, they're still humans, but I can tell you with certainty they are no longer humans. They're monsters. Furthermore, I can easily prove it to you. So, they must be sent elsewhere.

DG: 'Prove' it? Prove what? Prove what I feel inside?

HERMANN FEGELEIN: I'm not interested in 'what you feel inside,' because you're an American. I only think of our German people.

DG: You're talking as if these wounded boys are equal to the mass murderers that your men, the SS men, are!

HERMANN FEGELEIN: You're pretty accurate but not totally. No, they're not criminals, far from it. However, the average civilian, man, woman, and of course, children, cannot experience the actual sight of these hideously mutilated men. That's why I called them 'monsters.' I did not flippantly or insensitively use that term; instead, I'm afraid, for the 99% of any population, seeing any such creature would terrify them beyond their reason and senses. If you want to talk Hollywood language, I'll lie and say the hideously disfigured men and women are exactly like any non-disfigured man and woman. But I don't live in Hollywood land.

DG: But that's so hurtful, so immoral of your society!

HERMANN FEGELEIN: I don't know about your adopted country, but I know for a fact, all over western Europe, and even in England, I'm afraid that's the fact. Those hideously disfigured or restricted as to where they can live.

DG: You mean, even in England, they forcibly separated those sad, brave heroes from society?

HERMANN FEGELEIN: Yes.

DG: But why? After all that they've sacrificed for our societies, is that how we treat them?

HERMANN FEGELEIN: Again, this fact isn't because our politicians are wicked or uncaring. They've been obliged to enact these laws because our citizens complain vociferously against allowing these monstrosities to live and walk among the general population. They not only look like monsters, but they also have indeed, like it or not, become fleshy monstrosities that would offend the sensitivities of any human being unused to such the scenes of the mad world we soldiers belong in.

DG: Well, I guess, I think so.

~

Satan's Majestic Symphony!

Again and again, he asked me, "Are you sure about this? Are you ready for this?" and my veneer nodded or replied, "yes, yes."

I admit I was touched and surprised by this insistent concern shown by Fegelein for my feelings since I never saw a hint of softness in him, and how could I blame him or anyone, given the years of war he's been through? On the opposite, I fully expected Fegelein to be the man he was, strong, sturdy, and sound without melting into maudlin or pomposities. He was, in fact, by far the most robust character I personally felt, not the any of the others were 'weak; not at all, but Fegelein possessed a full roundness of character that seemed to be zipped tight in every aspect, allowing no leaks whatsoever, whereas, with the other officers and military, I could sense chinks of weakness scattered here and there.

We left the Bunker during a relative lull, and within minutes, he pointed to a building, and once entering it, he turned to me and said, "Downstairs." For the last time, he asked, "Are you sure?" I nodded, and so we descended into the belly of Satan.

Before we reached the intended destination, the stench almost tipped my body over. What the hell of a smell was that? God, Berlin, or the outside

Berlin stank to the limits of the universe, but this stench was of an entirely different flavor. These were odors of the earth's excrement, putrefaction, pus, gangrene, hydrogen sulfide, smelly feet, garbage, animal vomit [remember Daddy worked in a farm], human decomposition, decaying fish, rotten eggs, corpses, methane gas, stagnant water, sewage, bad breath, vomit, every other variety s of stench.

I threw up several times until I had nothing in my stomach.

And then, we entered the ward.

Fegelein was right. It was huge. Or, so it seemed to me. In front of me, as I expected, there were hundreds of wounded surgeons, doctors, nurses, and of course, the wounded.

Sounds. What an array of screams there are! I've never heard so many variations of screams, howling, shrieking, and you can imagine the rest. And the scariest part was that most of these sounds were not even comparable to animals. They sounded like aliens, and I have no words, much like the overwhelming stench.

Motion. Some were moving frantically, all four actors I mentioned — the wounded, surgeons, doctors, and nurses — while others were just sitting, lying on the ground, or standing motionless.

Words. Some spoke clearly; others garbled out their words.

This side of war I had not seen. In some ways, I felt shame because only now I'd come face to face with war. Until that moment, I'd seen clashes of war. I saw the consequences of it, such as the dead and dying soldiers and civilians, the destroyed cities, and so on. But, this was the only ghastly face of the monster, called war, which completely floored me.

I admit the hideousness paraded before me seared my nerves. To put it bluntly, what is more desperately frightening to behold than a blob of supposed 'human,' stabbed by holes, gashed with gapes in his body, noseless, lipless, eyeless, hairless, skinless. Was that a 'human' before my shivering eyes? A blob of flesh with only a tiny hole that tried to be a mouth, or maybe it was an eyeball. Some orifices urinated or defecated. This was Satan's Majestic Symphony.

I admit — again - Fegelein was correct. I didn't know if I was going to be able to endure this.

I was standing, motionless. What was I supposed to do in that situation? It was a zoo. I was, in effect, an utterly inconsequential being, totally unharmed with not a nip on me, while the extreme opposite of wounded humans stood or lay before me. But, I was terribly aware of one reality. One part of reality. Indeed, I had finally come face to face with war. This was the final truth, the face of war, and only now I could honestly say I had seen it.

But there was a price to pay. Of course. Nothing is free. Mind and body must violently react to this. I felt nauseous. Light-headed, dizzy - because all thoughts temporarily vanished from my brain, fearing that which they beheld. Homicidal hatred returned. Why? Because I hated these mass butchers who framed their entire guiding ideology in proclaiming themselves to be the only 'Master Race' on earth and in the latter's righteous name initiated these annihilatory wars throughout Europe.

How could this be, Man? No, from the sight before me, this proves Man is not the Man, one as Michelangelo sculpted with his David.

What caused Man to create this amount of bodily harm unto his fellow Man? What motivated Nazis to literally mutilate entire nations and populations such that when the afflicted and aggrieved returned to pay the compliment, they too unleashed their wrath, pound for pound?

Before me, they were not humans. These were Satan's followers, which is why they had mutilated each other to these paranormal, freakish levels. There was no way I could even entertain the idea those were children of God.

This was one truth.

Nothing mattered here in the realm of evil, but the of Nazi and nothing else. This was the triumph of evil. To be sure, a human corruption caused by Satan's minions, but an evil nevertheless.

I noticed Fegelein wanted to leave while I was philosophizing or whatever I was doing in my mind. I turned to him, motioning my willingness to get out.

HERMANN FEGELEIN: Now, you're ready to go?

DG [Horrified]: Yes. Has the Fuehrer seen this?

HERMANN FEGELEIN: Don't you think the Fuehrer has enough on his shoulders to have to see this?

DG [Revolted]: I suppose so. Maybe not. Hermann, we've got to leave –

My God, I felt startled at calling him by his first name and then by telling him what I thought he ought to do to save his life, and he too was visibly shocked at my unexpected outburst. Where did the sentence come from? How dare I speak in such a directly personal manner to him? I felt cheated. I felt something in my brain slipped out those words without my permission, and I was furious at my leaking brain. I tried to stitch up the mess I or whoever in my brain said those words.

Out we went, thank our Lord Savior!

DG: I'm sorry, my God, I didn't mean to say that –

HERMANN FEGELEIN: Doesn't matter.

DG: How come at each military conference you routinely carry on, telling Hitler on this move by that battalion and other such entirely meaningless words?

HERMANN FEGELEIN: You want me shot?

DG: But, for how long are all of you willing to tiptoe with Hitler's Dance of Death?

HERMANN FEGELEIN: I've been thinking about it, and so does everyone. I know everyone in that funeral chamber constantly thinks of their escape. But, we cannot disobey our Fuehrer. And, there's the end of that story.

DG: But what difference does it make now? It makes none. He will continue killing others until he ends his life. And how much time is needed before even he realizes the inevitable?, Sir, it's over, the war is over, and now shouldn't each one of you, men and women, civilian-military, finally get out of your 12-year long of being entranced by Hitler, and for once think of your own lives!

∼

Conversations with Hitler's Inner Circle

IV. Goebbels: "The Fuehrer Ought to Have Exterminated the Aristocratic Wehrmacht Generals!" Guderian Vehemently Disagrees

DG [To Halder]: I'm surprised you call him directly by his name and not 'Mein Fuehrer.'

Halder [Proudly and Angrily]: And *that* - is exactly my proof! How can anyone talk seriously if he spits absurd statements such as the Fuehrer is 'infallible'? Who froths such stupidities such as this except for our clergy and church?

Goebbels: Name one incident, speech, letter, or anywhere when I ever said the Fuehrer is an infallible man.

{Murmurs of Approval}

Guderian: Why then have I never heard you criticize your hero in his presence?

Keitel [Angrily]: Because heroes -such as our Fuehrer - are immune from criticism; what a stupid question!

Goering [Smiling]: Just as Catholics believe their Pope is infallible.

Goebbels: Oh, I think there are several reasons for that, my dear General Guderian. Number One: I know you were not invited to the hundreds of thousands of intimate, personal conversations I've had with the Fuehrer. Two; You talk tanks, guns, and war. We speak on every subject with our blessed savior. Thus I know him from different perspectives, whereas you know him only on war issues. Does that answer your question?

Guderian [To Goebbels]: You're right, but the most important conversations are precisely those I've had with him – that is, on military affairs.

Goebbels: And why do you elevate your narrow, limited knowledge above all other subjects?

Guderian [To Goebbels]: You don't know? Because it is precisely those issues that your holy savior erred in, thereby inviting the worse physical and human catastrophe in modern German history.

Fegelein: Is it true Catholics believe their Pope is infallible?

Keitel [Admonishingly]: Now listen and wait here, my boy, Fegelein; our Fuehrer is Catholic, so let us not tread on this kind of uncharted theological terrain because not one of us knows anything on this sacral subject.

Goebbels [To Guderian]: On the opposite, it was because you genius generals did not listen, nor obey the Fuehrer's counsel that has led us to be here in this dungeon. I think that would be pretty obvious to anyone, but not to you.

Keitel [To Goebbels]: What is so "pretty obvious"?

Guderian [Angrily to Goebbels]: I told you I accepted that –

Goebbels: What then is your argument, General Guderian?

Guderian [Angrily]: I admitted to you ... actually, I don't need to admit anything to you, Dr. Goebbels. The records speak for themselves. The Fuehrer and I had multiple and exhausting disagreements throughout the war. Every one of them was fruitless because of his pigheadedness since, to repeat, the man was not learned in military affairs for the millionth time; since he never rose above the loft rank of corporal.

Keitel: I can officially agree with General Guderian in his accurate description of our blessed Fuehrer's rank.

Himmler: But the man never questioned the question of the "Why?"

Ribbentrop [To Himmler]: What 'man'?

Himmler [Loudly to Ribbentrop]: Guderian, you fool!

Goebbels: Second, given your blind bias against National Socialism and specifically against our Fuehrer who does not belong to your aristocratic class, even if you were at any scene when I criticized him, your ears would be closed, given the aforementioned hatreds.

Guderian [Frustrated]: What 'hatreds' do you speak of?

DG: Dr. Goebbels, there's a contradiction here. If you're right in saying Hitler's generals were 'idiots,' how come these idiots successfully conducted invasion after invasion 1939 till the end of 1941?

{*Everyone: "Absolutely True!"*}

Goering [Laughing]: What a parade of midgets you all are!

Fegelein: Reichsmarschall, I thought only Dr. Goebbels was categorized as a "midget"?

DG: I don't understand what you mean, Reichsmarschall.

{*Silence*}

Keitel [Proudly]: The Fuehrer loves it when we behave as independent humans and not robots. Unlike Stalin's men, we are not lackeys.

Goebbels: You have no opinions, Keitel.

Goering [Laughing]: Gentlemen! I have a philosophical question!

{Everyone: 'Jawohl Herr Reichsmarschall Goring!"}

Goering [Laughing]: If the Fuehrer did not exist, would Keitel exist?

{Laughter}

Fegelein: Who invented philosophy and for what purpose?

Keitel [Angrily]: I know all of you think I am a so-called "Yes-Man" to our beloved Fuehrer.

{Everyone Nods in Agreement}

Goebbels [To Dorothy]: Let me answer your question. From 1939 till the invasion of Russia, these generals obeyed the Fuehrer's words and orders. You know our downfall began with Russia. They became dizzy with the successes our Fuehrer granted us.

DG: Who is 'they'?

Goebbels: Our esteemed generals. They wanted to have the lion's share of the military glory, especially since the Soviet Union is the biggest nation on earth. And that's when they created their own operational plans, countermanding the Fuehrer's orders.

Jodl: That's absolutely true.

Keitel: Well, I wish, or instead, I need to say something on this matter. I am not only proud; it is my most outstanding achievement in my earthly life to be a faithful servant unto our Fuehrer. Furthermore, our Reichsmarschall's question is meaningless, and I will answer him, given the fact -

Guderian [Laughing at Goebbels]: How convenient, the hour Germany suffers its first defeat, blame it on the erudite, elite generals!

Fegelein: I never knew Russia is the biggest country on earth; did everyone know that, and if so, I'm sure everyone must've thought twice about attacking that country.

Keitel [Proudly]: If the Fuehrer – God forbid – does not exist, then I must categorically state in no uncertain terms that I too would not live, and that obviously would be an absurdity, and therefore your words are entirely devoid of any meaning and that in turn also means none of you should not be wasting our time in speaking of these or on these meaningless words.

Himmler [To Fegelein]: Military strength has nothing to do with the size of a nation. In 1917, we destroyed Czarist Russia. China is the fourth largest country on earth, with nearly half a billion people. Look at Japan. China is twenty-times bigger than Japan. And now look at how Japan rolled all over China.

Guderian: True. It's not size but having the least corrupt, the least bureaucratic government. It's about having the proper, expert, professional allocation and productive, qualified management of a nation's economic, intelligence, transportation, military, manpower, increasing armaments and food output, and having a well-organized process of extracting natural resources for the war effort.

Goebbels [Referring to Keital]: For once, the idiot has a point. After all, if the Fuehrer did not exist, so to speak, not one of us would be where we are today.

Keitel: Finally, I must say this. Unlike many of you people here, I do not philosophize on questions such as whether the Fuehrer does exist or does not exist and I have already expressed my judgment on that specific question but I beg you not to fall into the hellish trap of speculative philosophy because apart from the known existence of the Fuehrer the rest of your philosophical in queries such as that of the question on God have no answer precisely because they can have no answer because they are speculative and so you will be wasting your precious time diving deeper in those abstract, meaningless holes and finally in reference to the Propaganda Minister I say this and briefly too and that is I remain steadfastly loyal to my Fuehrer and if being a 'servant' is an insult or matter of mockery for you gentlemen I will say this to you for I am like any of the apostles and disciples of Jesus Himself.

Fegelein [Smiling]: Listening to General Keitel can seriously damage one's brain.

{Laughter}

Goering [To Goebbels]: Your words are correct, but that's not what I meant with my question.

Keitel: Exactly as James, Peter, and the other disciples worshipped their leader, I too worship my Fuehrer, without questioning him, and I am willing to do so unto my death.

Goering [Bored, To Keitel]: Have you finished?

Keitel: Yes, I have -

Goebbels: Further to the question of our downfall, I don't say it was entirely the generals, though they played a gigantic role. Our Fuehrer, and here is a matter I have stated before - our Fuehrer ... and I am not committing any treasonous act, but the truth is, I had often urged our Fuehrer of the necessity in acting exactly as Stalin. That is, we must radically exterminate not only Jews, but we must also kill subhuman Germans living and thriving within Germany. The venal elites, the diplomats who worked as spies, the Ministries of Justice, Foreign Affairs, Reich Labor ministry, Postal, Reich Ministry of Finance, and Justice were all either utterly incompetent in their jobs or passed on every secret to our enemies; the inefficient, stupid, lazy men and women doing so-called administrative work within the Wehrmacht bureaucracy, the wealthiest magnates doing business with our enemies, the useless, corrupt gauleiters, the criminal and idiotic ministers, the leading families. They are as verminous as Jews ... Maybe not quite as bad as Jews, but their dysfunctional output of 'work' is one of the most significant reasons for our downfall. They were our cancer, and the Fuehrer would not remove one of them, let alone wipe them off the face of the earth like our friend, the Georgian Stalin.

{Shouts of Approval}

Goering: We can see the consequences that have by now befallen us.

Keitel: What 'consequences'?

Goering [Shouting at Keitel]: *The consequences of not exterminating German traitors!*

Himmler [Angrily at Keitel]: Why can't you understand what any of us says?

Fegelein: Because he is stupid.

{Laughter}

Keitel [Angrily to Fegelein]: Are you calling me "stupid"?

Himmler: He just did, yes.

{Laughter}

Guderian [Angrily]: The problem with you people is that you fixed your eyes on one man who you elevated to a god and –

Goebbels: What do such so-called poetic words mean?

Goering [Angrily]: Guderian, we know what you must say. Blame every wart and fart on the Fuehrer. And I have no doubt, the winners will devour your books because that theme of yours shall be littered throughout the pages you shall be writing – you and every other general.

{Angry Shouts of Approval}

Fegelein: Also, what else can they write, given the Americans and the British will be breathing down their throats.

Keitel [Angrily to Fegelein]: How dare you, a nobody in our military ranks, call me 'stupid?'

Fegelein [To Keitel]: Ask the same question, get the same answer.

Goering [To Keitel]: My man, what is this constipated distemper with you?

Keitel [Angrily]: I will not be insulted by –

Goering [Gleeful]: The man rightly called you 'stupid,' which should be the end of the matter.

Keitel [Fuming]: And you accept that?

Goering [Laughing]: Whom am I to deny truth?

DG: General Keitel, didn't you know Gruppenführer Fegelein is to marry Frau Gretl Braun?

Keitel [Shocked]: Excuse me?

{Laughter}

DG: You didn't know?

{Silence}

Keitel: Gruppenführer Fegelein, it is my earnest desire and hope you shall have a most blessed National Socialist union which I know will be blessed because you are indeed one of our stellar examples of National Socialism with the venerable Frau Gretl Braun, who I need not add in saying she too is another of our most stellar National Socialists.

{Everyone – "Congratulations, Fegelein!"}

{Silence}

DG: Gentlemen, can we resume our subject matter?

{Silence}

Guderian: My 'poetic' words mean the following. Whenever any race or regime, or culture chooses to follow slavishly, only one man blindingly, so then its end will be perdition.

Goebbels [Loudly To Guderian]: Here we go again! Focus on one man for a global war!

Ribbentrop [Puzzled to Guderian]: What in God's name are you talking about? 'Perdition?' But why? Why can't we talk optimistically?

Goebbels [To Ribbentrop]: So speaks a man suggesting we talk on optimism while he himself is undergoing a nervous breakdown, hopefully of a fatal variety.

Halder [To Goebbels]: Let me translate. When any society believes only one man has the truth and culture and proceeds to follow that same man fanatically, its destiny will be ruined. Is that now clear enough?

Ribbentrop: But optimism heals mental breakdowns.

Guderian [Loudly]: I am an independent man with my own thoughts. I idolize no one on earth! Unfortunately, the mental aberrations prominent and thriving in our sheepish German people, and you are prime examples of these sheep I refer to, have the same sickness that has infected our nation for the last twelve years. Nietzsche rightly called it, 'Herd Mentality.'

Himmler [Furiously Referring to Guderian and Halder]: Is it not a wonder hearing these traitors speak so freely and candidly of their blood-stained crimes against Germany?

{Silence}

Guderian [Angrily]: We're dead ... we're as death! Remember, you are mortal. We're mortal. Though we think of our lives as being immortal, remember your mortality.

Fegelein: What is the meaning of 'dead as death?' Death is death. Nothing else exists in the state of death.

Himmler [Chuckling]: I think the man is feigning insanity.

Goring [Laughing, To Himmler]: Rare it is indeed for me to agree with a disagreeable person such as yourself, Himmler – but in this precise moment, I must agree with you!

Guderian: It's *not* aristocrats, and it is *not* Jews who destroyed National Socialist Germany -

{Angry Shouts of Disapproval}

{Shouts of – "Who Else?", "Who Else?" "Who Else?"}

Guderian: My God! What has happened to you people?

Goebbels [Sarcastically Laughing]: What beautifully Biblical words, Herr Guderian!

Ribbentrop [Frightened]: When did you become a Christian, General Guderian? And which 'people' are you referring to, General Guderian? And do you think Salvation is coming for Germany?

Goering [Laughing Sarcastically]: You forgot to add the 'General Guderian' in your tripartite questions.

Goebbels: My dear General Keitel, our hero, Pastor Guderian, teaches us about our sins. So, please pay attention.

Goering [To Goebbels]: Pastors don't 'teach,' they 'preach,' idiot.

Himmler: Exactly. After all, who else is there in Germany to preach?

{Silence}

Guderian: Now imagine if that man was right! {Referring to Goebbels} Imagine men such as I and General Halder single-handedly destroying Germany. What does that say about the Fuehrer's leadership quality, meaning his control, management, and rulership over Germany? Of course, I am implying the man could not govern or rule Germany, as Stalin ruled over the largest nation on earth.

{Silence}

Goebbels: That is true. Because the Fuehrer was far too kindly in his interactions with all peoples.

Guderian [Violently]: You superior National Socialists men; you Herrenvolk whom God ordained to enslave the rest of the inferior masses! But of course, what other destiny can there be the Master Race except for being rulers of the earth!

{Angry Shouts of Disapproval}

Guderian [Violently]: What now? Do you deny the primary basis of National Socialist philosophy? You people before me, you deny we waged war after war with the fanatical belief we're superior to everyone else and that the latter deserved either extermination or mass enslavement?

Keitel [Indignantly]: *But we are the Master Race!*

{Silence}

Guderian [Violently]: A triumphal march was always called for whenever there was a military victory in ancient Rome. The victorious general in question drives throughout Rome's streets in his chariot, decorated with gold and ivory. Following him are his grand and proud troops. Behind them are the miserable prisoners and the spoils of war. This procession introduced the victorious and extraordinary opportunities for either creating or strengthening his self-publicity. That was one practical way he could increase his popularity with the people of Rome. For some people, the victorious general was divine, representing the god Jupiter.

{Silence}

Goebbels: What is this man now talking about?

Goering [Laughing]: He thinks ... speaking idiotic words, somehow the Allies will exonerate him from his own crimes.

{Laughter}

Keitel [Pompously]: The man, in my learned opinion, has not necessarily finished his pronounced and final judgment, so if we are to understand what he is talking about, please, in the spirit of National Socialism, please allow him to speak freely.

DG [To Keitel]: Did you allow Sophie School to speak her mind freely?

{Silence}

Fegelein: Who?

DG: You people do not know her?

{Silence}

Goebbels: Who are you talking about, dear?

I understood not one of these high-level Nazis had any idea who Sophie Scholl was, so I quit that question.

Guderian: I have no doubt whatsoever many generals believed they were Jupiter. Maybe, even Zeus. But that's not the reason I'm speaking of this factual event in ancient Rome. Behind the victorious general in the chariot, there was always a lowly slave. This wretch held a dazzling Golden Crown over his head. Amid the screams of the crowd and the sounds of the procession itself, the slave continually whispered in the general's ear –

- *"Memento Mori! Memento Mori!"* ["Remember, you are mortal! Remember you are mortal!"]

Guderian: This was to remind Jupiter no matter how outstanding your military achievements are, you are still but a mortal being like the rest of us, yes, even slaves too.

Goebbels: Wonderful story, General. Any more to fill our empty time with more?

DG: Can we go back to my question, please?

Goebbels: Absolutely, Frau Gale. In some ways, I admit it. And it stabs me to say it.

Ribbentrop [Nervously]: What stabs you, Dr. Goebbels?

Fegelein [Whispers to Himmler]: I never knew Guderian spoke Greek.

Himmler [Whispers to Fegelein]: First, it's Latin. Second, it's just a phrase or two he knows, nothing more.

Goebbels: I see the Fuehrer gradually surrendering not only on his duties but his life too. One by one. Why? I've asked him, "*Why?*" But we both knew the answer.

Guderian: Why do you ask the man a question if you both knew the answer?

Goebbels: With time, you see, Frau Gale, less and less men listen to him. Time. Fewer and fewer men obey his orders. And that's why only I understand his muted cries and lamentations.

Ribbentrop [Pleading]: But look at me. It wasn't just the Fuehrer whom no one obeyed. No one hears my muted cries and lamentations!

Goebbels: In these dying circumstances, what is a rational man to do? What can we do?

DG: Well, to be crude, you people are either condemned to death or given a prison sentence, depending on the gravity of your crimes.

Goebbels [Excited]: Should the Fuehrer go on giving orders and exhortations while everyone acts deaf? Can a leader bother to pronounce one word if his listeners are seditious creatures? That would be insane, and our saviour, our Fuehrer, knows the finality we are in. No one is interested in him, in his words. What a wretched, hideous hour this is! Maybe Socrates was correct —

"Death may be the greatest of all human blessings."

- Socrates

Guderian: Does anyone here admit the war is lost?

{*Silence*}

Guderian: None of you?

∼

V. Hitler's Highest-Ranking Men Cannot Understand Why Britain Fought a Suicidal War Against Germany and Dorothy Answers Them

Guderian: People are not deserting him because they are traitors. They're doing what's natural to every human and animal, and that's known as self-preservation—leaving a deflated dying entity—leaving him because that man willfully plunged Germany into this catastrophic abyss. A black abyss whose future properties none of us can know. Except to say for sure, it shall be as similar as Hell.

"Everybody wants to go to heaven, but nobody wants to die."

- Unknown

Speer [Laughing]: The 'hell' above us is as nothing compared to Germany's future?

Guderian: Precisely.

Fegelein [Chuckling]: Enjoy the war while it lasts; peace will be far worse!

Goering [Dryly to Fegelein]: Hilarious.

Ribbentrop [Nervous]: How can you people laugh at a time like this? None of this is *'funny.'* Where is the funniness you people find? I see you laughing. That means something, somewhere, must be funny; otherwise, no one would laugh. Do you know what 'funny' means?

Fegelein [To Ribbentrop]: I'd say something looking like you.

Keitel [Proudly]: Absolutely correct, Herr Foreign Minister von Ribbentrop. For anyone who dares to laugh when in truth and when they are in the actual state of reality of knowing what they are doing, so then there can be no official cause nor any official excuse that can conceivably create the aforementioned laughter in question and therefore they must officially be certified as insane and National Socialist Germany cannot accept insane 'people,' so such individuals must immediately either be sentenced to death or sent to a hospital where they would be euthanized since it is the Fuehrer's official National Socialist ideology not to tolerate any so-called 'human' who is unworthy of life.

{*Murmurs of Approval*}

Ribbentrop [Nervous]: General Keitel, you've not said to me one word of salvation. To get us out from this hell. Why don't you talk to us? The cripples, I mean.

Goering [To Ribbentrop]: My dear, when did you understand you're a "cripple"?

{*Laughter & Words Said, "The Day He Was Born!"*}

Ribbentrop [Frightened]: There must be hope. Please, will anyone speak anything positive? Why is it no one I see before me is scared? Do you people think we're going to survive? Because we are not going to survive. Neither the Soviets nor the Americans will leave us alone, as they did with the Kaiser and his government. Why is that? Why this criminal hypocrisy? How are we different from him?

Fegelein: From the Kaiser?

Ribbentrop: But the Kaiser died back in 1940! Do you mean his relatives? Yes, why not? Perhaps the Kaiser's family can be brought to make peace; what do you gentlemen think of that? As Foreign Minister of Germany, I can go and talk –

{*Laughter*}

Goering [Guffawing]: We can always exhume the Kaiser's corpse!

{*Laughter*}

Goebbels [Laughing]: Why not Bismarck's family?

{*Laughter*}

Didn't Ribbentrop even sense Fegelein was mocking him? But the ex-Foreign Minister was so far out; the poor idiot had no idea what or who was saying what and why. A train wreck.

Speer: Who knows the future? Some men speak with certainty. Very well. I do not. No one knows what will happen in one hour, let alone following the war. So, on what basis do you calculate -

Goebbels [Angrily at Speer]: Are you stupid?

Speer: I am not stupid.

Goebbels [Angrily at Speer]: If you think you're not stupid, why are you bothering us with your stupid words?

Speer [To Goebbels]: Sir, I am as 'stupid' and responsible for our downfall, so too is everyone else just as accountable for our catastrophic situation. And that just happens to include you.

Goering [Giggling]: For once, I agree with Black Dwarf! Goebbels played no role whatsoever in the history of National Socialist Germany. None! Why, does anyone think driveling words changed anything in our diplomatic, economic, and military affairs?

{*Murmurs of Approval*}

Goering: My dear man, why are you so intent on killing yourself? Never has a trial condemned a man for talk, and you must know that you shall be acquitted in the coming military trial.

{*Laughter*}

{*Silence*}

Guderian: Germany will be divided between the two superpowers, Russia and America.

Fegelein: What about France and Britain?

Goebbels: America controls those two chickens, though, for appearance's sakes, they'll be given crumbs of land.

DG: What about Poland and the other east European nations?

{*Laughter*}

Goebbels [Excited]: Oh yes, Stalin will back his men and tanks, especially from Poland. After all, that was what supposedly ignited this war – the honor, prestige, and independence of plucky Poland!

{*Laughter*}

Goering: If I were in Stalin's shoes, I certainly would never offer freedom to these East European countries.

For some reason, I thought about my old man. What was he doing with his 'life'? Well, nothing. He was existing. Nothing more. And that hurt me. And then I knew any day I'm bound to hear someone telling me, "Your Daddy's done dead." And I'd be sad, But then when I think about it, what difference would it mean for Daddy if he lived one more day when every day he just re-enacted every other day he lived? Every day, I know Daddy did or lived or whatever the verb is ... he just did or repeated the same routine, doing the same things. He'd eat, shovel shit, watch television, sleep, and so on. That was it. That was the entirety of his life. If you just repeat every pointless day of your dreary life in the exact same manner, why should we cry if the person in question dies?

Himmler: You're mistaken, General Guderian. There still exists the distinct possibility we can negotiate with the Allies, America. I cannot understand or imagine America will allow Bolshevism to conquer, occupy, and control Eastern Europe's entirety. It makes no sense!

{*Sounds of Shock*}

Goering: It makes no sense to us National Socialists, but to idiots in London and Washington, they believe this is the best solution for Europe's future.

Fegelein: But if it makes no sense, what 'sense' is the West acting on?

Goering [To Fegelein]: That was precisely what the Fuehrer could not understand, going back to 1940, when France fell. We offered England peace and publicly declared time, and again, National Socialist Germany not only does not want war with the West but that we had no quarrel with them. So, what are we fighting for? Now all you gentlemen remember Churchill refused our numerous pleas for peace, is that not so?

{Murmurs of Approval}

Goering [To Fegelein]: So, yes, it was baffling back then. Imagine if the Kaiser made the same proclamation to England and France!

{Everyone: 'Jawohl Herr Reichsmarschall!"}

Goering: And now you ask me in this final year of 1945 why London and Washington are fanatically determined to exterminate the remains of Germany and the German people?

{Silence. Everyone Pensive}

Speer: Baffling it is, indeed. And I cannot come up with any reason nor logic explaining the behavior of the West.

{Silence. Everyone Pensive}

Goebbels [Loudly]: Gentlemen, what is the matter with you?

Speer: If you know the answer -

Goebbels [Abruptly]: Let me finish, please. Have you forgotten the Fuehrer's words, ye so-called 'men' of no faith? When we say 'Great Britain' and the 'United States,' whom do we speak of?

Himmler: Jews.

Goering [Chuckling]: Rich for a club-footed Black Dwarf doubted we are 'men.'

{Laughter}

By the way, as per my last thought, that was during Daddy's final months. A stroke struck him, and I had never heard of that. Meaning, 'stroke.' But, golly, it transforms humans from electrifying, magnetizing personalities into zombies. And that was what happened to Daddy. In his autumnal years, he couldn't keep himself alive. Lame, mute, wild-eyed, and frightened. Frightened of what I couldn't know. I'd ask him, but his words were incomprehensible sounds.

Goebbels [Excited]: Exactly! International Jewry decided back in 1933 to exterminate the German people. And what a pitiful price it is for them if they must surrender half of Europe to Bolshevism? Think about our recent history. Remember, Churchill did not just seek war against us, as England did in the last war; they needed to exterminate Germany!

{People Saying – "True, True, But Senseless!"}

Fegelein: But why?

Goering: Goebbels is right. International Jewry and Bolshevism could not exist so long as National Socialism existed and not because we represented any military threat; that's the great lie. We represented a threat to them ideologically, challenging their putrid, self-destructive ideologies.

Goebbels: But that's why the Fuehrer begged us to question the motivations behind London and Washington in their fanatical need to exterminate the German people, culture, and civilization.

Goering: In the end, the people lose, be they in East Europe, West Europe, or America.

Himmler: The winners are indeed the Jewish-Bolshevik plutocrats.

Ribbentrop [Nervous]: Is this talk supposed to be helping our morale?

DG [To Himmler]: Weren't you just telling us there's still a chance of making peace with the West?

Himmler: That's true, but typically, since no one was interested in my words, I too decided not to press on with the matter. Dullards.

Goering: No, dear Himmler, it's not that we 'dullards' didn't notice your sacral words. You're mad. And so too, we'd be mad if we noted your words.

DG: Shouldn't we let the man explain his words?

Goering: Of course, there's no logic here when you think about it. But then, remember, when did the elites actually care for their people? Never! Except for the Fuehrer, of course.

Fegelein: Can't the British and Americans understand Russia will soon turn her aggressive eyes on them?

{Angry Shouts of Approval}

Goebbels: Of course they know. If anything, already we see ripples of confrontational incidents between the two camps.

{People Saying – "Senseless," "Idiotic"}

Speer: So, the question surely arises, where are the rational, educated, civilized Britons who could foresee that if they continued with their idiotic war against National Socialist Germany, they would end up not only losing their finances but their entire empire too?

Goering: You're assuming the average Briton has brains. More to the point, the average person throughout the world is an idiot.

Himmler: Racially, that is not strictly accurate, Herr Reichsmarschall, since you know some races exhibit higher intelligence than others.

Goering: Of course I know that, but on average, take the average American, Frenchman, or Briton – do you think they are clever enough to understand International Jewry and Bolshevism are destroying their nations for the sake of the elite plutocrats?

Goebbels [Agitated]: And gentlemen, that is precisely what happened in the last six savage years of unprecedented brutality against us.

{Silence}

Speer: And that's what stuns me to this hour.

{Silence}

Fegelein: Doesn't that mean people like Churchill is a traitor to the interests of his nation?

Goebbels [Loudly, to Fegelein]: Precisely! But the Jew offers many masks to his stooges. Churchill wears his fat face with that cigar, and Britons love the man they believe *'saved'* their country – when the truth is that that drunkard bankrupted and destroyed his Empire.

{Silence}

Goebbels: And now, having understood the story so far, what then can we conclude?

{Silence}

Himmler: England is controlled by the same Jews who control Russia.

Goering [Angrily]: Absolutely not! Stalin purged Jews from his regime, unlike Lenin, who loved Jews.

Jodl: The Reichsmarschall is correct. Jewish influence in Stalin's Soviet Union is practically non-existent.

DG: Excuse me, if that were true, why did your Fuehrer instruct the Wehrmacht to eliminate all commissars who were supposedly Jewish?

Jodl: You are correct in one instance - most Soviet commissars or political officers in the Red Army were infested with Jews. The

Fuehrer was right in demanding their liquidation. However, in the higher levels of office, Jewish influence was minimal.

{Murmurs of Approval}

Goering: Stalin is quite simple to understand, as per his impulses or motivations. He's a classic Bolshevik who wants his criminal ideology to conquer the world. And fundamentally, according to the depraved theories of Marx the Jew, there can never be any kind of co-existence between capitalist and communist nations. Therefore, it's only a matter of time when the latter must attack the former.

{Murmurs of Approval}

DG: You people astound me. You really do.

Goebbels: Do elaborate on your undoubtedly profound ideas by illustrating to us in what precise manner do we accomplish this extraordinary feat of having 'astounded' your sensitivities, dear?

{Everyone: "Exactly!"}

Speer: But, going back to the brilliant thesis of Dr. Goebbels - I still cannot understand anything here … Why didn't the elite, upper classes of England turn against that alcoholic Churchill?

Goering [Bombastically]: Because we under-estimated the matter of the power those Jewish elites had. And, to my regret, so did our Fuehrer, who thought the British people would somehow come to their senses and realize that it would be in their best interests to join us in this holy crusade against Bolshevism and America.

Ribbentrop [Timidly]: That was exactly what I was doing! But everywhere, I found people stopping me and distracting me. Why was that?

Guderian [To Ribbentrop]: I've always known you as an idiot, but not until now do I accept you are mentally deranged.

{Murmurs of Approval}

DG [To Guderian]: But who insisted that this "deranged man" remain his Minister of Foreign Affairs?

Keitel [Shocked]: Oh no, this is unacceptable! If it were true that Herr Ribbentrop, Foreign Minister of National Socialist Germany is mad as you claim, so then according to the laws of National Socialist Germany, the person must be euthanized and I do not know if that is what you gentlemen are actually proposing to do with our Foreign Minister of National Socialist Germany.

Ribbentrop: General Keitel, I thank you for your support. But please, the name is 'von' Ribbentrop.

Guderian [To Dorothy]: Look, please dispense with Ribbentrop because he was a non-entity. Now, I agree with you that countless people urged the Fuehrer to dispense with many pathetic, weakling idiots in his orbit.

Fegelein: Why euthanize a brain-dead person?

Himmler: Because he's a useless eater. A waste of Germany's precious resources.

Guderian: Though, as usual, the Fuehrer did not by nature like to sack miscreants. Certainly not outside the Wehrmacht ranks.

Goering [To Fegelein]: Lebensunwertes Leben ['Life Unworthy of Life'].

{Silence}

Himmler [Angrily]: Churchill ordered his people to self-immolate as a nation!

Goering [Loudly]: As the Fuehrer spoke time and again, how fortunate it is for so-called 'democratic nations' to have masses of entirely stupid people!

{Shouts of Approval}

{Silence}

Keitel: I still do not understand all these words. How can any people willingly choose suicide when they know suicide means self-extermination?

Goebbels: What else can suicide mean but self-extermination?

Speer [To Keitel]: I think the Reichsmarschall answered that question.

Keitel: He did? When?

"In our hatred, we are like bees who must pay with their lives for the use of their stingers."

- Friedrich Reck-Malleczewen. (1884-1945) *Diary of a Man in Despair*

Himmler [Frustrated]: Will someone, please bother to explain whatever needs to be explained to General Keitel?

Goering: What an idiotic request. No one has any interest in Keitel.

Jodl [To Keitel]: The British people are too stupid to understand what Churchill was doing. It is not that complicated.

DG: I have been listening to you gentlemen expressing your stupefied inability to understand why nations chose to fight Nazi Germany. You find it especially nonsensical why and what Great Britain's motivation in fighting Germany was, given the undoubtedly horrendous costs it would necessarily have to incur. And you rightly cited these gross costs as losing their entire empire and becoming a bankrupt nation.

Goebbels: What is your point, my girl? And I ask, because we fear being too bored given the history of your speaking drivel.

DG: What strikes me is that your mentality and mind-frames are no different from the Kaiser during World War One.

{Sounds of shock}

Himmler [Angrily]: Why are we even listening to this moronic girl?

Goering [Snapping at Himmler]: Let the girl talk!

{Angry Shouts of Approval}

{"She's the Fuehrer's Guest!"}

DG: Thank you, Herr Reichsmarschall. The Kaiser in his day wanted to conquer France. That was his aim. But stupidly, he did not think Britain would have to be involved. He thought London would just remain indifferent. My question is this; why did the Kaiser and his military people not understand the necessity for Britain to join in the war alongside France?

Fegelein: Continental Europe has nothing to do with England.

DG: Precisely so ... for that is how your predecessor military elites stupidly thought.

Guderian: The lady speaks the truth. The Kaiser and our generals should have known Britain had to become involved. Once we attacked France, specifically northern France, that posed an existential threat to Britain.

DG: Of course, it is not just that fact that propelled, that necessitated Britain in joining the war with France in 1914. If we think for a moment, had Germany conquered the West, that would have meant cutting off Britain's export enterprises with Europe. And so, it is with your beloved Fuehrer. He stated he did not want war in the West and, yes, to beginners, that sounded like fresh news. After all, if the Fuehrer did not attack France, why should France and Great Britain fear Germany? Well again, it is not difficult to see why London and Paris were compelled to fight. Hitler's foreign policy was to either conquer or make Europe Germany's sole sphere of interest. And that means Berlin would be the master of Europe on an economic basis. That equation meant nullifying France and England's role in their particular economic interests in mainland Europe. Can you now see the logic why Hitler's greediness in seeking to control Europe forced those two nations to fight Germany? And that was the same mistake Napoleon made by not only blockading England but, more importantly, with his strict insistence that no independent nation may trade with Britain. That, of course, fearfully hurt the economic interests of Czarist Russia, as you gentlemen should know. Napoleon was as strategically blind as your beloved Fuehrer.

Goering: Napoleon was lucky. He had no United States to confront us.

~

Goering's Response to Dorothy's Argument on Why Fighting Germany Is Pointless

Goering: Having said that, my dear Frau Gale, you do not see the larger context.

DG: And what is this 'larger context'?

Goering: Sooner or later, Germany will dominate Europe. By 'dominate,' I mean Germany will always be the strongest European nation. It will naturally be the dominant power in this continent. Now, how Germany achieves its natural function as the most significant economic power in Europe is immaterial because, as I said, one way or another, be it the Kaiser or the Fuehrer – none of that matters – in the long run, Germany will still be the only economic giant of Europe. I will provide you with a brief and more straightforward example. The Allies, that is, the enemies of Germany, created Czechoslovakia, as you know. Now, what is the function and purpose of that so-called state? It was designed to be deep within German territory, and thus you don't need to be a military genius to understand its threatening position within the heart of Germany. And I want you to know that I understand why our enemies created that artificial state. If I were an enemy of Germany, I, too, would have created Czechoslovakia. But there was one severe problem in that construct. Czechs hated Slovaks and vice-versa, much like the Goebbels marriage.

{Laughter}

Goering: In other words, the two races wanted no fake 'unity' imposed upon them by Great Britain, France, and the United States.

Both Czechs and Slovaks knew perfectly well they were created by the Allies, not in their interests — that is, for the beneficial interests of the Czech and Slovak peoples — instead, they were forced into this hated entity by the Allies serving the latter's interests. Now, Frau Gale, you know what happened with that nation, do you not?

DG: Of course, I do.

Guderian: Herr Reichsmarschall, I would like to interject here, if I may, for you have not asked our American friend if she agrees with what you have so far said or not?

DG: I can accept Czechs and Slovaks did not necessarily ... or did not want to be united.

Goebbels [Laughing Sarcastically]: Well, done, Frau Gale; how insightful of you!

Goering: So, when the Fuehrer arrived on the scene, he fully understood what he was facing. He knew that Czechoslovakia was an artificial state because its two races hated each other. The Fuehrer also fully understood the entire raison d'etre for creating this so-called 'state' — which, again, as I said, was to military be an existential threat to Germany.

DG: You're repeating yourself.

Goering: I think you should by now understand why our Fuehrer acted as he did not only during the Sudeten Crises but in ultimately dissolving that artificial state in March of 1939.

{Applause}

DG: But your Fuehrer ... didn't he promise no more territorial acquisitions?

Goering [Angrily]: What 'territorial acquisitions' do you speak of?

"It is not the length of life, but the depth of life."

Ralph Waldo Emerson

Goering: My young girl, don't you see a pattern building up here that's gradually clear enough for anyone to see?

DG: What 'pattern'?

Keitel [Loudly]: Exactly! And isn't that the point to be known in life – the specific patterns in life? Patterns that only the gods and prophets can see and interpret, such as our Fuehrer.

Goering: The Allies wanted to exterminate Germany.

DG: No, I do not accept –

Goering: That is principle number one. Next, they refuse Germany its natural rights to be the dominant power in Europe – and this is where we differ, and radically so.

DG: You must understand why nations such as Great Britain and France couldn't accept their existential rights extinguished by Germany's greedy insistence on being the sole power or arbiter over Europe.

Goering [Loudly]: And that's precisely my point too, my dear girl!

DG [Loudly]: Exactly!

Ribbentrop [Timid]: Do we have a sudden agreement here? We can send this agreement to Washington, Reichsmarschall ... I can do that.

Goering: Germany is the historically and the eternally strongest nation in Europe. So, by what right do weaker nations stand in our way? Do you or do you not understand that fact?

DG: I cannot accept one nation, just because it may be strong, stealing all the benefits with its commercial interactions in Europe. It must allow other countries the freedom to trade in Europe.

{Murmurs of "Rank Hypocrisy!"}

Goebbels [Sly]: Does the United States not economically control Central and South America?

DG: I do not know if that is a fact.

{Mocking Laughter}

Goebbels: Oh, dear me, the lady seems dumber than a cynic such as myself anticipated.

Speer: Frau Gale, we're trying to be reasonable with you, but you cannot say or pretend you don't know that your nation does not control the entirety of South American countries!

DG: Again, I've no facts to substantiate that point either way.

Goering [Shocked]: Are you playing stupid, my girl?

Himmler: If you have no facts, why do you insist on talking?

Speer: Isn't 'talking' her job?

DG: What evidence do you have?

Goering [Angrily]: Your nation installs pro-American puppets in every Latin American government. They do whatever Washington tells them to do. Meanwhile, most people in each country are entirely ignored, while these countries' only function is to serve your great, noble country.

Guderian: In other words, your country uses every Latin American country to make profits that go to its elites.

Goebbels [Shouting with Sarcasm]: Gentlemen! What is the point in this idiocy we are engaging in? Do you think our friendly Frau Gale has no idea America controls an entire continent? Do you believe our familiar Frau Gale has no idea that Great Britain controls a quarter of the earth's landmass, as per nations? Do you think this woman has no idea that France has had its colonial empire comprising at one time or another with the following countries, peoples, and territories - the Dominican Republic, parts of Canada, including Acadia, Newfoundland, Hudson Bay, Saint Lawrence River, Great Lakes, Lake Winnipeg, and Quebec?

{Mocking Laughter}

Goebbels: And how about territories in your nation, Frau Gale, such as - The Fort Saint Louis (Texas), Saint Croix, U.S. Virgin Islands, Fort Caroline in French Florida, Vincennes and Fort Ouiatenon in Indiana, French Louisiana?

{Shouts of Approval}

Goebbels: And how about Brazil - France Équinoxiale, the island of Saint Alexis, the Territory of Amapá, the city of Viçosa-Ceará (Territory of Ibiapaba), France Antarctique, to Fort Coligny (Rio de Janeiro Bay and the Île Delphine's island? And what about Haiti? Did France not conquer that island? And Suriname? And Grenada? Martinique?

{Laughter}

Goebbels: Morocco, Algeria, Tunisia, French Dahomey, Senegambia and Niger, Mauritania, Upper Volta, Chad, Gambia, Gabon, Cameroon, Madagascar, Seychelles, Djibouti, Laos, Cambodia, Vietnam, Syria, Lebanon, Papua New Guinea?

{Laughter}

Goering: Goebbels, your words remind of the Fuehrer's response to that idiot, Roosevelt! Do you gentlemen remember –

{*Everyone: Laughing, "Of Course, We Do!"*}

Ribbentrop [Laughing]: I have his words here! Listen, please –

President Roosevelt to the Chancellor of Germany (Hitler)
[40], [Telegram], 14 April 1939

THE WHITE HOUSE, April 14, 1939.

Roosevelt: You realize I am sure that throughout the world, hundreds of millions of human beings are living today in constant fear of a new war or even a series of wars.

{*Laughter*}

Goebbels: And now comes the marrow of his fears –

Roosevelt: Are you willing to give assurance that your armed forces will not attack or invade the territory or possessions of the following independent nations: Finland, Estonia, Latvia, Lithuania, Sweden, Norway, Denmark, The Netherlands, Belgium, Great Britain, and Ireland, France, Portugal, Spain, Switzerland, Liechtenstein,

Luxemburg, Poland, Hungary, Rumania, Yugoslavia, Russia, Bulgaria, Greece, Turkey, Iraq, the Arabias, Syria, Palestine, Egypt, and Iran?

{Laughter}

Goering: And then our Fuehrer gave his resoundingly victorious speech, illustrating the idiocy –

Hitler: If, however, President Roosevelt thinks that he is entitled to address such a request, in particular to Germany or Italy, because 'America is so far removed from Europe, we on our side might, with the same right, address to the President of the American Republic the question as to what aim American foreign policy, in turn, has in view, and on what intentions this policy is based-in the case of the Central and South American states, for instance. ***In this event, Mr. Roosevelt would, I must admit, have every right to refer to the Monroe Doctrine and to decline to comply with such a request as an interference in the internal affairs of the American Continent***. We Germans support a similar doctrine for Europe – and, above all, for the territory and interests of the Greater German Reich.

Goering: Do you understand, Frau Gale?

DG: I'm listening, but I don't accept a word you say. Anyway, go on.

Goering: Of course, you cannot agree with your bosses; how could you? If you did so, you would be fired –

DG: And what about you Nazis? Were you to disagree with your Fuehrer, wouldn't you too be fired?

Himmler: Shot.

Goering: Of course, we would, and so we *should* be fired. After all, anyone in an airplane and choosing to negate every pilot's act cannot be tolerated, am I right?

Speer: My young lady, do you not yet see the hypocrisy in your great leader's words?

Goering: More –

Hitler: Answers I have first taken the trouble to ascertain from the states mentioned, firstly, whether they feel themselves threatened, and what is most important, secondly, whether this inquiry by the American President was addressed to us at their suggestion or at least with their consent. The reply was, in all cases, negative, in some instances strongly so. Nevertheless, there were indeed certain ones among the states and nations mentioned, whom I could not question because they themselves – as for example, Syria – are at present not in possession of their freedom but are under occupation by the military agents of democratic states and consequently deprived of their rights.

{Laughter}

DG: I can accept FDR may have been misinformed on some details, but his … but the totality of his speech is intensely profound, meaning smaller nations ought not to be attacked by larger countries.

Goering: And we agree with your words, my good lady, but how can Germany guarantee the freedom and democracy of nations that your own peoples and allies brutally subjugate?

Goebbels [Shouting]: Gentlemen! That indeed is the question!

{Murmurs of Approval}

DG: I have already admitted that FDR was misinformed on specific details, but the totality –

Goebbels: So, what is his message, Frau Gale, if we discard the idiocies he mentioned?

DG: If you allow me to finish a sentence! Though it was not his fault, FDR was partially wrong because foreign affairs were never his priority. FDR's priority was to save us Americans from the catastrophic consequences of the 1930's Depression –

Himmler: Nobody is interested in that man's domestic policies, Frau Gale.

{Murmurs of Approval}

Himmler: So, try to stick to our subject matter, if you can.

DG: I am trying to tell you that he made a mistake in this or that speech. But what is the immoral value of those mistakes?

Fegelein [Confused]: What?

Goering: Did you not just hear that America, Great Britain, and France control much of the world through pure exploitation? And that is not 'immoral to you?

∼

Goering- "In the Eyes of the Hypocritical World, Our Greatest Sin Is Racism. But Do You Think the West Is Not Racist, Given Their Segregationist Laws and Colonies?"

Goering [Angrily]: You ask us what are the "immoral values" of our so-called "mistakes"?

DG [Sternly]: Yes, I do. Any nation, any civilization fighting against an exterminatory, racist regime such as National Socialist Germany has every moral right to eliminate you.

Goering: Wouldn't that be true if it were only us Germans carrying out these immoral practices?

DG: What?

Goering: You insist National Socialist Germany practiced immoral policies?

DG: Absolutely.

Goering: You imply, and correct if I were wrong; only National Socialist Germany carried out these hideously immoral policies, right?

"Men build too many walls and not enough bridges."

— Joseph Fort Newton

DG: Sir, even if other countries practiced immoral acts ... and by that, I am of course speaking of Stalin's Russia, because that man is as evil as your hallowed Fuehrer ... but even if the North Pole enacted barbaric, exterminatory policies so the civilized world would unite in unanimous condemnation.

Goebbels: I do not understand you, my dear, and I say that because as far as I happen to know with the utmost certainty, no one lives in the North Pole.

Ribbentrop [Excited]: Actually, that is a fascinating subject matter. Back in the thirties, I tried to get our nation territorial rights over large areas of the North Pole because my geologists told me there is oil in those areas.

Goering: Please continue hearing this magnificent Fuehrer speech that exposes the lies, idiocies, and hypocrisies of your beloved nation:

Hitler: With all due respect to Mr. Roosevelt's insight into the needs and cares of other countries, it may nevertheless be assumed that the Irish Taoiseach would be more familiar with the dangers which threaten his country than would the President of the United States. Similarly, the fact has obviously escaped Mr. Roosevelt's notice that Palestine is at present occupied not by German troops but by the English; and that the country is undergoing restriction of its liberty by the most brutal resort to force, is being robbed of its independence and is suffering the cruelest maltreatment for the benefit of Jewish interlopers. The Arabs living in that country would therefore certainly not have complained to Mr.

Roosevelt of German aggression, but they are voicing a constant appeal to the world, deploring the barbarous methods with which England is attempting to suppress a people which loves its freedom and is merely defending it.

{Laughter}

Goering: Frau Gale, how could Germany defend Palestine – when our enemy, Great Britain, occupied the poor nations?

{Laughter}

DG: We discussed Roosevelt's erroneous words. You can make jokes, but that hardly stretches the quality of our conversation.

Goering: We National Socialists are evil, vicious, and so on. Furthermore, because of these horrific attributes of our ideology, we deserve to be destroyed. But the question *you* have not answered, Frau Gale, is this - who is fighting National Socialist Germany? Presumably, it must be a country or nation with higher moral values than we do, correct?

DG: That goes without saying.

Goering: So, then, we back to our question; how can the Allied nation e counted as 'moral' nations when as we've just said, they control have the world?

DG: Let me tell you that many of us in the United States disagree with England's imperialist policies, such as exist in India. We condemn such racist practices because the English domination of India is an abomination. So, I agree with you. And I agree with you in that every imperialist conquest of any race, people, nation, or community is immoral and evil. But in time, I can tell you, thanks to our parliamentary system, wherein free thought is permitted, and it shall not be long before all these poor colonized peoples shall finally be given their rightful independence. Why? Because we have a democracy, other political parties are fiercely against Mr. Churchill's likes, and these liberal, progressive parties will throw him out of office. But, and here is the crucial, critical point, Sir, not one democratic nation exterminates its subject colonial people. That is the gigantic moral difference. I admit I cannot include Stalin in this camp because, frankly speaking, he is not much different from Hitler. But I am talking about Western democracies. Do you know, or can you kindly tell me if there are any extermination programs against anyone in these colonized countries? Do you now see the difference between democratic nations, where everyone is free, instead of your dictatorial system, where no one can speak against the beloved leader?

{Mocking Laughter}

Goering: My girl, do you really think the elites, the oligarchs of the capitalist nations, will allow independence or freedom of their colonies?

DG: Of course, because we Americans fought for the liberty of all human beings.

{Mocking Laughter}

Goering: Your illiteracy is astounding. What do you think your comrades, the French, are doing in Algeria?

{Everyone: 'Jawohl Herr Reichsmarschall Goring!"}

DG: Please, wait. Even if those criminal acts were true, are you saying that permits your Master Race to commit genocide?

Goering [Shouting]: I'm telling you, once more, *we did not commit genocide!*

{Everyone: 'Jawohl Herr Reichsmarschall Goring!"}

∼

Goering – On the Supposed 'Criminal Nature' of American and Russian/Soviet Culture

Goering: The Bolsheviks will automate us, annihilating souls. Robotised Germans cannot be classified as human beings. Meanwhile, your nation will convert us into Americans. Or you will Americanise us Germans, which means the same as Bolshevisatio, except American robots are a variant breed from the Bolshevik automaton.

Goebbels: It does not matter really, since whether you are Americanised or Bolshevised, you will still be a brainless puppet.

Keitel: Is there a difference for the German people between these two scenarios?

DG: And what's wrong with America?

Goering: Your nation floats in a moral vacuum because you have no culture. And you can never have a culture because America is not even a nation. However, the so-called 'culture; America created is depravity, which suits its elites perfectly well.

Speer: I agree.

DG [Indignant]: Excuse me? *We* have no culture?

Goebbels: The Reichsmarschall is correct. A nation composed mainly of Jews and Negroes cannot create civilization. It can mass produce brute, raw power, yes, just as Stalin can. But culture? Civilisation? No, that is the preserve of the dignified man, and Americans have no such thing as the ennobled Man. This is the sick tragedy being played out throughout this world. We are the bearers of civilization, yet we are now mournfully exiting the stage of existence, leaving only monkeys and cave dwellers ruling suffering Mankind.

{*Murmurs of Approval*}

DG: How on earth can you say we have no culture? We have the world's greatest philosophers, writers, scientists, artists, musicians, and more.

Goebbels: And they are all copycats of European culture, please. Let us not pretend for one moment you Americans created anything original.

Goering: They did.

"America is the only country that went from barbarism to decadence without civilization in between."

- Oscar Wilde (1854-1900)

Goebbels: What?

Goering: I said they *did* create original culture.

Goebbels: Such as what?

Goering: They have jazz, Hollywood, gangsters, drugs, promiscuity, and so on.

Goebbels [Angrily]: And you do not know who created those criminal movements and institutions?

Goering: What 'criminal' movements?

Goebbels: Jazz! Hollywood!

Goering: I do. Negroes and Jews. But that does not change the truth in what I said. Do you deny their popularity with the masses?

"All great movements are popular movements. They are the volcanic eruptions of human passions and emotions, stirred into activity by the ruthless Goddess of Distress or by the torch of the spoken word cast into the midst of the people."

— Adolf Hitler

Speer: You are correct, but that does not elevate jazz and Hollywood to the lofty realms of culture or civilizational.

Goering: I just said it is not culture. It is depraved culture. But no one can deny its global appeal. This is what the majority, the mobs want and love. And that is the genius of America. And when I say 'America,' I mean its leaders, the elites that govern that nation. Well, what do they do? How do they control their population? It is an ingenious strategy. They allow their masses to indulge in every vice on earth.

Goebbels: Well, now, I must again agree with you, Guderian.

Goering: By allowing the hoi-polloi total freedom to indulge in any vice they wish, they thereby deflect the minuscule intelligence residing within these idiotic classes away from any rational thinking. That is how they avert revolutions against their system of governance.

Speer: How correct you are, Reichsmarschall. In a way, that is precisely how the Romans neutered their population with Bread and Circuses.

Goebbels: But going back to morality, to truth, to the welfare of Man — is that what we want for our German people?

Speer: Of course not.

Goebbels: And yet, isn't that exactly what will happen to the miserable Germans who our friendly Americas will lobotomize

DG: Isn't it interesting how not one of you high-ranking Nazis recognizes one of our most outstanding achievements?

Keitel: Where?

DG: In the US!

Speer: What do you mean?

∼

Dorothy – "The Only Reason Why the 'Herrenvolk' Did Not Build the Atom Bomb Is Because You Expelled or Murdered Jewish Physicists – Which Proves You Were Dumber Than the Jews!"

DG [Laughing]: Which nation do you think is more scientifically advanced – Germany, England, the Russians, or Americans?

Goering [Sighing]: She's right.

Keitel: What do you mean Herr Reichsmarschall?

Goering [Wearily]: Apart from Keitel, will any of you leaders of National Socialist Germany please stand up and admit our catastrophic failure in the field of the sciences and specifically in the field of particle physics?

Himmler: We have our miracle weapons, but the only problem, Herr Reichsmarschall, is something I think you know much about. Were it not for our skies covered with Allied bombers, our output of the V-1 and V-2 rockets – to name but a few of our genius creations – would have obliterated the Allies.

{Murmurs of Approval}

Speer: Gentlemen, that's *not* what our Reichsmarschall is talking about.

Keitel: So ... will one of you please inform us of what is it that we do not know because I cannot know that which I do not know and that in itself also stands to sturdy reason that that which I say -

Goering [Loudly]: The atom bomb, idiots!

Fegelein: What's that?

{Silence}

Goering: Had we not expelled the Jewish physicists, we would've had our atom bomb by now.

Guderian: Herr Reichsmarschall, excuse me for saying this because I may be wrong, but weren't you one of the first instigators of expelling all Jews from Germany as early as 1934?

Goering: Of course, I was, and now when I look back, don't you think I regret it?

DG: You were absolute fools in expelling geniuses like Einstein, weren't you?

{Silence}

Himmler [Proudly]: Absolutely not! Jewish physics is cancerous, just as everything and anything connected with a virus is lethal and –

Goering [Roaring at Himmler]: What are you talking about, idiot? Had we kept our Jewish physicists, Germany would have been the first nation to create the atom bomb –

Goebbels: I hear the atom bomb causes cancer.

Himmler: We did not need criminals such as Einstein. We had our magnificent ranks of pure German scientists. The problem was not that National Socialist Germany lacked the brains to create an atom bomb. The problem was, which I just stated, thanks to the Luftwaffe's failures, our factories could not increase output in any new weapon – and you, Herr Speer, as Minister of Armaments should know that far more than I do.

Speer: I agree with you, but not one of our German scientists worked on the atom bomb with any efficiency as the Americans were, which is the subject we are supposed to be discussing.

~

Conversation with Three Female German Teens II – "What Is Happiness?"

Ilse Koch: If only the Fuehrer were harder, hard as leather without our effeminate, debauched people, we could've won the war.

Gudrun Ensslin: Idiotic as ever, blinded by fanaticism. If you look at the briefest statistics, an idiot will inform you Germany can never fight against the combined might of the United Nations of this earth.

Ilse Koch: And if you ever briefly acquainted yourself with military history so you would know how many times great men overcame overwhelming numerical odds.

Eva Gretl: Goodness me, you two! At least the war is over. Isn't that good for every German man, woman, and child?

Ilse Koch: You know, as much as I despise you, Gudrun, I must say my hatred is far fiercer for mongrels like Eva, for whom life means nothing but having babies and her one-person idiot whom she can only be a slave to.

Gudrun Ensslin [To Ilse]: That's rich coming from you! Aren't you too obsessed with your Fuehrer?

Ilse Koch: I love our Fuehrer, yes, but I'm not so idiotic to believe he is immortal or invincible. We lost the war. The war is over. I know many sisters who seriously tell me they cannot exist or 'survive' in a post-Hitler Germany. Idiots! These people have no personalities, no spine. They're nothing. So in many ways, Germany should see them commit suicide. I'm all for them doing it. Life goes on, with or without our Fuehrer.

Gudrun Ensslin [To Ilse]: That's not fair. You've got to ask, "Who devoided them from their minds, souls, personalities? Obviously, it's Hitler."

Eva Gretl: Is 'devoided' a real word?

{*Laughter*}

Ilse Koch [Laughing]: It's the Fuehrer's fault?

Gudrun Ensslin [To Ilse]: Obviously! If a person mesmerizes people into becoming automated murderers, you must try to rehabilitate these poor weak, impressionable people. What kind of society are we building when we have people like you believing in only one path; for any problem, the only solution is to kill.

Eva Gretl: Oh, you girls, twaddling on about irrelevant stupidities when life's so simple. What else is there in our life but to find love, comforts, security, and prosperity?

Gudrun Ensslin: Everything depends on how you define happiness and prosperity.

Eva Gretl: Why do you insist on complicating life when life is beautiful precisely because of its virginal simplicity?

Ilse Koch: I was going to say, 'only a virgin thinks stupidly like you,' but that's wrong because virgins are the most in-heat bitches, subverting their minds into an air-tight carnal sauna, disfiguring reality precisely because of their unsatisfied and unmet lusts.

DG [Giggling]: Some sentence that is.

Eva Gretl: Of course you know me, Ilse. Who am I to speak?

Ilse Koch: [To Dorothy]: Too wordy for your brain to follow?

Gudrun Ensslin [To Eva]: When I was a little girl, I too shared your viewpoints. Now that I'm a teen, albeit still young, I've learned several life-saving truths. Number one. I've learned that Stalinist or capitalist, ordinary people's lives will remain as they were before — forever voiceless, oppressed with low wages, over-worked and underpaid in alienating jobs. Second. I've learned that it doesn't matter if you're a capitalist or a Stalinist; both have one aim, and that is to create an automaton whose only existential reason for being on this earth is to serve the elites. Third and most importantly. All these factors destroy Man's soul, meaning his happiness and peace of mind are snuffed out.

Eva Gretl: I'm bored. I think this wonderful talk should be delivered to Ilse.

Gudrun Ensslin [Excited]: But you're ignoring your happiness! And if you don't nourish happiness, so it gradually metamorphizes into sorrow. Shouldn't you be concerned with that destructive factor in your life?

Eva Gretl [Angrily]: Now you're just like Ilse, thinking you know me! Who told you I'm unhappy? Who told you I'm oppressed? I'm not! I don't want politics in my life. Leave that for politicians, just as I don't talk about medicine. I don't want politicians in my life. I don't wish for any philosophy or ideology in my brief life because I - yes, me, Eva, and no one else - I know exactly the recipe for happiness, and all I need is to bake this happiness for my life.

Ilse Koch: Here's a cooking tip. Bake your brain.

∼

Guderian – "Goebbels Is a Nothing Man!"

Goebbels: Do you know talking to some of you is exactly as when our Fuehrer spoke with Franco?

DG: What?

Goebbels: When the Fuehrer met with that mouse of Spain, he told me, *"You know Goebbels, I would rather have my teeth pulled out rather than talk anymore with Franco!"*

{*Laughter*}

Speer: Yes, Dr. Goebbels is correct.

DG [To Goebbels]: Why are you looking at me?

Goebbels: Oh, how charming you are, my dear American; the land of idiocy unparalleled since the Stone Ages, I suppose.

DG [Angrily]: You still spit venom at America? In my country? America? Excuse me, gentlemen, but which nation has thoroughly thrashed you guys twice? Who powdered your superior race to bits and bobs? Who -

Goebbels: I think our guest is birthing a Star-Spangled speech.

DG [Snickering]: I suggest you gentlemen ought to be infinitely better acquainted with my glorious, first-rate power of a nation. But then again, why bother? How much more time do you people have on earth?

Goering: Indeed, how true are her words!

Guderian: And why not? Wasn't that your job for twelve suffocating years, Dr. Goebbels?

DG: If you insist on not learning from victors, what is there to learn from failures like your hero, Hitler? Odd, isn't it? Your greatest hero is the one man who has done the most extreme mass death, destruction, and damage to the German people and German civilization, by literally allowing his enemies to obliterate the face of Germany from the map.

{*Silence*}

Goebbels: Oblige our curiosity; what *are your* first impressions of our Fuehrer, Frau Gale?

{*Silence*}

DG: To be frank, I was shocked.

Himmler: Dr. Goebbels, apart from your theatrically based question, nobody cares.

Keitel: Cares about what?

Himmler: About this American's airy 'opinion.'

Goebbels [To Dorothy]: Shocked?

Goering [To Himmler]: She was asked for her 'impressions,' not 'opinions.'

Keitel [To Himmler]: I do not officially understand your question.

DG: We touched on this subject before you gentlemen went off on a tangent.

Goebbels: You too, my dear, went off on a tangent.

Himmler [To Keitel]: You don't need to understand my question.

DG: I expected to see a giant. A superhero of a man. To be sure, he is thoroughly sick. That's visible. Physically speaking.

Goebbels: No one informed us you were a physician, dear.

DG: I *didn't* say I'm a doctor. I specifically said that 'visibly' he looks sick, meaning —

Goebbels: Yes, yes, we understand you now. Plod on.

DG: And as for his mind, from what I have seen — and remember, mind you, I haven't yet spoken with him - but he doesn't seem to be fully coherent. You know, balanced. I expected to be greeted by a man of compelling prowess and bravura.

Keitel [Angrily to Himmler]: Oh no, that is most unacceptable! I am the one who tells the Fuehrer what may or may not have happened during these informal conversations, and therefore, please clarify your unnecessarily ambiguous question.

Goebbels: He certainly impelled Germany with his prowess and bravura.

Goering [To Keitel]: Since you're interested in matters of clarity, I must inform you that Himmler did not ask a question.

Ribbentrop [To Dorothy]: How can you *not* feel his overwhelming powers? I shudder every time I see him, in front of me, in my mind -

DG: I see the opposite. An infirm, almost invisible man. Do you know what I mean when I say 'invisible'?

Goebbels: I think most Germans understand the meaning of 'invisible,' yes.

DG: That was not my —

Speer: One needs time to be acquainted with eccentricities of the language and mind of Dr. Goebbels.

Keitel: I must insert here my disagreement, Minister Speer and of course, I can only speak of my impressions, but I find Dr. Goebbels a most personable and courteous gentleman and a most pleasing man and is, of course, the Fuehrer's conviction and h Hence what I have said is true.

Goebbels [Referring to Keitel]: It would be easier conversing with a monkey.

DG [To Goebbels]: Just out of interest, I'd like to know if you're just as sarcastic with your family?

Guderian: What family?

{Laughter}

DG: Excuse me?

Guderian: Why would do you assume the midget before us spends one minute with his family?

Goering [To Dorothy]: Your question would find much more receptive grounds were you to ask his mistresses and whores.

{Laughter}

DG [Impatient]: I'm speaking to you in the most open-hearted, honest manner I can. Meanwhile, is that all you can do? Is that the only manner you know how to interact with a lady? Constantly clowning, bickering, or being sarcastic with each other?

"Then we'll work a hundred years without physics and chemistry."

- Hitler's response shouted back to Carl Bosch (then still head of IG Farben), who had tried to advise him that if

Jewish scientists were forced to leave the country, physics and chemistry would be set back 100 years.

Guderian: It is buffoonery.

Goebbels: You mean baboonery.

Guderian [Angrily to Goebbels]: My man, *I choose my words, not you.*

Speer [Referring to Goebbels]: I never understood how why so many beautiful women were attracted to him.

Goebbels: Aha! You've just validated my worthiness, not just cerebrally but physically!

Fegelein: What women wouldn't be 'interested' in a man of wealth and power?

{*Murmurs of Approval*}

Goebbels: In all my speeches, I could've counseled my audience to jump off a cliff, and so they willingly would've done so.

Goering: We told you, Black Dwarf; words mean nothing.

Goebbels [Excited]: So, are you saying the Fuehrer's oratory powers are just as worthless?

Goering [Angrily]: What idiocy are you saying, my man? The Fuehrer mesmerized his audiences, rendering women to cry, swoon, scream while men of all ages felt their hearts exploding. Your speeches, on the whole, were met by polite applause. Furthermore, the Fuehrer isn't just the greatest orator in modern history; he just happened to back up his words with Germany's greatest achievements.

{*Everyone: 'Jawohl Herr Reichsmarschall!'*}

Jodl: Surely, the Minister of Propaganda speaks some truths?

Guderian: No, my dear. Nowhere Man is nowhere near anything of reality or truth. His stage role during this second global war was supposedly in using his awe-inspiring words.

Goebbels: Ich frage euch: Wollt ihr den totalen Krieg? Wollt ihr ihn, wenn nötig, totaler und radikaler, als wir ihn uns heute überhaupt erst vorstellen können?

DG: Dr. Goebbels, do you still deny that your nation faces defeat in a matter of days?

Goebbels[Excited]: We face a severe military challenge in the East.

Goering [Sarcastic]: Really?

{Laughter}

Goebbels: The crisis is broad, similar, but not identical in many ways to that of the previous years. Now, we must accept things as they are and discover and apply the ways and means to turn things again in our favor.

Goering [To Goebbels]: Are you rehearsing your latest speech on us?

{Laughter}

Goebbels[Excited]: There is no point in disputing the seriousness of the situation. I do not want to give you a false impression of the situation that could lead to false conclusions, perhaps giving the German people a false sense of security that is altogether inappropriate in the present situation.

Keitel: Since Dr. Goebbels is about to praise the Fuehrer it does not matter if the gentleman is offering a speech, a remark or an observation, or a comment -

DG: I've always wondered if Dr. Goebbels believes his words —

Goering: Of course not.

Goebbels [Excited]: The storm raging against our venerable people and soldiers overshadows all previous human and historical experiences. The German army and its allies are the only possible defense. In his proclamation on 30 January, the Führer asked in a grave and compelling way what would have become of Germany and Europe —

DG [To Goering]: How do you know?

Goebbels [Excited]: We tried to open their eyes to the horrible danger from Eastern Bolshevism, which had subjected a nation of nearly 200 million people to the terror of the Jews and was preparing an aggressive war against Europe.

Goering: Maybe initially, yes, he believed in his words. But certainly, after Stalingrad, everyone knew the truth.

Goebbels: When the Führer ordered the army to attack the East on 22 June 1941, we all knew this would be the decisive battle of this great struggle. We knew the dangers and difficulties. But we also knew that dangers and difficulties always grow over time; they never diminish.

Speer: So for whom is he talking now when all of us know the war is over?

Goebbels: It was two minutes before midnight. Waiting any longer could easily have led to the destruction of the Reich and a total Bolshevization of the European continent.

Guderian: Hitler's only purpose is to prolong his life. Meaning our simple people must continue to die or be wounded. While the criminal, knee-high, club-footed man goes on speaking of victory. Follow him to your graves.

DG: But isn't mass hypnotic power an 'achievement,' criminal though it may be?

Guderian: Not if it's used criminally; no, it is not. Goebbels only mesmerized Goebbels.

Goebbels [Angrily]: If the German people are unwilling to fight for their existence, their existence is worth nothing!

Goering: The Fuehrer already said that.

Speer: General Guderian, to be honest, we cannot discount some of the positive output our doctor created and throughout Germany too. Especially during our declining years. Given those deplorable years, it would be too harsh denying his remarkable gifts in rousing our wretched people.

Fegelein: Minister Speer, pardon me; didn't you say Dr. Goebbels is a Nowhere Man?

Speer: I said he is a Nothing Man.

Guderian: And what's the difference, Minister Speer?

Speer: The fact is our people still adore Goebbels. The same people who adore Hitler. Not on the same intensity, of course. Though, yes, you and I know he achieved nothing –

Goebbels [Bitterly]: I cannot accept such invective! I've achieved vastly, far, far more than nothing.

Goering: Anyone achieving vastly far more than nothing still adds up to nothing.

{Laughter}

Fegelein: This is becoming too philosophical -

Guderian: And Minister Speer, you are correct in everything you say. But how exactly does his ongoing popularity affect our remaining battle-unworthy units, our non-existent air forces, and our non-existent navy? Again, the answer brings us right back to my original point, which is nothing.

Goebbels [Stiffly]: I am not nothing. I am -

Speer: Gentlemen, if you believe the flighty morale of a general population is an irrelevant factor in determining the outcome of a war, I need only remind you of the mood of our people back in 1917.

Goering [To Speer]: There's no more fighting to be done. There's no men, no petrol, no tanks, no spare parts, no food, no artillery. What are you talking about? When the Kaiser surrendered, Germany wasn't even occupied! Therefore, your 1917 analogy is stupid.

{Laughter}

DG: Going back to our subject matter, if we may. Yes, of course, every now then, I saw flashes of his typical rage, as we say, but for the most part, I can describe -

Keitel [Angrily]: Please! We cannot continue discussing the validity or the invalidity of Dr. Goebbels as being a man of nothing because nothing can only yield a sum output of nothing.

DG: Gentlemen, I am *trying* to focus on Hitler and not -

Goebbels: You two gentlemen talk of absurdities; both of you think I am a Nowhere Man –

Guderian: The verb 'To think' is errant. The verb is 'To know.'

Dorothy Rats on The Rat Speer – And A Dreary Detour with General Keitel ...

Speer

Goebbels: Frau Gale! I think we have strayed from the original question.

Keitel: This question you mention of whether we have or if we have not digressed from the original question is only for the Fuehrer to settle and not for us flotsam characterless creatures to opine on either way.

Fegelein: The Fuehrer is not here, General Keitel.

Guderian: I have doubts as to you interviewing a man such as the Fuehrer. Or, to put it briefly, you lack the will, the emotions, and the knowledge to interview him.

DG [To Guderian]: You do your job, whatever it is ... and I'll do mine just fine.

{Laughter}

Goebbels: Splendidly stated!

DG: Going back to your leader -

Goebbels: Excuse me for interrupting, but what did you mean, 'every now then, I saw flashes of his typical rage'?

DG: I saw him once or twice in this room talking to officers. *Boom!* He suddenly flares up. Livid as lava. And do you know, those brief moments I saw him reminded me of the same mannerisms in our news films shown back in the United States? And now I am here, in his presence, I admit feeling degrees of the man's charisma. Even though, as I say, I have only seen him from a distance. But I do sense the aura of leadership. Then again, maybe what I have just described to you are only exceptions rather than the rule. I do not know.

Ribbentrop [Excited]: So you *did* feel overwhelmingly shattering personality! There's hope, gentlemen! Maybe this woman will understand and go back to America and convince Washington of our sincerity in seeking peace! What do you —

DG [To Ribbentrop]: This woman is not for turning.

Keitel: I must state that I am now officially confused because is it the case or the fact that you are saying the Fuehrer is or the Fuehrer is not a man of charisma and I ask you because we must be precise since we are National Socialists and ambiguity is not National Socialist.

Goering [Laughing]: What did you just say, idiot? Ambiguity is your essence!

{*Laughter*}

DG: Herr Speer, you seem rather quiet?

Speer: When I have nothing to say, my lips are sealed.

DG: Do you know for some queer reason you remind me of a psycho-killer?

Speer: I do not understand you.

Fegelein: She called you a *psychopathischer Mörder* ['psycho-killer'].

DG: Sorry, I'm mixing American to German. No, not a psycho-killer. That's Himmler. I'm mixing you, people, up. You're a Doppeldeutigkeit [double-dealing] man.

Himmler [To Dorothy]: How dare -

Speer: Excuse me?

Goebbels: Don't look at me, Minister Speer; I too have no clue what this American is trilling about.

Keitel: Do you need me to serve you with an official translator, Frau Gale because that may smoothen your linguistic difficulties, and so it may suit you better?

DG [To Speer]: When I first saw you, I thought you're a robot, and you're aware of that, right?

Goering: If he's a robot, how can he know he's a robot?

Speer: What on earth do you mean?

DG [To Speer]: But then I changed my mind. Unlike many Nazis, you're one of the few who is *not* an automated man. You're a political chameleon.

Goebbels [To Speer]: Why do you look at me when your question is for our fair lady?

Fegelein: I think that was a compliment, Minister Speer.

Guderian: Herr Reichsmarschall, your question is *most* interesting. It goes to the heart of consciousness. Are animals conscious? Are they self-aware? How about plants? And so on. The answer, I presume, must rest with neuroscientists.

DG: Without a doubt, I think you're the best actor in this Bunker. Most cannot switch masks as convincingly and as rapidly as you. They are who they are. Fictitious or not. But you're not whom you seem.

Keitel [Frustrated]: So now, since none of us seems to know whom Herr Speer is in truth, it seems to me that you are now proclaiming yourself or self-crowning yourself as the only individual in this Bunker who knows the answer as to who is what and therefore, now it must be your official duty to inform us whom you believe Herr Speer seems to be.

Speer: I am who I am!

Goebbels: Meaningless words, Speer.

Fegelein: Can anyone steal any identity, role, profession, and morality?

Goering: Now, isn't that interesting of you to say, Fegelein?

Fegelein [To Goering]: I'm not sure why, Sir, you say that.

Goering: One more traitor in our hallowed dung mound.

DG [To Speer]: You have ulterior motives, entirely and only self-serving your life –

Speer: I believe our conversation has shifted to Herr Fegelein but if you insist in talking about me, go ahead.

DG: [To Speer]: No, no, no … don't try distracting me. That won't do! …

Guderian: Her German is wretched. She's speaking English, using English idioms.

Ribbentrop [Incredulous]: She's prophesying the future; can't you gentlemen feel that? But what exactly she is saying; I too do not understand one word!

Goebbels: Exactly, Foreign Minister; she's our Divine Prophetess whose words none understands.

Fegelein: All prophets are by definition 'divine.'

DG: Oh no, Herr Speer fully understands me, gentlemen - not that the rest of you do.

Keitel: If the Fuehrer understands her, then I too must conclude her German is perfect. So, there should be no more twaddle talk on that illicit subject matter. It is absolutely forbidden.

Guderian [To Dorothy]: That's why we're finding it difficult to follow you, dear.

Jodl: But that's been her problem from day one.

Speer [Sighing]: I don't understand what or why this lady is attacking my integrity.

Keitel: Herr Speer, please do correct me if I am wrong but, when you -

Goering: You're wrong.

Keitel: I believe our German ... excuse me ... our American lady has discovered you to be one more rat or traitor in our government. Is that not the factual case or not? Please clarify.

Speer [Angry]: What evidence —

Goering [Laughing to Keitel]: Why do you ask Speer that question instead of Dorothy?

{Laughter}

Guderian: You see, Frau Dorothy? Here's the necessary evidence from the mouth of Herr Speer proving without a shred of doubt that he's one more bastard pretending he doesn't understand your words.

Speer [Angrily]: Excuse me! I'm being verbally hanged while I'm not even given a chance to —

Goebbels: Your future is not necessarily limited to a verbal hanging, Speer.

Speer: I would like to interject here if I may. She's accusing me of being a weasel, and I have -

Goering [Smiling]: But you *are* a weasel.

Speer: Having heard that, I can only reject her unworthy accusatory words, and that's enough as far as I am concerned with this matter.

Himmler [Loudly]: That's strictly a matter for our Fuehrer to decide!

{Everyone: "Long Live the Fuehrer!"}

Keitel [Pleased]: Excellent then, there it is! Herr Speer has kindly chosen to submit himself to a court, whereby any disreputable accusation arraigned against his honorable work will be judged —

Speer [Angrily]: I have not agreed to be put on any court, and I will not -

DG: Others play out their roles and nothing else. One role. But you, Herr Speer, you're different. You're the only personality changing every minute as the occasion suits you. You're charming, suave, and terribly 'considerate' in the ways you interact with people, while your hideous past is corpse-laden with the millions of slave workers you worked to their early grimy deaths.

Goebbels: I think the noun 'affable' would suffice here, my dear lady.

Goering: 'Affable' is an adverb.

DG: You have one thought in your mind. I mean, now. These days. You know that, and I know that.

Speer: Know what, dear?

DG: Your neck.

Goering [Laughing]: If Speer escapes the noose, I bet you, gentlemen, one day he'll write a money-making, National Socialist-scourging book on our supposedly criminal 'slave society' while he was in charge of the very same 'slave society' itself"!

{Laughter}

Keitel: How odd of you to say that. Oddly enough, because I am also constantly plagued in my neck with odd pains and odd itches.

Himmler [To Keitel]: I have these same problems, and my masseuse tells me it is entirely due to stress.

DG: "All the perfumes of Arabia will not sweeten this little hand."

Speer: I think you daydream too much, Frau Gale ...

DG [Sternly]: I certainly daydream and a lot too. You're right, there. Though not when looking at you.

{Laughter}

Goering: Frau Dorothy, you must know Speer is quite enamored of himself.

Speer [Dry]: Why don't you get on with your questions, dear girl?

Keitel [IExasperated to Dorothy]: Can you please confirm what you are saying? What is your final, irrevocable verdict - is Minister Speer an actor or a robot or a minister or a nobody or a somebody or what?

Guderian: The ex-Reich's Armaments Minister is supremely taciturn. That's his quintessential nature. That's the entirety of your personality, ex-Minister Speer. The girl's right, though.

Speer: Was that a compliment or an insult, General Guderian?

Keitel [Angrily]: Gentlemen, please! There is too much confusion here! We National Socialists do not accept confusion since confusion confuses people while the Fuehrer strictly abides by the divine rule of being radically transparent in all of his edicts, admonishments, and wisdom, in general! What a mess!

DG: Why are any of you confused? All I'm saying is that Herr Speer will be one of the few, if not the only high-ranking Nazis who will charm his way during the trial and convince the judges of his innocence.

Himmler [Puzzled]: How is that to be achieved when he's regarded by the enemy as a 'War Criminal' since he was as involved as the rest of us during the war?

Goebbels: And if you think 'charm' is enough to get yourself away from the noose, you're mistaken, Frau Gale.

DG: Oh no, it won't just be charm. Herr Speer is far too clever, knowing his path far from the hangman.

Goebbels: Meaning?

Goering: Meaning he's made deals behind our backs in exchange with a relatively light sentence.

{*Sounds of Shock*}

DG: Look, in every trial, when you have several guilty individuals, the courts strike a deal with one of the guilty people; it's called a 'plea deal' in my country. Anyway, the courts offer this one chosen individual a reduced sentence if they are willing to rat on everyone else —

Goebbels: What does 'rat' mean?

DG: To snitch.

{*Sounds of Shock*}

DG: And so, they thereby ensure for the prosecution that they will get exactly what they demanded in the first place, again, as per the rest of the accused defendants.

All Along the Watchtower

"There must be some kind of way out of here,"
Said the joker to the thief
"There's too much confusion
I can't get no relief.
Businessmen, they drink my wine
Plowmen dig my earth
None of them along the line
Know what any of it is worth."

- Bob Dylan - 1967

Goebbels: Going back to the Fuehrer, I agree with your impressions, Frau Gale. Our noble leader suffered enormities incalculable to the ordinary man or woman. Do we know what it's like to be a Mozart or a Schopenhauer? Of course, we do not! And why not? Because we're piddling ants in an unknowable scurrilous play of life. Let us never be inebriated by arrogance or by a lust for power, privilege, or wealth. Let us not seek to emulate our heroic masterminds.

Guderian: My goodness me. The dreariness of this empty balloon staggers me to -

Goebbels: None of us understand geniuses like the Fuehrer. Monumental giants of history. And let us not deceive ourselves into thinking we could view the complexities of his life and its reality from his dizzying heights.

Goering: The dwarf tries to be poetic in his final hours; let him diddle.

Keitel: General Guderian, to *whom* do you refer?

Guderian [Laughing]: Goebbels.

Goebbels: God only knows what goes on in his tormented mind this minute. God only knows what created this occasion, one that momentarily enjoined you and him, so he can finally, freely, and expansively deliver his final Testament unto this forever dithering Mankind.

DG: Herr Speer, how do you —

Goering [Staring at Goebbels]: Black dwarf! Now, if the Fuehrer's final words are, as your eloquence so put it, to be delivered unto a "forever dithering Mankind," then of what use is there in your undeniably heroic words to be passed on to future generations?

Goebbels: Maybe I'm being overly pessimistic, Herr Reichsmarschall. But then again, I am utterly exasperated by the fact that ... isn't it one of the most distasteful of truths, this imprisoning reality that after all his years of struggle, our Fuehrer still cannot find one man to deliver his Final Sermon?

Himmler: Too wordy, Dr. Goebbels.

Fegelein [Whispering to Himmler]: I think Goebbels is copying the Fuehrer's style of monologuing.

Keitel [To Guderian]: I must, in the name of our Fuehrer, officially disagree with you, General Guderian, because Dr. Goebbels is well known as one of the favorites of our Fuehrer.

Goebbels: What does that say of our people? What does it say but that they chose *not* to listen to his worldly guidance?

Himmler [Whispering to Fegelein]: But there *is* a vast difference. With this black dwarf, we can shut him up.

Goebbels: That is why we're here in this dungeon. I say, and I speak of this awful matter and circumstance, partially in response to Guderian's question. Now you have your answer laid bare and valid for all to see.

Guderian: Are you done?

Fegelein: I once had to see a Shakespeare play. And the only thought or memory I have of that miserable experience is watching Dr. Goebbels talk.

Keitel [Angrily to Guderian]: I will not warn you anymore, given the foul manner you speak -

DG: Herr Speer, how do you see your leader today, especially since he's been in this miserable deathly Bunker?

Speer: Having lambasted me, now you seek my counsel?

DG: You heard Officer Fegelein, didn't you? You could've taken my swords as compliments, Herr Speer.

Speer: Frau Gale, I am not comfortable with your duplicitous nature.

Goering [Laughing at Speer]: *"Duplicitous nature?"* Dorothy? And you don't think you're one of Germany's most duplicitous bastards?

{Everyone: *'Jawohl Herr Reichsmarschall Goring!"*}

DG [To Speer]: When speaking with Satan, you must improvise to attain your target.

Fegelein [Whispers to Himmler]: Are they flirting?

Speer [Angrily]: And what exactly is your "target"?

Himmler [Whispering to Fegelein]: No, idiot, of course not!

DG [To Speer]: You don't know, Minister of Slave Munitions?

Speer [Angrily]: Look, do you wish me to answer your question or not? I'm not a man of games. I'm a man of wealth and taste.

DG: Laugh at yourself.

Speer: Excuse me?

Keitel: Now come here, this is not National Socialist behavior. Frau Gale, you must let the man defend himself. That is how our National Socialist judicial system was created by our Fuehrer.

Himmler [To Keitel]: No, it wasn't.

Speer: I see him fading. And that accords with your words, Frau Gale. His limbs tremble: he walks stooped, with dragging footsteps. Even his voice quavers, having lost its old masterfulness. Its force has given way to a faltering, toneless manner of speaking. When he becomes excited, as he frequently does in a senile way, his voice starts to break. He still has his fits of stubbornness, but they no longer remind one of a child's temper tantrums but of an old man's. You have seen him.

Goering: My goodness me, Dorothy thinks Speer has the answers in knowing the heart of our Fuehrer!

Guderian: But Herr Reichsmarschall, that's her job —

Goering [Angrily]: What *"job"* do you think she has, Guderian?

Guderian: With respect, Herr Reichsmarschall, if you insist on being angry, I have no interest in pursuing this conversation.

Goering [Shouting]: Speak, man! Speak!

I was surprised at Goering's loss of temper. It was rare seeing him losing his temper. Plus, I didn't think whatever Guderian was babbling was worthy of his anger. To be honest, I didn't notice what Guderian had said that so annoyed Goering.

Speer: We've all seen his complexion is sallow, his face is swollen; his uniform, which in the past he had kept scrupulously neat, is often neglected. His clothes are stained by the food he eats with a shaking hand. All these mental tribulations result from his awareness that this is explicitly his final moment on earth.

Ribbentrop [Fearful]: Gentlemen! What exactly is the point of this talk? Can we try to find solutions? Can we resolve … try to create a diplomatic breakthrough … I mean, with the West but necessarily with latter because I'm still highly regarded by Marshall Stalin and —

Goering: Wonderful idea, Ribbentrop! Why don't you fly off and see your friend, Stalin?

{*Laughter*}

Himmler [Laughing]: Excellent idea! I wonder how many minutes would it take for Stalin to have Ribbentrop dead?

Speer: This condition undoubtedly touches his entourage, who've been at his side during the triumphs of his life. I'm constantly tempted to pity him, so reduced is he from the Hitler of the past. Perhaps that is why everyone still listens to him in silence when, in the long since hopeless situation, he continues to commit non-existent divisions or orders units supplied by planes that can no longer fly for lack of fuel.

Himmler [Referring to Speer]: What a brilliant liar, I must admit!

{Murmurs of Approval}

Speer: Perhaps that's why no one says a word when he more and more frequently takes flight from reality and enters his world of fantasy when he speaks of the clash between East and West, which must be on the point of erupting — when he bids us to realize that it is inevitable.

Keitel: Even I feel bored by this.

Speer [Emotional]: Having said that, although the entourage can scarcely be blind to the imaginary character of these ideas, his constant repetitions still do have some *hypnotic effect*— as when, for example, he still claims he's somehow able to 'conquer' Bolshevism purely using the strength of his personality and in an alliance with the West. It sounds believable to some simple-minded fanatics when he assures us that he continues to live only for this turning point.

Fegelein [Whispers to Himmler]: Never has a moment been more appropriate than to execute this dog.

Speer: The same composure with which he looks forward to the end intensifies sympathy and commands respect. Besides, he has again become more amiable and more willing to drop into his private mood. In many ways, he reminds me of the Hitler I had known at the beginning of our association twelve years before, except that he now seems more shadowy.

Goebbels: Herr Speer, I'm fascinated with the certainty with which you single out the unfavorable aspects of our shared situation, some of which is true. But can't you speak of the valuable lessons the Fuehrer has shown not only us here in this dungeon but to all Germans?

Speer: I believe you misheard me, Dr. Goebbels. I spoke on both sides of his personality, so to speak, since I mentioned the twelve years.

DG: What are these 'valuable lessons'?

Goebbels [Sarcastic]: You don't know?

DG: No, I don't.

Goebbels [Irritated]: How can you not know?

Keitel [Angrily to Goebbels]: The lady has just stated to you in a most direct manner, and therefore there can be no misunderstanding on your part. She stated before all of us and in a clear voice, if I may say so, the following distinct words - *"I do not know."* The latter crystal clear statement on the part of our invited guest, Frau Dorothy, was in direct response as per and as to your entirely pointless question of *"You don't know?"* So why would you deem it necessary to bother us by asking her another equally meaningless question, this time adding the word, 'how,' as in *"How can you not know?"* If the girl in question does not know, that should provide you with enough and with sufficient knowledge for you to see or to know that she does not know, and so you must then proceed to the next constructive question, but it is regrettable that you surrender in being repetitive, Herr Doktor.

Guderian [Sarcastic]: Ah, but, General Keitel, what *just happened* to your love and respect for Goebbels?

Keitel: Dr. Goebbels, you always baffle me.

Goebbels: That's not difficult, General Keitel.

Speer [To Keitel]: I believe you have not answered General Guderian's question.

Keitel: What question?

Goebbels [Murmuring to Himself]: Oh dear ... what a mishmash of dunces.

Speer [To Keitel]: You were just exalting Goebbels, and now you're asking him a demeaning question.

Keitel [Irritated]: I know that! But what is ... what is ... or what are the questions or words you wish to pose?

Guderian [Angrily]: What's so difficult for you to understand?

Keitel: I cannot accept such a disreputable tone.

DG: Gentlemen, does all this matter? Can we continue with the more important matters?

Keitel [Haughtily]: Oh no, Frau Gale, you do not understand us, Herrenvolk Germans. I believe I have been insulted, and we must clear this grave matter up; otherwise, I shall inform the Fuehrer of this egregious incident which, I assure you that it shall not bode well for my uninformed accusers! We Germans are diligent lovers of strictness, rules, and orders. That is why we are Herrenvolk Germans.

{Silence}

Fegelein: Did you, General Keitel ... did you say ... or did you *not* say that our hero Dr. Goebbels is one of the Fuehrer's favorites?

DG [Bored]: Oh Lord ...

Goering [Laughing to Dorothy]: Now wait here, girl! Weren't you the one who wanted to see what our National Socialist government looks like? Girl, you're witnessing our final scenes being played out before your eyes, my good girl.

{Laughter}

Keitel [Angrily to Fegelein]: Indeed, that was my official pronouncement. And proudly so. And *who* officially designated you to interrogate me as regards to my eternal loyalty to our Fuehrer?

Fegelein [Firmly to Keitel]: With respect, Sir, but now you're telling us that our Propaganda Minister is *'baffling.'* Is that correct or not? How do you square that?

Keitel: Square what?

Fegelein [To Keitel]: Don't you notice a contradiction in what you have said as per your description of Dr. Goebbels?

{*Silence*}

Goering [Loudly]: *Clowns! Clowns! Kein Wunder, dass wir diesen verdammten Krieg verloren haben!* ["Clowns! Clowns! No wonder we lost this damned war!"]

DG: Looking and hearing you high-ranking Nazis, how did you ever think you could win the war?

~

Conversations with Himmler – Explaining His 'Historic' and Most Difficult 'Burden' That None Could Bear nor Do

Heinrich Himmler

I. Himmler: "Do You Think any General, Officer, Diplomat, or Minister Could Have Done What I Achieved Without Having a Nervous Breakdown or Committing Suicide?"

I was lonely. Himmler walks into my cell or room. What contrasting realities! Me with dizzying emotional anxieties and some unexpected next moment, Nazi Germany's second-worst mass murder appearing before me, seeking to talk 'sense' about genocide.

Himmler [Smiling]: I heard you witnessed a battle.

DG: Yes.

Himmler: Life, good and bad, must be understood in their rational perspectives, my girl. The opposite would be exaggerating life's attributes.

DG: I'm in no mood for philosophizing.

Himmler: I heard you were aggrieved. May I ask why?

{*Silence*}

I had no appetite to look at him, let alone converse. It was, after all, my off-duty hour.

Himmler: My girl, war is not for everyone.

DG: You think you're one for war?

Himmler: Have I ever said I was 'one for war?'

DG: You act like one.

Himmler: I do not understand your German.

DG: What are your achievements, apart from murdering millions of innocent men, women, children, and babies?

Himmler: Do you know ... why ...or how the SS began?

DG: No.

Himmler: Do you know how or why the SA was constantly attacking us?

DG: I don't care. You enacted the mass murder of six million Jews, and now in these final days of your venomous life, you're trying to interest me in the origins of your criminal organization? What relevance do you think that has compared to the monumental criminality you have committed – an act unseen in modern history?

Himmler: What a child you are! My girl –

DG: Don't address me as 'your child.'

Himmler: Every event, historical event, and simple human event can only be understood when we listen and understand the specific context within which the event occurred. Unfortunately, you simply look at any event, such as the purging of Jews. You then conclude that was a 'crime.' But, again, I know that being an American, a Jew, or a communist, you have no interest in learning the essential facts that created or pushed us to do what we did against these lethal parasites. I alone carried out the most psychologically, emotionally, and spiritually challenging operations necessary for our National Socialist ideology. No man could do what I did. No man had the steely nerves for what I did. Our Fuehrer knew that. Do you think any general, diplomat, or minister could have done what I achieved without having a nervous breakdown or committing suicide? He alone saw in me that unique ability to carry out Germany's most burdensome task, a task necessary for Germany's survival. And that is why he appointed me for that glorious task.

DG: Are you proud of your genocidal deeds?

Himmler: Absolutely! I was trying to explain to you, though you insisted on not allowing me to speak the truth.

DG: Go on.

Himmler: The raison d'etre of the SS was that we were not like the SA. The latter was entirely made of drunkards, convicts, homosexuals, and rabble. And that infuriated the Fuehrer. We were supposed to be National Socialists. That meant we were the party of not only law and order, but even more importantly, we were the party representing the dignity of the German soul, meaning orderly, disciplined, well-organized, humane respectable men.

DG: Those aren't quite the adjective I'd use when describing men whose only task was to enact genocide.

Himmler: And throughout that ordeal, I retained my humanity. I never stole from any Jew. I did not become a criminal or become evil as so many of my SS men and officers became. On the contrary, I maintained my dignity as a virtuous, honest human being, given the enormity of the task I had to do. And with me, of course, I speak of my men. Of course, here and there, you will find riff-raff such as the SA-types of ruffian idiots. But on the whole, it is to the eternal glory we carried out our grisly, gruesome tasks with a humanity that will be a beacon for humanity for a thousand years!

DG: I don't even know if you can hear me, let alone understand my words, but I'll say it anyway. How on earth can any genocide be 'humane'?

Himmler Visting A Concentration Camp

Himmler: You do not and cannot conceive the mighty burden God and the Fuehrer placed upon my men and I to do it efficiently and without resistance from those unworthy of life. From nothing, I built up thousands of camps, all of them fully functioning with all the required equipment, housing, water, food, soldiers in place. In addition, I created a gigantic network of railways to connect each camp to deport any Jew anywhere and ensure within a matter of days, and they reach their destination. I created this network stretching from France, Europe, and throughout Russia. I placed efficient camp commandants who expertly did their duties. There was never a glitch or breakdown in our operations to eliminate that satanic race until, of course, the army began to withdraw thanks to the failures of the Fuehrer's generals and officers. At the same time, Germany's skies were naked, thus speedily destroying our rail and road links. That, in turn, meant we could no longer feed any concentration camp with food, water, medicines, and whatever else they needed, such as clothes, wood to build huts, and so on. Thus, my work was struck down, and you can see for yourself whose fault that is. Still, despite these handicaps, I alone succeeded in wiping off the majority of European Jewry, and for that, I know the Almighty will forever be grateful for my sacred deeds.

DG: What do you think of Jack the Ripper?

Himmler: In one sense, he was certainly adept in not being caught. However, you must ask yourself, who and what made that individual kill and how? Crimes or so-called crimes have reasons behind them, motives, and so on.

I honestly didn't think he would take my question seriously - as I was sarcastic. I guess being tone-deaf to sanity; he surprised and shocked me by seeming to imply Jack the Ripper's motives may be decent.

Himmler: He murdered prostitutes. That was all. Well, that is not necessary. One can reform these fallen women. I understand executing prostitutes who are repeat offenders; that is most certainly necessary since they have evidenced unto society they cannot behave morally and must thereby be done with. We, on the other hand, were liquidating a virus whose existence threatened our own life. Thus, you can see, I think, the vast difference in whom we knew we had to eliminate and that man's targets who did not necessarily need to be killed. So, that is point one. Point two is that we liquidated Jews in the most humane, dignified manner possible. Jack the Ripper, as his name indicates, horrifically mutilated his victims, and that is a clear indication the man himself was insane. So, he, too, would have been executed in National Socialist Germany. And in fact, I can offer you our own character, as Jack the Ripper, Paul Ogorzow. He worked on our trains, and he too killed only women, but any woman. He bludgeoned them, raped them, stabbed them, and threw their bodies wherever he may have been. In total, he murdered eight, and in 1941 he was captured, put on trial, found guilty, and duly hanged. So, you must understand, though it is impossible, to comprehend the scope of my work. A European-wide systematic program with thousands of offices, officers, soldiers, and secretaries interacting and communicating to carry out the latest request. Thus, I'd order 500 Jews to be deported from Copenhagen and immediately deported to Belsen. And it is done without any trouble. And yes, I will not deny how strong I had to carry out these European-wide tasks.

~

II. **Dorothy To Himmler: "Since So Much of Your Ideas are Rooted in Biology, Can You Explain How Exactly Does the 'Degradation' You Speak Of, Occurs in the Medical or Biochemical Sense?"**

I chuckled, remembering what Misch told me about Himmler's chicken nerves when Hitler gave him the command of an army. I didn't want to antagonize him, so I switched subjects.

Himmler: War calls on us all to remain steely as the mightiest steel on earth. Only I had the nerves of steel in Germany! Though I'm not a military man, not one man in the Wehrmacht nor the SS had the –

DG: So, let's not talk about military affairs.

Himmler: Going back to your question, I'd like to respond to it if –

DG: Which question?

Himmler: You are unaware of questions or words you speak?

DG: No, it's called memory. People sometimes forget. I know the Master Race is unaffected by this silly plague we subhumans have.

Himmler: My dear, you're German! You must –

DG: What question?

Himmler: Remember, you asked, "How on earth can any genocide be 'humane'?"

DG: Yes.

Himmler: A surgeon operating on a person with a life-threatening illness can be a malicious or a benevolent human being. It is not the operation that is in question. The latter must be done, or the patient expires. The question is —

DG: Can you give a dumber answer than that?

Himmler: I beg your pardon?

DG: The good surgeon seeks to save his patient's life, whereas the bad surgeon is presumably uninterested in doing his job and so lets the patient in question pass away. Mind you, I'm not sure there are so many of these 'bad' surgeons. Overworked, alcoholics, depressed, yes. And that's called negligence, and it does happen. But I don't think there are many surgeons who deliberately seek to murder their patients. Meanwhile, genocide by definition has only one function, and that is the biological annihilation of an entire race or community.

Himmler: You are so stupid, my dear. Genocide, too, can have dual purposes, that is justified or not. For example, the Ottoman extermination of the Armenians was justified but not to the extent they carried it out. Why because the Armenian race is not a lethal race. Absolutely not. That genocide was politically based. In our case, we had to physically eradicate Jewry because, among other threats, the most serious one is the biological one. That is why we had to wipe them out. There was no choice — either Jews remain and infect the German population, and we degenerate, or we liquidate them and keep our racial purity.

DG: How exactly does a human who happens to be a Jew 'infect' a human who happens to be a German?

Himmler: Can you repeat your question?

DG: Well, you're talking, or sounding as though whenever a Jew and a German interact, a biological act occurs, whereby the German's racial purity is degraded, right?

Himmler: Precisely.

DG: Since so much of your words are rooted in biology, can you explain how exactly does that 'degradation' occurs' in the medical, chemical, or biological sense?

Himmler: Biologically, the obvious answer is miscegenation. It is the eternal instinct of the Jew to create mixed offspring with our German women. And that is not just a sickly primal instinct that is the preserve of Jews. Negroes have a much higher thrusting need to father children with white women. Like the Jew, the offspring will, on the whole, be copies of the bastard race, the Jew or Negroe father. That is what our Fuehrer meant by the eloquent and supremely important term, "bastardization of the German race." If a government takes no action to stop this racial bastardization, then our nation will become as Brazil or as your great nation is becoming. That is, they are being negrified. And what does that say about such a 'government'? A government that allows its racial purity to be blackened and Judaized?

~

III. **Himmler Insists Katharina Esser Was A 'Moron'**

Himmler: Would you like to know what happened to that young girl on the street, Frau Gale?

What? What a quick change of subject. Now I was actually interested to hear what he had to say.

DG: What? Do you know? How do you know? What happened?

Himmler: Her name is Frau Katharina Esser.

DG [Excited]: Katharina! Exactly, so you know about her! I know her. What happened to her? Please?

Himmler [Smiling]: One moment, you tell me you "know her," and then you ask me what happened to her.

What a sickly smile.

Himmler: I am afraid she did not make it.

DG: No prophet succeeds.

Himmler: Excuse me?

DG: You wouldn't understand in a million years.

Himmler: What 'prophet'?

I realised I sounded hysterical.

DG: What happened to her? Why did she die?

Himmler: I think the answer is rather apparent enough, wouldn't you think?

Suddenly my emotions switched. I hated Himmler. And the crazy thing was my hate for him wasn't because of his particular job, which arguably had to be the worse in the entire Third Reich. I just hated his looks. His sneering personality. His meticulously created self-pufferies.

DG: She's dead?

Himmler: I believe I have already stated that fact.

DG: But why?

Himmler: God acts in mysterious ways, doesn't He?

DG: You sound happy she died.

Himmler: I sound incredulous at your stupidity.

DG: Why did no one help her? She could have been saved.

Himmler: Again, we do not understand each other.

DG: Excuse me?

Himmler [Angrily]: Who cares if one human died, albeit a German, when millions have our people have been massacred, mutilated, and slaughtered by your criminal people?

DG: You're right; I lost my sense of perspective.

Himmler: Both our men and from the enemy side turned up trying to help her. But her wounds were fatal. Furthermore, you will be happy to know she was *not* a Jewess. But my goodness me, her intellect must have been that of a worm.

DG: Why?

Himmler: A woman trying to see her so-called fiancé, driving through on an ongoing battle zone!

{*Silence*}

DG: Why? Do you doubt he was her fiancé?

Himmler: Countless Germans, unfortunately, and this is not proper National Socialist behavior, but countless German soldiers, especially those in their teens, propose marriage, hoping thereby they would seduce them to bed.

DG: But you don't know that. You don't know if he were honorable or not.

Himmler: You're correct; I don't. I'm only telling you numbers or statistics. But assuming he was indeed a white knight in shining armor, what brain thinks it necessary to be driven to see him, meaning driving through a battle?

DG: What about the driver?

Himmler [Smiling]: What about him, apart from being dead too?

DG: Why did he accept taking Katharina on that fatal drive?

Himmler: I cannot believe he drove solely at her request, and if that were the case, he too shared a similar quality of a brain with that young lady. But that is unlikely. Meaning, statistically speaking, how likely is it to have two retarded individuals together simultaneously? You see, as a detective, I suspect he *must* have had his own interests in going to the spot where the fiancé lived. Now I have a question for you. How can you equate the fact she was stupid with your belief that she was a Prophetess?

DG: Death does not end the life of prophets.

Himmler: That was not my –

DG: Secondly, your other assumption is false since I do not think she was stupid.

Himmler [Laughing]: When a half-brained woman chooses to be driven through a fierce battle, and for the most idiotic, senseless, and sole purpose of seeing her fiancé, who is in all likelihood, not an honorable man, and when even a child would know chances of driving through a battle and being shredded to mincemeat is around ninety-nine percent, does that indicate a spark of intelligence on her part?

DG: We don't know for sure –

Himmler: Assuming he is honorable. Wouldn't her excursion still suggest idiocy?

DG: Do you enjoy humiliating and hurting people?

Himmler: I regret watching fools.

{*Silence*}

DG: Why are you staring at me?

Himmler: Am I?

DG: And you continually smile.

Himmler: I apologize. This is the structure God built me —

DG: Do you feel any humor in this tragedy?

HH: I do, and I've already indicated to you why. Again, you are slow. But that is to be expected. You are Americanized, after all. I told you it is funny when a moron thinks she can survive driving through a fierce battle zone and all for the pointless purpose of seeing a man, and for what purpose? To have sex with him? She may as well have blown up her empty brain with one clean bullet. So, in simpler terms, I laugh at her stupidity. And yes, I think stupidity is often hilarious.

DG: You don't know she was going for sex. That's a damned lie.

HH: Do you suppose she was risking her life to play hide and seek with him?

DG: No, she wanted to remain with him in these last days of this damned war.

Himmler [Laughing]: Hirohito would've been honored to have her as a kamikaze, and the first female one too!

{*Silence*}

DG: You look homicidal. There it is again. That weird smile. I swear if ever any woman were to walk past you in any street accidentally, she would feel the same as I do.

Himmler: Talking of stupidities, I will relate to you another story. After all, that's why you're here, scribbling our 'stories.' One day, an officer frantically tells me or asks me, "Reichsführer, a commandant — I forget which camp — was about to burn corpses. Jew corpses. He was shocked to find one female corpse fully clothed. Approaching her, he was startled, finding her to be fully alive. He asked her, "What are you doing here?"

DG: Great question.

HH [Laughing]: Astonishingly, the Jewess replied, "Do you think I'd want to live when all my people are either dead or being killed?"

Suddenly the loathsome cockroach hurled it a burst of laughter that startled me. And that continued for a few seconds before he composed himself, returning to his typical cold, flat person. I didn't bother thinking about that 'story' that so tickled his ribs.

DG: Who shot her? Was it Germans or Russians?

Himmler [Laughing]: Or we back to your Prophetess?

DG: Yes.

HH [Giggling]: As a racial man, even I think that in this specific instance, the racial origin of the man who pulled the trigger, releasing the fatal bullet, is entirely irrelevant, and thus your question is downright stupid.

{*Silence*}

Himmler [Laughing]: Well, I must admit, I have not laughed as much as this moment. You entertain me. You do.

DG: Do you know the answer?

Himmler: Still? More questions on that irrelevant incident? What's so fascinating to you about her? You never even knew her! Or maybe, in your eyes, she is famous. Well then, why is she famous? Did she write a Bible or Koran?

DG: It doesn't matter my obsession … or fascination.

HH: I believe it has always been Fate. Fate seals lives, and Fate creates life.

DG: What?

HH: I meant life is beyond our meaning. The procedures of events are beyond our comprehension. Who would have known one Asiatic gangster literally heaved the entirety of Soviet industry from western Russia to the Urals and in the space of a few months while simultaneously being delivered the worse military assault in Russian history? Now that is a worthy question to be asked. Though I have no answers, that's what I mean. Understanding life is impossible. And that is what I have learned with certainty — yes, certainty - during this war of extermination.

DG: Did you enjoy mass-murdering people?

Himmler: Stupid woman! Didn't you just ask me that question?

He was, in truth, correct, but I had to move my soul from that pervert. Even though I think he had my answers, I didn't or couldn't relax talking to him alone. Not that I thought he was sexually bothersome. If anything, his femininity was too much to suggest a predator. But there was something loathsome about him, and that made me think. Why did I find Himmler loathsome? The simplest answer would be because he's, or he was, the man in charge of the Holocaust. But that's not really my answer. That wasn't my reason for loathing him. After all, I had no feelings of disgust with the other Nazi men, whose crimes were as equal as Himmler's crimes. That made me feel immensely guilty.

How could I feel 'comfortable' with not one mass murderer but a mass murderers — men, such as Hitler, Goering, Jodl, Guderian, Goebbels, Fegelein, Speer, Keitel, Ribbentrop, and others? Surely, being or feeling 'comfortable' with those genocidal bastards must incriminate me in the moral sense; isn't that correct? At least, an accessory to criminals? But no, that's silly. I was only interviewing them. I wasn't a spectator while they committed their acts of mass rape, torture, murder, and genocide. Therefore, I am innocent. My God, Dorothy, stop thinking. You're going to eat yourself alive!

Himmler: I had to serve my people as per their physical, mental, and spiritual health. Now, do you remember my answer?

DG: Yes, you're right. I forgot. But did you ever think twice and doubting your belief Jews are verminous?

HH [Smiling]: Belief brooks no doubt.

DG: Even Our Blessed Lord Jesus had His Moments of doubt in His faith.

HH: I am not Jesus. I'll tell you a major source of disagreement between myself and the Fuehrer. I always knew Jesus was a Jew, and from that, you can extrapolate my understanding of that Man and Christian philosophy. Meanwhile, the Fuehrer believed Jesus was an Aryan, and the text's corruption came from Paul, who was, of course, a well-known Jew.

DG: When you say 'text,' you mean the Bible?

HH: Yes. That's why the Fuehrer was not only uninterested in pagan German history; he also disagreed with my endless pagan parades and pagan festival days, which I did in coordination with Goebbels.

As the man droned on, I noticed I hadn't answered my earlier question — how come I only felt uncomfortable with the former chicken farmer and not the rest of the Hitler gang?

~

Guderian – "The War Is Over! My God, What Is Wrong with you Fanatics?"

Guderian [To Goebbels]: We are facing annihilation. This hour is by far the worst in Germany's modern history. You know that. No German has ever left Germany in the annihilated state it's in save for that Austrian corporal.

Goebbels: How do you know that? Attila the Hun ravaged Germany –

Guderian: I'm speaking in modern times. Or modern history.

{Silence}

Guderian: Meanwhile ... and you're still seeking ways to weasel your way from our reality? You're still lying to the poor German people, speaking of 'victories.' Do you think our people are idiots? Everyone knows we're not only facing defeat; we're facing mass extermination by the Russians.

Ribbentrop [Nervous]: No, there must be hope! Please do say this to me, will you? There is yet hope still, no?

Keitel [To Ribbentrop]: I believe your sentence is structured in an entirely incorrect format, so far as the German language goes. However, to give you the benefit of the doubt, aren't you supposed to be our eloquent, worldly diplomat? Because I must inform what you said was quite a demolishing of the purity of our precise German syntax.

Guderian [Angrily]: Can't you for once and in this final scene of our lives — just for once, speak of the truth, Dr. Goebbels?

Guderian [Angrily]: Is that too much for your stomach and sensitivities? To speak the truth? We hear your lying broadcasts urging boys to stand up to T-34 tanks!

Goebbels [Laughing Sarcastically]: The defeatists drone on! Do you not hear them, comrades?

Ribbentrop [Nervous]: Do you think our situation is like the Titanic?

Goebbels [Loudly]: Defeat is not the end! Only stooges and dullards think in bleak and pessimistic, pointless manners.

Guderian [Angrily at Goebbels]: Do you know in what conditions and circumstances eighty million Germans live in at this moment?

Keitel: Why do you look at me when you say "stooges and dullards"?

Goebbels [Angrily]: Of course, I do! I have been out on the frontlines many times, so don't you lecture —

Guderian [Angrily at Goebbels]: What are the essential concerns of the remaining Germans?

Goebbels [To Guderian]: As the Fuehrer stated, the so-called "essential concerns of the remaining Germans" are of no concern to us. Only military matters must interest us.

Goering [Smiling]: So, speaks a crippled man who has never served a day in the military.

DG: Herr Speer. If I may change the subject.

Speer: Yes.

DG: How do you now see Hitler's social interactions?

Speer: He centers his amiability on the few women who had been with him for years. For a long time, he had shown a particular liking for

Frau Traudl Junge, the widow of his servant who had been killed at the front; but he also favors his Viennese diet cook. His long-time secretaries, Frau Wolf and Frau Christian, also form part of this private circle. For months now, he has shown a preference for taking his teas and meals with them. Scarcely any men still belong among his intimates. I, too, have long since ceased to be invited to his table. The arrival of Eva Braun also introduced several changes in his habits, although it didn't stop his probably innocent relations with the other women around him. He must be motivated by the simple belief that women are more loyal in misfortune than men could be. Indeed, he sometimes seems to distrust the show of faith by the men of his staff. The exceptions are Bormann, you, of course, Dr. Goebbels, and Ley, whom he seems still to be sure of.

DG: Anyone else?

Speer: Not that I have noticed.

DG: Any military men?

Guderian: Of course not! He despises all of us to his marrow.

DG: I spoke to one individual telling me it is remarkable how the government machinery is still somehow functioning.

"There is a better chance of seeing a camel pass through the eye of a needle than of seeing a really great man 'discovered' through an election."

- Adolf Hitler. *Mein Kampf - My Struggle:* **Unabridged edition of Hitler's original book -** *Four and a Half Years of Struggle against Lies, Stupidity, and Cowardice*

Speer: Around this shadowy man, the apparatus of command continues to run mechanically. That is true. Apparently, there is still some momentum here that operates even when the motor is running down. This residual force seems to keep the generals moving along the same track even at this very end when the radiation of Hitler's will is beginning to weaken. Keitel, for example, continues to press for the destruction of bridges even when Hitler is now willing to spare them.

Goering [Smiling]: Why would you even mention Keitel? Talk of a piss-drenched doormat.

Keitel [Angrily]: Excuse me? I am a proud doormat for the Fuehrer, certainly, but I am certainly *not* urine-soaked and never have been.

Fegelein [To Keitel]: What if the urine in question were the urine of the Fuehrer?

{Laughter}

Ribbentrop [Nervous]: But there is hope, I know that. Am I correct? Or not?

Keitel [Proudly]: Yes, Foreign Minister, there is hope.

DG: There's 'hope' when the Russians stand a mile or two from you?

Keitel: My dear, you do not understand. The Fuehrer stated in a Kantian categorical manner there is hope; therefore, there is hope.

Goebbels: Using your words, General Guderian, a true 'fanatic,' gives up only upon his death.

∼

How Hitler Seduced Everyone Around Him

By now, I had far more understanding of Hitler and how he seduced millions of ordinary Germans and non-Germans to follow his genocidal words.

Everyone admired him. Stupefied by his presence. And there was nothing feigned in their reaction to his existence, to his company. I said he had a controlling presence. Let me offer you a simple though shocking example of what I am trying to relate.

The minute he leaves a room, going God knows where, I tell you, the minute he disappears, you notice the existing energy in the Bunker is suddenly disconnected. Instantaneously every personality changes to whomsoever they were before he was physically there. And then, for once, despite the war outside, you feel a semblance of 'normality.' As though all the acting and feigning are defused.

During my first brief encounter with that man, I had a bizarre feeling. It was not one I expected to have. I pushed myself to 'rationalize' why a dispirited nation such as Germany was in 1933 adored him. I think I understood why the German people were so dreamily agog with this one man throughout the last twelve years. I will be criticized for these words.

But I sure would be vile if I say otherwise. As I said, I did not expect such feelings to exist in my mind. The man was unconditionally evil, and that was the end of it. So, therefore, why on earth or how could I dare to have any sympathy for the Devil?

But that was not Adolf Hitler! I'd be lying to myself and to you, the readers, if I was going to restate what every historian has been saying since 1945 simply — that is, Hitler was uniquely evil, and that's where the story ends. Hitler was far, far more complicated and multi-dimensional than being evil. And remember, I'm in no diminishing his evil insanity. I'm telling you that that man had absurdly magnetic energies that sucked you towards him, and to deny that or to omit writing about it or to say minimize that makes light of the man in question. And that's dangerous because if we only think of Hitler's evil, that reduces his uniqueness. And he was unique in modern history. That's precisely my point.

We must forever remember with horror his supernatural abilities to suck you in. Speaking about myself, he sucked an unknown sympathy for him that I felt arose from my untouched womb. Extricating imperceivable compassion I never knew existed. How did he even know, let alone discover the whereabouts of these attributes of mine were? Who let the thief inside my womanhood?

The Rolling Stones

"Sympathy for The Devil"

> Just as every cop is a criminal
> And all the sinners saints
> As heads is tails
> Just call me Lucifer
>
> Cause I'm in need of some restraint
> So if you meet me
> Have some courtesy
> Have some sympathy, and some taste
>
> Use all your well-learned politesse
> Or I'll lay your soul to waste, um yeah
> Pleased to meet you
> Hope you guessed my name, um yeah
>
> But what's puzzling you
> Is the nature of my game, um mean it, get down
>
> - Mick Jagger & Keith Richards - 1968

Naturally, I struggled with those feelings. I denied their relevance or credibility. I ignored my feelings. Hitler's evil, and that's it. But that's a Fool's Paradise. Face the truth, girl. Face them as an addict or a phobic face their addiction or terror. But then, the other side of my mind countered back - *blasting* me for having compassion for any of the machinations of that man. Rantingly screaming, the mind of mine bellowed out, *'This behavior means you're an accomplice!'*

No, I'm not an accomplice. I'm trying to understand how evil humans think, feel, and operate. To do that, I had to journey straight into their mental landscape. I had to be a tourist, dwelling in the Hell of insanity and evilness. There was no other way of understanding the viewpoint of an extremist if you don't look at it entirely from their mind and eyes. If you want to understand the nature of cancer, don't you have to learn how and where that disease is created in the first place? And don't oncologists need to know how cancer survives in the body of the unfortunate victim? And to do that, don't they have to get in there in situ, and that is when and where they can confront cancer and how it operates? Or am I lying to myself? So, what I was doing didn't imply *I* had sympathy for the Devil.

Dorothy, girl, you've got to establish your thoughts more succinctly. Hitler could be impressively convincing, given his totality. Conventional, respectable historians omit that in their books, lectures, debates, and so on. The 'totality of his personality' was not just when he whipped his people with his furies, far from it. And having experienced it myself, I understood Germans. It was not the man – Hitler - who aroused in me these exotic tensions. He was the lighter of unknown needs. The Firestarter of my repressed impressions, memories, and aspirations. The arsonist of the forgotten parts of my soul. Ablazing not one but a thousand rebellions and contradictory emotions, intuitions, needs co-existing existing in my mind.

When he poured out his exculpatory arguments, defending Man's most abominable deeds, everything seemed so damnably, elegantly simple – I could hardly not believe him. He'd vary with combinations of mixed tempos of rage and passionate love. You were lavishly subsumed with his mostly unknown wicked humor, and you loved it, despite its sinful insinuations. And yes, here he did arouse carnal sensations – but not for him. That's important to know. At least, I'm speaking for myself. I know for a fact many German women did have sexual feelings for him. Not me.

He doused his harangues with stinging sarcasm at one moment, next turning to grave admonishments warning us the way we're living our lives, we're heading for a catastrophic disaster. He vividly illuminated the hypocrisies he saw in his nation, searing the cauldrons of our brains with freshly cooked raw vindictiveness, making you feel as though all of your life you've been a victim, and now that you hear these raw words, you feel you've been awakened. My mind screamed, "My God! What have I done all those years? Nothing but destroying myself!" And that was true in my case, and it was true for millions of Germans. You feel a need to scream, *"Why have you, 'my' so-called society, family, my neighborhood, my education, my job – why have you all been stomping on my neck all my life?"* Yes, go on and deeply pity yourself for being unheard, oppressed, and having never thought of counteracting, let alone taking revenge against all those bastards that have systematically verbally and spiritually and mentally and bodily abused you. And my God, that feeling of needing to take revenge was physically shattering, firing off shivers throughout my body, toes to head. That was one secret of his success in arousing the German people. And remember the man spellbound all Germans, from every socio-economic, cultural, class, rural, city, sectarian, and educational background.

Hitler

Remember the depths of German grievances against what they viewed as their atrophying Weimar nation and against a world that viciously robbed them of victory and then proceeded to dismember Germany itself.

It may be difficult for modern readers to understand how Germans felt in the post-1918 years, but that's one methodology if you want to understand their feelings for Hitler. The fact is a significant number of Germans believed foreign powers deliberately planned and managed their inflation unemployment and so rendering their nation no different than any other backward country. Many Germans believed Weimar culture was prostituting German civilization and culture. Many Germans believed Weimar culture deliberately destroyed people's love and pride in their country, culture, and heritage. Many Germans believed Weimar culture deliberately sought to destroy all memories of German identity. Many Germans believed Weimar culture deliberately sought to bring black men, inter-marry with German women, and decrease the number of white Germans. Many Germans believed Weimar culture deliberately sought to create and swarm Germany with brothels, pimps, rent-boys, homosexuality, lesbianism, and an overall state of sexual permissiveness. Many Germans believed Weimar culture deliberately introduced US culture, such as jazz, to devalue the culture and people's dignity. Many Germans believed Weimar culture deliberately sought to destroy pre-1918 education from primary, high school to university levels. And the most essential part in this mesh of beliefs is this – most Germans believed it was a 'conspiracy' by the democratic West, Jewish financiers, and Bolsheviks – for they were 'in charge' of all these attributes that was afflicted upon their prostrate nation.

I think you get my drift by now.

And suddenly, this awkward-looking Austrian who comes from nowhere speaks to what people need to hear – *"You do not have to put up with these fatally destructive forces! Stand up and fight for Germany's right to be proud of its culture, civilization, society, folklore et al.!" "No more mass unemployment, widespread homosexuality! No more pittance wages! No more prostitution of our people and our culture!"*

Perhaps now you can sense how liberating it was to hear this man speaking those words? Now, whether you happened to agree with the actual contents of the man's words or not is not the relevant point here.

This undeniable ability to touch your most private and rawest parts and emotions to liberate and alleviate your awful living conditions and making your nation once more a global power.

That is how I felt, and that is how people who met or saw him felt. I can only speak and write what I experienced. What I experienced was *my* truth. Indeed, were I to omit or dismiss these feelings, I would be writing a false narrative for you.

I believe all those who met the man and denied his attractive characteristics lie when writing their experiences. Or maybe not every one of them lied. Maybe, I'm too extreme. Perhaps some people genuinely felt no thrills nor sparks when meeting him. But I'll say this to my final breath. That man affected a majority of anyone who met him, even from distances.

Before some of my readers tear my words and pages, I'm not saying the dictator automatically convinced me of every word he said. If that's what some of you have assumed, you've missed my intention. The man said words, ideas, themes, concepts, thoughts, complicated questions that I never thought about, and they were astonishingly truthful. This is an essential fact because no historian will ever say what I've just said. Remember, for the established, published, conventional historian, dare not say anything positive about that man. He's pure evil. End of conversation. End of research.

It was an undeniable fact when I tell you the man in question had a stunning and thrilling ability to simplify complex problems. He had a refreshing ability in making complicated matters not just understandable but somehow, and I do not know how or why, but he'd render these tediously intricate and alarmingly complex problems appear not only easily coherent but even thoroughly pleasing to hear! And that's one more reason why as he spoke, you couldn't help but feel degrees of simmering pleasure. You felt confident. He elevated you to the heights of geniuses as he graciously explained to you their complex ideas and theories. Yes, now I, too, understand what all those so-called geniuses were talking about. I understand their theories and philosophies. I felt power. Intelligence. Foresight.

And when he wasn't orating, believe it or not — and sorry for some of you to hear this — but yes, he terribly pleasing to be with. He cared for you. He asked about your concerns and interests. He charmed you. Yes, if you want, his presence, his mannerisms, his gestures, his body language, his words, his facial expressions, his behaviors, his eyes, and that eccentrically deep voice deeply comforted you. As I said, he made you feel you were valuable and important not only to him but, far more importantly, you felt you felt righteous about your mind and your life. You weren't just one more pointless, worthless speck of a brick with no meaning in your ordeal-riddled existence.

The man made you feel and believe your presence was vitally necessary for the organism known as your nation and community. You are important. You are needed. Can one not feel these inspirational words and beliefs? All your worries and problems had and have a purpose. To serve the greater reality, which is the living nation of Germany. And you have duties to do. It is no good just 'being' German. You had to be a fully participatory human working for Germany's health. You had to be in the Hitler Youth. You had to join the Wehrmacht. You had to be a one unified community. That was the only diagnostic method for

Germany's survival. And, in case you think, 'Well, what is this abstract Germany thing?' The man reminds you Germany is not only you. Germany is your future wellbeing and the for the direct safety and goodness of *your* children. Therefore, working for Germany meant you are paving better roads and more fabulous ladders for your children's future aspirations.

"Our strength consists in our speed and in our brutality. Genghis Khan led millions of women and children to slaughter—with premeditation and a happy heart. History sees in him solely the founder of a state. It's a matter of indifference to me what a weak western European civilization will say about me. I have issued the command —and I'll have anybody who utters but one word of criticism executed by a firing squad —that our war aim does not consist in reaching certain lines but in the physical destruction of the enemy. Accordingly, I have placed my death-head formation in readiness — for the present only in the East — with orders to them to send to death mercilessly and without compassion, men, women, and children of Polish derivation and language. Only thus shall we gain the living space (Lebensraum) which we need. Who, after all, speaks today of the annihilation of the Armenians?"

— Adolf Hitler

How odd, isn't it? Because of all people, I think psychopaths are best able to make you forget their criminal nature. Invisible enticements luring you into your mind and forcing you to think about your life. . Charming you with their wit and humbling you with their compassion, and startling you with their erudition.

To wit, it was not so much *what* he was saying as his overall performance, exactly as you would feel when listening to an opera. Of course, you may not even understand the text nor remember this meaning at that moment or the purpose of that staged scene in some other moment. Still, the overall effect was undoubtedly one of exhilaration and security.

∼

MANY REAL LIVES

A MAN STUMBLES ACROSS A STREET,

FINGERS GRIPPING THE BROWN PAPER BAG,

A WOMAN PACES BACK AND FORTH,

MAKING SILENT OFFERS TO PASSING DRIVERS.

UP THE BLOCK ANOTHER MAN,

SLUMPS OVER A SIDEWALK BENCH,

HIS BODY HANGING ON SOMEHOW,

BETWEEN THE BENCH AND CONCRETE.

- TOMMY LYNN SELLS - American Serial Killer (1965-2014)

~

FAQ III - "Did I Just Sit There & Ask Questions and Hear His Answers?"

I have since been asked:

- *"Did I just sit there and ask questions and hear his answers?"*

No, not at all.

How did I see Hitler in the Bunker? Once now and then, officers seemed to query or question him, and these interactions lasted no more than seconds to minutes at most. Indeed, no conversations. He never walked around in the Bunker; I know that sounds strange. He never joined in any conversation or even any kind of banter among the Bunkerites. Instead, he was either in his private room or conducting talks in the military conference room; finally, in that latter room, when no military conference was taking place, he allowed me to interview him. That was when I observed him in action, so to speak—watching his slow, halting shuffle. Making the few steps, he did undertake. Laden with a weighty gait that was varying and varying between lethargic disgust and weariness.

I could not help but wonder, time and again, what on earth was this supposed creature of God thinking when he was detached from everyone else? Surely, he knew these were the last moments of his life on earth? Obviously, he knew. Never mind all his pep talks on victory and all that rubbish. The man knew, damn it! And so, in those ending hours, sitting in his private room, maybe lying in his bed, what did he think? He had no audience. There was the need to act or impress anyone. I am sure he reminisced about his life; I believe he must have thought again and again about the mother he so adored. Did he recall his youthful days in Vienna and Munich? Was he rejoicing in his deeds of genocide? Did he have any regrets, any remorse for the atrociousness he unleashed from Paris to Stalingrad? Were his only regrets in not being able to complete his Final Solution? Or did he ignore ugly thoughts?

But wait, that makes no sense! For Hitler, the extermination camps must have been a source of pride since that was the only 'achievement' he partially succeeded in. Do you see what I'm trying to do? Trying to understand, visualize his mind. During our conversations, oddly enough, he once insisted on showing me an architectural model of his hometown of Linz [modeled by one of his architects, Hermann Giesler].

I thought to myself, well, why would this man be showing me all this pointless nonsense? What was his purpose in showing me his *future* plans, given the apparent actuality that his future was coming to its immediate end? That question puzzled me back in 1945, and, to this day, I have no answer.

~

Finally, I'm Allowed to See Hitler During His Military Conference, Though I May Not Speak

I. Military Conference – Evening Situation Report – March 2nd, 1945

His military conferences usually lasted five or six hours. But why in the first place ... or let me rephrase this - what exactly was the point in having a 'military' conference when the dimmest form of reason would bark at you, stating that your end is well-nigh? It seems laughable to me to propose the obvious question, 'Didn't he know the war was over?'

However, in retrospect, as I look back, I understand why he did what he did. Let me explain. Today I'm an old woman. Any day, I may die. And every night, as I go to bed, I know I may not wake up alive. And you know what? Even in my advanced age, I still cling to life, though logic, science, science, biology tells me it is futile to think I will last on for much longer. And yet, like Hitler, I still adamantly refuse to believe that fact or facts.

Anyway, going back to the conferences. Usually, Hitler had two conferences; the first began at around 4.00 pm, and the second would start at midnight, lasting till around 3.00 am. Remember Hitler woke up by 2.00 pm, meaning his lunch was served around 3.00 pm. So please re-orient your mind to his worldview.

To my surprise, I was finally permitted to join one of those military conferences. So far, I met Hitler only once … actually, I did not 'meet' him. I saw him close up, but we were not introduced, and I don't think he even noticed me. And as I told you before, I would complain a million times when I would interview him, and they would reply, 'Soon, soon.' Well, at least now, I will not be interviewing him, but at least I would be seeing him in action, so to speak. I was harshly told not to utter a word during the military conference.

Hitler allowed only one older general, Rundstedt, to sit in these sessions – plus Goering. The rest stood facing the leader.

I must confirm one matter. His astonishing knowledge of a million subjects, from the most tedious details in architecture to the most minute technical matters, was true. He could not hide his delight whenever he corrected the supposedly professional men, bringing *him* the latest 'news'. He effortlessly juggled differing statistics on differing subjects, typically comparing and contrasting them, proving his point of view. I know that for many of our readers, this isn't pleasant to hear.

Hitler had an unbelievable ability to recollect and analyze obscure statistical information that would buffer and augment his arguments in front of his baffled audiences. Time and again, he would rapidly interrogate officers, firing off multiple questions on where such and such a regiment was, the number of its men, excruciating details on their weapons. He would follow through with these questions endlessly.

Having said that, contrary to what you might think, standing there watching the Fuehrer having his final military conferences, there were many hours of trivial exchanges that I can only kindly describe as tortuously tedious. Why? I'm no army person. Obviously, but, as I said, I couldn't understand what point or purpose was there in these sometimes-heated arguments involving bitty bitsy 'details' having no bearing on the overall situation outside in the real world? And I'm not just talking about when Hitler corrected his staff. All his conferences boiled down to the leader asking worthless questions such as the whereabouts of this mostly destroyed regiment or how many operable tanks did that crippled division have? I knew the answer – remember what I said about clinging to life? The man was clinging to dear life, his precious life, though life had no more time for him. What about these men standing before him? Surely, logically, rationally, these collections of the top army officers and generals must have been able to speak candidly to Hitler, stating the simple fact that the war was over. 'Over' – so far as Germany was concerned. And yet, not one man dared to speak what was glaringly obvious – except for Guderian.

Such questions would, of course, be necessary for leaders like Churchill, FDR, and Stalin. But for Germany, what did it matter if this shriveled-up panzer division was here or how guns this shattered regiment had?

There he sat in his chair; maps neatly laid out on the table in front of him. These maps were impossible for me to understand. Too many meaningless differently colored signs, arrows, pins, notes, rulers all over.

I couldn't even tell you what geographic location the map in question was representing. I knew they were showing him Berlin maps, but I couldn't judge where the frontline was. Hitler intensely scrutinized these maps with his magnifying glass, sometimes staring at them for minutes in total silence. As he poured over these maps with his magnifying glass, he reminded me of a surgeon operating on a patient.

I'm not sure if by that time he could write, given his hand shaking. No, wait. He was right-handed, and it was his left arm and hand that shook uncontrollably. But maybe his right hand was also partially affected because he would only point out whatever location he had in mind with his fingers. He seemed overworked, burdened, heavy – not just his personality but his body - do you know what I mean? For long periods [or what appeared to me to be long stretches of time], nothing seemed to interest him. He would switch to a zoned-out state of mind, allowing the military men to discuss whatever subject matter was at hand. I thought he was either blanking out or imagining happier moments in his life. I could be wrong; I'm conjecturing.

However, that impression was joltingly blown out of existence as his laser-like focus and intensity resumed activities. That was when he would behave in the following different manners. One was when he chose to stare at any one of his military staff; second, is when he angrily shouted at someone reproaching them that because he did not appreciate their answer; third, was when he fired off a thousand questions a minute at any of the poor men and finally, he sometimes orated a bellowing speech that made me feel as though we were back in Nuremberg during those rallies in 1938, with a much healthier Fuehrer rasping out his sermons. That is when you realize a hurricane was overwhelming the small conference room, appreciating the fear and trembling of many of these men. That is when I reminded myself *not* to be too over-hasty in judging the man as a has-been, frail figure.

∼

Military Conference I – Midday Situation Report. March 2nd, 1945: Tedious Numbers

- [3.12 pm]

Hitler: I have thought it over, recently – I don't know if it's been reported to the Reichsmarschall or not – I have thought the whole thing over recently, and I've come to the following conclusion. Eighty aircraft have been shot down recently.

Generalleutnant Herbert Büchs: Mein Fuehrer, 82.

Hitler: Of these 80, the fighters shot down 50, and anti-aircraft guns shot down 30. These 30 we must leave aside for the movement. 490 aircraft have engaged in aerial combat.

Herbert Büchs: Mein Fuehrer, 305!

Hitler: All right, 305 have engaged in aerial combat. You recently said 490.

Already I felt sleepy at these tedious words and numbers.

Hitler, Goering & Behind Hitler, Fegelein

Keitel [To Herbert Büchs]: Get your numbers correct, man!

Goebbels [To Herbert Büchs]: Arithmetic is not one of your strong points, I suppose.

Herbert Büchs [Stiffly]: I have my numbers correct, General Keitel. The number is 305. None of the Frankfurt fighter wings had aerial combat, and of the 4th Fighter Wing –

Hitler [Angrily]: All right, 305! *It does not matter*, including an assault squadron, which was deployed with 42 aircraft. This assault squadron alone has shot down 30.

Herbert Büchs: Mein Fuehrer, both assault groups. There were two assault groups.

Hitler: With altogether -?

I was already lost as to what the meaning of the conversation was about.

Herbert Büchs: Mein Fuehrer, with altogether 62 airplanes. Sixty-one of them have engaged in aerial combat.

Hitler: All right, 61!

Herbert Büchs: Mein Fuehrer, they have shot down 30 four-engine planes.

Hitler: So, there are 20 left. If you subtract the 60 planes from 305, there are 240 left. So, 240 planes together have shot down only 20 in aerial combat band have themselves lost: the assault squadron 30 –

Herbert Büchs: Mein Fuehrer, the assault squadron: 30.

Keitel [Angrily to Herbert Büchs]: You are irritating our Fuehrer.

Himmler: Not a good attribute.

Hitler: And the others have lost 90. So, with 90 losses, they have shot down 20 altogether in 240 sorties.

{Everyone: 'Jawohl Mein Fuehrer!'}

Keitel: Never argue against the Fuehrer. Do you not know that by now, Generalleutnant Büchs?

Herbert Büchs: Mein Fuehrer, I am not arguing –

Hitler [Angrily]: Never mind, continue.

Herbert Büchs: There is something else. The assault group has another group with it to give them cover.

Hitler [Angrily]: I do not care. I say the covering group must shoot as well – it's not just bombers that have been shot down, but also fighters.

Herbert Büchs: Of course, Mein Fuehrer.

Hitler: So, the result is totally unsatisfactory.

Herbert Büchs: Mein Fuehrer, the deciding factor in this issue is that the 30 shot down by the assault groups –

Hitler [Angrily]: *Is there anyone among you who goes through all these matters and analyses everything closely?* The Reichsmarschall does not know this anyway. He didn't even know that our losses are bigger when he was here recently because they confuse the whole picture with those damned 'failed-to-land reports.'

Goebbels [Sarcastic]: Where is the Reichsmarschall, Mein Fuehrer?

{Murmurs of Laughter}

Why were they arguing about the difference between having 305 or 300 planes? Did they think that the supreme question would alter the balance of forces in Germany's favor? Unfortunately for them, the reality was the Luftwaffe itself was non-existent. Our combined air forces ruled supreme over German skies. So never mind those noisy facts and let these gentlemen continue in their labyrinthine esoteric conversations.

I did not think any leader could be so persistently aimless in these dry conversations. Weren't there weightier matters to discuss? Such as how soon is it going to be before a million merry Soviet soldiers are banging on the Bunker's door?

And you may ask yourself
How do I work this?
And you may ask yourself
Where is that large automobile?
And you may tell yourself
This is not my beautiful house!
And you may tell yourself
This is not my beautiful wife!

- *Talking Heads. Once in A Lifetime. 1981*

The prominent group attendees were Jodl, Keitel, Fegelein, Himmler, Guderian, Goering [though rarely], and oddly enough, Goebbels. I say this because the latter had no connection whatsoever with anything remotely connected to military matters. Anyway, there he certainly was in every conference.

I must say this since we are on this subject, and I couldn't understand how much Hitler indulged Goering for the life of me. Can you imagine, he was the only man who would often sit [remember, only older gentlemen were allowed to sit, and Goering was 52]. Only he could *sleep* during these conferences without provoking a whisper from the Fuehrer.

~

Military Conference II - Evening Situation Report - March 24th, 1945

Hitler [Shouting]: "Are We Blind? Is That What you Wehrmacht Geniuses are Telling Me? If you Cannot Even Produce One Report That You Can understand On Our Frontline Situation, Why Then are We Having This Conference?"

- [2.26 am]

Sturmbannfuehrer Goehler: Mein Fuehrer, the Ukrainian Division has an authorized strength of 11,000 and an actual strength of 14,000.

Hitler [Frustrated]: What are you saying? Why is the so-called 'actual strength' greater than the so-called 'authorized strength'?

Sturmbannfuehrer Goehler: Mein Fuehrer probably it means they have many more Ukrainian recruits than the target, so they have integrated them. They have the following actual stock of weapons: 2,100 pistols, 610 submachine guns, 9,000 rifles, 70 guns with telescopic sights, 65 machine carbines, 434 light machine guns, 96 heavy machine guns, 58 trucks, four armored personnel carriers –

Hitler: We could equip most of the two divisions with that. What do they have?

Sturmbannfuehrer Goehler: Mein Fuehrer, 22 flame-throwers, one medium antitank gun, 11 7.5 cm antitank guns, 17 light infantry guns, three heavy infantry guns Model 33, 9 3.7 cm anti-aircraft artillery pieces, 37 light field howitzers, and six heavy field howitzers.

Guderian: What 'Ukrainian unit'?

Hitler & His Generals & Officers

Sturmbannfuehrer Goehler: General, I do not have their specific details.

Goebbels: Aren't details by definition 'specific'?

Goering [Sarcastic]: *Who* creates these meaningless terms, such as 'actual strength' as opposed to 'authorized strength'?

Keitel: Very good question, Herr Reichsmarschall. Apart from you, of course, only the Fuehrer would have detected that.

Sturmbannfuehrer Goehler [Nervous]: Herr Reichsmarschall, I do not know.

Goebbels: How is it possible to read a document which you admit you do not understand?

Sturmbannfuehrer Goehler [Nervous]: I received this telegram, but that does not mean I understood every word.

Goebbels: Are you telling us you're an idiot?

{Silence}

Hitler [Angrily]: I must know *what* they are worth! We must go through every word conscientiously to determine what can be expected from a unit like that.

{Everyone: 'Jawohl Mein Fuehrer!'}

Hitler [Shouting]: Are we blind? Is that what you Wehrmacht geniuses are telling me? If you cannot even produce one report that you can understand on our frontline situation, why then are we having this conference?

{Silence}

Hitler [Shouting]: If we can't expect anything, then it makes no sense; we cannot afford the luxury of having units like that, and I still don't understand what you're saying! You create words to camouflage the truth, and we need the correct information for us to know how and where to proceed and react!

Keitel [Angrily]: Absolutely true, Mein Fuehrer! Only we men of the Wehrmacht can deliver empty reports because we're just as empty-headed.

Sturmbannfuehrer Goehler [Nervously]: Absolutely, Mein Fuehrer. I will get the detailed, most accurate information immediately.

Fegelein: Well, Sturmbannfuehrer Goehler, it seems I made a mistake in promoting you. If you knew you were to present your report today, why is it only now you admit your account is worthless as per its clarity?

Sturmbannfuehrer Goehler [Nervous]: Standartenführer Fegelein, I was unaware the report lacked clarity.

{Mocking Laughter}

Goering [Roaring with Anger]: So, it took the Fuehrer a matter of seconds to make you see your report is pointless?

{Tense Silence}

Sturmbannfuehrer Goehler [Nervous]: Reichsmarschall, I did not ... I admit, I did not have the time to study this report as I am mainly involved with my unit, SS-Kavallerie-Regiment 1.

Goering [Angrily]: Now you've changed your excuse, my man! First, you were apparently "unaware" of the contents of the report that you wrote. And now you confess you didn't have the time to research information for the report. So which is?

Sturmbannfuehrer Goehler [Nervous]: With respect, Herr Reichsmarschall, both. Because I was at the frontlines, I did not have time to do the requisite research. Further, at the same time, knowing I was called to this conference, I had to write something, and that's why my report is lacking.

Fegelein: You mean 'frontline.'

Goering [Angry]: You think that idiotic answer absolves your shame?

How dare you appear before the Fuehrer admitting you wrote nothing?

{Tense Silence}

Guderian: Mein Fuehrer, we may go on grilling this man, but the critical point here is that we're endlessly discussing what are essentially units that are simply not even battleworthy.

Goebbels: That's not the point.

Guderian: Oh really? What is the 'point' then, my dear?

Goebbels: The point is the man before us dared to write a report containing nothing while knowing he had the honor to be before the most outstanding leader in history.

{Tense Silence}

Goebbels [Sharply]: Meanwhile, *who* informed you of that supposed fact, General Guderian?

Guderian [Sharply]: *My staff.* I wasn't at the front if that's what you're asking.

Hitler [Shouting at Guderian]: Then it must be *your* job to make them fit for combat!

{Tense Silence}

Guderian [Icily]: *How can I make inexperienced boys and old men battle-worthy soldiers?*

Hitler [Screaming]: Age does not matter, Guderian! Whenever I suggest a method to increase our offensive capabilities, you diminish the idea, creating defeatist excuses!

{Everyone: 'Jawohl Mein Fuehrer!'}

My God, the tension in that room was boiling, with every officer or general or whatever they were either shaking or sweating.

Hitler [Screaming]: I will *not* have my orders disobeyed!

{Tense Silence}

Goering: Sadly, Mein Fuehrer, your orders have been disobeyed since we came to power back in 1933.

Jodl [To Goering, Frustrated]: I don't think you're defusing the existing tension ...

Goering [Shouting at Jodl]: What damned *"defusing the existing tension"* do you mean, Jodl, eh? Do you ... didn't you hear what I just said?

Jodl: I did.

Goering [Angrily]: This has been the cancerous history of the Third Reich since January 1933, and you dare speak of "defusing the existing tension"?

Keitel [Nervous]: Gentlemen, can we please –

Goering [Shouting at everyone]: All of you bastards! All of you! Every word the Fuehrer speaks has been directly, specifically, willingly and enthusiastically countermanded by every non-SS military staff member, from Manstein, Guderian, Fedor von Bock, Günther von Kluge, Erwin von Witzleben, Paul von Kleist, Henning von Tresckow, Rudolf Christoph Freiherr von Gersdorff, Axel von dem Bussche, Ewald-Heinrich von Kleist-Schmenzin, Eberhard Freiherr von Breitenbuch, Hans Oster, Ludwig Beck, Erwin von Witzleben, Carl Friedrich Goerdeler, Henning Hermann Karl Robert von Tresckow, Friedrich Olbricht , Fritz Erich Fellgiebel, Friedrich von der Schulenburg, Erich Hoepner, Carl-Heinrich von Stülpnagel, Caesar von Hofacker – you want more?

DG: As I said, I am not a military expert. But let us observe the shocking negligence in that one chunk of a conversation. Hitler was correct in being angry, given the supposed military men's incompetence in front of him. First, that Ukrainian unit was not even near Berlin itself. Its commander had no interest in coming to Berlin to help anyone for a dying cause. Second, it's clear Sturmbannfuehrer Goehler himself had no idea why that unit was structured in its manner. So much for that man. But this pathetic showing by Goehler does raise obvious questions. Why was Goehler in a military conference if he was not competent to produce any credible news? Why are these reports using meaningless doublespeak? And who in the first place is allowed to write babbling reports? In other words, my first impression was that there was much of anarchy, no control, no proper management as per the functions of the Wehrmacht.

On the other hand, I can also fully understand — and this directly contradicts my first impression — why none of these military men had any accurate or credible reports — as I said, the war was lost, and their priority was to save themselves. Photons — being both a wave and a particle. Complimentary in the face of odd contradictions!

~

Watching and Observing Hitler, Trying to Think What He Was Thinking & Feeling

I have been talking about Hitler, and one colossal subject has so far been entirely absent from all my words. You do not know?

Jews.

One of the vastest oddities in observing Hitler's mind during his military conferences was that not once did I hear him mention the subject of the Jews, the concentration camps, or the mass shootings. Not once. I say that because even on several occasions, Himmler or Kaltenbrunner would be the attendees, presumably to give him the latest statistics on how many undeserving people were murdered. And yet, to my surprise, they were the only ones who remained either silent or, when speaking, they would discuss purely military matters.

The gigantic gorilla in the room was invisible. Quite odd not only for a man whose lifelong 'ambition' was the extermination of that gorilla but for one who had by 1945 carried out the murder of six million innocents, civilian men, women, and children who just happened to be of the Jewish faith or Jewish traditions.

Further, while these conferences dragged on, my mind wandered. Within this space, place, and setting, it was evident the man had no friends, no intimates. Apart from Eva Braun and his dog 'Blondi,' I'm not sure I saw much of any affection. Another oddity. The man — at least as far as I saw him - never engaged in give-and-take conversations. There were no discussions as normal people would understand a 'discussion' to be. Instead, he would either deliver hours-long monologues. Or he would ask a few highly polite questions to whoever and then curtly end such an interaction in a matter of minutes. As I say, I never witnessed him having normal, healthy discussions, debates, or even civil arguments. Except with his military staff, and those were, of course, talks of an entirely different context.

"To study history means to search for and discover the forces that are the causes of those results which appear before our eyes as historical events. The art of reading and studying consists in remembering the essentials and forgetting what is inessential."

— Adolf Hitler. Mein Kampf

And maybe that was a trait that went back to his youthful days. I don't think the man enjoyed much of any human company, except perhaps when that company happened to be a fawning audience. But even in those contexts, I'm not sure Hitler was content. You know he was a teetotaler. And a vegetarian. He hated traveling anywhere outside Germany. Essentially he lived an austere life – the opposite, if you like, of Churchill. But then again, living in Berchtesgaden was a luxury – so his housing was far from the frugal lifestyle.

Essentially I felt he was a loner, just as he was in his youth, back in his Vienna and Munich years. He had no friends then. Apart from Kubizek, and that was a temporary one. But even if we were to say Kubizek was his best friend, that still means that throughout his youth, teens, and right through his four years of trench warfare, he still could not or did not want any friend. And then, if we look at the entirety of his political life, he still had no friends. So is it an exaggeration of me saying he remained a solitary, lone man throughout his life?

Now you've got to remember the context of this tragedy-horror situation.

The Hitler I was witnessing was experiencing *his* final days. And so, it was for most of the Bunkerites. Therefore, we must modulate our understanding of how these people felt and behaved from their catastrophic viewpoint, given that they faced rape, mutilation, torture, and God knows what else. I mean for those who choose *not* to commit suicide.

The next point I need to make is the tricky part for me to describe and explain. But I will try, and so here I go.

The man I saw only superficially 'resembled' the 'Hitler' of the millions of films and photographs we have all seen. I said that already. But only now did my words have a more significant impression in my mind. Isn't that odd? I mean, you say something, and you believe it to be true. But then, after circumstances change, you find that what you previously said has a much greater depth of significance than when you initially said it.

The man I spoke to 'resembled' the man I visualized in my imagination and memories. But this man before me, talking to me, looked nothing like the living, real man I saw in those films and textbooks. And that made no sense to me.

And my following words will sound crazier than what I've just said. As Hitler and I talked many times, I thought, 'Well, how could this really be the same Adolf Hitler?' How could it be that this was the same man bombastically beaming before an adulatory, shrieking mass of German men and women in gigantic event after gigantic event? How could this man once have controlled, managed, and had the power of life or death over the lives of millions of human beings?

I ask this question because the two men did not appear to be the same person. Yes, he was, as I said, commanding, mesmerizing, and yet, still, the man before me did not or was not the same individual I saw in all those newsreels. But then, having just said that, what else was there for Hitler to do in these circumstances?

Think Dorothy! I witnessed the final days of a man—one man who just happened to have ignited the Second World War. I witnessed the last days of a man who was now obviously aware the final curtains of his entirely mismanaged stagecraft were coming down. A man who knew his stage was ending. His one-person play, his global theatre of genocide, tyranny, and mass murder, was coming to an end. I was witnessing the final days of a man who knew the horrors he created. I witnessed the last days of a man who now knew all his dreams and ambitions had now come to the point of extinction. Yet, once again, I tried to put my mind in his mind while ignoring the enormity of our differences. Remember when I told you if I wanted to understand his mind, I had to plunge deep into the muck of his mind? After all, if I did not try to see the world and reality as *he* saw and experienced them, how could I understand *his* visions and ideas?

Ah! So near, yet so far!

It is easy for many pundits, neuroscientists, psychiatrists, scholars, self-proclaimed geniuses, bookworms, musicians, philosophers, historians, artists, and practically everyone and anyone to assume – 'We know Hitler automatically.' But can you know the contents of a man's mind? I ask this because not one Hitler historian had ever met him, let alone had in-depth discussions with him.

But historians calmly assure us, "We know Hitler. Obviously, he was evil and mad. That's all you need to know." But *how* do people, be they historians or not, who never met the man in question get to know the intricacies of his motivations, impulses, emotions? How do people who never met Hitler know where, when, why, and the evolution of his personality and ideas were formed? Was his life story and, therefore, world history an inevitable trajectory? Was his life a purely Newtonian, mechanical series of events or not? Was his life decidedly deterministic in its paths?

Can we say each of Hitler's life's thoughts, passions, events, and episodes and their inevitable consequences were predetermined to be what we know them to be? And if that determinism were true, then we must also state that we could do nothing to have changed that man's life trajectory. And then what? Where do we stand? Or do we stop since there is nothing more to discuss?

"The time will come when men such as I will look upon the murder of animals as they now look on the murder of men."

— Dmitry Merezhkovsky (1865-1941) - *Romance of Leonard da Vinci*

The war was lost.

And so, nothing he did or did not do mattered anymore. Nothing his generals did or did not do mattered anymore. Indeed, nothing his entire nation's infrastructures did or did not do mattered anymore. So, even when saying 'Germany,' what did that mean if we were to be a tad bit more precise?

First, most of her cities no longer existed. Except if you wish to define a city as nothing more than mountains of rubble, refuse, debris, ruins, corpses, and the living, mainly women and the elderly. Second, when speaking of 'Germany,' how much did Hitler even control when I was there in March 1945?

Well, not much. In fact, his actual orders ranged not more than a square kilometer or two in Berlin, and that was it. The rest of Germany was fully occupied. Most of Germany was in a state of lawlessness. Some parts were still under the gangster rule of fugitive Gauleiters and runaway *SS* officers. So, Hitler was defending nothing but his bare skin. And yet, I suppose, to keep up appearances, he was in many ways forced by circumstances to continue saying something and doing - anything. After all, what was the alternative?

There was no alternative. The show had to go on, so to speak. And it did go on. The alternative reality would be the truth of his futile existence— the pointlessness of his presence on earth. And what man dared to confront that woebegone truth? Sometimes, hopeless reality can be far too glaring for humans to witness for themselves.

~

What Were the Remaining Options for Hitler by April 1945?

Here is my thought experiment. I think there were four options for Hitler in April 1945.

1. If he were brave and knew the war is over, he would kill himself.

2. If he were a coward and knew the war was over, he would not kill himself.

3. If he were brave and thought there was still a chance for some kind of 'relief,' he would live on.

4. If he were a coward and still thought there was a chance for some kind of 'relief,' he would live on.

If *he* genuinely thought there was a chance, we can understand why the man would hang on for some helpful twist of fate. And that would explain and answer the oft-heard question, so many people ask:

- 'Why did Hitler just not kill himself when he knew, and the entire world knew the war was lost?'

Forget what I said earlier — all, or most, humans cling to life.

The crazy question becomes number two. Imagine if Hitler privately knew the war was over and yet continued the fight. *Why* would he do that? One answer would be the conventional, standardized, and typical response from traditional historians, and that is, the maniac [in their words] loved war; he loved destruction. Therefore, he continued with this game literally till the Russians were a few hundred meters from his Bunker so he could enjoy more destruction and deaths.

But if we were to accept that response, why would the man bother with those long-winded and laborious military conferences? If we accept that answer, our Corporal should do nothing with his remaining days. Instead, he could lounge about, eating his favorite cake. He could idly chat away with his fellow Bunkerite dwellers. Or he could've offered more of his one-man shows, such as his monologues. In others, he would basically be doing nothing except for the act of waiting for the Russians to arrive and kill him.

Is that believable? Can you imagine Hitler sitting around and doing nothing? So, we are back to seeing the mas furiously dictating his orders and questioning in excruciating details on every military matter down to the lowest rank. But in that case, this question arises - why would the man bother with military conferences if he knew the war was lost deep in his heart? One response can be this — he had to pretend he was working. He had to pretend he was the Fuehrer, giving out orders and examining every detail in the war. He had to pretend Germany was not a mere spectator in the war, and that is why he forced himself to sit through those hours-long conferences.

Sounds convincing? You judge. Others will say if a man believes there is a *shred* of credible evidence of hope out there, he will choose life over death. And not only in Hitler's mind but to many, if not everyone in that Bunker, for the faintest rumors of supposedly 'good news' inflamed them to heights of vivifying exuberance — as happened when they heard of FDR's death. Again, all too natural for human behavior given their disastrous context.

In hindsight, we know it's nonsensical because *we* know there was no hope. But from *their time* and perspective, believing in a hope which can potentially save their necks from the gallows is a powerful incentive. Their dire situation forced people to grasp at the most comical straws out there, believing salvation is at hand.

~

FAQ IV – "How Can One Man Mesmerise Millions of Germans and Not Only in Germany?"

That was one of the most critical questions. Indeed, how did this one provincial, uneducated, uncultured, one-time homeless man, a man who flunked High School, a man who never worked a day in his life succeed? How could a man who lived an entirely aimless, careless, and vagrant lifestyle in his youth succeed in leading his nation? How could a man as unsophisticated as he was, one who lived in men's hostels or homeless shelters? How could an essentially untaught, uninformed character create a practically non-existent political party that would eventually control the entire nation of Germany? How could this unlettered man create a loyal, disciplined, and ardently obedient population? How could this man's failure generate a nation willing to serve his every whim and act, no matter how morally repugnant they were?

Everyone knows and has seen the mass hysteria, especially among females, when they saw their leader appear before them. But the question that is rarely asked is this - *has there ever been anyone remotely equivalent in modern times where and when a political leader is greeted with wild-eyed screaming, crying, shouting, and even fainting, fans, audiences, and crowds?*

No.

Why do historians and people, in general, forget this critical dimension of Hitler's overall personality when we speak of him? Suppose we insist on only describing the man in the traditional, conventional manner. In that case, we are consciously or unconsciously [depending on the individual] introducing and inviting ourselves to live the life of a lie.

And what a lie! The problem here is the consequences of just such a gigantic lie, given the subject's historical enormity and severely counter-productive. Why do I say they are severely counter-productive? Precisely because if we go on as we are doing, ignoring the totality of that one man's facts, we become directly and indirectly responsible for diminishing his incalculably complex attributes. Think about it — is it not difficult for many of us who just cannot understand our children, spouses, and friends? Now imagine trying to understand one of the most colossal humans in modern history.

"How fortunate for governments that the people they administer don't think."

- **Adolf Hitler**

And this is precisely the paradoxical situation we are in today. What a crucial statement to make. Why? Because, in essence, every politician, every actor, influencer, talk-show-host — every human who needs to convince a crowd to buy their products or services or ideology must believe the masses are idiots. Think about it. If salespeople felt their audiences or customers were intelligent, they would know they'd have no hope in hell or heaven to convince anyone to buy their products, services, or ideology.

The classy and well-paid famous historians blabber on repeating the same replicated words on Hitler. And so, the greater is the force of our contained boredom. So far from interesting us studying or understanding Hitler, the natural result from all this empty talk is people will turn off and switch off. Because tedious, repetitive dialogue deadens interest and consciousness. And that's precisely what has happened, especially among the new generation.

The standard, famous conventional historians, have immersed themselves in millions of primary historical sources. But they either choose to omit, or they deliberately ignore one of the most critical facts of relevance and significance to our detriment.

Do we know why these famous historians and society, in general, have been doing this? [We can excuse the general public, for they are rarely interested unless when they are instructed by the gibbering top-high wizards of our elites and the establishment]. It's because no one dares to illuminate Hitler's great attributes. Even saying the word 'great' will *shock* people and cause the establishment to call up their lawyers to defame any of our days.

'Great'?

How *dare* you say Hitler had any characteristic that could be described as 'great'? You must be an anti-Semite! ... You must be racist! ... You're a criminal! .... Worse, you must be as mad as Hitler! Lock them up!

The fact that one uncouth, lazy, uneducated, homeless man was able to spawn an almost mad following – yes, 'mad,' precisely, because some of his policies were mad - among those screaming adherents of his, spawning an actual mass hysteria, not seen in our modern times is or requires a genius of a personality to achieve. If the sanctimonious bearers of the only permissible truth think my words are felonious and unlawful wrong, fine, go and do what you must do. But I cannot accept the continual and ongoing mass production of the same trash our respectable scholars, historians, and writers write and present on Hitler.

~

Finally, Interviewing Hitler! And My Lousy Start ...

Finally, I was offered my first interview with the man himself. Was I nervous? No, not really. I entered his study, and there he was, sitting in his armchair, staring at me. Quite a different character than the man I had experienced during his military conferences; I mean, there was no rage or hatred, as he so typically evinced when facing his military staff. However, as I say, his eyes betrayed that 'calm' demeanor of his, given their natural intensity.

Remember, please, this was the first time I was sitting directly in front of the man. Eyeball to eyeball, so to speak. I understood what I had heard a million times before. His eyes were not only naturally intense, but without making any effort, they bored into your eyes. Usually, most people must expend some concentrated energy to stare at you with any effect but to this Austrian man, his eyes, as I say, naturally emitted a strikingly incisive look into your eyes.

We were not alone. As usual, there were his what I assume favorite characters, Speer, Goering, Goebbels, and others.

DG: Good evening, Herr Hitler.

Hitler [Barely Smiling]: Good evening. You speak good German, I am told.

DG: Yes, Sir. My father emigrated from Germany when I was around seven or eight years. I am proud to have retained my German language.

Hitler [Smiling]: Good girl, good. But now you must tell me this. Do you think of yourself as German or American?

Keitel [Loudly]: Indeed, Mein Fuehrer, that is the ultimate, existential to-be-or-not-to-be question that all Germans must answer in the correct form or else they are traitors!

DG: Why do you say ask me that question?

{*Everyone Seems Stunned*}

{*Silence*}

Goebbels [Condescendingly]: The Fuehrer believes knowing and appreciating one's identity is of paramount importance to one's physical and mental health.

Himmler: Knowing one's blood, one's racial origins is the definition of Man. I assume you know your identity.

DG: I do not understand ...

Goering [Laughing]: My girl, if you find this question tricky, I suggest you fly off back to your country.

{*Laughter*}

Keitel: It is really a remarkably simple question. But I will help you because even that which the Fuehrer enunciates, which may appear to be officially categorized, is 'simple' may not be an accurate statement since, in fact, everything the Fuehrer says in private requires rigorous analytical thinking because of his profound thoughts, and of course, being who he is, that is, the greatest son Germany has ever been gifted with, what else would you expect or in simpler words, the Fuehrer wishes to know if you think of yourself as German or American?

Hitler [Chuckling]: Just because a human physically moves his person from his homeland to a foreign one, blood does not change. Never forget for a moment, my young one, for you are still the bearer of the most fantastic blood on earth, one that has created the highest known civilization and culture in the history of Mankind!

{*Everyone: 'Jawohl Mein Fuehrer!'*}

Fegelein: Do you realize you are an Americanized German?

DG: I don't think of 'blood,' as you say. Nor do most people that I know think of blood. Not in rural Kansas anyhow. Maybe out in New York or Los Angeles. I don't know. But racists are an obnoxiously sad part of American law; that is true.

Goebbels: Well, it seems to me that the obnoxious tragedy imbued within your mind is that you have no interest in the science of the identity of Man.

Goering: Goebbels, my boy, I know you love adding and sticking words in sentences, but what does 'obnoxiously tragic' mean?

{*Laughter*}

DG [Shocked]: What 'science'? Blood has no science nor races! We're all humans.

{*Laughter*}

Goebbels: If your words are valid, you must tell us why blacks are segregated from whites in your land of democracy?

Himmler: Because she's a liar! Do you think she doesn't know the laws of her land?

DG: I do.

Goebbels [Angrily]: So why are you pretending to be astounded at our 'obnoxious' racial questions?

Himmler: If she has lost her German heritage, so that means, so she has also lost her integrity, humanity, and intelligence.

Fegelein: Maybe it's like taking a cub lion from the wild and raising it in a zoo. Soon, the adult lion won't know how to hunt a rabbit nor even defend itself.

DG [Nervous]: I feel I'm being looked at as if I'm an animal in a zoo.

Hitler: Not all, my young girl. You are most welcome here. I have personally asked Fegelein to protect wherever you and from anyone who dares to be insulting in any manner. I will not accept that! And despite the admittedly difficult circumstances wherein we meet and find ourselves, I assure you we shall make every effort to make your stay here as comfortable as we can afford to give you.

{*Everyone: 'Jawohl Mein Fuehrer!'*}

DG: Thank you, Sir.

Himmler: Mein Fuehrer, with your permission, should we not ascertain what her mind thinks of her Germanic blood?

DG: I know my identity. I know the laws of my country. You ask me about my identity. My upbringing and background are that of what I guess you would call rural American culture. I also know of segregationist laws -

Hitler [To Himmler]: That *can* be changed in a week, believe me.

DG: Are you talking about me?

Goebbels: Yes, dear, the Fuehrer, the Reichsfuehrer, Fegelein, and the Reichsmarschall – all of them – are talking to and about you.

Keitel: I'm in the room too.

Goebbels: Why do you feel insecure, General Keitel? We know you are here. So is General Guderian, Minister Speer, and others.

Ribbentrop [Nervously]: Nice to me you, Frau Gale, I'm the Reich Foreign Minister, von Ribbentrop.

DG: Nice to meet all of you. But I don't understand then -

Fegelein: What do you not understand?

Keitel [Haughtily to Fegelein]: The lady just stated in the most explicit terms that she fails to understand the Fuehrer's complex words, ideas, and sentences and I just officially stated that it is not easy for humans who are not accustomed to being near the Fuehrer in being able to understand him given his extraordinarily complex mind and ways of expressions given that is a genius and therefore mainly incomprehensibly difficult to understand for the average human being and now you must understand or know why so many of what our Fuehrer said or ordered was not carried out and that is because it was too complicated for mere mortals such as -

Goebbels: *I* find the Fuehrer's questions quite simple.

Keitel [Angrily to Goebbels]: Did I not just say that people who are accustomed to being near the Fuehrer can partially understand his intricately woven expressions? And are you not one of those people?

Himmler: Why is this becoming so complicated?

Goebbels [To Himmler]: You started it, asking your initial question. The girl is American. She stated she does not think of blood. I believe she has answered your question, Himmler. Furthermore, isn't she here to interview the Fuehrer rather than you interrogating her?

{*Everyone: 'Jawohl Herr Reichsmarschall Goring!'*}

Himmler: Mein Fuehrer, with your gracious permission, allow me to explain to our young American guest what you meant to convey to her inexperienced brain. The Fuehrer believes you can change from being a corrupt, criminal, racially degenerate American, and hopefully, on some sunny day, you too may once more become a pure German.

Keitel [Confused]: Meaning what?

Himmler [Firm]: What *cannot* be changed is precisely what you find to be of no importance, and that is blood and only blood!

Goebbels: Why didn't she understand that from that start?

Himmler [To Goebbels]: Because she is an American

Goering: Mind you, many white Americans are also extraordinarily racially sensitive and aware of the biology involved. Blood is life.

{Silence}

Guderian: I believe the young lady before us admitted that in her town ... I forget where ... they are not racially conscious, while major cities like New York and others may be racially aware.

{Silence}

Hitler: Mind you, if you transplant a German to Russia for twenty years, he remains a German, whereas if you transplant the same German to America, he will become an idiot.

{Laughter}

Goebbels: Mein Fuehrer, it seems to me that this American intruder —

Hitler [Sharply]: No, she is *not* an intruder! I invited her; therefore, rectify the words you intend to express, or else such language will not be accepted.

{Tense Silence}

Goebbels [Categorically]: I apologize, Mein Fuehrer.

Guderian [To Goebbels]: Shouldn't you apologize to whom you insulted, Herr Doktor?

{*Laughter*}

Goebbels: I sincerely apologize, Frau Gale. Please accept –

DG [Frustrated]: I do ... I accept it all; can we move on with our conversation?

Keitel: Of course, you may. Because you have fully acceded to the orders of our Fuehrer.

Himmler looked awfully frustrated, not allowing me to squeeze further with his tedious race question, but I just smiled at him. The man, Ribbentrop, was by far the oddest of the look because he looked – well, how can I put it? He looked as though he were suffering from some form of hysteria. Goebbels looked consistently sly, and that suited his features. He was by far physically the most petite man, like a rat, and maybe to compensate for his un-Germanic features, he strove to be continually acerbic with his words. Goering was easily the most relaxed, comforting of all of them. I mean, I felt calm when conversing with him. Himmler looked like a pervert. Speer struck me as overconfident and yet detached from everyone. Who else was there? Oh yes, Keitel. Well, I had nothing to say about him because he didn't strike my mind with anything in particular. Jodl looked stiff. Fegelein, of course, was the smooth, heroic, charming one whom everyone looked at as 'their boy.'

DG: I shall begin asking you broad questions based on the agreement made by our two nations, allowing me to ask you on any subject matter and without hindrance.

Hitler: Yes.

{*Silence*}

DG: Do you believe a dictator has the *right to kill* any race he defines as being unworthy of life?

Hitler: No National Socialist thinks like that.

{*Silence*}

DG: All right. Now if –

Goebbels: Goodness me! Was *that* your first question?

Goering [Laughing]: What exactly do you gentlemen expect from our American guest? The overture to *Götterdämmerung* (Twilight of the Gods)?

DG: Do you believe any dictator has the right to *exterminate* any race he deems deserving to be rendered extinct?

"Often, the fear of one evil leads us into a worse."

- **Nicolas Boileau-Despréaux, *L'Art Poétique* (1674).**

Hitler: No.

{*Laughter*}

DG: No?

Keitel: I believe it is clearly evident in that our Fuehrer fully answered your utterly meaningless question with his exquisitely succinct response, which, to repeat, since you seem to find difficulty in understanding him, happened to be the well-known word 'No' which has no meaning but it's one meaning and again the Fuehrer is speaking in this manner so it will be as simple as is possible for you to understand him since it is not in his manner and soul to be wordy.

Wait! Isn't that the most critical question? Why are they rushing me to change subjects?

Goering [Yawning]: Let's move on matters.

DG: Can you elaborate, please?

Hitler: A leader can only decide which race needs to be physically *removed* from the nation in question.

DG: Physically removed?

Hitler: Yes.

Fegelein [Laughing]: My God, Mein Fuehrer, this lady seems intent on repeating every word you say!

{Laughter}

DG: *Not* to be exterminated?

Speer: Maybe her German has been tarnished, having lived in America for so long.

Hitler: No. As I told you, it is obviously necessary for any undesirable race to be physically removed from one's living spaces for racial hygiene purposes.

Goering: Speer, do you think you need to be a German to understand the word 'Ja' ['Yes']?

DG: What if that so-called 'undesirable race' *cannot* be physically removed from the nation in question?

Fegelein: We kill them.

{Laughter}

Hitler: In that case, we must localize them in specified areas, waiting for the opportune moment to physically shove them off and as far away from our homeland.

DG: What do you mean by 'localize them'?

Hitler & Goering

Goebbels: Oh dear. The lady's German is already showing signs of stress.

Hitler: They must be contained in restricted areas, wherefrom there can be no escape, so no contamination affects us.

DG: Would you imprison an entire race?

Hitler: Absolutely.

DG: I hear you say, 'racial hygiene,' but I don't understand what that means. Can you kindly explain what this act of 'localizing' is for?

Goebbels: My dear lady, the answer is in your question! We 'localized them for 'racial hygiene' purposes.

Suddenly and I do not why, I swung to another topic, far from the subject we talked about. I swear I sensed the inadequate, stupid manner of my questions where there was no linearity, no sequential questions being forwarded to that man.

DG: What was the cynically named *Gesetz zur Wiederherstellung des Berufsbeamtentums* for? ['Law for the Restoration of the Civil Service]. And before you respond, for our audience, I need to remind our audience what that infamous law was about.

I noticed everyone uncomfortably perked up because this was the first time I used a specific fact in my question, whereas before, they assumed I was retard country girl, which is, of course, what Hitler had wanted.

DG: That law banned all people who happened to be of the Jewish faith, even secular or atheistic Jews, from working in any profession – such as judges, lawyers, army, diplomats, dentists, film-makers, poets, playwrights, psychologists, musicians, artists, mathematicians, philosophers, engineers, accountants, novelists, professors, doctors, scientists, surgeons, professors and anyone who works in governmental positions. Quite a fair law, isn't it, Herr Hitler?

Hitler: Of course, yes.

DG [Shocked]: Yes?

Goebbels: The Fuehrer answered your question. Move on, girl.

DG: Do you seriously believe – and I ask you this question because I cannot believe anyone would say the –

Goebbels: Calm down, dear.

DG: The words you say – do you believe, say a Jewish pianist or cellist would be harmful to the nation?

Hitler: Not the way you phrase the question. Were I to understand your question as you prejudicially framed, well, of course, I would be the first to stand up and loudly protest! It's the negative influence of the collective whole that is pernicious in their reality.

DG: So, individually, Jews can be decent people?

Goebbels [Angrily]: Good Heavens, dear! The Fuehrer just explained it, and now you want another explanation for his explanation?

{*Laughter*}

Hitler: Not quite. There are some individual Jews who are harmless, just as there are some Jews who are nefarious. However, that is not our concern. We must preserve the purity, integrity, and value of our blood, which means we must remove all infectious parasitic blood from other certain races. Thus, the totality of the Jewish race is potentially fatal for us Germans were we not to remove them from midst physically.

{*Everyone: 'Jawohl Mein Fuehrer!'*}

Goering: Ask any chef, and he'll tell you the same as I tell you.

Goebbels: In that statement, we must acknowledge your vast knowledge since all chefs bow to your every word, Herr Reichsmarschall.

Himmler [To Goebbbels]: I don't understand.

Goering: You must always separate good beans from bad beans.

DG [Excited to Hitler]: You've still not provided me with any evidence proving why, for example, Germans needed to be segregated from Poles. What catastrophe would happen if these peoples were given their inalienable right to choose and mix with whomsoever they wanted to?

{*Sarcastic Laughter*}

Goebbels [To Himmler]: I'm saying how apt it is for a larger-than-life man to speak of chefs and food.

{*Laughter*}

Fegelein [Whispers to Himmler]: What does the Reichsmarschall mean, 'separating beans'?

Himmler [Whispering to Fegelein]: Meaning we must separate the races as per their hygienic standards.

Goering: My dear young girl, the whole purpose of National Socialism is to keep one's blood as clean as possible. That is why we separate Germans from Poles.

Goebbels: Didn't we just remind you of your own country's racial laws?

These people's laughter really enervated me. For some reason, I did not expect laughter of any kind coming from these men. I thought we'd be having dry conversations with faceless technocrats. And I was baffled at the sight of these men quibbling over trivial matters when I expected them to be in a rushed state, and by that, I mean, given their catastrophic situation, I didn't expect relaxed banter. Maybe I'm wrong. Anyway, Dorothy, think! Next question!

DG: Would these unfortunate peoples be forced to live in camps suitable for human habitation?

Goering: Inasmuch as we can, given our limited resources.

DG: And if you come to a point in time where and when Germany can no longer adequately feed, shelter, and provide the basics for their sustenance, what would your country do in that situation?

Himmler: They will make do with whatever they are given. That is your short, sharp, and to-the-point answer.

Fegelein: The point is we never cared if they remained tethered in their leper colonies.

This vulgarity dumbfounded me. I admit it — the shocking language. What is worse is that we both knew what we were talking about. The Holocaust. The deliberate mass murder of six million Jews. And they are casually talking as though we are speaking on farm animals that need to be tethered.

Goebbels: I am convinced our poor Pucelle has not yet been satisfied.

Goering [Laughing]: Don't you gentlemen feel assured hearing this club-footed midget assuring us that he is 'convinced' and therefore we too should be 'convinced' — whatever that means?

{*Laughter*}

And this was another unexpectedly annoying thing I found — they laughed a lot, and I had no idea what was so funny!

Goebbels: Do you need to nap, my dear?

DG: That was not my question.

Keitel: Who is *Pucelle*?

Goering [To Dorothy]: Repeat your question for us old men, won't you, dear?

DG: I asked you, what if there is not enough food? Would you still imprison them? Would you accept a situation whereby they would be starving while Germans eat?

Goebbels: Are you now advocating we must 'abandon' our people while only serving our enemies, these murderers, and kindly offer them a figmental liberty, one to which they have no rights to?

DG: I did not understand a word you said, Minister Goebbels.

Keitel: Oh dear, Mein Fuehrer, maybe our dear guest is not competent enough in her language skills?

Goering [Laughing]: Twaddle! No one understands when that midget speaks!

{*Laughter*}

Fegelein: Humans are not so distant from animals. We always manage to survive even in the harshest and in the extremes of circumstances. I have seen that for myself.

Guderian: Have you, really, my boy?

Fegelein: Yes, out in Russia.

What happened to me? I feel invisible. They're talking as though I were not in the room, and I know why. It's because they regard me as zero. Therefore my physicality is equally a zero.

Goering [Laughing at Fegelein]: How absolutely fascinating your wild west experiences must have been! And now we await you to regale us with more of these assumed brave fables of yours.

Goebbels: Russia is in the east, Herr Reichsmarschall.

Keitel: One must never confuse between these two directions. It is officially known as a matter of truth; the twain shall never meet.

Fegelein: Howling lunatics. Hideously ugly creatures yelping for food. Of course, we wouldn't deign giving them so much as our precious spit, even if we were forced to. And yet, they survived. Somehow in all these harsh conditions, they survived. And that is my point.

Guderian: Spare us wordy dreams, Fegelein, will you?

Goering [Laughing]: No, Fegelein is actually correct! I myself heard it said many times Russian POWs were eating each other!

{*Laughter*}

DG: That's funny?

Speer: I think you're exaggerating Gruppenführer Fegelein. Most perished.

Goebbels [Angrily]: Anyway, whatever the circumstances afflicted these inmates, it wasn't our responsibility nor our fault.

Fegelein [To Speer]: Herr Minister, who perished?

Himmler: All you must do is look at Stalin's Gulags in Siberia.

{*Murmurs of Approval*}

Himmler: How can those beasts survive in temperatures of minus fifty centigrade? Well, gentlemen, they did. And I tell you more.

Hitler: True.

DG: Poor creatures.

Himmler: Those hardy Bolshevik dogs succeeded in getting this mass mob of criminals to work night and day and produce everything Stalin needs. I think, gentlemen, we can all agree they accomplished a magnificent job for Stalin.

{*Murmurs of Approval*}

Hitler: So true.

Goebbels: Depressingly accurate, indeed.

{*Silence*}

Goering: We know what you're talking about. And the pity you feel, Frau Gale.

DG: I beg your pardon?

Goebbels: What's the matter, Herr Reichsmarschall? Are you trying to seduce us into thinking you cared for those Russian dogs?

Keitel: I am in a state of confusion. I thought the dogs in question were the Bolshevik prisoners themselves. Or are the Bolshevik dogs in question the soldiers in charge of the Russian inmates? Or what? But, what gives here?

Goering [Indignantly, to Goebbels]: *'Seduce'*? What is this filthy language you use, Arschgesicht? I said *Frau Gale* feels pity for Stalin's prisoners. *Not I!*

DG [Astonished]: Do you gentlemen really believe German blood is biologically 'superior' to Polish or Czech blood?

{*Groaning Sounds*}

Himmler [Angrily]: My girl, are you feeling all right?

Goering [Derisive]: Himmler, why of all people would you ask a 'compassionate' question, while your forbidding voice, your unsightly eyes, your yellow complexion, and your perverted demeanor remain repulsive to behold unto all Mankind?

{*Laughter*}

Himmler [Icily]: I do *not* have a yellow –

Keitel: But I must lodge an official National Socialist protest in this instance and moment, Herr Reichsmarschall, and of course, I do that with my utmost respect for you because –

Fegelein [To Keitel]; What is the nature of your official National Socialist protest?

Keitel [To Fegelein]: Excellent question, indeed!

Goering [To Keitel]: For whom is your official query necessary?

DG [Frustrated]: Gentlemen, please! ... Can we just have the questions answered?

Keitel: Well -

Goering [Roaring with Laughter at Himmler]: Are you telling us you *don't* look Chinese?

{*Laughter*}

{*Someone said: The 'Chinaman' thinks he's the model of the Germanic looks!"*}

Goebbels [To Dorothy]: No, we cannot.

DG [Indignant]: Why not? After all, why do you think I am here? To banter and joke?

This was the first time I showed anger in front of Hitler. Though, of course, it was not aimed at him.

Speer: I think there is a general though an unannounced consensus among the gentlemen here that your so-called 'questions' are so ridiculous, so dreary such that they inevitably cause digressions which is what I assume is or must be bothering you, Frau Gale.

Hitler: Gentlemen, the young girl has only just come here. It must be daunting to speak to so many people, so bear patience with her.

{*Everyone: 'Jawohl Mein Fuehrer!'*}

~

Dorothy to Hitler – "Why Did You Force Jews into Concentration Camps, Where Thanks to Your Restrictions, the Majority of Jews Either Starved to Death or Were Sick to the Point of Death?"

DG: I would like to go back to this subject matter of ours, please. That's why I'm here. To ask a question which many ... or all of you will find childish if not idiotic. Well, there's nothing I can do about that, but all I can add is that maybe you, too, ought to learn something from my silly questions.

Goebbels: Oh dear, are you now preparing to be our teacher, Frau Gale?

{Laughter}

Goering: I'm confused, Frau Gale. How and what is the point of us learning from you when you admit your words are entirely "silly"?

{Laughter}

Fegelein: Maybe she wants us to learn how to be silly.

Guderian [Loudly]: Now, come here, gentlemen, please! All of us need education, given our catastrophic failures in the past six years.

Goering [Angrily]: What a pompous ass!

Guderian: An 'ass?' Yes, that I have been. Possibly. And many times too. But 'pompous'? No, Sir, that I have been not.

DG: Relative to you, my questions are stupid. Relative to your enemies, or the world, they think the reverse is the opposite.

Keitel [Shocked]: My dear, are you daring to actually state that we National Socialists are 'stupid'?

Goebbels: That is what precisely she said, General Keitel.

DG: No, not in those words. I meant since you see my questions being feeble, silly, ludicrous, or whatever, so too the world sees your opinions in the same manner.

Fegelein: The lady is correct; after all, why else have we been in this life-or-death war for six years? They see us as evil, just as we see them as evil. Mirror facing mirror.

Speer: Will you gentlemen allow her to ask her questions, stupid, ludicrous, or not?

Goebbels: Whoever knew Fegelein was a philosopher?

Goering [To Goebbels]: No one. Rest assured.

DG: Thank you, Minister Speer. Going back to my questions - why did Germany allow some races in concentration camps or ghettoes to the point where they were starving? Implicit in my question is the immoral situation whereby your nation enables millions to rot and starve to death. I've deliberately ignored the fact your guards murdered most of those inmates, focusing on the starvation aspect for now.

Goering [Angrily]: The terrible conditions raging in these camps was no fault of ours! The blame is entirely on your side! *You're* the mass criminals who wilfully chose a continental-wide blockade on us exactly as the British did on Napoleon's Europe. Your peoples, the British and Americans, acted in the same criminal manner during the Great War. Your peoples choose to bomb every nook and cranny of our civilian infrastructures. Night and day. And that is the core reason why conditions are so hideous. Our road and highway networks have been destroyed, same with bridges; in short, transportation of food and vital requirements for our people cannot move anywhere, thanks to the direct, deliberate Allied bombing that succeeded in destroying our transportational networks.

Goebbels: Remind me, Reichsmarschall, but wasn't it you who was the direct commander of the Luftwaffe whose job was to protect German airspace from the enemy aircraft you mentioned that was allowed to destroy Germany?

{*Tense Silence*}

Goering [Loudly]: You can see for yourself the life-shattering results before your eyes and our eyes. This blasphemous league of nations has succeeded in eradicating our national infrastructures throughout Germany. Of course, that was their intention since the Fuehrer came to power!

{*Everyone: 'Jawohl Herr Reichsmarschall Goring!"*}

{*Silence*}

Goering [Shouting]: And yet, now you come here all the way from America, daring to wag an accusatory blood-stained finger at *us?* Germany's transportation system is now entirely broken down. We know that. Your people know that. One can say it entirely broke down last year, in 1944. What does that mean for a nation with living human beings? Do you know?

{*Silence*}

DG: I suppose that's why *I'm* sitting opposite *you*, while your every enemy is hundreds of meters from this bunker.

{*Silence*}

Goering: Today in Germany, we can no longer speak of any transportational links.

Goebbels: You already said that Reichsmarschall.

Goering: Well, now she must know what that means even for an American mind.

DG: Excuse me?

Goebbels: Let me help our good dame, please. The Reichsmarschall is telling you –

DG: Sir, I understood what I just heard, thank you.

Keitel [Shouting]: Exactly! And that has been the heart of the matter! The fact of the case I am referring to is the fact that our Luftwaffe failed to cover Germany's skies from your enemy aircraft, fighters, and bombers and hence our complete destruction and that due entirely to our failure in protecting our skies and that was the responsibility of the Luftwaffe and there the story ends.

Guderian: What do you think happens when a division cannot receive its supplies? I mean, essential supplies. How can a panzer division drive with no oil? How can soldiers thrive if they don't have enough food, water, and medical supplies? And so too, it is the same with your obsession with these labor camps.

DG: 'Labor camps'?

Goebbels: Did we ever claim concentration camps were Hollywood mansions? This is our reality! Forget your American reality. You are here in Berlin now. Adjust to our existence. It is only to be expected that we see multiple outbreaks and explosions of epidemics given our undeniably and insufferably unhygienic conditions.

Guderian: Reichsmarschall, why so silent?

Goering [Laughing]: Who else but this midget thinks a comparison between Germany's devastation with 'Hollywood studios' is valid?

Goebbels [To Keitel]: The Reichsmarschall cannot critique his exemplary failures; instead, he slyly blames the Allies for the damages they've caused, yet without continuing the equation. Meaning he is the man who is the most responsible character allowing our enemies to conquer German skies. Do you deny that Herr Reichsmarschall?

{*Tense Silence*}

Suddenly, out of the blue, Hitler woke up and turned to Goebbels –

Hitler [Angrily]: Goebbels, how correct you are. Goering, why are you faulting the enemy? Whose fault is it, allowing them to penetrate our skies?

{*Murmurs of Approval*}

DG [To Hitler]: But that takes me back to my point, Sir. Why would you force any human being into camps when you admit Germany could no longer provide for them?

Goebbels: I think the Fuehrer answered that question, dear. Your memory may not necessarily be serving you well.

Himmler: Why is everyone skirting the point?

Keitel [Indignantly]: Are you daring to say our Fuehrer is 'skirting the point'?

Himmler: Of course, I am *not* speaking of our Fuehrer. I'm wondering at you lot, gentlemen, with your great timidity. The lady asked us a question. So, well, then – answer the lady's question! The answer is because they're a racially unacceptable species.

Ribbentrop [Nervous]: I don't understand .. what's the point in this talk or conversation. We are facing terror .. Extinction. Russian armies are -

Fegelein: Being straightforward is delightfully refreshing!

Hitler: Correct.

DG [Confused]: What are you all talking about?

Goebbels: The truth of National Socialism - and I assume you have read a paragraph or two on this subject matter – is to maintain the absolute and unwavering necessity for racial hygiene.

I cannot believe it. I heard it. Finally, they admit their ridiculous belief in racial superiority.

Himmler: She really must know nothing of our philosophy; otherwise, she wouldn't be asking simplistic questions.

Goebbels [Smirking]: I think it's all an act. Mein Fuehrer, she's a spy, and I'll go down to my grave believing that!

Guderian: That won't be long.

Guderian [To Goebbels]: Small man, that's rich coming from you! Just a few days ago, you were still saying how our brave Luftwaffe aces were fighting the enemy. Do you deny that?

{*Mocking Laughter*}

DG [To Gioebbels]: Actually, Sir, I may or may not know answers to questions I pose. However, and either way, we, the people, want to hear the words from yourselves, even if these questions are simplistic. That should be clear enough, correct?

Goebbels [Angrily]: How dare you title me 'Sir'? I'm a 'doctor'! And how dare you ask a question in that scandalous tone, scoundrel!

Hitler: She is but a girl, please.

Goebbels [Rapidly]: How correct of you to remind me of the truth, Mein Fuehrer; again, I apologize to you and you, our dear guest, Frau Gale.

'All fleshe is grasse, and all the glory of man is as the flower of grasse, the grasse withereth, and the flower falleth away, but the worde of the Lorde endureth forever.

Christ is to vs life and death to vs advantage.'

- A short discourse of man's fatal end with an unfeigned, commendation of the worthiness of Syr Nicholas Bacon, Knight, Lord Keeper of the great Seale of England: who deceased the xx. day of February. 1578. Ramsay, Laurence.

DG: I accept your apology. It's obviously a tense time for all of you. We will discuss this concept of 'racial hygiene' later, but we shall move on for now.

∼

Dorothy – "Herr Hitler – What Do You Think Your Legacy Will Be?"

Hitler In His Final Days

DG: Do you know what your legacy will be?

Hitler: My legacy?

DG: Yes.

Hitler: It seems we are losing the war. I shall be reviled. It shall be the victors who will be the only ones who shall dictate what history is.

DG: During your twelve-year reign, you plunged the entire continent of Europe and North Africa, from glittering Paris to the ruins of Stalingrad, from snowy Oslo to the deserts of Tunisia, Libya, and Egypt, plunging all these lands and nations into one of the most beastly, malevolent eras in modern history.

Ribbentrop [Mumbling]: God have mercy on Germany. Is there mercy?

Goebbels: God have mercy on your miserable self.

DG: Your reign, thankfully brief, has been one wherein mass murders, atrocities, and planned genocide were the daily routine. Given what I say to you and those daunting facts, I would like to know, again, if you realize or are aware of the evil you and your minions bequeathed to human history?

Fegelein: Shouldn't that be one of her last questions?

Goebbels: Did Roosevelt write that script for you, dear?

Goering [Angrily]: Don't be more foolish than you are, Goebbels! Roosevelt is a cripple, idiot.

Hitler: When you insist, I am 'evil,' are you referring to the eradicating of those Jews?

Fegelein [To Goebbels]: Of course, who else – that is the only interest of the Jewish-dominated West.

Keitel [To Goering, Talking about FDR]: Not his lips. The man can talk. So, he is not or cannot be categorized as a total cripple. Please … please! We pure Master Race National Socialists are ideologically committed not only for racial purity but also unto and for the linguistic purity by which I mean speaking soundly the most extraordinary language on earth, that is to say, German, in the most eloquent and the most grammatically perfect form; otherwise, we could not legally be categorized as National Socialists. So please be accurate in your words. I mean, if he were a total basket case, how did the man communicate with Churchill?

DG [To Hitler]: It's not *only* killing '*of those Jews*' – as you put it. That mammoth crime, of course, makes you one of history's most evil humans – and I'm on shaky grounds when I use the latter adjective because 'evil' doesn't adequately can define you.

Goering [To Keitel, laughing]: His mouth is not crippled!

Goebbels: Mein Fuehrer, Nietzsche's spirit praises you, for you are now officially beyond evil.

DG: The fact is that *you*, the man sitting next to me, the man politely conversing with me, the man who seems utterly 'normal,' civil and composed - you deliberately ignited a world war that's consumed the lives of around fort six million men, women, and children.

Goebbels: I know he *is* a cripple, Herr Reichsmarschall. So, what's your point?

DG [Firmly]: And I'm no amateur, Herr Hitler, on this terrible subject. I have come prepared to meet you.

Goering [To Goebbels]: Only his legs are dead, as far as I know.

Keitel [To Goering]: But at the time when you originally spoke about Roosevelt, you *did not* clarify what you said. There was no clear enunciation from you as to what extent his crippling status is. Indeed, your words indicated or inferred he could not write, which is soundly untrue since the man has full use of his arms, hands, and fingers.

Fegelein: Now I believe those rumors he has a mistress stored somewhere.

Goering: When you have a manly-'wife as Roosevelt has, would you blame him for having mistresses?

{*Laughter*}

Goebbels: She's a lesbian, so you're correct, Herr Reichsmarschall.

Fegelein: Really, Dr. Goebbels? She's a lesbian?

DG: What is the relevance -

Goering [Angrily to Keitel]: I didn't need to go into the details of his physical status because it's of no interest to me. And when something is of no interest to me, I don't talk about it in detail – is that clear enough for you?

Keitel [To Goering]: Yes, Sir. I apologize.

DG [To Hitler]: Though I am by no means a professional historian, I've read numberless primary and secondary sources on you, your ideology, your regime, and your deeds.

Fegelein: But wait, if Roosevelt is a cripple, how come he has children?

DG [To Hitler]: I have listened to your audio recordings of lectures and speeches. They are all, collectively, a mass of incomprehensible words were it not for the fact, you succeeded in implementing the intricacies of your will unto the millions of humanity.

Keitel [To Fegelein]: Did I not just declare to you that we do not officially know what is the extent of his crippled status is?

Goering: Shut up, Goebbels.

Himmler [To Fegelein]: He became a cripple later in his years, boy.

"He who does not punish evil commands it to be done."

- **Leonardo da Vinci**, *Notebooks*.

DG: Now, I also hesitate in using the adjective 'mad' because, on the surface of it, there is no appearance of madness.

Goebbels [Excited]: Wonderful news, Mein Fuehrer! You're unlike King George III! Thanks to Frau Gale, we've been officially informed we are not mad after all!

Himmler: I thought Frau Gale was only accusing our Fuehrer and not the rest of us.

Ribbentrop: What is this? Jokes? How can the mad joke in this hour of our finality?

Himmler [To Ribbentrop] The mad obey whatever their irrepressible mad instincts tell them to do. That's why they must be euthanized.

DG [To Hitler]: And I'm facing you, which is the first time in my life.

Goebbels: Everyone knows that, dear.

DG: In this hour, I see you, and I don't see evil nor madness. Odd, isn't it, Herr Hitler?

{Silence}

Keitel [To Himmler]: We and the Fuehrer are one. Therefore, your remark is severely erroneous. Appearances are not always deceiving.

DG [To Hitler]: I want you to know my purpose is to understand the nature of your game.

{Mocking Laughter}

DG [Proudly]: And I'm going to discover what it is that makes a human evil! Like Dr. Frankenstein did, yes, I will determine what made you people become the killers you are today. And further, I wonder, are you even aware of your guilt?

{*Mocking Laughter*}

Goebbels: Who knew we'd be having the undisputed honor of having the daughter of a dead Jew, Dr. Sigmund Freud, freely giving us a Jewish lecture?

{*Laughter*}

DG: A murderer is one who kills one human. A serial killer kills several people. A mass murderer kills in the hundreds. A genocidal killer kills millions of people.

Hitler wasn't responding to anything I was directly saying to him. That really aggravated me because I thought I could switch him on or off, but I was wrong. Obviously, another failure on my part. Again, I know why. He regarded me as an idiot. And that day, he was in no mood to converse. Because I was sure, when he would be in the mood to talk, he would be volcanic – and I speak having seen him act volcanic.

Goering [To Goebbels]: What does the Jew Freud have to do with Mary Shelley?

Goebbels [To Dorothy]: My dear, I think all of us proudly understand what 'mass murderer' means.

Fegelein [To Goebbels]: I've never knew the dead can 'teach.'

Goebbels [Angrily to Fegelein]: I said the 'daughter,' not the father.

Keitel [Confused]: Isn't Freud's daughter in one of our camps too? I am assuming he had a dead daughter, did he? Or not? I must check if you so want me, Mein Fuehrer!

Himmler [To Keitel]: Your words are meaningless since the enemy has overrun every camp.

Goering [Sarcastic to Keitel] What is this mumbo jumbo, Keitel, my man? If you don't know if the Jew Freud has a daughter, why would you then presume his daughter must be in one of our concentration camps?

Keitel: I don't know. This is really becoming confusing.

Himmler: General Keitel; they left Germany back in the year 1937.

Keitel: Who left?

Speer: The Freud family.

DG: They didn't 'leave' – they were deported – the old man and his entire family.

Fegelein [Confused]: I don't understand. Why do you, General Keitel, express surprise Freud had a daughter?

Himmler [To Fegelein]: The daughter is still alive, my boy!

Goebbels [To Fegelein]: Who told you General Keitel expressed surprise concerning the dead Jew Freud had a living daughter, Fegelein?

Fegelein: Because he said he "had a dead daughter."

Ribbentrop [Frantic]: Stop this madness, will you ... people ... we face death if we do not act and try -

Goering [To Himmler]: You're wrong. They left the following year, in 1938.

Goebbels [To Dorothy]: My dear, we know what those words mean. Spare us the language lesson.

Keitel [Indignantly]: I did *not* register surprise, Gruppenführer Fegelein, as regards my German emotions; I merely wanted to know for our official records. So she may have been dead, she may be alive. I do not know, nor can I know, the living status of every inmate. Furthermore, linguistically even saying "had" does not necessarily imply the act of death. You really worry me with your lacking knowledge in German affairs.

Goering [Laughing]: No wonder the Fuehrer is dozing ... and you make fun of me when I doze – who wouldn't with all this monkey talk!

Keitel: To be frank, I must confess, I have no memory of who this Freud is. I admit to being haughty. I apologize.

Actually, Goering couldn't have said it better – it was like seeing squabbling chimpanzees!

DG [To Hitler]: Now the end of this war is near; we know around six million European Jews have been murdered; more than one million victims are children. What category of a human does that make you? *You* tell me. Finally, the 'end of this movie' will be me waving farewell to your dangling corpse from the gallows.

Goebbels: The lady is finally revealing the end of this movie, much to our surprise.

Goering: Mein Fuhrer, why are we putting up with this repetitive talk? And you, my young girl, I advise you not to repeat yourself.

Hitler [Chuckling]: She brings in fresh air!

Himmler: Frau Gale, you're a lucky one. After all, the Fuehrer never permits anyone to blabber so long.

Goering: Really? I would've thought only your presence is enough for anyone to cast you as far away as possible, my Chinaman Himmler.

Goebbels: Mein Fuehrer, why have you acceded to the terms set by the Americans for these interviews?

Keitel: The Fuehrer knows exactly what he is doing, Dr. Goebbels, please. Refrain from seeking to understand the endless mysteries of truths within the heart of the Fuehrer.

Fegelein: Is Roosevelt Jewish?

Keitel: I will check as per your decent question. But at least, we achieved significant proh=gress in this hour. We have definitively ascertained he is a cripple.

Feghelein: But we knew that.

~

Dorothy – "To Be Blunt, Herr Hitler, Are You Aware of Your Crimes?"

DG: If I'm repeating myself, it's because I don't hear answers.

Goebbels: No, dear. You *are* hearing answers. It's just that you only listen to answers your masters want to hear.

Goering [Giggling]: What 'answers'? No one has answered anything so far because we haven't heard any meaningful questions.

DG: Why are you, Herr Hitler, disinterested in what I'm saying to you? I notice you do not answer or respond to any of my questions. And isn't this my purpose being here in Berlin? To interview you?

Hitler [Chuckling]: I'm unresponsive precisely as our Reichsmarschall just said, I do not hear any reasonable question.

I had enough. My patience was out. Dead. I know it was far too early to get angry directly at that man, but Dorothy couldn't help herself. I decided to be deliberately confrontational with that man and let him kick me out if he gets angry. I do not care. What's the point of my being in this revolting place if the idiot in question was not prepared to my questions since he deemed them to be 'reasonable'? Damn it, I was raging, and at the same time, I knew how crazy I was behaving because the essence of a decent journalist is not to react or become emotional.

DG: You seem unmoved by facts. I'm accusing you of mass murder, and you haven't twitched a muscle. No emotions. You say my questions are 'unreasonable.' Sir, that's not for you to decide. An interviewer has the right to ask questions, even if the questioned regards the questions –

Goebbels: My goodness me! Are you lecturing us?

{*Laughter*}

DG: What's my purpose in being here if you -

Hitler [Smiling]: I know you need me to accept your truths, and you need me to confess I'm the Devil, no less!

{*Laughter*}

DG: That's not what ... Sir. I'm trying ... I'm asking you to contemplate the extent and scope of your crimes.

Hitler In His Final Days Congragultating Boy Soldiers For Their Achievements

Goebbels: What kind of interview is this? You accuse the greatest son Germany has ever produced without a proper discussion of the facts?

{Murmurs of Approval}

Hitler: This proposition is senseless, my young girl. How can I contemplate falsities when they are, by definition, non-existent? So, until you come up with a good question, there is nothing for me to answer.

DG: Those 'falsities '*are* facts —

Hitler [Angry]: 'Facts' for whom?

Suddenly he turned wild. I regretted it. I poked the sleeping lion too many times, and now he was wide awake, staring at me with grilling eyes. But I'd never betray my true insecurities. I chose to confront the bastard mass murderer. I don't know what got in my mind. But I was sick of his ambiguities and other crap.

DG [Angrily]: What do you mean? Facts are facts. You murdered six million Jews. Are these falsities?

Hitler [Angrily]: Understand now this truth on the eternal nature of life. You have *your* perceptions which you implicitly and without thought believe is truth. So, too, we National Socialists have our beliefs. Now the question before us is. Who told you *your* beliefs are true and *our* beliefs are false?

DG [Angrily]: What 'beliefs' are you talking about? I'm telling you the fact you ordered the extermination of six million Jews, and I'm seeking a response from you on that fact.

Hitler [Shouting]: *But that is not a 'fact'!*

Everyone suddenly seemed concerned for Hitler. I didn't know why at that time, but later I learned they feared if he got too angry, he might suffer a heart attack. So, I backed down.

Himmler: Those are *opinions*, my dear.

Keitel: The Fuehrer cannot discuss the anatomy of anything without facts. Without facts, everything is meaningless, and the Fuehrer is not here to discuss empty words.

Himmler: Maybe she's unaware of the difference between 'fact' and 'opinion'?

Goebbels: Gentlemen, it seems we must do a better job in explaining the difference between an opinion and a fact. Otherwise, we cannot proceed in the desired manner.

Speer: It is natural opposing ideologies cannot understand each other.

Goebbels [To Dorothy]: My young lady, your trivial, insulting words are *not* based on truth.

DG: Explain to me the nature of your confusion.

Goering: The only 'confusion' resides entirely within your befuddled mind.

Goebbels: What's puzzling you is the nature of our game.

Ribbentrop: Instead of using the verb 'to rest,' I believe it is worthier to employ 'imprisoned.'

Goering [Wearily to Ribbentrop]: In the name of God, go.

Keitel [Indignant]: *But where can he go?* His home has been bombed. Germany is bombed to near extinction. Therefore, he has nowhere to call home but here. No, Sir; the man in question has nowhere to go. Thus, your order, Herr Reichsmarschall, cannot conceivably be attained.

DG: Perhaps we're in a peculiar situation wherein there's a reality within which only a majority of sane people live. And then there's another twisted reality wherein, thankfully, only a minority of mentally ill individuals live and breathe within. And it seems the two cannot communicate.

Keitel [Angrily]: Atrocious language! Mein Fuehrer, I, for one, cannot breathe in the presence of such undignified language!

Fegelein [To Dorothy]: Are you being philosophical again?

Goebbels: Who knew that! I certainly did not; Gentlemen, Keitel's brain needs oxygen!

I decided I'd challenge that man again. He's no wimp. Heart attack – please!

DG: Herr Hitler, will *you* kindly tell your officers or gentlemen that prior to me coming here to interview you, both parties agreed that nothing would be off-limits, neither language nor any subject matter?

Hitler [Sternly]: I said this before ... She is correct. Give her the freedom to speak as she wishes!

{*Everyone: 'Jawohl Mein Fuehrer!'*}

DG: Will you now tell me if you have any remorse, any regret for the crimes -

Hitler [Loudly]: *My reality*, as you put it ... the only truth I have sought throughout my life was simply and solely to serve the interests of the German nation, its historical civilization, and its sacred blood. Now any other reality and truth that may or may not exist doesn't concern me. Understand this, then of what I speak to you. This reality – *my Deutschland!* - is the only reality that interests me, and whatever your personal truth is, it remains far and away beyond any of my concerns or interests!

{*Everyone: 'Jawohl!'*}

DG: There is only one reality, Sir.

Fegelein: I knew philosophy's coming back in this conversation.

Hitler: Look at our enemies. Look at England. A nation defending democracy, liberty, and non-aggression for all peace-loving nations, is that not so?

DG: Absolutely.

Hitler [Loudly]: Three hundred years earlier, England gradually built her Empire, not perhaps through the free will or the unanimous demonstrations of those affected, but for 300 years, this World Empire was welded together solely by force. War followed war. One nation after another was robbed of its freedom-one state after another was shattered so that the structure which calls itself the British Empire might arise.

I didn't expect the intensity of the rebuttal from the criminal who was supposedly nearly having a heart attack from my prosecutorial words. But on he went, in effect, giving a tedious speech.

Hitler [Loudly]: Democracy was nothing but a mask covering subjugation and the oppression of nations and individuals. This State cannot allow its members to vote if today, after they have been worked upon for centuries, they should freely choose to be members of this Commonwealth. On the contrary, Egyptian Nationalists, Indian Nationalists in their thousands, are filling the prisons. Concentration camps were not invented in Germany; the English were the ingenious inventors of this idea. By these means, they contrived to break the backbone of other nations, to remove their resistance, to wear them down, and make them prepared at last to submit to this British yoke of democracy. Is this not Great Britain?

DG: I agree with your points on England's colonies, and they should be free nations.

Goering: So on what grounds do you favor England?

DG: On the grounds, it does not exterminate millions of human beings.

Goering: Are you stupid? At the end of the blood-stained path of British history, after three centuries, stands the fact that 46,000,000 Englishmen dictatorially rule about a quarter of the globe. This means that there are 46,000,000 men for about 40,000,000 square kilometers. It's essential to shout this out to the oppressed world again and again. Because you people, the Allies, are the most brazen undemocratic liars, asserting your 'right' to conquer the world. And Germany has only been in existence since 1870, or for 75 years! You call National Socialist a 'dictatorship.' Very well. What 'democratic rights' do the colonized peoples of England, France, Belgium, and the United States have?

{*Angry Shouts of Approval*}

DG: I agree with you. I'm not condoning –

Goering: Therefore, I ask you again, why do democratic nations fight to exterminate Germany?

{*Everyone: 'Jawohl Herr Reichsmarschall Goring!'*}

DG: I hope that colonialism will end but for now -

Hitler [Hushed]: I started a struggle against everyone in those days, against the individualist and against the humanitarians. And in this struggle, we slowly conquered the German nation for fourteen years. The mere one thousand faithful members which this piddling movement counted at the end of its first year of life witnessed a number which was to increase steadily -

these followers were Germans who had come from other movements. Still, we were insignificant.

I wondered what on earth did this boring story have to do with Hitler's global crimes? Who cares about the history of his political party?

Anyway, I chose not to confront him on this matter. Let him drone on.

Hitler: Hundreds of thousands of my SA and SS had been fighters in other organizations, whom we had all convinced and conquered by winning their inner allegiance. *That was perhaps the greatest battle of souls in our history.*

{*Everyone: 'Jawohl Mein Fuehrer!'*}

Hitler: I could not force anybody to go with me to enter my organization – they ... they all had to be inwardly convinced, and this conviction caused them to make great sacrifices.

∼

Conversations with The Infanticidal Adele Sorella

I. The Background – Adelle Murders Her Two Daughters And A Day Later Stages A Car Accident after which She's Taken To The Police & Thinks She's Been Investigated for The Car Crash

Adele Sorella.

A still-existing German court found her guilty of first-degree murders of her two daughters, Sabrina, aged eight, and Amanda, aged nine. Her case shocked the war-shattered Germany. How could a German woman, mother do such a deed? Her daughters were found dead inside the family's home. The mother either convinced or forced her daughters to remain inside a hyperbaric chamber until they died of asphyxiation. Sorella had purchased the chamber to treat Sabrina's juvenile rheumatoid arthritis. While Sabrina responded to her treatment, the girls liked to pretend it was a tent they could camp out in.

A day after the murder, the mother crashed her car into a utility pole.

Sorella was not at her home when Sabrina and Amanda's bodies were discovered. Their grandmother and uncles Enzo and Luigi Sorella found the girls lying on the playroom floor wearing their school uniforms. They called emergency and tried resuscitating the girls, but the bodies were already dead cold. There was no sign of a struggle. There was no mark on the girls' bodies, save for a bit of bruise on the side of Sabrina's head. They were perfectly healthy little girls, apart from being dead.

Who else but Adele placed the innocent little girls inside the hyperbaric chamber? Who zipped them in, closed the outlet valve, and left them to die?

Where the mother was on the day or night of the filicide remains unknown. The first person to arrive on the scene where Adele Sorella crashed her car into a utility pole said the woman behaved in a 'strange manner for someone who just survived a car crash.' In other words, she faked it. A lot of murderers play that same scene. Faking suicide. Pretending God knows what. But, somehow, they never succeed in killing themselves. Believe me, a serious suicidal individual will get the relatively easy task done. She was a faker.

Firefighter Mathieu Dubreuil said the accused appeared to be "on the moon" when he arrived to help her after the car she was driving and crashed, splitting a utility pole on a rural road sometime before 3 a.m. on April 1st. Her vehicle came to a stop in a field with severe damage to the driver's side, but she was unscathed.

The day before, at around 4:30 pm, Sorella's daughters — Sabrina, 8, and Amanda, 9 — were found dead inside their family home. Sorella was nowhere to be found when her two brothers and mother made the tragic discovery. She left her home.

Dubreuil stated he found Sorella seated in the passenger seat of the sport utility vehicle. He said he tried to talk to her while seated, but she muttered two words he did not understand.

Otherwise, "she didn't say anything. It looked like she was waiting for someone," Dubreuil said while describing his first impression of Sorella. He testified that he convinced her to get out of the vehicle when he expressed concerns the passenger-side airbag might deploy and injure her. However, the driver-side airbag had already been deployed. When she stepped out of the Lexus, the first responder asked Sorella a series of questions to verify if she was injured. He said she replied with "very brief responses — always no." Sorella said she was not injured and turned down an offer for an ambulance, which was dispatched anyway. Dubreuil said Sorella's reactions puzzled him, and he tried to determine why a woman would be traveling alone in a remote part of Laval at 3.00 in the morning.

While answering questions from prosecutor Maria Albanese, Dubreuil said Sorella refused to identify herself with him when the ambulance arrived. "I asked her, 'Can I have your name?' She replied, 'No, you won't get that,' " he said.

"She wasn't all there. She was on the moon. She had the appearance of someone whose mind was somewhere else. I wondered why she was so preoccupied."

Previously, while being questioned by defense lawyer Pierre Poupart, Dubreuil said he was surprised at how Sorella *showed no signs of being in shock*. Poupart also asked Dubreuil to consult a written statement he gave to the Laval police shortly after talking to Sorella. The firefighter said that he walked over to a police officer who arrived following the strange experience. He recalled having heard earlier in his shift about the girls' deaths and that the police were looking for their mother. "I told (the police officer) ... 'This might be the person you are looking for,' " Dubreuil said.

Why am I talking about Adele Sorella?

She's another murderer. So, what? A million murders are going on every day. All right, not millions. Thousands. Thousands of murders throughout this world of ours. And we know female murderers are rarer than male murderers. And how many of those female murderers are mothers? And how many of those murdering mothers commit filicide as opposed to killing other people? So, it is at this point we reach a rarefied world.

Filicide.

At first, my shock was because I had never heard of a mother deliberately, willfully, and intentionally murdering her children. This was, for me, an unusual territory. And you know, I have admitted to this, I was never sophisticated in the knowledge of Man's mind when it comes to this specific subject of evil and madness. But I want to show you why this story is quite rare; it is so bizarre. You see, my real shock was when I interviewed her. You'll see what I mean.

Wouldn't you think one had to be mentally disturbed if someone went ahead and killed their own two daughters? Once upon a time, I thought there were no such people as Adele Sorella. Even my abusive Mother, I could not say she was evil. Nasty she was, yes. But evil? No! Of course, if you wanted to find such creatures' dwelling places, you would have to read horror novels and movies.

But, as I sat there quietly in my Bunker room in wartime Berlin, as I intensely read her news, for some reason or other, that woman ... Adele Sorella ... beckoned me to view her reality. A reality I had never thought existed before. Or perhaps, a reality I chose to ignore throughout my early years.

Eventually, I *did* see her reality. I understood her crime. I say 'understood' when I mean I understood the acts she did.

I think so. Now you might be saying - 'Come on, Dorothy, thankfully filicide rare as it is, does occur, and what's up with your mystified incredulity?'

That is *not* what dragged down my consternated disgust and disbelief to the pits of my rawest nerves as I read more of the incoming news articles on this lady in question. What is worse than killing your children? But there *was* something worse than filicide. Evil is layered. And most people tend to believe in the first signpost of evil in a rotten character and stop there. But that's just the first layer of the Devil's cake. There was something far more sinister to this 'woman.' A more profound evil. I will tell you why.

~

II. Dorothy - "I Regret to Inform you Both of Your Daughters Are Dead."

During our interview, *she does not react* in a manner that evokes remorse, panic, fear, shock, or hysteria. She sits there in front of me throughout it all as though she were in a café or chatting to her neighbor about her latest shopping that day. Well, not really. I'm exaggerating. She was flat. Dead. Emotionless. Instead, her mind expresses a cocktail of denial, disregard, and boredom, though to balance that, occasionally, we see the shock and hurt in her face, especially when I showed her photographs of the corpses of her two daughters.

Dorothy Gale's Conscience: 'What the hell is this? Is this Man? Is this a human being?"

And don't you see how Adele Sorella ties in so firmly with the entire regime of her country, the Nazis? I had to show this footage and transcript to those freaks in the Bunker and see their reaction to Madame Sorella. How would they react? Would they feel an affinity with her or not? And if not, why not? Or would they pretend to be revolted at her?

Here's my conversation with her, and remember at this point, she's pretending her daughters are fine, and I'm pretending that too.

DG: I'm worried about how you feel now because I find it a little bit odd that you're not upset.

AS: Well, I'm being accused of something serious, and I reserve the right to remain silent.

DG: You can stay silent, but you're confirming my point.

AS: What is your point?

DG: Ma'am, I just find it strange that you're not upset by everything going on right now.

AS: I find it very strange being in this situation. I don't know what to think of it. I'm just trying to stay calm. That's it. But it's only a car crash or accident. Why all this worry?

{*Silence*}

{*AS Sighs*}

DG: What's 'strange'?

{*Silence*}

AS: It's hell to have *an accident*, and the next thing I know, I'm here, in the Police Interrogation Cell. So, what else would you expect?

DG: Is that what's so 'strange' to you?

AS: Yes.

DG: You're concerned because of your accident?

AS: Yes.

DG: *Do you think you're here because of an accident?*

{*Silence*}

AS: Anyway, I refuse to … you know, talk … that's what my lawyer said.

I'm thinking, is this lady so dumb as to believe the police would interrogate her for a car crash on some pole, where no one was hurt? Or is she acting?

DG: Why do you say "it's hell to have an accident"?

AS: I don't understand.

DG: Wouldn't a normal mother, a normal human, be grieving for their two kids instead of thinking about their car accident?

Using the verb "grieving," she would have to understand that something serious must have happened to her kids.

AS: I am.

DG: *Do you think you are here because of the accident?*

AS: No. *I don't know why I am here. They're telling me it's because something has happened to my kids.*

That's a lie.

DG: Who told you?

AS: I don't know.

DG: Okay, but what *do you* believe?

AS: About what?

DG: Why you're here?

AS: Right now, like I just said ... I'm staying calm, and I'm waiting to go to court tomorrow and follow my lawyer's advice.

DG: Don't deflect from my question. You still claim you've no idea why you're here, Ms. Sotrella?

{*Silence*}

AS: No, I don't.

DG: You don't believe me?

AS: No.

DG: *What do you believe?*

AS: *What I like.*

DG: Which is?

AS: I said, I am here right now –

DG: I know you're "here right now." What does that have to do with my question? Ms. Sorella, are you on drugs? Can you concentrate or don't you want to contrate on this urgent matter?

AS: I don't know.

I was trying to be cool, detached, but in truth, I myself felt murder in my heart. Little things made me want to snuff the life out of her, just like she snuffed the life out of Sabrina and Amanda. Things like the number of times she said, *"I don't know ..."*

DG: *Do you believe Sabrina and Amanda are alive?*

AS: *Yes. So, but I am staying calm.*

DG: Why would you need to be "calm" if you know Sabrina and Amanda are fine?

AS: I don't know.

DG: *I must regret to inform you that they are dead. Both of them.*

Having decided to tell her that her children are dead — which we knew that she knew — I was hoping she'd act horrified since she pretended she had no reason to be worried about them. Remember, the only thing she thinks brought her to the police is her car 'accident.'

AS: No, that is not true.

DG: Excuse me? What do you mean by "that's not true"?

AS: Just that. Not true.

DG: Is that why you're not upset?

AS: I told you I am staying calm.

DG: T*hey are both deceased ... both of them ... and you are under arrest for killing them.*

{Silence}

DG: You've got nothing to say? Did you hear what I just told you?

AS: I hear.

~

III. Switching To Playing Good Cop

I decided to switch to nice cop, hoping to get her to trust me and hopefully open up.

DG: What is this machine for pressure? What do you use it for?

AS: It's for my daughter's arthritis; she has juvenile rheumatoid arthritis. We were able to get rid of it –

DG: Sorry, which daughter?

AS: Sabrina.

DG: It works?

AS: Yes.

DG: That's wonderful.

AS: It's done very well for her. She's grown a lot. So, she's very, very, very well.

DG: And so, Sabrina doesn't need it now?

{*Silence*}

AS: No, she's in remission, so she's doing very well. She's grown four inches though she never gains weight.

You couldn't but notice she never names her daughters while I deliberately named them, trying to remind her they had names.

DG: If I may ask, why?

AS: Why what?

DG: Why doesn't Sabrina gain weight?

{*Silence*}

AS: Because of the sickness, I think. Not sure, though. She's not talkative, you know. Very introverted girl. So we never talked much. She was already an adult. You can say that, I suppose.

If that were true, I wonder where got those 'introverted, word-shy' genes from.

DG: Is she under any medication?

AS: No, no more, but I saw progress, you know. She was getting healthier by the day. It was making me happy, you know.

I noticed she lapsed back into the past tense when talking about her daughters.

DG: We would do anything for our kids, that's for sure.

{*Silence*}

AS: Yes.

DG: We want the best for them.

{*Silence*}

AS: Yes, we do.

DG: Are they doing well in school?

{*Silence*}

AS: Amazing.

DG: Amazing.

{*Silence*}

AS: What do your questions about my kids have to do with the car incident?

DG: Absolutely nothing.

AS: So, why are we talking?

DG: You don't like talking?

AS: I meant, why aren't you doing your job and ask me questions about the car?

DG: I think it's time I'm going let you in on a secret.

{*Silence*}

DG: You don't want to know the secret?

S: I don't know.

DG: I'm not a police officer.

AS: All right.

{Silence}

She wasn't talking much.

~

IV. Dorothy – "Don't Your Daughters Look Beautiful, with Rigot Mortis Having Their Arms Outstretched to God, With Lividity and Decomposition Eating Their Faces?"

DG: There's going to be a lot of anger at you. People hate you, do you know that?

AS: How can I know?

DG: Can you focus on the reason why you did it. Do you agree?

{*Silence*}

DG: You disagree? You're difficult to read. But I'm asking you a question. Do you disagree with what I am saying?

{*Silence*}

AS: What question?

DG: Adele, you know my question. Quit playing this act. You can tell me. Don't be afraid.

{*Silence*}

AS: Because they have the right to say whatever they want.

DG: Who is "they"?

AS: You, the police —

DG: I just told you I'm not a police officer.

AS: It does not mean it is accurate or not true. It is their perception to think what it is. And it does not matter because they have already decided what it is, no matter what you say or what you do.

Now I decide to show Sorella four crime-scene photographs taken inside her home where Sabrina and Amanda's bodies were found. The photos are of the girls' bodies after the paramedics tried to revive them. Both are in a state of rigor mortis and slight decomposition.

DG: There is one thing we need an explanation for. You need to explain this.

AS: I need to talk to my lawyer.

DG: Look at this. *This is the truth.* These are your daughters, Sabrina and Amanda. Now, something in the course of your life must have brought you to do that to them. You weren't born a killer. You were once just like Sabrina and Amanda. Playful, giggly girls. In love with an enchanting world. Exploding with innocence. Bubbling with silliness and laughing hysterically at anything. And that's the beauty of childhood. You remember that? Do you remember when you, too, were a young girl?

AS: My childhood was no happiness.

DG: I believe that. I can believe that. My childhood wasn't all milk and honey.

AS: You just told me about the greatness of being a child.

DG: No, I was just speaking in generalities. Right?

{*Silence*}

DG: You wouldn't want someone to kill you when you were the age of Amanda and Sabrina, would you?

AS: I don't know.

Again, I felt I was losing my control, my coolness.

DG: *You don't know?*

{*Silence*}

DG: How can you explain this?

AS: Explain what?

DG: How can you explain the deaths of your two beautiful daughters?

{*Silence*}

DG: *How can you explain that this could happen? What is it in your life that brought you to that? We have to explain this. Look at that!*

{*Silence*}

DG: *You gave them life. You brought them up. They trusted you. Can you still say it's not true?*

{*Silence*}

DG: Why don't you want to explain that? *How come you don't have any reaction?*

AS: I am not saying anything.

DG: *This is the truth. This is the reality.*

{I show her another photograph}

DG: This is what happened. Don't they look beautiful, with lividity and the decomposition eating their faces?

I admit that was not professional. But I was only a twenty-year-old maiden, please. And I've already said I wanted to shred her face look a woodchipper. With delight.

{Silence}

DG: This is how you left them. This is Sabrina, and this is Amanda. Because I'm not sure if you remember their names. And you left them there to be found by your brother. You forgot to try to revive them. Why did you not call the police and the ambulance?

AS: I wasn't there.

DG: Who killed them?

AS: I don't know.

{Silence}

DG: Why did you leave them? Why did you leave them there alone? You told me you loved them.

{I show her the third photo}

{Silence}

DG: *You do not even react to that? Do you deny this? Do you feel this? What are you doing?*

Sorella still maintains her daughters are alive, despite having been shown photos of their lifeless bodies.

{Silence}

DG: You want to say something? I'm listening.

AS: No, I don't want to say anything. I don't believe that it's them on the floor.

DG: Excuse me? *Did you just say, "you don't believe that these two girls are Amanda and Sabrina lying dead on the floor?*

AS: These are your words.

DG: And what are your words, so no one gets you wrong?

AS: I said, I don't believe that it's them on the floor.

DG: You don't recognize them? Is that it? I know you forgot their names, but are you now pretending you don't even recognize Amanda and Sabrina?

AS: Yes, I do not believe that is them.

DG: Okay. So, who do you believe they are? *Let's play this game.*

AS: I am not playing a game.

DG: *You say that is not them on the floor. Okay. Who are these girls, then, in your sound opinion? Actors?*

AS: I am going to think of my kids.

DG: What?

{Silence}

DG: I don't understand what you just said.

{*Silence*}

DG: *Okay, do you think the police took actors there? Is that what you think? The police took these child actors and lay them on your living floor? Do you think they found actors with the same build, with the same hair? Same face? And they told them to pretend to be dead? Is that what you're saying?*

AS: That could well be, yes.

DG: Are you mad? Why would the police frame you?

AS: And I am telling you that ... those pictures are *not* my babies.

DG: They are actors or perhaps mannequins?

AS: Anything can be created

{*Silence*}

DG: Didn't you see those pictures? Didn't you recognize Sabrina and Amanda? Want to take another look? *You are not serious when you say that it is not them on the floor.*

AS: I just want to back to my cell, so that is it.

DG: There's one more picture I want to show you. There is no logic in what you are saying.

{*Silence*}

DG: Do you know what day it is today?

{*Silence*}

AS: I don't need to say anything.

DG: Do you know what day it is today?

AS: Yes.

{*Silence*}

AS: I do not want to see any of that stuff [meaning the photos]

DG: No, I'm not showing you anything. I'm just asking you if you know what today is?

{*Silence*}

DG: Today is the first of April. April Fool's Day. *You* believe what you want.

It was this question that that rattled my brain -

DG [Frantic]: *How can you explain that this could happen? What in your life brought you to that? We have to explain this. Look at that!*

I immediately noticed she presents no defense for herself. Nowhere and at no time does she say —

'*No, I did not commit these acts of murder.*'

Instead, she chooses the bizarre tactic of denying the existence of the murders. They did not die. My daughters are alive. They're somewhere playing and still living with God knows whom. When I informed Sorella her daughters had been murdered, she negates my declaration.

Is she stupid? Or intelligent? Does she think that is the necessary strategy, one that will convince the jury of her innocence? The absurdity of this woman's case stunned me. What is the answer? Why would anyone kill innocent human beings? Babies or adults? And how do we describe such people?

Is Sorella mad or clinically insane? Is she evil? If so, wherefrom did this Evil come to possess her spirit? Was she born evil? Or is Evil nothing but one more Man-made fancy fable?

Finally, is there a difference in the minds of Magda Goebbels and Sorella?

FINISH

www.ingramcontent.com/pod-product-compliance
Lightning Source LLC
Chambersburg PA
CBHW071425070526
44578CB00001B/4